PROCEDURAL REVIEW IN EUROPEAN FUNDAMENTAL RIGHTS CASES

Traditionally, courts adjudicate fundamental rights cases by applying substantive tests of reasonableness or proportionality. Increasingly, however, European courts are also expressly taking account of the quality of the procedure that has led up to a fundamental rights interference. Yet this procedural review is far from uncontroversial. There is still a lack of clarity as to what 'procedural review' really means, what its potential for judicial decision-making is, how it relates and should relate to substantive review and what its limitations are. Featuring contributions from experts in the field, this book is the first in-depth study into procedural review, considering the theoretical and conceptual issues at play, as well as the applicability of procedural review in different legal systems. It is thereby of great importance to scholars and practitioners interested in fundamental rights adjudication in Europe, judicial reasoning and procedural justice.

JANNEKE GERARDS is a professor of fundamental rights law at Utrecht University. Her research focuses on European fundamental rights, judicial review and constitutional law. She is also a deputy judge in the Appeals Court of The Hague, a member of the Human Rights Commission of the Netherlands Advisory Council on International Affairs and a member of the Royal Netherlands Academy of Arts and Sciences.

EVA BREMS is a professor of human rights law at Ghent University. She has published widely in many areas of human rights law, in particular on the European Convention on Human Rights. She is an ERC Starting Grant Laureate and a member of the executive committee of the International Association of Constitutional Law.

PROCEDURAL REVIEW IN EUROPEAN FUNDAMENTAL RIGHTS CASES

Edited by

JANNEKE GERARDS

Utrecht University

and

EVA BREMS

Ghent University

CAMBRIDGE UNIVERSITY PRESS

CAMBRIDGE
UNIVERSITY PRESS

University Printing House, Cambridge CB2 8BS, United Kingdom

One Liberty Plaza, 20th Floor, New York, NY 10006, USA

477 Williamstown Road, Port Melbourne, VIC 3207, Australia

4843/24, 2nd Floor, Ansari Road, Daryaganj, Delhi – 110002, India

79 Anson Road, #06–04/06, Singapore 079906

Cambridge University Press is part of the University of Cambridge.

It furthers the University's mission by disseminating knowledge in the pursuit of education, learning and research at the highest international levels of excellence.

www.cambridge.org
Information on this title: www.cambridge.org/9781107183773
DOI: 10.1017/9781316874844

First published 2017

A catalogue record for this publication is available from the British Library.

Library of Congress Cataloging-in-Publication Data
Names: Gerards, J. H. (Janneke H.), author. | Brems, Eva, author.
Title: Procedural review in European fundamental rights cases / Janneke Gerards and Eva Brems.
Description: Cambridge [UK] ; New York : Cambridge University Press, [2017] | Includes index.
Identifiers: LCCN 2016046814 | ISBN 9781107183773
Subjects: LCSH: Human rights – Europe. | Civil rights – Europe. | European Court of Human Rights. | Proportionality in law. | Subsidiarity. | Complementarity (International law)
Classification: LCC KJC5132 .G47 2017 | DDC 341.4/8094–dc23
LC record available at https://lccn.loc.gov/2016046814

ISBN 978-1-107-18377-3 Hardback

CONTENTS

CONTRIBUTORS

MALU BEIJER is a research fellow to the Radboud University Nijmegen, the Netherlands, and a judicial assistant.

EVA BREMS is Professor of Human Rights Law at Ghent University, Belgium.

JANNEKE GERARDS is Professor of Fundamental Rights Law at Utrecht University, the Netherlands.

FAY KARTNER contributed to this chapter as a junior lecturer in EU Law at Radboud University Nijmegen, The Netherlands. Since 16 January 2017, Fay works as a legal advisor (privacy law) at ICTRecht (Amsterdam).

ROGER MASTERMAN is Professor of Law at Durham Law School, United Kingdom.

ANNE MEUWESE is Professor of European and Comparative Public Law at Tilburg University, The Netherlands.

ANGELIKA NUSSBERGER is judge at the European Court of Human Rights.

PATRICIA POPELIER is Professor of Constitutional Law and Vice-Dean of the Law Faculty at Antwerp University, Belgium.

ARUNA SATHANAPALLY is a barrister. She is the legal adviser to the Australian Parliamentary Joint Committee of Human Rights and a visiting lecturer at the University of Sydney.

ISABELLE VAN DAMME is référendaire at the Chambers of Advocate General Sharpston, Court of Justice of the European Union and a visiting lecturer at the Université Catholique de Louvain, Belgium.

1

Procedural Review in European Fundamental Rights Cases: Introduction

JANNEKE GERARDS AND EVA BREMS

1.1 Background

In deciding on cases about infringements of fundamental rights, such as the right to privacy or the freedom of expression, it is generally expected that courts protect the substance of these rights through reasonableness or proportionality review. When confronted with a question to review a legislative measure, an administrative decision or a court ruling which allegedly interferes with a fundamental right, courts should identify which legitimate societal aims are served by the measure or decision, they should assess their effectiveness and necessity to achieve these aims and they should examine whether (overall) the body responsible for the interference has struck a fair balance between the interests concerned. Hence, courts are interested mainly in the content of a decision or measure, not in its coming-into-being.[1] Indeed, substantive reasonableness review in cases on fundamental rights is common to many national and supranational or international courts – it is deeply engrained, for example, in the judicial reasoning of the German Federal Constitutional Court, the US Supreme Court, the Canadian Supreme Court, the European Court of Human Rights (ECtHR) and the Court of Justice of the European Union (CJEU).[2]

[1] I. Bar-Siman-Tov, 'The Puzzling Resistance to Judicial Review of the Legislative Process', 91 *Boston University Law Review* (2011) p. 1915 at p. 1923.

[2] The prevalence of this particular type of review in fundamental rights cases is well illustrated by the various contributions to A. Jákab, A. Dyevre and G. Itzcovich (eds), *Comparative Constitutional Reasoning* (Cambridge, Cambridge University Press, forthcoming 2017). See also e.g. D. Law, 'Generic Constitutional Law', 89 *Minnesota Law Review* 652–742 (2005); D. Grimm, 'Proportionality in Canadian and German Constitutional Jurisprudence', 57 *University of Toronto Law Journal* (2007) pp. 383–397; T. Hickman, 'Proportionality: Comparative Law Lessons', 12 *Judicial Review* (2007) pp. 31–55.

Scholars have argued, however, that it could be valuable for courts to take a 'procedural turn' in their argumentation in fundamental rights cases.[3] Instead of (only) reviewing the substantive reasonableness of interferences with a fundamental right, they might (also) expressly take account of the quality of the legislative, administrative or judicial procedure that has led up to the alleged violation.[4] This idea of procedural review is far from uncontroversial and it has been heavily contested.[5] Nevertheless, in recent years, the approach increasingly can be seen to have emerged in the case law of European courts dealing with fundamental rights issues, in particular in that of the European Court of Human Rights (ECtHR) and the Court of Justice of the EU (ECJ).[6]

[3] Classically, such procedural review has been advocated for the Supreme Court of the United States, although it has been contested there, too; see e.g. J.H. Ely, *Democracy and Distrust* (Cambridge, Mass: Harvard University Press 1980); L. Tribe, 'The Puzzling Persistence of Process-Based Constitutional Theories', 89 *Yale Law Journal* (1980) p. 1063; L. Lusky, 'Footnote Redux: A Carolene Products Reminiscence', 82 *Columbia Law Review* (1982), p. 1093; B. Ackerman, 'Beyond Carolene Products', 98 *Harvard Law Review* (1985), p. 713; M.C. Dorf and S. Issacharoff, 'Can Process Theory Constrain Courts?', 72 *University of Colorado Law Review* (2001), p. 924; M.V. Tushnet, 'New Forms of Judicial Review and the Persistence of Rights- and Democracy-Based Worries', 38 *Wake Forest Law Review* (2003) p. 813; Bar-Siman-Tov, *supra* n. 1; J.S. Schachter, 'Ely at the Altar: Political Process Theory Through the Lens of the Marriage Debate', 109 *Michigan Law Review* 1363 (2011). More generally, see e.g. A.L. Young, 'In Defence of Due Deference', 72 *Modern Law Review* (2009) pp. 554–580; P. Craig, 'Substance and Procedure in Judicial Review', in Andenas, M. and Fairgrieve, D. (eds), *Tom Bingham and the Transformation of the Law: A Liber Amicorum* (2012) at www.oxfordscholarship.com; J.H. Gerards, 'The Prism of Fundamental Rights', 8 *European Constitutional Law Review* 2012 (2) pp. 173–202; I. Bar-Siman-Tov, 'Semiprocedural Judicial Review' 6 *Legisprudence* (2012) p. 271; A. Alemanno, 'The Emergence of the Evidence-Based Judicial Reflex: A Response to Bar-Simon-Tov's Semiprocedural Review', 1 *Theory and Practice of Legislation* (2013) p. 329; E. Jordão and S. Rose-Ackerman, 'Judicial Review of Executive Policymaking in Advanced Democracies: Beyond Rights Review', 66 *Administrative Law Review* (2014) pp. 1–72. More recently, there is also a debate on the possibilities for procedural review on the level of the national courts in European states; see e.g. Th. Poole, 'Of Headscarves and Heresies: The Denbigh High School Case and Public Authority Decision-Making under the Human Rights Act', *Public Law* 2005, p. 685; G. Davies, 'Banning the Jilbab: Reflections on Restricting Religious Clothing in the Light of the Court of Appeal in *SB* v. *Denbigh High School*', *European Constitutional Law Review* 2005, p. 511. A Kavanagh, 'Proportionality and Parliamentary Debates: Exploring Some Forbidden Territory', 34 *Oxford Journal of Legal Studies* (2014) (3) pp. 443–479.

[4] There are different possible variations of this procedural review; see e.g. Bar-Siman-Tov, *supra* n. 1, pp. 1923–1924, who distinguishes between procedural and semi-procedural review.

[5] See the sources mentioned *supra* n. 3.

[6] For analyses of this emerging trend, see the various chapters of the current volume. On the ECJ, see further e.g. A. Alemanno, 'A Meeting of Minds on Impact Assessment. When Ex

The procedural approach that is currently surfacing in the case law of the European Courts appears to have two different guises.[7] Firstly, the European Courts have formulated a number of procedural obligations for the states. For example, the ECtHR has required that national legislation provide for sufficient opportunity for individualisation and it has consistently asked national courts to take due account of the standards and criteria it has formulated in its case law.[8] Similarly, the ECJ has set a number of obligations for the national authorities, as well as the EU institutions, to be met when dealing with fundamental rights. They should respect the right to be heard, decisions should be transparent and sufficiently reasoned and there should be access to effective judicial remedies.[9]

Secondly, it appears that European supranational courts, in particular the ECtHR, increasingly take account of procedural shortcomings, but also of procedural quality, when determining whether a substantive right has been violated.[10] Sometimes the ECtHR draws negative

Ante Evaluation meets Ex Post Judicial Control', 17 *European Public Law* (2011) pp. 485–505; P. Van Cleynenbreugel, 'Judge-Made Standards of National Procedure in the Post-Lisbon Constitutional Framework' 37 *European Law Review* (2012) pp. 90–100; K. Lenaerts, 'The European Court of Justice and Process-Oriented Review', *College of Europe*, Research Paper in Law 1/2012 (2012). On the ECtHR's approach, see e.g. O. De Schutter and F. Tulkens, 'Rights in Conflict: The European Court of Human Rights as a Pragmatic Institution', in Brems, E. (ed), *Conflicts between Fundamental Rights* (Antwerp: Intersentia 2008) p. 169; P. Popelier, 'The Court as Regulatory Watchdog: The Procedural Approach in the Case Law of the European Court of Human Rights', in P. Popelier et al (eds), *The Role of Constitutional Courts in Multilevel Governance* (Antwerp, Intersentia 2012) pp. 249–268; P. Popelier and C. Van de Heyning, 'Procedural Rationality: Giving Teeth to the Proportionality Analysis', 9 *European Constitutional Law Review* (2013) pp. 230–262; J.H. Gerards, 'The European Court of Human Rights and the National Courts–Giving Shape to the Notion of 'Shared Responsibility', in J.H. Gerards and J.W.A. Fleuren (eds), *Implementation of the European Convention on Human Rights and of the Judgments of the ECtHR in National Case Law. A Comparative Analysis* (Antwerp, Intersentia, 2014), pp. 13–94.

7 For more detail, see the chapters by Eva Brems, Janneke Gerards, Malu Beijer, Angelika Nussberger and Fay Kartner and Anne Meuwese.

8 For more detail, see the chapter by Janneke Gerards in the present volume; see further e.g. E. Brems & L. Lavrysen (2013), 'Procedural Justice in Human Rights Adjudication: The European Court of Human Rights', 35 *Human Rights Quarterly* 2013, p. 176–200 and E. Brems, 'Procedural Protection: An Examination of Procedural Safeguards Read into Substantive Convention Rights', in E. Brems and J.H. Gerards (eds), *Shaping Rights in the ECHR. The Role of the European Court of Human Rights in Determining the Scope of Human Rights* (Cambridge University Press, 2013) pp. 137–161.

9 For more detail, see the chapter by Malu Beijer in the present volume.

10 See the chapters by Eva Brems, Angelika Nussberger and Janneke Gerards in the present volume.

inferences from the lack of procedural quality, in that it may more easily find a violation of a fundamental right if it turns out that an interference was not carefully considered by the national authorities. In other cases, the effect may be more positive – when the ECtHR finds that the national authorities have made a great effort to take all relevant interests into account, they have balanced these interests well and they have provided for sound judicial review of the resulting legislation, it 'would need strong substantive reasons' to set aside the outcome of such procedures.[11]

In combination, the two guises of procedural review may be seen to constitute a feedback loop.[12] When national authorities realise that meeting their procedural obligations under the Convention or under EU law helps to improve their record of protection of fundamental rights, this may provide an important incentive for them to pay attention to fundamental rights in national procedures in the first place. In turn, this may increase the level of protection of fundamental rights on the national level, which clearly is a desirable consequence.

Focusing on procedural quality may have some other advantages. Firstly, procedural review has since long been advocated by proponents of democratic deliberative theories.[13] Rather than looking into the substance of the matter, courts should analyse whether procedural requirements related to transparency, accountability, participation and fact-finding were met in the legislative or executive decision-making procedures. The advantage of such procedural review is that courts are not seen as substantively intervening in matters on which (national) governments, parliaments or administrative bodies have particular legitimacy or expertise.[14] Instead, they are regarded as regulatory watchdogs that will intervene only, and for good reason, if the legislative or administrative decision-making reveals important shortcomings.[15]

Secondly, a high level of procedural quality may bolster procedural fairness, which in itself is of great importance to the legitimacy of

[11] For more detail, see the chapters by Janneke Gerards and Angelika Nussberger in the present volume.

[12] This feedback loop is mainly discussed in relation to EU law, in relation to cases where impact assessments have been made in preparation of legislation; the judicial response to this is discussed in more detail in the chapter of Fay Kartner and Anne Meuwese in the current volume. See also e.g. Alemanno, *supra* n. 6.

[13] See in particular Ely, *supra* n. 3 and C.R. Sunstein, *The Partial Constitution* (Cambridge, Mass.: Harvard University Press 1993).

[14] cf. Bar-Siman-Tov, *supra* n. 1, p. 1940.

[15] cf. also Van de Heyning and Popelier, *supra* n. 3.

(supranational) judicial decisions.[16] Social psychology research on procedural justice has established that when it comes to institutional legitimacy in the eyes of individuals, the perception of procedural justice (was the case dealt with in a fair manner?) is more significant than the perception of distributive justice (was the outcome of the case fair?).[17] The same research suggests a strong autonomous value of procedural justice, as it is provides individuals status recognition and hence is related to their feeling of self-worth. Among the crucial components of procedural justice for courts are participation ('voice'), neutrality and accuracy. A recent study has argued that procedural justice is of particular relevance for the ECtHR, albeit as a complement rather than as an alternative to substantive justice.[18]

Thirdly, procedural review may have institutional and pragmatic value. It may help supranational courts to avoid the need to get deeply involved in debates on sensitive and delicate topics, which the national authorities may be better placed to deal with.[19] In line with principles of primarity and subsidiarity, it should be up to the national authorities, including the national courts, to ensure that fundamental rights are protected in an appropriate manner.[20] If a supranational court is seen to restrict its assessment to looking at the quality of the procedure and the extent to which national authorities have taken account of the standards the court has set in earlier cases, this could enhance its legitimacy in the eyes of national authorities, to the extent that it is not actually seen to interfere with the substantive policy choices made.

Including (aspects of) procedural review in fundamental rights cases by supranational courts thus may be commended. Nevertheless, a range of questions and points for debate arise as soon as the notion of procedural review is looked at in more detail.[21] Such undesirable effects may

[16] See further the contributions by Eva Brems and Aruna Sathanapally to the current volume. See also e.g. Bar-Siman-Tov, *supra* n. 1, p. 1931.

[17] In more detail and with references, see E. Brems and L. Lavrysen, 'Procedural Justice in Human Rights Adjudication: The European Court of Human Rights', 35 *Human Rights Quarterly* (2013) pp. 176–200.

[18] Brems and Lavrysen, *supra* n. 17.

[19] See in particular Popelier, *supra* n. 6.

[20] See further, with references, J.H. Gerards, 'The European Court of Human Rights and the National Courts – Giving Shape to the Notion of 'Shared Responsibility', in Janneke Gerards and Joseph Fleuren (eds), *Implementation of the European Convention on Human Rights and of the Judgments of the ECtHR in National Case Law. A Comparative Analysis* (Antwerp, Intersentia, 2014), pp. 13–94.

[21] For a more complete discussion of arguments, objections and questions, see Bar-Siman-Tov, *supra* n. 1; see also the other sources mentioned *supra*, n. 3. See also hereafter, in particular the chapters by Angelika Nussberger, Aruna Sathanapally and Roger Masterman.

present themselves in particular when procedural review is used to replace substantive review, rather than as a supplementary type of review. In this regard, it has been mentioned, for example, that a lack of substantive review may lead to reduced standard-setting, since the courts would in many cases no longer indicate what kind of outcomes are considered reasonable. Moreover, even highly sophisticated procedures may lead to unfair outcomes, which procedural review may be unable to redress. A stronger focus on procedure arguably could result in an unwarranted increase of formalism and window-dressing on the national level, instead of an increase in substantive protection of fundamental rights. Finally, there is still a lack of clarity as to what 'procedural review' really means. A wide range of variations can be conceived, such as 'full' procedural review (where the content or outcome of the decision-making process does not play any role at all), semi-procedural review (where elements of procedural and substantive review are combined), strategies where negative or positive inferences are drawn from the existence or lack of procedural quality and fairness or 'evidence-based review', where a court mainly assesses whether the legislator or administrative body based its decisions and measures on a sufficient set of facts.

1.2 Foundations and Rationales, Practical Value and Judicial Application

Against the background sketched above, the current volume aims to provide for an analysis of the possibilities for the use of procedural review by the European supranational courts in fundamental rights cases, looking into the foundations and rationales for such review, as well as the practice of its application. The main question thereby is to what extent and how the 'argument from procedure' could be used in fundamental rights case law of the European courts in a legitimate and practical manner. To answer this question, this volume centres around three central themes that merit in-depth exploration. Read in their entirety, the chapters relating to these three themes provide a broad and deep insight into the meaning and potential of procedural review for European supranational courts deciding in fundamental rights cases.

1.2.1 *Foundations and Rationales for Procedural Review by Supranational Courts Deciding Fundamental Rights Cases*

To be able to answer the main question of the current book, it is important to provide for a better understanding of what 'procedural review' could entail, as well as explain the theoretical basis of this type of review and the normative value of its use in judicial reasoning. The issues to be addressed in Part I of this volume therefore are of a normative and theoretical nature, investigating the foundations and rationales for procedural review.

To this end, Eva Brems in her chapter seeks to identify several potential motivations for the ECtHR's recent turn to a quality assessment of domestic procedures and processes. In addition to assessing the merits of each of these motivations, her chapter investigates their respective implications as concerns the desirability and modalities of such an assessment. Brems thereby critically assesses four different 'logics', intuitions or rationales underlying procedural-type review: the notion of process efficacy, i.e. the reliance on obligations for procedural due care as a proxy for reaching reasonable outcomes; institutional reasons for relying on procedural arguments; the right to be treated fairly and procedurally correctly as a value of its own; and the notion of procedural fairness as a means to bolster legitimacy, compliance and social cohesion. Although these four rationales are derived from the ECtHR's approach, they have a wider theoretical relevance. This means this chapter, in fact, provides for a general overview of the possible theoretical rationales for procedural review, thereby offering important starting points for distinguishing between different types of use of procedural arguments in judicial reasoning.

The chapter by Aruna Sathanapally continues to critically examine the procedural turn in fundamental rights jurisprudence from a theoretical standpoint. Sathanapally draws on scholarship on the role of courts in relation to constitutional rights, as well as deliberative democratic theory, to examine the normative case for a particular variety of procedural review, or semi-procedural review, but also asks whether this is a type of review that a court – and specifically, a supranational court – can effectively develop through its jurisprudence. She explores this question by reference to an illustrative case study, concluding that the promise of procedural review in a fundamental rights context is a modest one. A court that takes into account the deliberative process leading to the decision under challenge is likely to do a better job of deciding when to exercise restraint, and this is likely to provide some incentives for better deliberation at the national level. However, given the difficulties in applying uniform standards to deliberation, procedural review of this kind may need to be impressionistic, rather than systematic, and ought to be understood as a secondary, rather than primary, consideration in fundamental rights review.

1.2.2 The (Potential) Value of Procedural Review for Supranational Courts Deciding Fundamental Rights Cases – Political Science Perspectives

Procedural review is often associated with notions of 'better regulation' and quality and legitimacy of legislation. As was explained above, there is an assumption (sometimes implicit) that procedural review is part of a continuous 'feedback loop'. The express judicial approval or disapproval of the process of decision-making may provide an incentive to legislators, administrative bodies or (national) courts to improve the quality and legitimacy of that process. Eventually, this may be beneficial to the quality of legislation and judicial and administrative decisions, presuming that better procedures contribute to better decision-making. If inclusive, transparent and open procedures for decision-making lead to better outcomes and to stronger protection of fundamental rights, it may indeed be desirable for the European courts to pay attention to procedure in addition to substance. At the same time, the question arises whether the assumptions and presumptions mentioned above are correct. Over the past years, for example, many efforts have been made in States and in the European Union to improve the quality of regulation, for example through fundamental rights impact assessments, public consultations based on greenbooks or internet consultations. The question remains, however, whether such improvements actually help to enhance compatibility with fundamental rights standards, or whether compliance with such standards is mainly due to other factors. Moreover, an important empirical question is whether and how such approaches can be transposed to the reality of supranational adjudication, so whether is it feasible for supranational courts to create incentives to raise attention for fundamental rights in national procedures. These questions are addressed in Part II of the current volume.

In her chapter, Patricia Popelier aims to answer these empirical questions by closely investigating the relationship between the recent surge of evidence-based legislative models worldwide, and the trend towards procedural or evidence-based judicial review. She concludes that these trends may indeed reinforce each other, but she also points out that other factors may be important in determining the degree of mutual influence. In particular, she finds that the legal, administrative and political context, as well as institutional design and constitutional values, may either stimulate or discourage the adoption of evidence-based policies. Based on her research, she also recommends that the ECtHR will most probably be more effective if it appeals to national courts rather than national legislators and policy-makers. Moreover, instructions to take an evidence-based approach must take into account political context and constitutional values to be most effective, if only in awareness raising on the national level.

The analysis made by Patricia Popelier is complemented by an empirical study of the European Union's better regulation programme by Fay Kartner and Anne Meuwese. After an analysis of fundamental rights aspects in impact assessments and scrutiny thereof by the newly established Regulatory Scrutiny Board, they note that the ECJ sometimes draws positive inferences from the fact that EU legislation has been prepared with particular care. The authors also signal that the legitimacy of such positive inferences may be connected to the question of whether indeed there is a clear link between quality of legislation and quality of preparation. Their chapter mainly aims to answer the questions as to which fundamental requirements of regulation are set in the European Union, what barriers exist to making legislation responsive towards judicial review and how the preparation of EU legislation affects judicial review. To this end, by using the case study of the Data Retention Directive, as well as some other examples, Kartner and Meuwese analyse the different 'Better Regulation' instruments available to the EU legislative bodies, and they examine the extent to which these instruments can enhance the awareness of (intended and unintended) impact on especially fundamental rights. They also identify certain aspects of the EU legislative process that seem to hinder the effective collection of information on fundamental rights impacts, and the appropriate use of this data. Finally, they make an assessment of the consequences the degree of fundamental rights-responsiveness can have for judicial review, in particular by the ECJ. Their analysis shows that indeed there is room for procedural review when EU legislation has been prepared properly, and also that there is scope for incentivising EU legislative bodies to be more responsive to fundamental rights impacts.

1.2.3 Application of Procedural Review – Supranational and Comparative Perspectives

Procedural review evidently has normative value for supranational courts deciding in fundamental rights cases, as well as practical potential. In addition, it often has been observed that courts increasingly rely on this type of review in their argumentation. Nevertheless, a close analysis of the various ways in which procedural review may play a role in judicial decision-making and judicial reasoning has long been missing. For that reason, Part III of this volume presents a number of critical analyses of the approach currently taken by the European courts, supplemented by two analyses of other legal systems in which procedural review increasingly plays a role.

Firstly, Janneke Gerards' chapter aims to provide for a typology of procedural review in the case law of the ECtHR. The typology presented is based on a distinction between the two main aspects of the Court's 'procedural turn', i.e. (1) setting procedural positive obligations and (2) relying on the quality of national decision-making in reasonableness review. Next to providing a brief review of the different types of procedural positive obligations the Court has developed in its case law, the chapter looks into the ways in which the Court has woven procedural elements into its judicial reasoning, with the objective of clarifying in which types of cases and to what effect the Court already uses elements of procedural review. Gerards concludes that it is possible indeed to distinguish some general lines in the Court's case law, yet overall, it appears that the Court uses a 'pick and choose' approach, selecting only those arguments that it considers useful in reasoning its judgments. These arguments sometimes may be of a procedural nature, for instance, if a procedural flaw or quality is particularly striking, but sometimes they may not.

Angelika Nussberger, the present judge for Germany in the ECtHR, makes an assessment of the usefulness and legitimacy of the different uses of procedural review from the perspective of the ECtHR, drawing on the typology presented in Gerards' chapter, as well as on her own practical experience. She both clarifies the reasons why the ECtHR relies on procedural review in some cases, but not in others, and critically reviews whether the ECtHR's practice actually achieves its aims. She also places the use of procedural review in the context of the ECtHR's work and thereby provides more depth to the possibilities and risks for relying on the 'argument from procedure'.

Just like the ECtHR, the ECJ has paid quite some attention to procedural safeguards in its case law. It has developed a variety of standards to ensure effective respect of EU law in relation to judicial remedies and powers at national level, and it has set important procedural requirements for administrative authorities in the member states and at the EU level. Malu Beijer in her chapter addresses the question to what extent the ECJ has developed and applied procedural standards to ensure that good decisions on fundamental rights are reached. She first discusses why and what kind of procedural review can be considered useful for the ECJ in fundamental rights cases, having regard to the particularities of the European Union's legal order. Subsequently, she presents an analysis of some cases where the ECJ has developed procedural obligations, and of cases where it can be seen to apply a procedural type of review. Her conclusion is that a strongly procedural approach is not really feasible for the ECJ, because of its specific task to develop uniform standards of protection and provide for an interpretation of the fundamental rights notions in the EU Charter of Fundamental Rights. In relation to preliminary questions referred by national courts, substantive standard-setting is its main task, rather than reviewing the reasonableness of national decisions. In relation to the ECJ's review of EU secondary legislation, this is different, and there, the ECJ, in Beijer's view, could benefit from more explicitly relying on procedural review.

The WTO Appellate Body has to decide on the legality of non-trade measures adopted by States in furtherance of environmental and human health considerations which impact on trade. Such topics are often highly sensitive and relate to the delicate interrelationship between an international body and national authorities, just like the cases dealt with by the European supranational courts. In her chapter, Isabelle Van Damme therefore looks into the question if, to what extent and how the Appellate Body uses procedural arguments in its review. While hardly any clear foundations for procedural review appear to be present in the European treaties and the ECHR, the WTO treaties appear to provide for much more precise yardsticks for assessing national procedures, which this chapter discusses and of which it assesses the (perceived) legitimacy.

Finally, it is often considered that one of the drivers of procedural review in European fundamental rights cases is a concern with subsidiarity. Indeed, these past years have seen a raging debate on subsidiarity in European fundamental rights justice that has Europe-wide implications, yet in its concrete manifestations, was mostly focused on the United Kingdom and its relationship with the ECtHR. For that reason, Roger

Masterman presents the United Kingdom as a case study to look at procedural review in national jurisdictions, and how this is impacted upon by supranational developments. His chapter shows that procedural review is at once orthodox and alien to United Kingdom constitutional law. Fair process lies at the heart of the common law of judicial review of administrative action. Traditionally, by contrast, legislative review has not been a feature of United Kingdom constitutional law and the courts have long regarded the propriety of legislative processes as effectively non-justiciable. Importantly, however, the enactment of the Human Rights Act 1998 has facilitated, and rendered constitutionally permissible, a species of legislative review in the United Kingdom. Taking their lead from the supposed 'outcome orientated approach' of the European Court of Human Rights, the House of Lords and United Kingdom Supreme Court have in recent years placed the focus on the proportionality analysis. Nevertheless, at the same time, a closer engagement with legislative deliberative process than has traditionally been permitted has been evident, with courts taking the quality of the legislative decision-making process into account when assessing whether legislation is compatible with Convention rights.

1.3 Main Findings

The analyses provided in this volume show at once the potential and the limitations of procedural review as a suitable approach for European courts having to decide on fundamental rights cases. The chapters on the logics and rationales underlying procedural-type review and on the theoretical validity of this approach show that there may be good reason indeed for European courts to include arguments from procedure in their judicial argumentation. It is also clear from the various chapters, however, that there are important risks and disadvantages involved in the use of this type of review. It may be safely concluded that there is no sufficient basis for the European courts to engage in full procedural review, which means that a court would not at all look into the substance of a measure or decision infringing a fundamental right, but only at the quality of the decision-making procedure. Other forms of procedural review are much more legitimate, such as drawing negative or positive inferences from procedure, or combining elements of substance and procedure in judicial reasoning. Indeed, it is apparent from the empirical chapters in this book that such attention to procedure, as well as the formulation of procedural requirements, may incentivise national authorities to step up their efforts to provide for better regulation and evidence-based decision-making.

The question then arises as to what form of procedural review would be the most appropriate for the European courts to apply. The comparative analysis of case law shows that a great variety of approaches can be conceived. The typology of the ECtHR's approach provided by Gerards shows, for example, that this Court refers to elements of procedure in many different ways and to different effects. The various chapters in Part III of this volume also demonstrate that the impact of arguments from procedure may depend on the circumstances of each case, such as the subject and nature of a measure or decision, and the way in which a case has been argued. In addition, variations in approach may be due to differences in judicial style, legal culture and procedural and legal context, as has been expressly remarked by Popelier. Masterman shows, for example, that the traditional differences between judicial review of administrative decisions and statutory legislation in the United Kingdom may explain the British courts' initial reluctance to use a procedural type of review. The changes in this approach are mainly due to the particular legal context created by the UK Human Rights Act 1998. Likewise, as is clear from Beijer's chapter, the ECJ may rely on arguments from procedure in cases about secondary EU legislation much more easily than in cases concerning national measures of implementation. For the WTO Appellate Body, this is different, as Van Damme has demonstrated, as this body finds a rather clear legal basis for inserting elements of procedural review in its argumentation, thus providing for better yardsticks than are available to the European Courts.

Hence, there is no straightforward and easy answer to the main research question of this book, which is to what extent and how the 'argument from procedure' can be used in fundamental rights case law of the European Courts in a legitimate and practical manner. It will be necessary to conduct further research into the specific possibilities and limitations for each individual legal system, taking its own intricacies into account. Given the theoretical and practical significance of further development of methods of procedural review, and given the potential that is already apparent from supranational and national case law, it would appear to be of great value to indeed conduct such further studies.

PART I

Foundations and Rationales for Procedural Review by Supranational Courts Deciding Fundamental Rights Cases

2

The 'Logics' of Procedural-Type Review by the European Court of Human Rights

EVA BREMS

2.1 Introduction

In the case law of the European Court of Human Rights (ECtHR, or 'the Court'), a 'procedural turn' can be noted. That is to say it seems that in its assessment of the compatibility of a particular measure or situation with the European Convention on Human Rights (ECHR, or 'the Convention'), the Court increasingly includes an appreciation of the quality of the domestic processes that led to this measure or situation. This concerns administrative and legislative processes, as well as procedures before domestic courts. The latter have been involved in most cases, given the admissibility requirement of the exhaustion of domestic remedies.[1] Scholars have noted this procedural turn, and have started to analyse it, by mapping and assessing its various manifestations.[2]

Building on the mapping exercises conducted by other scholars,[3] this chapter adopts a normative approach. It explores several potential motivations for the Court's turning to a quality assessment of domestic procedures and processes. In addition to assessing the merits of each of these motivations, the paper explores their respective implications as concerns the desirable nature and modalities of such quality assessment.

1 Article 35 (1) ECHR.

2 Eva Brems, 'Procedural Protection: An Examination of Procedural Safeguards Read into Substantive Convention Rights', in Eva Brems and Janneke Gerards (eds), *Shaping Rights in the ECHR; The Role of the European Court of Human Rights in Determining the Scope of Human Rights*, Cambridge: Cambridge University Press, 2013, pp. 137–161; Janneke Gerards, 'Procedural Review by the ECtHR–A Typology', draft paper 2015; Patricia Popelier, 'The Court as a Regulatory Watchdog: The Procedural Approach in the Case Law of the European Court of Human rights', in Armen Mazmanyan, Werner Vandenbruwaene and Patricia Popelier (eds), *The Role of Constitutional Courts in Multilevel Governance*, Intersentia, 2013, pp. 249–267; Matthew Saul, 'The ECtHR's Margin of Appreciation and the Processes of National Parliaments', working paper 2015.

3 In particular, Gerards, o.c., Popelier, o.c., Saul, o.c.

2.2 Why Would the ECtHR Take an Interest in the Quality of Domestic Process?

Good process can classically be valued for its own sake ('process value'[4]), or for instrumental reasons. Among instrumental reasons, the classical account is one that considers that good process produces good results ('process efficacy'[5]). Yet, social psychology research has also linked 'procedural fairness' to other important values, including legitimacy, compliance and social cohesion. In addition, for a supranational body such as the ECtHR, there may be institutional reasons for turning to (a certain type of) procedural review. In the ECtHR context, such institutional reasons may be found in the principle of subsidiarity.

In what follows, the dynamic of each of these rationales will be presented, in general terms as well as in its application to ECtHR review of the quality of domestic parliamentary, administrative and judicial process. For each of these rationales, this chapter will also examine what *type* of procedural review they can be expected to lead to, taking into account the purpose and the internal logic of that particular rationale. This entails exploring what would be the focus of procedural review within this rationale, i.e. which procedural elements the Court would look at when it conducts procedural review from within that particular rationale. In that respect, the paper distinguishes between procedural review *sensu stricto* and an assessment of the quality of domestic human rights scrutiny.

In addition to exploring the type of procedural review that fits each rationale, the examination will also look into the appropriate *role* of procedural review from within each of these four rationales. This implies assessing within the logics of each rationale how much weight the procedural review would merit within the Court's overall assessment, and what kind of consequences may be attached to a positive or negative assessment of the quality of domestic process.

After analysing each of the four rationales separately (2.2.1 to 2.2.4), the paper will explore whether and how they can be aligned, in an attempt to minimise conflicting dynamics between different rationales and to optimise their respective benefits (2.2.5).

[4] Jonas Christoffersen, *Fair Balance: Proportionality and Primarity in the European Convention on Human Rights*, Martinus Nijhoff Publishers, 2009, 462.

[5] Ibid.

2.2.1 *Process Efficacy: Good Process for Good Outcomes*

2.2.1.1 The Process Efficacy Rationale

The classical instrumental reason for valuing the quality of process conceives of good process as an important way to guarantee good outcomes. In the Convention system, good outcomes signify domestic norms, decisions, actions and inactions that respect, protect and fulfil Convention rights.

Looking at the ECtHR's practice of reading procedural safeguards into substantive Convention rights as a whole, the process efficacy function stands out as the prime purpose and merit of this development. Christoffersen, in 2009, stated

> Procedural obligations that only have process value do not add anything to the effective implementation of the ECHR. The end purpose of proceduralization is to implement the ECHR in domestic law. The effective implementation by means of procedural obligations thus logically presupposes an obligation to apply the substantive content of the ECHR in the course of the proscribed procedures.[6]

In a 2014 overview paper of the Court's tendency to 'proceduralise' substantive rights, I found that whenever the Court motivated its turn to proceduralisation, it did so on the basis of efficacy arguments. It would seem that from the perspective of the Court, the identification and scope of procedural obligations are in most cases designed to optimise protection of substantive rights.[7]

2.2.1.2 Process Efficacy in Parliamentary, Administrative and Judicial Process

When it comes to *judicial* process, the instrumental process efficacy rationale is prominent even when decent procedures have been made the object of autonomous human rights, as in Article 6 ECHR. For example, one important reason why there has to be equality of arms and a right to an attorney is because this will increase the quantity and quality of factual claims and legal arguments before the judge, who is therefore in a better position to make a good judgment. Likewise, one of the reasons why judges have to be impartial and independent is because it is considered that sheltering judges from the interference of factors that are not related to the merits of the case is important to reach a good outcome in that case. The Convention's fair trial guarantees apply in

[6] Christoffersen, o.c., 463. [7] Brems, o.c., 159.

most court cases, in particular in ordinary civil and criminal cases. When a judicial procedure concerns the protection of fundamental rights, the stakes are raised significantly higher for any factor, including fair process, that is considered conducive to the best possible outcome. The perceived link between fair process and fair outcomes may explain why the Court sometimes chooses to assess under substantive provisions procedural elements that might also have been assessed under procedural Convention provisions (in particular, Article 6), such as the length of proceedings, equality of arms or the impartiality of the bench.[8]

In relation to *administrative* decision-making, the process efficacy rationale is no less relevant. In fact, historically, fundamental rights have been conceived in the first place as checks on the exercise of administrative power by kings or feudal lords. This function directly translates into a procedural rule; the Court has often requested guarantees against the arbitrary use of administrative powers.[9] This appears to emanate from a process efficacy rationale, the assumption being that arbitrariness in the exercise of administrative powers will lead to violations of human rights. Similarly, many of the specific positive obligations concerning administrative process that the Court has stated are manifestly aimed at the prevention of human rights violations. This is the case, for example, in the context of the regulation of hazardous activities that may threaten the right to life,[10] or with respect to secret surveillance, that may interfere with the right to privacy.[11]

When the Court surveys the quality of *parliamentary* process, there can be little doubt that the process efficacy rationale applies as well. The very concept of a parliamentary democracy relies, among others, on certain premises of process efficacy, i.e. the idea that certain procedural features such as broad representation and checks and balances improve the quality of outcomes.

2.2.1.3 Type and Role of Procedural Review under the Process Efficacy Rationale

There can be many different interpretations of what is and is not in general terms a 'qualitative' outcome of a domestic process. There is no need to go into that discussion however, as the ECtHR's yardstick for measuring the quality of domestic outcomes is obviously centred on

[8] Brems, o.c., 158. [9] Gerards, o.c., footnote 61.
[10] E.g. ECtHR, *Namat Aliyev* v. *Azerbaijan*, 8 April 2010, para. 81.
[11] E.g. ECtHR, *Petkov a.o.* v. *Bulgaria*, 11 June 2009, para. 63.

Convention compliance. Hence, the Court's interest in process efficacy is an interest in procedures that further compliance with the rights and freedoms of the ECHR.

This has implications for the *type* of procedural review that is warranted from a process efficacy perspective. From this angle, it does not seem particularly relevant for the Court to attach importance to formal elements, such as the mere fact that certain bodies or persons were consulted, the respect of time limits or publicity requirements, or the length of parliamentary debates. In the context of the process efficacy rationale, what matters is that the process is organised in such a way as to optimise Convention compliance. Rather than focusing on the technicality or factuality of specific procedural features, it is therefore relevant for the Court within this rationale to check whether the impact of a proposed measure on Convention rights has been expressly and extensively discussed, whether the reasons invoked to justify interference with a Convention right are among those that the Court accepts, and whether and how domestic actors have assessed the proportionality of such interference. Hence, within a process efficacy rationale, a review of the quality of domestic process is best conceived as a review of domestic human rights scrutiny.

The process efficacy perspective also has implications for the *role* of procedural review in the Court's overall analysis. First of all, it is submitted that the fact that quality of process is assessed under this rationale because of its assumed close relationship to substance legitimises an integration of procedural control within the Court's substantive human rights assessment. This means that substantive inferences can be drawn from the assessment of the quality of domestic process. This may go up to the point of justifying the finding of a violation of a substantive right on the basis of serious procedural shortcomings, in particular when these shortcomings stand in the way of the Court's being able to thoroughly assess the substantive aspects of the case. Yet, precisely because under this rationale, procedural control is instrumental in the light of substantive human rights outcome, this does not seem to apply the other way around. It has been noted that when procedural review is not added to or integrated into substantive scrutiny, but is instead used to replace substantive review, there is a real risk that a tendency towards proceduralisation of review would lead to weakening substantive rights protection.[12] This risk does not manifest itself when the Court draws

[12] Brems, o.c., 159; Christoffersen, o.c., 455.

negative substantive inferences from bad procedure, yet it is problematic when positive substantive inferences are drawn from good procedural practice. Hence, if process efficacy drives the Court's monitoring of the quality of domestic process, positive inferences from process should not be decisive towards the outcome of the case.

2.2.2 Institutional Reasons for Procedural Review: Shaping Subsidiarity

2.2.2.1 The Subsidiarity Rationale

Recently, scholars,[13] as well as ECtHR judges,[14] have situated procedural review by the ECtHR in a new context, i.e. the institutional debate about the appropriate role of the supranational court *vis-à-vis* national authorities. Protocol 15 to the ECHR will entrench the principle of subsidiarity in the Convention's Preamble. In the specific context of the ECtHR, the subsidiarity principle means that 'the task of ensuring respect for the rights enshrined in the Convention lies first and foremost with the authorities in the Contracting States rather than with the Court. The Court can and should intervene only where the domestic authorities fail in that task'.[15] While the entry into force of Protocol 15 is pending, it may be assumed (and some judgments seem to suggest)[16] that inside the Court, reflection and discussion is going on as to the implications of this emphasis on subsidiarity. These concern the two faces of subsidiarity, turned respectively to the ECtHR and to domestic authorities. A focus on the one or the other has an impact on the conclusion one is likely to draw with respect to the way in which the Court should perform its role. Echoing the Court's terminology of negative and positive obligations, this chapter distinguishes these two faces as 'negative subsidiarity' and 'positive subsidiarity'. Negative subsidiarity refers to the issue of judicial restraint by the ECtHR, the Court leaving room to domestic authorities to perform their own human rights scrutiny. From a rationale of negative subsidiarity, the question is whether the Court should increase its reference to and the width of the 'margin of appreciation' of the States Parties.

[13] Gerards, o.c.; Saul, o.c.

[14] Robert Spano, 'Universality or Diversity of Human Rights? Strasbourg in the Age of Subsidiarity', Human Rights Law Review, 2014, pp. 487–502.

[15] Jurisconsult of the ECHR, *Interlaken Follow-Up: Principle of Subsidiarity*, 8 July 2010, at www.echr.coe.int/Documents/2010_Interlaken_Follow-up_ENG.pdf, 1.

[16] ECtHR, *A.K.* v. *Latvia*, 24 June 2014; Eva Brems, 'Making Subsidiarity Work: Struggling with Procedural Review – *A K.* v *Latvia*', www.strasbourgobservers.com.

Positive subsidiarity, on the other hand, concerns the need for States Parties to take up their first-line responsibilities for the protection of Convention rights. From the perspective of the Court, the challenge of positive subsidiarity is not so much about restraint, but rather about providing incentives for domestic authorities to optimise the quality of their human rights scrutiny. From both angles, the argument has been made that increased use of procedure-type review might be the way forward. In the spirit of negative subsidiarity, the idea is that when the Court reviews domestic procedure and finds that the claims based on Convention rights have been carefully considered at the domestic level, there is no reason why the Court should conduct an additional substantive review.[17] From the perspective of positive subsidiarity, the reverse idea may be advanced, namely that when the review of the domestic procedure that was supposed to address the claims based on Convention rights shows serious deficiencies at this level, this should contribute to (or even suffice for) the finding of a violation, without the need for additional substantive review.

2.2.2.2 Subsidiarity and Parliamentary, Administrative and Judicial Process

The debate about *negative subsidiarity* and the ECtHR has not engaged much with domestic administrative decision-making. It has been mostly about domestic courts and legislatures invoking institutional reasons to claim the need for ECtHR restraint.

Especially the highest domestic *courts* may consider that they are better placed than a supranational court to assess restrictions of fundamental rights within their specific legal and societal context, and may not welcome the ECtHR substituting its own proportionality assessment for theirs.[18]

Focusing on *parliamentary* process, the claim for negative subsidiarity may be even louder than with respect to administrative or judicial process. This is the case especially in contexts in which a strong doctrine

[17] Janneke Gerards, 'The European Court of Human Rights and the National Courts – Giving Shape to the Notion of "Shared Responsibility"', in: J.H. Gerards & J.W.A. Fleuren (eds), *Implementation of the European Convention on Human Rights and of the Judgments of the ECtHR in National Case Law. A Comparative Analysis* (Antwerp), Intersentia, 2014; 52 ss.

[18] See, on the 'judicial dialogue' between the ECtHR and the House of Lords, as well as the German Federal Constitutional Court, Markus Fahlbusch, *European Integration in the Field of Human Rights Protection. The Interaction on the Basis of Different Constitutional Cultures*, Ph.D. dissertation Université Libre de Bruxelles, 2014.

of parliamentary sovereignty reigns.[19] Moreover, in certain types of cases in which hard choices have to be made, democratic legitimacy, or domestically rooted judicial legitimacy, is considered particularly important. Indeed, in her chapter in this volume, Gerards finds that the Court is most inclined to attach value to the quality of legislative or judicial process (including positive as well as negative inferences) in two types of 'cases with a high degree of sensitivity', i.e. 'cases relating to complex choices in socio-economic policy fields', and 'dilemma-cases, in which conflicting interests of rather similar weight are at stake or which relate to moral issues, or cases in which the national authorities are particularly well-placed to take decisions'.[20] It seems that in such cases, negative subsidiarity is least controversial, as the case for a wide margin of appreciation is a strong one on policy grounds, and procedural review can provide at least some European control where otherwise none might occur.

When it comes to *positive subsidiarity*, there are solid reasons to focus on each of the three branches of government. *Parliaments* may be a priority focus for positive subsidiarity. This may be the case because parliaments make general rules that affect large numbers of people, but even more so because the incorporation of human rights guarantees in those general rules prevents the occurrence of human rights violations, which is manifestly to be preferred over a situation in which violations occur and one can only attempt to remedy them. Some of the most noted and notable cases in which the Court draws strong inferences from procedural review do indeed concern parliamentary process. These concern positive inferences, as in *Animal Defenders*,[21] as well as negative inferences, as in *Hirst nr 2*.[22] Yet, it is important to encourage decent human rights scrutiny also among *administrative decision-makers*, as these are often in key positions with respect to preventing or remedying specific human rights violations. Finally, a thorough and high-quality human rights scrutiny of legislative and administrative acts by the domestic *judiciary* is a *sine qua non* for the viability and sustainability of the Convention system. If the ECtHR is to achieve and maintain a workable caseload, it is vital that the domestic judiciaries should deliver excellent human rights justice. Hence, it is worthwhile for the ECtHR to

[19] Cf. the United Kingdom. [20] Gerards, o.c., 13 (legislatures) and 17 (courts).

[21] ECtHR, Grand Chamber, *Animal Defenders International* v. *United Kingdom*, 22 April 2013, para. 111.

[22] ECtHR, Grand Chamber, *Hirst* v. *United Kingdom* (nr 2), 6 October 2005.

examine the domestic judiciary's scrutiny and to provide guidelines for improving it.

2.2.2.3 Type and Role of Procedural Review under the Subsidiarity Rationale

Looking at the *type* of procedural review that is mandated by a subsidiarity logic, it seems that this rationale leads to the same preferences as those under the process efficacy rationale, i.e. a review that scrutinises domestic human rights scrutiny. Such a review is appropriately called procedural, because it does not autonomously engage with substantive arguments. Yet, at the same time, it is more substantive than formal in focus. The reasons for this preference are different from those under the process efficacy logic though (where they were linked to the idea that good process is instrumental for good outcomes). The subsidiarity logic is interested in the division of work between national authorities and the supranational court. The 'work' at issue is the scrutiny of the compatibility of a (proposed) norm with the Convention. Hence, the procedural review that operates from this logic, whether from negative or positive subsidiarity, focuses on 'whether the national authorities do their part of the job', and aims at identifying what is good or bad in the way these national authorities take up their responsibility for human rights scrutiny. Except where it is found that human rights scrutiny was simply omitted, such a review should focus on 'whether the impact of a proposed measure on Convention rights has been expressly and extensively discussed, whether the reasons invoked to justify interference with a Convention right are among those that the Court accepts, and whether and how the proportionality of such interference was assessed' (cf. *supra*, 2.1), that is to say that it should scrutinise domestic human rights scrutiny.

It is to be noted that a negative subsidiarity logic is suspicious of any interference by the Court in matters that are considered to be the appropriate domain of the domestic authorities. It therefore would not be inclined to accept the Court expressing normative preferences about certain more strictly formal matters, especially where the work of the legislature is concerned and where a strong doctrine of parliamentary sovereignty is adhered to. From that perspective, it may be highly problematic to attach positive or negative inferences to issues regarding the organisation of parliamentary work, such as the discussion of a matter in committees, the organisation of hearings, the consultation of certain people, etc. All of these issues fall outside the commitments that states have entered into when ratifying the Convention, reason for which states may challenge the legitimacy of the Court's scrutinising these matters. A strong stance on negative subsidiarity may resist also the less formalistic type of procedural review advanced here, i.e. the review of domestic human rights scrutiny. It is submitted, however, that this viewpoint does not stand on solid ground, as from the institutional subsidiarity angle, the review of domestic human rights scrutiny is the European Court's core business. The reason for creating a supranational court is the assumption that domestic human rights scrutiny will occasionally be deficient. The way a supranational court functions should therefore enable it to point out these deficiencies, so that they may be remedied. Even more than an autonomous assessment of the substance of a case, the assessment of the domestic authorities' treatment of the substance enables the Court to engage in such a dialogue with the national authorities. In other words, a dynamic of negative subsidiarity cannot go so far as to undermine the core idea of positive subsidiarity. In that sense, the two faces of subsidiarity are inextricably linked.

As for the *role* of procedural review as envisaged by a subsidiarity logic, it is to be noted that, different from the process efficacy logic, a negative subsidiarity logic would support a decisive role of a positive assessment of domestic process for a finding of no violation, in addition to – reluctantly (cf. *supra*) – accepting the reverse, i.e. a decisive role of a negative process assessment for the finding of a violation. In a positive subsidiarity logic, the important thing is to create leverage to nudge states towards improving domestic process. This would require that important (though not necessarily decisive) positive/negative consequences are attached to a positive/negative assessment of domestic process.

Drawing negative or positive inferences from the quality assessment of domestic process can be phrased or framed in the Court's reasoning in many different ways. However, within a subsidiarity logic, more particularly within a logic of negative subsidiarity, the most coherent approach would seem to be one that works with the width of the national authorities' margin of appreciation. That is to say a framing, as found in some of the Court's case law,[23] in which a positive quality assessment results in a widening of the margin of appreciation, whereas a negative quality assessment leads to narrowing the margin.

[23] Saul, o.c.

2.2.3 *Autonomous Process Value*

2.2.3.1 The Process Value Rationale

Generally speaking, the reasons for valuing good process are not purely instrumental; instrumental reasons are often intertwined with autonomous reasons of 'process value'.[24] Similarly, the institutional motivation discussed above does not necessarily point towards a procedural approach; if such an approach is put forward, it is because good process is (also) valued for its own sake.

2.2.3.2 Autonomous Process Value in Parliamentary, Administrative and Judicial Process

The European Convention on Human Rights explicitly attaches autonomous value to a decent *judicial* process. The right to a fair trial is a human right, not only in the ECHR, but in international human rights law as a whole, as well as in domestic bills of rights. In the ECHR, the right to a fair trial is developed in some detail, including multiple sub-rights, in Article 6. This is by far the most frequently invoked provision of the ECHR. An overview of the Court's case law until 2011 shows that no less than 45 per cent of its judgments concerned Article 6.

Additional procedural guarantees relating to court procedures are found in Article 5 ECHR with respect to arrest and detention, and in ECHR Protocol N° 7 with respect to the right of appeal in criminal matters (Article 2), compensation for wrongful conviction (Article 3) and the right not to be tried or punished twice (Article 4).

Moreover, the ECHR and its additional protocols include a number of specific procedural rights that do not exclusively concern courts, but rather extend to administrative remedies. In particular, Article 13 ECHR enshrines the right to a remedy in case of a violation of another Convention right, and Article 1 of Protocol 7 provides procedural safeguards relating to the expulsion of aliens.

When it comes to *administrative* decision-making or parliamentary process, a similar elevation of standards of good procedure to human rights cannot be found in the ECHR. Yet, a broader look at international human rights standards reveals that a fundamental right to fair treatment by administrative bodies has gained recognition internationally. In particular, it has been enshrined in Article 41 of the Charter of

[24] Christoffersen, o.c.

Fundamental Rights of the European Union.[25] Hence, there can be little doubt about the relevance of attaching autonomous process value to fair procedures before administrative bodies.

Zooming in on parliamentary process, it is also clear that a strong case for process value can be made here, as the value of good parliamentary process is directly related to the value of a well-functioning democratic system. The ECHR protects fundamental rights, not democracy per se. That is to say, the protection of Convention rights can be seen as a matter of substantive democracy, yet as far as the formal or procedural aspects of democracy go, only the right to free elections is included (Article 3, First Additional Protocol to the ECHR). Hence, as a free-standing motivation for its interest in reviewing the quality of parliamentary process, the argument from process value may be prone to legitimacy challenges. Yet as a supportive argument that is mobilised in combination with the instrumental and institutional arguments discussed above, it has undeniable strength, given the recurring emphasis on the importance of (the preconditions for) a well-functioning democracy throughout the Court's case law.[26]

2.2.3.3 Type and Role of Procedural Review under a ProcessValue Rationale

The *type* of procedural review, i.e. what exactly is being reviewed, from the angle of process value, concerns procedural features in the strict sense. For the judicial process, these relate among others to the right to a public hearing within a reasonable time by an independent and impartial tribunal (cf. Article 6 ECHR). For the administrative process, relevant procedural features would include a number of similar issues, such as the right to impartial treatment, the reasonable time requirement and the right to be heard (cf. Article 41 CFREU). When it comes to the parliamentary process, relevant features would have to be related to what Saul has described as the 'core components

[25] Article 41 provides in its first and second paragraphs:

1. *Every person has the right to have his or her affairs handled impartially, fairly and within a reasonable time by the institutions and bodies of the Union.*
2. *This right includes:*
   - *the right of every person to be heard, before any individual measure which would affect him or her adversely is taken;*
   - *the right of every person to have access to his or her file, while respecting the legitimate interests of confidentiality and of professional and business secrecy;*
   - *the obligation of the administration to give reasons for its decisions.*

[26] Popelier, o.c., 256; Saul, o.c., 12 ss.

of democracy: representation, participation, deliberation'.[27] Hence, a review of the quality of parliamentary process that is driven by process value concerns would focus on process features that are related to those core components. This may include, for example, the question whether the range of opinions on a certain issue found in society is included in the parliamentary debates, whether stakeholders have been able to make their case and whether discussions have been thorough, rational and balanced.

As such, the focus of procedural review under a process value rationale would be clearly different from that which is driven by process efficacy or by institutional motives.

As for the *role* of procedural review from a process value angle, it seems difficult to justify strong inferences from the quality assessment of domestic process in either the positive or the negative sense. For the judicial process, the text of the Convention has attached important value to these process features. Yet the fact that, in the Convention, they have been made the subject of a separate provision, may plead against giving them an important role in the interpretation of other, substantive Convention provisions. For judicial procedures (e.g. immigration cases or tax cases) that fall outside the scope of application of Article 6 ECHR, the situation is even more difficult, as attaching strong value to an assessment of procedural features in such cases might be considered as a way of circumventing the textual restrictions of the scope of Article 6. For the administrative process, the mirror argument can be made, i.e. that procedural guarantees have not as such been included in the Convention or its additional protocols, and that therefore their autonomous value is not a good basis for the ECtHR to attach much weight to them. Similarly, because promoting a well-functioning democracy is not part of the explicit mandate of the Court, this motive alone cannot justify strong inferences from good or bad parliamentary process in the Court's case law.

2.2.4 *Procedural Fairness: Good Process for Legitimacy, Compliance and Social Cohesion*

2.2.4.1 The Procedural Fairness Rationale

The autonomous value of good process (cf. *supra*) has been repeatedly confirmed in empirical research from the discipline of social psychology.

[27] Saul, o.c., 5.

Moreover, this research points towards additional instrumental reasons for valuing procedural review, as well as pointing to specific focal points in such review that differ from those that result from the process value and other perspectives.

The concept of procedural fairness (sometimes called 'procedural justice') was developed by American social psychology researchers and has gained worldwide recognition.[28] Its central empirical finding is that in people's contact with the law, they care not only about the outcome of their case, but also about the way in which it is handled.[29] In fact, the perception of procedural fairness (was the case dealt with in a fair manner?) is a more significant factor determining the perception of the legitimacy of the institution concerned than the perception of distributive justice (was the outcome of the case fair?). Moreover, it has been shown that perceptions of procedural fairness are linked to outcome compliance, and to overall satisfaction with the law, which in turn is beneficial for social cohesion. Legitimacy, compliance and social cohesion are important goals of the Parliament, the administration and the judiciary. Hence, they have a strong stake in the protection of procedural fairness.

2.2.4.2 Procedural Fairness in Parliamentary, Administrative and Judicial Process

These findings have been confirmed across a wide range of legal settings, including courts,[30] administrative decision-making and the lawmaking process.[31] A number of process features have been identified as crucial for perceptions of procedural fairness. These coincide to some extent, but not fully, with some of the values that are protected under provisions that have been adopted from a process value perspective (e.g. fair trial provisions). Yet from the viewpoint of impacting on fairness perceptions, the emphasis is not so much on compliance with specific technical rules as with the overall impression that is communicated. First among these process features that determine procedural fairness perceptions is the issue of voice or participation. In the judicial context, this largely coincides with the right to be heard. In the administrative and legislative contexts, it translates into the expectation that

[28] J. Thibaut and L. Walker, *Procedural Justice: A Psychological Analysis*, Erlbaum, 1975, vii.
[29] Ibid., 1.
[30] Tom Tyler, 'Procedural Justice and the Courts', *Court Review*, 44 (1/2) (2008).
[31] Amy Gangl, 'Procedural Justice Theory and Evaluations of the Lawmaking Process', *Political Behavior*, 25, 2 (2003).

one's interests are taken into account.[32] The second criterion of trustworthiness refers to the sincerity of authorities' intentions (do people see that they care?).[33] Another feature is neutrality. In the judicial context, this is largely covered by the concepts of impartiality and independence of the judiciary. For lawmakers and administrative decision-makers, it implies that the interests of the whole population are taken into account. All views should be considered and no one view should be granted an obvious advantage in the policy debate.[34] Neutrality also requires accuracy: informed decisions based on accurate information.[35] The final criterion is about treating people with respect.[36] People should be given the feeling that they and their concerns are taken seriously by the legal system. They must be treated as people and as valued members of society.[37]

I have argued elsewhere that there are several good reasons for the ECtHR to take the findings of procedural fairness research seriously, and that it should not only apply procedural fairness in its own work, but in addition take up a watchdog role concerning procedural fairness at the domestic level.[38]

Even if one does not consider such a procedural fairness watchdog role as a priority for the Court, a strong case can be made that, since the Court is expanding procedural types of review for other reasons, it would be wise to consider the findings of empirical research in this field that may enable it to maximise the benefits from procedural review for individuals, institutions and society as a whole.

[32] Margaret Levi, Audrey Sacks and Tom Tyler, 'Conceptualizing Legitimacy, Measuring Legitimating Beliefs', *American Behavioral Scientist* 53(3) (2009). p. 360.

[33] Tom Tyler, 'What Is Procedural Justice?: Criteria Used by Citizens to Assess the Fairness of Legal Procedures', *Law and Society Review*, 22 (1988), p. 129; Tom Tyler, *Why People Obey the Law*, Yale University Press, 1990, p. 164; Tom Tyler, 'Procedural Justice and the Courts', *Court Review*, 44(1/2) (2008), p. 30.

[34] Tyler, 'Procedural Justice and the Courts', o.c., 30; Saila Ouald Chaib, '*Suku Phull* v. *France* Rewritten from a Procedural Justice Perspective', in Eva Brems (ed), in *Diversity and European Human Rights: Rewriting Judgments of the ECHR*, Cambridge: Cambridge University Press, 2013), p. 223.

[35] Tom Tyler, 'Governing Amid Diversity: Can Fair Decision-Making Procedures Bridge Competing Public Interests and Values?', *Law and Society Review*, 28, (1994), p. 824.

[36] Kevin Burke and Steve Leben, 'Procedural Fairness: A Key Ingredient in Public Satisfaction', White paper for the American Judges Association (2007), 7; Tyler, *Why People Obey the Law*, o.c., p. 152.

[37] Tyler, *Why People Obey the Law*, o.c., p. 149.

[38] Eva Brems and Laurens Lavrysen, 'Procedural Justice in Human Rights Adjudication: The European Court of Human Rights', *Human Rights Quarterly*, 2013, pp. 176–200.

2.2.4.3 Type and Role of Procedural Review under the Procedural Fairness Rationale

The procedural fairness logic points to a *type* or focus of procedural review that is more similar to the process value logic than to the process efficacy or subsidiarity logics. From this perspective, the point is not so much to scrutinise the domestic authorities' human rights review, but rather to scrutinise the extent to which they have valourised the above-mentioned features that are crucial in procedural fairness perceptions. Hence, were the ECtHR to review the quality of domestic process from within a procedural fairness rationale, the procedural quality control would have to examine among others whether the domestic process has included all relevant perspectives, whether it has relied on accurate information and whether it has acted in a transparent manner, free from bias and etc.

As for the *role* of procedural review, the conclusion from the procedural fairness rationale is similar to that from the process efficacy rationale. Procedural fairness does not replace substantive fairness, but complements it. Hence, while a finding of a lack of procedural fairness can support the finding of a violation, a positive record of procedural fairness cannot be decisive for finding that a rights infringement does not constitute a violation.[39]

2.2.5 Aligning the Different Rationales for Procedural Review

In their goals and dynamics, the above-described different rationales under which the ECtHR might resort to assessing the qualities of domestic process do not contradict each other. Yet the weight of the consequences that may justifiably be attached to such an assessment varies according to the motives. In particular, the case for far-reaching consequences will be stronger as the ultimate objective of the turn to procedure is closer to the core business of the ECHR system, i.e. the human rights scrutiny of domestic measures. In that sense, the different motives can be ranked as follows, starting with the one that makes the strongest case for attaching far-reaching consequences to process quality assessment:

First comes process efficacy, because under this rationale, the concern with process is motivated directly by a concern with outcomes in terms of human rights scrutiny.

[39] Ibid., 200.

Next follows the subsidiarity rationale, because the concern with subsidiarity is about the Court's core business of human rights scrutiny. However, it is not a concern about the quality of human rights scrutiny, but rather about the division of work in this respect between the national and the supranational levels.

The rationales of process value and procedural fairness close the line. They make the least strong case for attaching far-reaching consequences to procedural quality control, because the motives behind the procedural control are only indirectly related to the Court's core business. The procedural fairness concerns of legitimacy (of domestic institutions), compliance, overall satisfaction with the law and social cohesion are peripheral to the Court's core concern of human rights protection. It may nevertheless be argued that for the ECtHR, procedural fairness is the procedural mirror of the substantive work it is trying to accomplish, and that it is part of the value system the Court represents.[40] Therefore, the procedural fairness rationale is compatible with substantive inferences from procedural quality assessment.

Under the rationale of autonomous process value, the quality of procedure is by definition valued for its own sake and hence detached from any other concern, including the protection of substantive human rights. Yet, within the Convention system, this autonomous process value is explicitly recognised in some cases, either in the treaty text (fair trial) or in the Court's case law (the importance of democracy). Hence, also under this rationale, there is still sufficient ground for drawing substantive inferences from the procedural quality assessment.

Overall, from within each of these rationales, there is a wish to draw at least some substantive inferences from the quality assessment of domestic process. The internal variation concerns mostly the desirable weight of these inferences. There is one exception, however, in that a negative subsidiarity logic, especially when it is based upon a strong dogma of parliamentary sovereignty, resists ECtHR scrutiny of parliamentary process (cf. *supra*). Arguably, the degree of resistance is stronger when this concerns an assessment of the quality of Parliament's organisation of its work, as opposed to an assessment of the quality of Parliament's human rights scrutiny. Yet, in practice, ECtHR scrutiny of the quality of parliamentary human rights scrutiny may also meet with strong resistance, and the same can happen with respect to ECtHR scrutiny of

[40] Brems & Lavrysen, o.c., 185.

the quality of domestic judicial human rights scrutiny.[41] It is submitted, however, that while in a logic of subsidiarity, resistance to ECtHR interference with formal procedural aspects deserves some credit as it is not explicitly within the Court's mandate; resistance to ECtHR scrutiny of domestic human rights scrutiny cannot carry much weight within the Convention system. It is indeed hard to see how the Court might pursue its core business in a framework of subsidiarity without scrutinising the human rights scrutiny that took place at the national level. Such exercise would be incomplete – and hence not fair – if it did not include human rights scrutiny performed by national parliaments or constitutional courts.

Moreover, there is a conflict between different logics when it comes to the desirable weight of positive inferences to be drawn from the process assessment. From the negative subsidiarity angle, there is support for strong inferences, even for a decisive role of positive inferences from the procedural assessment towards the outcome. At the same time, such a decisive role for positive inferences from procedure is not acceptable from the logic of process efficacy, nor is supported from the perspective of procedural fairness. However, it is submitted that a middle ground can be found if procedural review, especially when it leads to positive inferences towards the outcome, is focused on scrutinising domestic human rights scrutiny, rather than on scrutinising procedural elements in the stricter sense. Both from the process efficacy perspective and from the procedural fairness perspective, resistance to strong inferences from a positive procedural review is based on the need to avoid that procedural review replace substantive review by the Court. However, if procedural review takes the shape of 'scrutiny of scrutiny', it is in fact more aptly described as a mixed review that is procedural and substantive at the same time. If a sufficient substantive component can thus be introduced in the procedural review (cf. *infra*), this type of resistance might be overcome.

2.3 Optimal Procedural Quality Control in Practice

The analysis in the previous section points towards a particular kind of procedural review, i.e. a review of the quality of the human rights scrutiny performed at the domestic level, rather than a review of procedures or

[41] See the chapter by Angelika Nussberger to the current volume (7: 'Procedural Review by the European Court of Human Rights: View from the Court').

processes in the strict sense of those terms. It was called above a 'mixed' type of review that is procedural and substantive at the same time; below it will be called a 'substance-flavoured' procedural review.

This is the preferred type of review on the basis of a process efficacy logic, as well as the subsidiarity logic. Moreover, this type of review avoids any direct clash between the different logics (see 2.55). Below, it will first be examined, building on existing ECtHR case law, what such a review might look like in practice. Next, the question will be asked whether/how it might be possible to enrich this type of review with additional elements, so as to optimise its benefits by including autonomous process value, as well as the promotion of procedural fairness.

2.3.1 Substance-Flavoured Procedural Review: Strasbourg Scrutinising Domestic Human Rights Scrutiny

In the ECtHR case law, at least three types of 'substance-flavoured procedural review' can be identified.

In a number of cases in which the Court has drawn substantive inferences from an assessment of the quality of the parliamentary process, the Court has adopted a *broad approach* to this assessment. Notably in *Hirst (No 2)*, the Court checked whether the national parliament 'sought to weigh the competing interests or to assess the proportionality' of the restrictive measure at issue, and whether it had had a 'substantive debate' on that specific issue.[42]

Such a broad-brush approach to the quality of domestic human rights scrutiny, however, has the disadvantage of offering little guidance to national actors. In terms of lessons that can be learned from these cases, it is clear that some 'weighing of interests' and some proportionality analysis need to be done, yet it is not clear what is required for the Court to be satisfied with the quality of such weighing or proportionality analysis, nor what it would consider to be the requirements of a 'substantive' debate. In its case law to date, the Court has moreover given contradictory signals in this respect, focusing on occasion on a general finding that there has been a lot of debate (and/or reflection, consultation) about all kinds of (social, ethical, legal) aspects or consequences of the measure,[43] and in other cases requiring evidence that Parliament has sought to weigh competing interests and to assess the proportionality of the measure in

[42] *Hirst* v. *UK*, o.c., para. 79.
[43] ECtHR, Grand Chamber, *Maurice* v. *France*, 6 October 2005, para. 121.

Convention terms.[44] This lack of clarity is problematic both from a perspective of legal certainty and because it partly undermines the incentives for better scrutiny in a positive subsidiarity logic, as it is not clear what precisely should be done to get a better assessment next time.

In some cases, the Court has complemented a broad-brush approach to reviewing human rights scrutiny with a specific substantive focus, that is to say, a requirement that authorities show that they have explicitly taken into account certain relevant elements. In particular, the Court has required evidence of taking into account the minority status, as well as the specific vulnerability of affected persons. This can be the case for administrative measures,[45] but also for legislation, as appears from the Court's statement in *Aksu*: 'the vulnerable position of Roma/Gypsies means that special consideration should be given to their needs and their different lifestyle, both in the relevant regulatory framework and in reaching decisions in particular cases'.[46]

Though this certainly offers more concrete guidance to domestic authorities, it is not clear on what basis the Court has singled out some substantive elements to the exclusion of others. While this tendency in the Court's approach shows that substantive debate, weighing competing interests and assessing proportionality, may imply a number of very concrete requirements, it also covers only (a small) part of the ground and leaves a fog over what further specific expectations there might be.

Yet, if it so chooses, the Court can be a lot more concrete and complete in stating its expectations towards national authorities' human rights scrutiny. The Court has notably shown this in its review of human rights scrutiny by domestic *courts*, in a few lines of its case law where it has drawn very concrete checklists of criteria that are supposed to guide proportionality analysis. The Court has done so in particular in defamation case law,[47] as well as in Article 8 case law concerning expulsion of foreigners.[48] The Court has declared its willingness to draw far-reaching positive inferences from a positive quality assessment along these lines, stating that 'where the balancing exercise has been undertaken by the national authorities in conformity with the criteria laid down in the

[44] ECtHR, *Grand Chamber, Shindler* v. *United Kingdom*, 22 April 2013, para. 117.

[45] ECtHR, *Yordanova and others* v. *Bulgaria*, 24 April 2012, para. 133.

[46] ECtHR, *Grand Chamber Aksu* v. *Turkey*, 15 March 2012, para. 75.

[47] ECtHR, Grand Chamber, *Axel Springer AG* v. *Germany*, 7 February 2012; ECtHR, Grand Chamber, *Von Hannover* v. *Germany* (Nr 2), 7 February 2012.

[48] ECtHR, *Grand Chamber, Üner* v. *the Netherlands*, 18 October 2006; ECtHR, Grand Chamber, *Maslov* v. *Austria*, 23 June 2008.

Court's case law, the Court would require strong reasons to substitute its view for that of the domestic courts'.[49]

A human rights scrutiny check list for a legislator or for executive authorities might look somewhat different as compared to a checklist for a court. In particular, as legislators or administrations cannot be expected to reason in a legal way, criteria designed for them would have a much lower level of detail. They might include basic issues such as 'has the human right on which a measure will impact been named', 'has the need to resort to criminal law or to make a blanket ban been argued in a relevant manner' or 'has there been any consideration of whether the same goal might have been reached without infringing upon the human right or with a lighter infringement'. However, there appears to be no reason of principle why some type of checklist approach that concretises the requirements of a good proportionality analysis with respect to a specific issue would not work for administrations and parliaments as well. It is of course not a realistic or even meaningful goal to have concrete checklists for each possibility; yet if the Court were to start developing a number of such lists, it is expected that soon the nature of the expectations *vis-à-vis* domestic human rights scrutiny would become significantly clearer.

Yet, a checklist approach is not a panacea. In order for its message to get across to the national authorities, it is desirable to attach some weight to a finding of respect or lack of respect for the Court's checklist. Blind application of a checklist risks resulting in substantively unfair outcomes. Negative inferences from blind application of a checklist may be unjustified to the extent that the domestic authorities may have performed a qualitative human rights scrutiny along different lines than the ECtHR had envisaged. Positive inferences from blind application of a checklist also cannot be decisive without a consideration of the concrete facts and context of the case, which may raise issues that have not been anticipated by the ECtHR. The checklists themselves should be considered a work in progress. They are based on case law, and should be open to being refined through further case law.

2.3.2 *Adding More Flavours: Bringing in Process Value and Procedural Fairness*

If the Court's turn to procedural review, motivated by institutional reasons and/or by reasons of process efficacy, continues, it is worth considering

[49] *Von Hannover (No. 2)* v. *Germany*, o.c., para. 107.

enriching such procedural review with elements that would yield beneficial results in other logics, that is to say, for procedural fairness and for democratic parliamentary process, fair trial and fair treatment by administrations. As noted above, the focus of procedural review is a slightly different one from these angles, in that it is about process or procedure in a stricter sense of the word. Nevertheless, there appear to be many points of contact between the fields of interests from different procedural logics. For example, the procedural fairness issue of 'voice' is close to the democratic concern with participation and the fair trial concern of getting a hearing, and both echo the 'good human rights scrutiny' concern of weighing all relevant interests. Moreover, it seems possible to read most procedural fairness and process value concerns into (interpretations of) 'good human rights scrutiny' criteria. For example, both the democratic concern with proper deliberation and the procedural fairness focus on accuracy can be integrated into the expectation of 'substantive debate'.

It is submitted that an ideal scenario is one in which the Court's procedural review of domestic human rights scrutiny is thus enriched so as to optimise the autonomous beneficial effects of high-quality procedures, as well as their positive impact on people's perceptions of procedural fairness.

2.4 Conclusion

On the basis of the literature and the case law, this chapter has identified four different rationales that may explain the 'procedural turn' in the case law of the ECtHR. It has then proceeded to 'think through' the internal dynamics of each of these rationales, in terms of their application to the quality control of judicial, administrative and parliamentary process, and in terms of the type and role of procedural quality control they would ideally envisage.

In the Court's actual case law, there is not much explicitation of its motives to turn to procedure. It may be assumed that in reality, the rationales of process efficacy, process value and institutional concerns (subsidiarity) combine and or alternate to explain why and how the Court decides to scrutinise domestic procedures. Whether the Court also contemplates procedural fairness is not even certain, even though it is submitted that there are good reasons why it might wish to do so.

Given this reality of competing and interacting rationales, it is crucial to note that this chapter has identified a type of procedural quality control that allows for all rationales to be aligned. This is moreover the preferred type of control from the institutional as well as the process efficacy perspective. This 'substance-flavoured' procedural control scrutinises domestic human rights scrutiny, and in so doing, offers guidelines to domestic courts, administrations and parliaments on how to organise and implement high-quality human rights scrutiny. It is submitted in this chapter that the emergence of this type of procedural control by the ECtHR is a positive development, and that it is justifiable to draw substantive inferences from the result of the procedural quality control. The most difficult issue remains the possibility of drawing decisive positive conclusions from a positive procedural assessment. This scenario, in which procedural scrutiny substitutes for substantive scrutiny, is difficult to accept from a procedural fairness logic, as well as from a process efficacy logic.

3

The Modest Promise of 'Procedural Review' in Fundamental Rights Cases

ARUNA SATHANAPALLY

3.1 Introduction

One of the concerns of this volume is to better understand the recent orientation of supranational courts engaged in human rights review towards examining the '*fair procedures*' or '*deliberative processes*' undertaken by national authorities. This chapter interrogates whether and in what way it may be of value for a court – particularly the European Court of Human Rights (ECtHR) as the foremost supranational human rights court – to focus on the deliberative process leading to a decision or action that is subsequently challenged on human rights grounds. As a matter of normative human rights theory, is this a promising development, which ought to be developed doctrinally?

Drawing from theoretical scholarship on constitutional rights and political theory on democratic deliberation, a normative case can be made for a court undertaking a form of human rights review that has some regard to the deliberative processes leading to the decision under review. The *promise* of this practice is that a court leaves appropriate space for other institutions' decisions on difficult questions concerning fundamental rights, and does so in a way that supports and incentivises institutions of government towards better deliberative practices.

However, while this is appealing as an abstract proposition, it raises some concrete questions: is this more procedural type of review something that a court can effectively develop through its jurisprudence? If so, from where is the court to draw standards of good deliberation? How, in particular, is a supranational court such as the ECtHR to identify markers of good process applicable across different national systems, and will reference to process draw such a court into a more wide-ranging supervision of national authorities than is its remit?

This chapter examines these questions through a real-world example of a human rights decision (from the United Kingdom), one that has received attention precisely because it raises questions of how a court is to have regard to the processes followed by a respondent to a human rights complaint. The focus on a case study allows us to move from abstract propositions regarding the operation of institutions, to illustrate the different ways in which the process leading to a decision that is challenged on fundamental rights grounds may (or may not) be considered relevant to a court's consideration of whether a fundamental right has been infringed. It also allows us see the challenges facing a court that seeks to assess the quality of that process within the course of human rights review.

This chapter argues that, ultimately, the promise of procedural review in a fundamental rights context is a modest one. A court that takes into account the deliberative process leading to the decision under challenge is likely to do a better job of deciding when to exercise restraint, and this is likely to provide some incentives for better deliberation at the national level. However, given the difficulties in applying uniform standards to deliberation, procedural review of this kind may need to be impressionistic, rather than systematic; and ought to be understood as a secondary, rather than primary, consideration in fundamental rights review. Finally, as with any innovation aimed at changing behaviour, the effectiveness of procedural review in achieving even this modest promise is an empirical question, and one that can only be answered in time.

3.2 Theoretical Foundations: Fundamental Rights Deliberation beyond Courts

3.2.1 The Nature of Fundamental Rights Deliberation

Sometimes, though not all the time,[1] courts engaged in human rights-based review of legislation or government action face hard cases.[2]

[1] Human rights scholarship, particularly the scholarship surrounding the *design* of human rights review, is generally focused on fraught human rights cases, such as cases involving moral disagreement or difficult choices between political goals. Not all human rights cases have this character. While, when one is interested in institutional design, it makes sense to consider hard cases – cases that test the system – it is important to recall that not all human rights cases are hard cases; nor should principles that govern judicial involvement in human rights cases be designed solely with hard cases in mind. See the author's work elsewhere regarding 'quiet cases': A. Sathanapally, *Beyond Disagreement: Open Remedies in Human Rights Adjudication* (Oxford: Oxford University Press, 2012).

[2] See R. Dworkin, *Taking Rights Seriously* (Cambridge, MA: Harvard University Press, 1977), Chapter 4 for early use of the concept of a 'hard case' in constitutional theory.

The difficulty may be that the limitation on a litigant's human rights has been instated to protect the human rights of some other group, so the court may be in a position of effectively balancing rights against each other. It may be that the limitation on the litigant's rights is justified by reference to an important policy need, or a shortage of resources, so the court may be in a position of evaluating a policy justification for limiting rights. It may be that the situation before the court is one where a litigant seeks to push the previously judicially- or socially-accepted boundaries of a right into new territory. Or, it may be that the court must make its decision in the face of vehement disagreement from the political branch, perhaps attended by the significant unpopularity of the litigant's case before the court, so there are political realities external to the law that may affect the wider reception of the court's decision.

In such situations, above the immediate, substantive case that the court faces, sits an institutional question: Are courts the best forum for the polity to resolve this issue?

Some consider the answer to this question to be evidently 'yes'. Rights are legal entitlements to be determined by a court, in human rights law as in all other areas of the law. This is the juridical paradigm of fundamental rights, interpreted and enforced by independent courts as limits on the choices of political bodies. In virtually every Western democracy, courts are given the responsibility for determining and enforcing the fundamental rights guarantees granted to the population, against the administration and, in most cases, against the legislature.

However, fundamental rights principles are not exclusively or inherently legal standards of conduct. They are also moral or ethical claims on the exercise of power. As explained by Amartya Sen:[3]

> The admissibility of a domain of continued dispute is no embarrassment to a theory of human rights ... the possibility of such debates – without losing the basic recognition of the importance of human rights – is not just a feature of what can be called human rights practice, they are actually part of the general discipline of human rights ... An acknowledgement of the ethical necessity to pay attention to human rights, far from obliterating the need for such deliberation, actually invites it.

As formalised in national constitutions or international conventions, constitutional or international human rights are the general norms that States have agreed govern the fundamentals of a free and democratic

[3] A. Sen, 'Elements of a Theory of Human Rights' (2004) 32 *Philosophy and Public Affairs* 315, 322–323.

society. They are open-ended and necessarily underspecified for the range of circumstances in which they are claimed. Well-established civil and political rights, such as those in the European Convention of Human Rights (ECHR), have a clear core that can readily be identified. However, cases arise where the requirements of a given human right are open to varied interpretations and to reasonable disagreement over which interpretation is best. This may be because the scope of the right is, as a matter of law, indeterminate at the relevant time. The situation before the court may be one in which the right has not yet been considered or specified, or there may be potential for progressive development of the right from previous understandings of it. Or, it may be because the incursion is claimed to be a proportionate limitation on rights based on evidence of a social need, or that the individual's human rights claim raises systemic policy consequences or resource allocation issues beyond that of the immediate case.

There are those, most famously Ronald Dworkin, who favour courts as the forum best-placed to resolve issues of moral principle.[4] To Dworkin, once courts have determined the legal requirements of constitutional rights, it is for political decision-makers to decide questions of policy and resource allocation within those bounds. This argument relies on three features of courts: the independence of courts, the requirement for courts to engage in public, principled reasoning in reaching their conclusions and the courts' focus on matters of long-term principle rather than the short-term exigencies of politics and popular sentiment. It is the *deliberative character of courts* that attracts legal theorists like Dworkin. Equally, political theorists concerned with 'public reason', such as John Rawls, have portrayed the highest courts as exemplars of public reason.[5]

However, court-centred models of fundamental rights interpretation have been the subject of extensive criticism. It is difficult enough to delineate questions of 'principle' from questions of policy and resource allocation.[6] Where a human right is defined in a way that allows for proportionate limitation on grounds of a social need, then it is virtually

[4] Dworkin, *Taking Rights Seriously*. A more recent attempt by Dworkin to draw a line between sets of issues appropriate for majoritarian decision-making, and those appropriate for protection by courts against majority sentiment, is the concept of 'choice-sensitive' and 'choice-insensitive' decisions: R. Dworkin, *Sovereign Virtue: The Theory and Practice of Equality* (Cambridge, MA: Harvard University Press, 2002), pp. 203–205.

[5] J. Rawls, *Political Liberalism* (New York: Columbia University Press, 1993), § 6.

[6] K. Greenawalt, 'Dworkin's Rights Thesis' (1976) 74 *Michigan Law Review*, pp. 1167–1199; N. MacCormick, *Legal Reasoning and Legal Theory* (Oxford: Oxford University Press, 1978), pp. 259–264.

impossible to separate questions of 'policy' from the task of determining the scope of the protected right. Further, and most importantly for present purposes, when difficult cases arise, they are not uniquely problems that interest lawyers and courts – in healthy democracies, disagreement over the scope of the fundamental ethical and moral principles governing a democratic polity invites deliberation both inside and outside court rooms.[7] Hard cases can also involve trade-offs between different rights, decisions that need to be made in conditions of uncertainty, value pluralism and the pursuit of social goals that are incommensurable. These are problems that are worthy of consideration by public institutions beyond courts. Some of the features that make cases difficult are intractable in modern, plural democracies and cannot be 'solved' by reasoning alone, no matter the calibre of the judge or, indeed, philosopher. But while they may not have a 'correct' answer, these types of questions do have 'better' and 'worse' answers. The puzzle then is how to design our institutions such that we get better answers more often.

At the supranational level, there is a further dimension that makes the task of a human rights court difficult: there is a longstanding debate over the extent to which the content of international human rights safeguards must be uniform or may permissibly, even desirably, vary across countries.[8] This raises questions about how a supranational court should exercise its role as the final arbiter of what broadly worded rights require of national governments. Nowhere has this interest been more prominent in recent times than in relation to the role of the ECtHR, with State parties recently expressing formal support for the principles of 'subsidiarity' and 'the margin of appreciation' as guiding the court's jurisprudence,[9] principles which delimit the role of the court relative to national institutions.

[7] A. Gutmann and D. Thompson, *Democracy and Disagreement* (Cambridge, MA: Belknap Press, 1998). See also Habermas and Benhabib, who both argue that human rights are a major support for moral and political discourse: J. Habermas, *Between Facts and Norms* (Cambridge, MA: The MIT Press, 1996) and S. Benhabib, *The Rights of Others* (Cambridge: Cambridge University Press, 2004).

[8] For a discussion of challenges on the grounds of religious identity, see C. Cerna, 'Universality of Human Rights and Cultural Diversity: Implementation of Human Rights in Different Socio-Cultural Contexts' (1994) 16(4) *Human Rights Quarterly* pp. 740–752.

[9] Izmir Declaration on the future of the European Court of Human Rights, Council of Europe, 27 April 2011; Brighton Declaration of the future of the European Court of Human Rights, Council of Europe, 20 April 2012; Council of Europe Treaty Series, No. 213, Protocol No. 15 amending the Convention on the Protection of Human Rights and Fundamental Freedoms, Strasbourg, 24.VI.2013.

If a court, in particular a supranational court, is to restrain itself so as to leave space for other institutions to reach answers on what human rights require, the practical question that immediately arises is in what circumstances is it appropriate for the court do so? This chapter explores one method by which a court may decide when to weigh in, and when to exercise restraint, in the context of human rights adjudication. This is to do so by reference to the quality of the deliberative process undertaken by the body whose decision is under review.

3.2.2 *The Phenomenon under Consideration*

This chapter takes as its point of departure the turn towards procedure in the decision-making of the ECtHR documented in this volume and other recent scholarship.[10] The term 'procedural review' provides a useful, if somewhat imprecise, shorthand to refer to a type of review that focuses on the procedure followed by national authorities in reaching a particular decision or taking particular action, as distinct from the decision or action itself. This chapter is not directed towards the full range of judicial behaviour that has been described as procedural review by others. It is important therefore to establish the bounds of the phenomenon that I am interested in here.

There are several ways in which the description '*procedural*' may be understood in the human rights context. Certain human rights, archetypically the right to a fair trial and the right to due process of the law, are procedural in their essence. Other generally worded rights have been translated by courts into procedural obligations in particular circumstances, such as the duty to investigate all deaths caused by State actors as a component of the right to life. Therefore, a human right may itself be a procedural right or have a procedural component.

On the other hand, procedural review by courts of governmental action is well-known to national administrative lawyers. The ideals of democracy and the rule of law, which underpin Western administrative law systems, give rise to a set of predominantly procedural principles such as the right of affected persons to be heard before a decision is made,

[10] See in particular E. Brems, 'Procedural Protection' in E. Brems and J.H. Gerards (eds), *Shaping Rights in the ECHR. The Role of the European Court of Human Rights in Determining the Scope of Human Rights* (Cambridge: Cambridge University Press, 2014) and P. Popelier, 'The Court as Regulatory Watchdog: The Procedural Approach in the Case Law of the European Court of Human Rights', in P. Popelier et al. (eds), *The Role of Constitutional Courts in Multilevel Governance* (Antwerp: Intersentia, 2012).

the right to be heard by an impartial decision-maker, the requirement that the decision-maker give reasons for a decision or the requirement of transparency as to information relied upon.[11] These procedural requirements may be judicially developed, or codified by the legislature, depending on the national system.[12]

Typically, the remedy for a violation of administrative procedures is that a decision is invalid for having been improperly made. A court reviewing administrative action polices the procedure; the *outcome* remains a decision for the public official and may be remitted for the official to make in the correct way. This aspect of national administrative law is a reflection of the separation of powers between the administration and the courts. It is for the courts to hold the administration to the law and the procedural standards of administration that are either judicially developed or mandated in legislation. Procedural invalidity is distinct from illegality of governmental action on the grounds that a substantive decision was prohibited by law. Procedural invalidity does not generally allow a court to determine the correct outcome.

This is an important difference between (non-human rights-based) national administrative review and fundamental rights review conducted by a national or supranational court. Taking the example of the ECHR, the ECtHR has been tasked with upholding the substantive rights in the ECHR. The requirement of international law is that State parties uphold ECHR rights in their jurisdiction, not simply to take them into consideration in a particular manner. Human rights law is not agnostic as to outcomes; the ultimate issue before a court engaged in a fundamental rights case is whether the particular State action or decision that is under challenge complies with the substantive right claimed.

[11] In attempting to identify a core of shared administrative law principles across systems, Harlow observes 'in most systems, administrative law has evolved as primarily concerned with procedure': C. Harlow, 'Global Administrative Law: The Quest for Principles and Values' (2006) 17 *European Journal of International Law*, pp. 187–214. In the European context, see M. Shapiro, 'The Institutionalisation of European Administrative Space' in A. Stone Sweet et al. (eds), *The Institutionalization of Europe* (Oxford: Oxford University Press, 2001).

[12] From country to country, the selection of principles and emphasis of administrative law may vary. For instance, the procedural focus in American administrative law is participation, while Scandinavian systems emphasise transparency. However, a core list of administrative law values has been suggested to be 'openness, fairness, participation, accountability, consistency, rationality, accessibility of judicial and non-judicial grievance procedures, legality and impartiality': M. Aronson and M. Groves, *Judicial Review of Administrative Action* (Sydney: Thomson Reuters, 2013), [1.10].

Therefore, a general objection may be taken to a court referring to decision-making procedures when reviewing a decision on fundamental rights grounds, which is that how a decision came to be made or an action was chosen by the respondent does not matter in principle. The most admirable parliamentary decision-making process should not save from censure a decision that clearly infringes, say, the right to life. And conversely, whatever one may think about the poor quality of deliberation leading to a particular action being taken, if that action is in substance compatible with, say, freedom of religion, then the action cannot be said to fall foul of freedom of religion for reason of process alone.

This objection is well made insofar as it demonstrates that, by contrast to general administrative review, in a fundamental rights context, a court cannot and should not adopt a wholly procedural approach focused only in the procedure leading to the decision under challenge and not the substantive right claimed.

However, a court may find itself faced with a hard case, in the sense described above. One may take the position – adopting the juridical paradigm of fundamental rights – that the only thing that matters is the court's determination of the substantive question of human rights principle. However, in light of the criticisms of that paradigm of fundamental rights protection in hard cases, we may ask whether a normative case can be made for a court having reference to the calibre of the deliberative processes of other institutions, leading to the decision under review, in the course of deciding the scope and application of the substantive right claimed.

The phenomenon that this chapter considers, and refers to by the shorthand 'procedural review' for ease of reference, is one in which a court takes into account the quality of the procedures followed by the decision-maker in satisfying itself whether the decision complied with a substantive fundamental right. This aligns with the second aspect of the 'procedural turn' in the ECtHR's jurisprudence set out in Gerards' helpful typology of procedural review.[13] In particular, this type of procedural review has arisen in relation to whether a limitation on rights is proportional and thereby justified. However, conceptually, such an assessment

[13] See Chapter 6: 'Procedural Review by the ECtHR: A Typology'. Popelier refers to this as 'procedural rationality review' (see Chapter 4: 'Evidence-Based Lawmaking: Influences, Obstacles and the Role of the European Court of Human Rights'), and it has also been referred to as 'semiprocedural review': I. Bar-Siman-Tov, 'Semiprocedural Judicial Review' 6 *Legisprudence* (2012), p. 271.

need not necessarily be limited to proportionality analysis; the process followed by the decision-maker may be considered when a court is deciding the scope of a right, or whether the exercise of a right has been interfered with.[14]

The relevance of the procedures followed by the decision-maker may be in order to draw an inference in favour of human rights compatibility, or to draw an adverse inference.[15] The ECtHR has considered the procedures followed by national authorities – including national legislatures – to be relevant to its decisions in both senses. It is not suggested by those who have studied the Court's jurisprudence, such as Brems and Gerards in this volume, that the Court is applying a wholly procedural approach, but the more qualified understanding – one where procedures followed by a decision-maker are taken into account – fits the burgeoning practice that has been identified. This practice has not to date been systematically applied by the Court. In contrast to the Court's extensive use of '*the margin of appreciation*', the procedural elements of its decisions, where they emerge, have not yet been explained as part of a principled doctrine.[16] Nonetheless, given the Court's role in upholding States' obligations under the ECHR, this phenomenon raises the question of whether the Court *should* have reference to the procedures followed at the national level when evaluating the human rights compliance of the outcome under international law. As a matter of normative human rights theory, is this a promising development, which ought to be developed doctrinally?

3.3 The Promise of Procedural Review in Fundamental Rights Cases

3.3.1 Institutional Humility on the Part of the Courts

There are two lines of normative scholarship in constitutional and political theory that may support recourse to procedural review in fundamental rights cases as a way for a court, particularly a supranational court, to share responsibility for the development of human rights with

[14] In relation to which, see the case study below in Part 3.4.

[15] See Chapter 6: 'Procedural Review by the ECtHR: A Typology'.

[16] According to Angelika Nussberger, the practice has to date been reactive, that is, in response to submissions about the national deliberative procedure being made by parties, rather than initiated by the Court: see Chapter 7: 'Procedural Review by the European Court of Human Rights: View from the Court'.

national actors. The first advocates judicial restraint in fundamental rights adjudication. These scholars caution against excessive reliance on judges to elucidate the meaning of fundamental rights and freedoms, and to weigh up how these rights and freedoms are to be balanced against competing social goals. Procedural review presents itself as a potential method by which a court may limit its intrusion on conclusions that other branches of government have reached regarding the scope and proportionate limitation of constitutional rights.

3.3.1.1 Judicial Restraint in Fundamental Rights Adjudication

There is a long tradition of scepticism and criticism of the juridical paradigm of fundamental rights protection.[17] Without necessarily accepting the full range of this criticism, for present purposes, there are three types of shortcomings of judicial review that can be argued to support a court exercising restraint – or being restrained as a matter of constitutional design – when deciding the scope of fundamental rights guarantees and whether limitations on rights are proportionate.

The first is the challenge to the legitimacy of courts overriding decisions made by political decision-makers who are electorally accountable to the polity. In response, theorists have sought to distinguish questions of law and principle suited to judicial resolution from questions of policy suited to majoritarian decision-making,[18] as a way of demarcating questions that are more legitimately answered by a court. However, as set out above, this view is hard to sustain and ultimately unhelpful in the face of formulations of fundamental rights that allow for proportionate limitations of rights, which openly draw courts into an evaluation of the requirements of policy. In any event, criticism of the legitimacy of courts deciding fundamental rights cases has not been limited to courts deciding

[17] There are those who reject rights themselves as prioritised norms (notoriously, philosopher Jeremy Bentham), but the argument from a 'rights-based' philosophical perspective as to why an elected legislature is to be preferred as the institution to protect rights is articulated in J. Waldron, *Law and Disagreement* (Oxford: Oxford University Press, 1999). This chapter does not enter into the challenges to this view, but for an analysis, see Sathanapally, *Beyond Disagreement*, p. 54. For a collection of sceptical perspectives on judicial review, see A. Tomkins et al. (eds), *Sceptical Essays on Human Rights* (Oxford: Oxford University Press, 2001), arguments which several of the authors renew in A. Tomkins et al. (eds), *The Legal Protection of Human Rights: Sceptical Essays* (Oxford: Oxford University Press, 2011).

[18] See text accompanying note 4.

issues of 'policy', but has extended to courts making decisions in the face of societal moral disagreement over issues of principle.

This legitimacy-based shortcoming relates to the court's lack of responsiveness or accountability to the polity and therefore its credentials, in comparison to other branches of government, to resolve societal disagreement. Jeremy Waldron has set out one prominent philosophical criticism of the legitimacy of judicial decision-making regarding fundamental rights, in his case, relative to the legitimacy of an elected legislature. However, a similar form of reasoning has been employed in relation to administrative agencies, who have been given responsibility within a constitutional scheme for making the decision under review, and have their own routes of accountability to the polity for their decisions.[19]

The second type of shortcoming concerns how well-equipped courts are, relative to other institutions, to work out the correct, or best, answer when faced with a hard case. The issues raised before the court may concern interests other than those represented by the parties involved in the dispute (what has been referred to as 'polycentricity')[20] or may involve assessments of the preferences of the polity as a whole, where the court may have limited means of determining views or preferences beyond the parties to the dispute before it. There may be technical aspects to a problem that are better understood by the relevant administrative agency or social conditions better understood by the local government official. There may be, and often are, conditions of uncertainty faced by the decision-maker,[21] and subsequently, the court. In short, this *epistemic* limitation is concerned with whether, by reason of its particular institutional features, a court is the most capable institution to weigh up the available choices.

Finally, there is a realistic constraint on the ability of a court to reach decisions that thwart the other branches of government and defy popular sentiment. This is a pragmatic limitation, as any court needs to maintain

[19] In a Westminster context, see M. Taggart, 'Proportionality, Deference, *Wednesbury*' (2008) *New Zealand Law Review* 423, 457; in the United States context, see J.L. Mashaw 'Between Facts and Norms: Agency Statutory Interpretation as an Autonomous Enterprise' (2005) 55 *University of Toronto Law Journal*, p. 497.

[20] L.L. Fuller, 'The Forms and Limits of Adjudication' (1978) 92 *Harvard Law Review* 353; though see Allison's analysis of the deficiencies of Fuller's articulation of the concept in J.W.F. Allison, 'Fuller's Analysis of Polycentric Disputes and the Limits of Adjudication' (1994) 53(2) *Cambridge Law Journal*, pp. 367–383.

[21] On how conditions of empirical uncertainty affect legal interpretation, see generally A. Vermeule, *Judging Under Uncertainty* (Cambridge, MA: Harvard University Press, 2006).

a certain degree of comity with other institutions of government to ensure that its decisions are implemented and that its role does not come under attack.[22]

For these reasons, there has been sustained interest amongst constitutional theorists, and, in recent decades, in the field of constitutional design, in limiting the role of judicial review under fundamental rights instruments. In those Commonwealth countries that have been late adopters of a Bill of Rights, traditional methods of constitutional judicial review have been modified so as to limit the extent to which judges necessarily have the final word on what is or is not constitutionally permissible. Structural modifications range from giving the legislature the power to override judicial determinations and reinstate legislation found by the courts to violate fundamental rights (or pre-emptively protect legislation from adverse judicial review),[23] to preventing the courts from invalidating legislation at all and leaving the decision on whether and how to change the law to the legislature.[24]

However, even without any formal limitation or weakening of judicial powers, a court may, despite having full powers of substantive human rights review, be restrained in the exercise of those powers; that is, courts may and do exercise *self-restraint*. Faced with a case that is fraught or difficult, a court exercising restraint errs on the side of respecting the decision made by the body under review. Indeed, it can be seen, most clearly in the jurisprudence under the UK *Human Rights Act 1998* ('*Human Rights Act*') that judges may exercise self-restraint in interpreting and applying fundamental rights even when their powers to override legislative choices are constrained under the Bill of Rights.[25]

A court that routinely shies away from interrogating the adherence of public action to the rights which it is entrusted to uphold, without

[22] See the discussion of self-preservation in M. Tushnet, 'New Forms of Judicial Review and the Persistence of Rights- and Democracy-Based Worries' (2003) 38 *Wake Forest Law Review* 813, pp. 829–830 and what Kavanagh calls prudential reasons for deference in A. Kavanagh, 'Deference or Defiance? The Limits of the Judicial Role in Constitutional Adjudication' in G. Huscroft (ed) *Expounding the Constitution: Essays in Constitutional Theory* (Cambridge: Cambridge University Press, 2008), pp. 184–215.

[23] In Canada and South Africa.

[24] In the United Kingdom, New Zealand, at the sub-federal level in Australia, and with respect to ECHR rights specifically, Ireland.

[25] Sathanapally, *Beyond Disagreement*, Chapter 5, and cf: Mark Tushnet's hypothesis that courts may be more robust in their interpretations of constitutional rights if their powers are weakened: M. Tushnet, *Weak Courts, Strong Rights* (Princeton: Princeton University Press, 2008), pp. 242–252.

offering a reason for doing so, can be criticised as effectively abdicating the role given to it by a constitution (at the national level) or State parties to an international convention (at the international level). For this reason, courts (and commentators advocating restraint) have considered it valuable to finesse the exercise of judicial restraint through jurisprudential approaches which determine when self-restraint by judges is or is not appropriate.[26]

For instance, a court may identify certain subject matter that is considered unsuitable for judicial scrutiny (matters that are *non-justiciable*),[27] such as foreign policy, war powers or national security. A court may engage in *judicial minimalism*, that is, narrow its reasoning to the minimum required to do justice between the parties before the court, and hold back on setting out broader views on the scope of the right at issue. Alternatively, a court may exercise *remedial restraint*; that is, after finding a violation of a fundamental right, instead of prescribing a substantive remedy, the court may leave decisions regarding corrective action to another branch of government. In this way, the court can avoid making decisions on how to translate its judgment into broader prospective action.[28]

Relevantly for present purposes, a court may simply defer to another institution and hold back from engaging in searching review of its decision or conduct on institutional grounds, that is, on the basis of (real or perceived) institutional failings of courts relative to the particular institution whose decision or action is under review. In an administrative law context, courts in the United States and Canada defer to administrative decision-makers' interpretation of the law on this basis, only intervening if the decision-maker's interpretation is not reasonable or

[26] Notwithstanding the existence of various doctrines of judicial restraint, restraint may also be exercised in an ad hoc manner in controversial cases. Such restraint is pragmatic and unstated, and may be identified only in hindsight with the benefit of historical research or through the observation of patterns in decision-making. For instance, see the work of Dinah Shelton in relation to the European Court of Human Rights's remedial restraint in relation to politically sensitive cases and unpopular litigants, drawn from personal interviews with judges of the court and analysis of patterns in decided cases: D. Shelton, *Remedies in International Human Rights Law* (Oxford: Oxford University Press, 2005), Chapter 7.

[27] G. Marshall, 'Justiciability' in A.G. Guest (ed), *Oxford Essays in Jurisprudence* (Oxford: Oxford University Press, 1961), 265–268; L. Sossin, *Boundaries of Judicial Review: The Law of Justiciability in Canada* (Toronto: Carswell, 1999). In a similar vein, see the 'political question' doctrine in United States constitutional law: *Baker* v. *Carr* 369 US 186 (1962).

[28] There are a variety of such remedies across different jurisdictions, which I have written about elsewhere as *open remedies:* Sathanapally, *Beyond Disagreement*, Chapter 1.

is contradicted by clear instructions in the legislation.[29] In the United Kingdom, with the advent of the *Human Rights Act*, the courts attempted to identify circumstances in which it was appropriate to exercise deference towards the primary decision-maker, notwithstanding that the courts had been given powers of substantive human rights review.[30] In each of these national systems, the doctrines of restraint can be understood both on the basis that the primary decision-maker has been given constitutional responsibility for making the relevant decision (the legitimacy-based rationale for restraint) and is well-placed to determine the best answer (the capability or epistemic rationale for restraint).

The ECtHR's margin of appreciation doctrine is an example of a doctrine of judicial restraint based on institutional grounds, that is, allowing national authorities room for some variation within the requirements of the ECHR. The foundation for the doctrine of the margin of appreciation was set out in the judgment in *Handyside* v. *United Kingdom:*[31]

> By reason of their direct and continuous contact with the vital forces in their countries, State authorities are in principle in a better position than the international judge to give an opinion on the exact content of these requirements as well as on the 'necessity' of a restriction or 'penalty' intended to meet them.

What constrained judicial powers by design and judicial self-restraint share is that both give effect to the notion that responsibility for developing the meaning and scope of human rights protections in a given polity is not solely the province of the courts. One potential – and passive – method to expand responsibility for the protection of human rights beyond courts is for courts to step back, or be held back, and recognise and give respect to other institutions' assessments of what human rights require. In both contexts, it has been suggested that this may support a 'dialogue' between courts and other institutions over the meaning of fundamental rights.[32]

[29] In the United States, this is referred to as the *Chevron* principle: *Chevron USA Inc.* v. *Natural Resources Defence Council*, 467 US 837 (1984) at pp. 865–888. In Canada, it is referred to as judicial deference to agencies' own interpretation of their own laws, see *Baker* v. *Canada (Minister for Citizenship and Immigration)* (1999) 174 DLR (4th) 193.

[30] Sparking in turn academic commentary on appropriate principles of deference: see P. Craig, *Administrative Law* (London: Sweet & Maxwell, 2012), pp. 628–632.

[31] *Handyside* v. *United Kingdom* [1976] 1 EHRR 737 at [46].

[32] For references and a roadmap through the extensive scholarship, see Sathanapally, *Beyond Disagreement*, Chapter 2. This metaphor of dialogue has been applied to the exercise of judicial restraint by the ECtHR: see the text accompanying note 54 below.

3.3.1.2 Procedural Review as a Variant of Judicial Restraint?

The processes leading to the decision or action under review are a further reference point that a court may use when deciding whether or not to exercise restraint in a fundamental rights case. To the varieties of judicial restraint identified above, can we then add procedural review?

It is clear that, in certain cases, procedural review may operate as a form of restraint on the substantive human rights issue before the court. By directing its attention to the deliberation leading to the decision or action under review, the court may identify reasons not to disrupt the conclusion reached by the decision-maker. Moreover, if these reasons are process-based, they indicate to other decision-makers that there is a latitude available in terms of substantive conclusions on what rights require, *if* a diligent process is followed in reaching that conclusion.

So, where procedural review results in a positive inference as to rights compatibility, it operates to leave space for political decision-makers to interpret fundamental rights. Moreover, there is an appeal to using procedure as a basis upon which to respect government decisions that comes naturally to administrative lawyers: a careful, well-informed decision should be entitled to greater respect than one made hastily or carelessly.

What then of procedural review that results in a *negative* inference?

On the one hand, a 'negative inference' may amount to no more than a court declining to exercise restraint, exposing the decision to searching human rights review. Here, the reference to process is still being used to identify the extent to which, in the circumstances, restraint is appropriate.

In fact, there is a logical connection between procedural review and the exercise of judicial restraint on institutional grounds. Where institutional reasons for judicial restraint has been considered in academic scholarship, justification for restraint have centred on the need for institutional humility on the part of courts, when faced with a case that is not straightforward.[33] However, institutional humility on its own is not a sufficient reason for a court to step back from engaging in full and proper review of a decision, if it is empowered to do so, because all institutions are imperfect, and institutional choice is *relative*.[34] Therefore, an institutional

[33] For example, see Kavanagh, who focuses on 'deficits' of institutional competence, expertise and legitimacy: Kavanagh, 'Deference or Defiance?' at pp. 194–200. Similarly, J. King, 'Institutional Approaches to Judicial Restraint' (2008) 28 *OJLS*, pp. 409–441.

[34] N. Komesar, *Imperfect Alternatives: Choosing Institutions in Law, Economics and Public Policy* (Chicago: University of Chicago Press, 1994).

approach to judicial restraint ought to be based on *relative* incapacity or fallibility on the part of the court compared to the body that made the decision under review.

Even if a court suffers from limitations and is not the ideal institution to resolve a particular type of human rights problem, it may be the best or only institution to take that particular problem seriously and approach it diligently. The advantage of a court having reference to the manner in which a decision-maker has in fact acted is that this helps to give the decision-maker's conclusion the weight it deserves, rather than assuming the strengths of the particular decision-maker based on formal or abstract attributes alone. It helps courts identify circumstances where judicial restraint is appropriate, not simply on the basis that other institutions may theoretically have strengths that judges lack, but on the basis that those institutions have in fact employed those strengths.[35] By contrast, if a court defers to a decision-maker on institutional grounds without any reference to the actual deliberation of that institution, a court may absolve that decision-maker from the requirement to justify why their decision is compatible with fundamental rights, in circumstances where that decision was not the product of careful consideration in the first place.

It is therefore possible for the court's reliance on process (in drawing either positive or negative inferences) to operate not as a variety of judicial restraint *in itself*, but *within* judicial restraint on institutional grounds, furnishing reasons to amplify (or alternatively, mute) the respect that the court gives to the decisions of another institution of government.

On the other hand, procedural review is not necessarily an exercise in *institutional humility* on the part of courts, unlike the other methods of judicial restraint. Even if courts do not actively, or openly, draw negative inferences, procedural review necessarily draws courts into an evaluation of how other institutions of government operate. It opens the door to something beyond the primary conclusion of the court on the substantive human rights question before it, that is, a secondary conclusion as to the adequacy of decision-making processes of the respondent before the court.

Whether procedural review is an exercise in judicial restraint on institutional grounds, or instead a more expansive supervision by courts

[35] Dyzenhaus makes the sensible point that it is hard to separate the attributes of institutions from their decision-making processes: D. Dyzenhaus, 'Proportionality and Deference in a Culture of Justification' in G. Huscroft et al. (eds), *Proportionality and the Rule of Law: Rights, Justification, Reasoning* (Cambridge: Cambridge University Press, 2014), 234.

over other institutions of government, depends on how a court engages in the evaluation of process. A systematic form of procedural review may be highly prescriptive. Alternatively, the reference to process may be a more impressionistic evaluation to the effect that the matter before the court is a hard case and, its dimensions having been conscientiously deliberated by the respondent, it would be unwise for the court to disrupt the respondent's conclusion. I explore these two options further in section 3.4.

3.3.2 *Incentivising Deliberation*

Those advocating institutional humility on the part of courts (or institutional design that de-emphasises judicial review) have not generally directed the same critical lens to the decision-making processes of other institutions. The second line of normative scholarship that can be employed in support of procedural review is more actively concerned with improving the calibre of democratic processes in formally democratic systems of government. This is a more positive rationale for procedural review; the concern is not with keeping courts *out*, but rather how to guide and incentivise deliberation and reason-giving across the polity, and thereby enhance (a particular account of) democracy.

Often when arguments are made for courts to respect the decisions of the political branches of government regarding fundamental rights, they are based on formal characteristics of the legislature and, occasionally, the characteristics of the executive. The reasoning is routinely along the lines that, in contrast to judges, legislators are elected and representative of the polity. Even where the legitimacy of legislative decision-making is the subject of sustained reasoning – for instance in the work of Jeremy Waldron[36]– it is the *formal* and *indirect* manner in which an elected body gives effect to the right to participation that grounds the democratic legitimacy of legislative decisions, not the *actual degree of civic participation* in any given decision.

Equally, where arguments are made about the superior capabilities of the legislature to determine certain questions, general claims are made without much attention being paid to their empirical foundations. There are various features of the legislature that may be relied upon: the representative and amateur nature of the legislature; the assumption that the legislature engages in public debate and reflects a range of diverse

[36] Waldron, *Law and Disagreement*.

viewpoints; and the social policy information available to the legislature, by way of the executive, communication with constituents or the backgrounds of legislators themselves. Within a particular system of government, the general attributes of the legislature can be identified without great difficulty, such as whether it is elected. However, attention is not ordinarily given to comparing the actual public debate, or the diversity of opinion or information available, with the diversity of views or information that may be before a court in a particular proceeding as a result of evidence from the parties or interveners.

Formalistic arguments for courts to exercise judicial restraint either do not engage with democratic theory or political science, or assume a minimalist, majoritarian approach to democracy that is based on electoral accountability alone. These arguments are not especially useful for our concern here, which is whether a case can be made for a court to have reference to the actual deliberative process followed, in the course of fundamental rights adjudication.

For this, we can turn to deliberative democracy theory, which is a school of normative theory that, at its core, rejects the idea that democratic decision-making is simply the aggregation of private, pre-political interests. Preferences are not given and static, but are capable of transformation through deliberation. Moreover, political views are not a purely private matter. Rather, political engagement requires citizens to adopt 'a civic standpoint, an orientation to the common good'.[37] As a consequence, the 'democratic will' is not an aggregation of existing private preferences,[38] but rather an outcome once citizens' views are subject to reasoned argument in the public sphere.[39]

Under a deliberative conception of democracy, democratisation is an ongoing project to advance the processes of public reason-giving and the inclusion of multiple perspectives in the public sphere, either through alternative sites for deliberation or better access to governmental institutions.[40] For this reason, it is a school of thought that is not averse

[37] J. Bohman, 'Introduction' in J. Bohman and W. Rehg (eds), *Deliberative Democracy: Essays on Reason and Politics* (Cambridge, MA: The MIT Press, 1997).

[38] J. Elster, 'The Market and the Forum: Three Varieties of Political Theory' in Bohman and Rehg (eds), *Deliberative Democracy*, p. 10.

[39] J. Cohen, 'Procedure and Substance in a Deliberative Democracy' in S. Benhabib (ed), *Democracy and Difference* (Princeton: Princeton University Press, 1996).

[40] J. Dryzek, *Deliberative Democracy and Beyond* (Oxford: Oxford University Press 2000), pp. 28–29.

to judicial review, as judicial reasons may themselves contribute to public reason-giving and thereby enhance public deliberation.[41] However, multiple sites of deliberation are to be preferred to a single site of deliberation.[42] If one takes this approach, institutional design or innovations that incentivise deliberation are to be welcomed.

A deliberative conception of democracy can be contrasted to majoritarian, social-choice or minimalist conceptions of democracy, each of which centre on processes of voting and electoral accountability. To a deliberative democrat, the processes leading to public decision-making are important for two types of reasons; one, because public deliberation is necessary for these decisions to truly reflect the democratic will, and two, choices made after due deliberation are better decisions. While the first proposition is a normative one, the second proposition is an empirical claim. Therefore, even if one does not accept the normative claims of deliberative democrats, one can still accept that it is valuable to support more deliberative decision-making. This point is readily made in relation to decisions carrying a fundamental rights dimension. There is a potential systemic benefit to regular attention to human rights principles in the ordinary workings of parliaments and government agencies, particularly bearing in mind that a significant body of human rights law is not controversial, and day-to-day infringements of human rights may not be matters of principled disagreement, but inattention.

Procedural review presents itself as one strategy to encourage institutions to persuade courts of the calibre of their decision-making.[43] It is an approach by which a court rewards careful deliberation with the stability of not having a decision overturned or otherwise disrupted by a court and subjects hasty or uninformed decisions to searching review and, in the event of an adverse finding, policy disruption.

It has therefore been argued that where courts insist that decisions be made the right way, they improve the standard of decision-making in

[41] J. Knight, 'Constitutionalism and Deliberative Democracy' in S. Macedo (ed.), *Deliberative Politics: Essays on Democracy and Disagreement* (New York: Oxford University Press, 1999). The notable exception is Cass Sunstein, who has linked judicial minimalism (discussed above) to the project of supporting a deliberative democracy: C. Sunstein, 'Beyond the Republican Revival' (1988) 97 *Yale Law Journal*, p. 1539.

[42] See Benhabib's concept of democratic iterations across multiple institutions: Benhabib, *The Rights of Others*, pp. 176–181.

[43] M. Cohen-Eliya and I. Porat, 'Proportionality and the Culture of Justification' (2010) 59 *American Journal of Comparative Law* 463, pp. 466–467.

public authorities.[44] Certainly this has been advanced as one important function of national administrative law: to promote 'good governance' by incentivising officials to follow procedures that lead to better, fairer decisions.[45] This potential to guide and incentivise better decision-making differentiates procedural review from other methods of judicial restraint.

However, this raises the challenge as to what it means to make decisions 'the right way'. What constitutes good deliberation and how is a court to assess it?

I have argued previously that one can derive five general features of public decision-making process that can be used to indicate the quality of public deliberation:[46]

1. The effort and time taken to make the decision: Was the decision made after due consideration, or hastily?
2. Reason-giving: Did deliberation proceed on the basis of public-regarding reasons, rather than self-interested motives?
3. Information: Was the relevant information available to decision-makers in their deliberation?
4. Diversity: Was there deliberation that encompassed or invited a diverse range of viewpoints?
5. Openness to change: Were decision-makers open to changing their viewpoints in the course of deliberation; that is, was the deliberation genuine, or only symbolic?

Specifically in the fundamental rights context, several of the modified bills of rights enacted in Commonwealth countries (referred to above) have included procedures of human rights scrutiny in the administration and the legislature, such as requiring human rights review in the pre-legislative process, requiring statements of human rights compatibility to accompany proposed legislation, and establishing dedicated parliamentary committees to engage in human rights scrutiny in the legislative process.[47]

[44] Dyzenhaus, 'Proportionality and Deference in a Culture of Justification', p. 248; J. Beatson et al., *Human Rights: Judicial Protection in the United Kingdom* (London: Sweet & Maxwell, 2008), pp. 234–238.

[45] Harlow, 'Global Administrative Law'.

[46] The derivation of the criteria to evaluate non-judicial deliberation is developed in Sathanapally, *Beyond Disagreement*, Chapter 3.

[47] For a discussion of these methods, see J. Hiebert, 'Interpreting a Bill of Rights: The Importance of Legislative Rights Review' (2005) 35 *British Journal of Political Science*, pp. 235–255.

There is the potential for this type of human rights scrutiny to operate as the application of judicial standards by lawyers and as a form of legal advice as to compatibility or not.[48] If done diligently, this serves to expand the reach of human rights law and avert human rights violations before they reach the court. However, if we are focused on *hard cases*, the more human rights scrutiny resembles legal analysis in anticipation of what a court would decide, the less likely it is that the institution – be it the legislature or the administration – will be drawing on any unique deliberative capabilities. Moreover, an approach that is too focused on judicial decision-making risks reducing consideration of human rights concerns to anticipation of how a court may treat a particular matter, rather than the type of deliberation that human rights – as fundamental ethical commitments – ought to invite.[49] This risk of distorting democratic deliberation and encouraging self-limitation to legal standards has been referred to as '*judicialisation*'.[50]

While regular reference to judicially developed standards is seen in the operation of regular governmental and parliamentary consideration of human rights, what can also be observed is the introduction of proportionality reasoning into the legislative process. Where a potential to limit rights is identified, proportionality analysis requires administrators and legislators to ask what the purpose of the limitation is, what evidence there is to support the necessity of the measure to achieve this purpose, and whether there are other less rights-restricting means to achieve this purpose. Put in this way, these questions need not be matters of legal art.[51] Instead they provide a principled framework for the justification of public decisions that affect rights before limitations are imposed, rather than a *post hoc* justification of a decision, and generation of an evidence base, if and when the decision is challenged on human rights grounds.

[48] J. Hiebert and J. Kelly, *Parliamentary Bills of Rights: The Experiences of New Zealand and the United Kingdom* (Cambridge: Cambridge University Press, 2015).

[49] See Sathanapally, *Beyond Disagreement*, p. 71.

[50] M. Shapiro and A. Stone Sweet, *On Law, Politics and Judicialization* (Oxford: Oxford University Press, 2002).

[51] This was the suggestion made by Francesca Klug in her report into the working practices of the United Kingdom's parliamentary Joint Committee on Human Rights: *Twenty-Third Report 2005-06, The Committee's Future Working Practices* HL 239, HC 1575 (24 July 2006) Appendix 1, [12.6].

3.3.3 *The Supranational Dimension – Subsidiarity and National Courts*

The literature referred to above draws almost exclusively from a national context, and is concerned with how a State converges on its constitutional position in relation to the ethical questions thrown up by human rights cases.

The types of hard cases that face national courts when interpreting and balancing fundamental rights are equally faced by the ECtHR. The ECtHR shares significant similarities to a constitutional court – in a position of dominance, if not supremacy, in relation to the interpretation of the ECHR.[52] However, as a supranational institution, the Court faces a patently different situation than that of a national court. Instead of a single constitution and system of government, the Court deals with a varied group of legal systems and traditions of politics and government (including States with a shorter history of liberal democracy).

Above, I listed three reasons why a court may exercise restraint when faced with a hard case: its democratic legitimacy, its institutional capabilities and maintaining comity with institutions subject to review. Each of these reasons translate to the supranational context of the ECtHR. The Court is in the position of passing judgment on measures enacted by democratic governments, and the approach of progressive development of the ECHR as a 'living instrument' over time necessarily draws it into evolving moral and ethical debates. Under the rubric of institutional capacity, as set out above, the Court is open about the fact that national authorities may be better equipped to assess national conditions as they may arise for consideration. Finally, maintaining comity between the ECtHR and national institutions has been a necessary feature of the ECHR system over time.[53] While the Court is in the position to rule authoritatively on the requirements of the ECHR in its judgments, those judgments only have effect given to them by national authorities. Political resistance to implementing judgments of the Court, as well as the sheer volume of complaints generated where States do not act to address systemic violations, are major challenges for the Court.

[52] Alec Stone Sweet, for example, has argued that the ECtHR effectively has the functions of a constitutional court and acts like a constitutional court, albeit one that has to deal with constitutional pluralism. See A. Stone Sweet and H. Keller (eds), *A Europe of Rights: The Impact of the ECHR on National Legal Systems* (Oxford: Oxford University Press, 2008).

[53] See N. Krisch, 'The Open Architecture of European Human Rights Law' (2008) 71 *Modern Law Review* 183, pp. 206–210.

When the distinguishing feature of greater heterogeneity that comes with being a supranational court is added to the shortcomings that courts may face generally, it can be seen that at least as strong a case may be made for judicial restraint by the ECtHR compared to the national constitutional context. Indeed, the recognition of the ECHR system as *subsidiary* to the national systems safeguarding human rights has long represented a principle of shared responsibility between national authorities and the institutions of the ECHR. In recent times, subsidiarity has been linked by judges and commentators to something beyond burden-sharing to a 'dialogic' approach between the Court and national authorities, in which the Court has regard to national views on what Convention rights require.[54]

However, there are some further distinguishing features to be borne in mind in the context of a supranational court exercising judicial restraint or encouraging national deliberation.

First, the nature of review by an international court assessing State compliance with an obligation under international law is that the Court assesses the whole of the State's conduct. This includes national *courts*. Therefore, an element of procedural review at the international level, not present at the domestic level, is review of the national judicial process. The 'dialogue' is of a different kind to the interaction between courts and legislatures at a domestic level. Instead, we are speaking of an interaction between national and international courts tasked with applying the same legal instrument. This is recognised in the Brighton Declaration of the Committee of Ministers of the Council of Europe, which stated that the Brighton Conference:

> welcomes the development by the Court in its case law of principles such as subsidiarity and the margin of appreciation . . . and welcomes and encourages dialogue, particularly dialogues between the Court and the highest courts of the State parties.

Second, if a supranational court is to look at the decision-making processes leading to an alleged human rights violation, it faces a diverse range of traditions of government and democratic societies of very different stripes. A national court holding legislators or the administration to a particular standard of deliberation faces an easier task than

[54] H. Fenwick, 'Enhanced Subsidiarity and a Dialogic Approach – or Appeasement in Recent Cases on Criminal Justice, Public Order, Counter-Terrorism at Strasbourg against the UK?' in K. Ziegler et al. (eds), *The UK and European Human Rights: A Strained Relationship?* (Oxford: Hart Publishing, 2015).

a supranational court trying to identify the indicia of good process applicable across different national systems. One may ask if these indicia can effectively be developed through a supranational court's jurisprudence and whether doing so risks drawing such a court beyond its proper remit.

3.3.4 *The Promise of Procedural Review*

What I have set out above are two halves to the promise of procedural review in the fundamental rights context. The first is that looking to the quality of the deliberation undertaken by a respondent will assist courts to identify appropriate circumstances to exercise restraint in fundamental rights cases, or alternatively, subject a decision to robust and searching review. The second is that, if a court is responsive to the quality of deliberation of respondents, this will encourage careful deliberation by those institutions in the future and provide guidance as to what constitutes careful deliberation.

In the supranational context of the ECtHR, the promise is somewhat bolder. Given the diversity of States subject to complaints before the Court and the principle of subsidiarity, the Court already operates in circumstances where it is required to leave some latitude for national authorities. Yet, at the same time, the Court must provide guidance to national authorities to support the resolution of human rights complaints without resort to the Court. Procedural review is potentially a way to marry these two imperatives.

However, I have also raised two related challenges faced by this type of procedural review. First, it has the potential to engage courts in a more expansive supervision of the processes of a respondent than is contemplated by the court's jurisdiction over fundamental rights. Secondly, insofar as procedural review relates to the decisions of non-judicial entities, a court will need to identify what qualifies as good deliberation, and this is not a straightforward question. I have suggested above the general components of good deliberation, as well as processes that may be adopted specifically in the context of human rights scrutiny.

In the following section, I explore the case for procedural review in fundamental rights adjudication through an example of a hard case (in the sense described in section 3.2), one in which the deliberative process followed by the decision-maker was open both to praise and censure.

3.4 Exploring the Promise: The Case of *Begum*

3.4.1 *R (on the Application of Begum)* v. *Headteacher and Governors of Denbigh High School ('Begum')*[55]

In 2006, the UK House of Lords (as it then was) decided the case of *Begum*. The interaction of process and substance in human rights review was front and centre of the House of Lords' reasoning, and its disagreement with the decision under appeal, made by the Court of Appeal of England and Wales.[56]

The case concerned a complaint made by Shabina Begum, a 14-year-old student, against Denbigh High School, under the *Human Rights Act*, which directly incorporates ECHR rights into the law of the UK. Begum claimed that the school had, among other things, unjustifiably limited her right under Article 9 of the ECHR to manifest her religion or beliefs.

Denbigh High School is a coeducational community school (not a faith school) in England with, at the relevant time, a significant majority of Muslim students. Ms Begum sought, on the grounds of religious belief, to wear a particular garment known as a *jilbab*, which was a full body covering claimed to hide the shape of the body. The school insisted that she adhere to the school uniform. The school offered three uniform options, one of which was a *shalwar kameez* (a loose-fitting garment traditional to the Indian subcontinent). It also allowed students to wear a headscarf of a specific colour. The school claimed that its uniform options accommodated Islamic dress requirements in a manner that struck a balance with other goals, namely, supporting unity across an ethnically and religiously diverse school community, as well as enabling other Muslim girls to resist any potential pressure to adopt more restrictive forms of Islamic dress.

The accommodation of religious expression within liberal societies, particularly within public institutions, has been a notorious source of hard cases in human rights jurisprudence, and *Begum* is one such example. The difficulties of the question before the Court were well explained by Baroness Hale, in her separate reasons.[57] Baroness Hale pointed out that we can assume that an adult woman wears Islamic dress as a free choice. She acknowledged that strict dress codes for women may be

[55] [2006] UKHL 15.

[56] This decision is well-known to UK public lawyers and well debated within the academic commentary on the UK courts' approach to process considerations in human rights review: see Chapter 10 of this volume by Roger Masterman for references to this debate.

[57] *Begum* [2006] UKHL 15, [92]–[99].

imposed to serve the ends of others, deny women equal treatment to men and be premised on ideas about women belonging in the private, domestic sphere, rather than the public sphere. Still, believing the form of dress to be a symbol of oppression is not a good reason to deny a person the choice to wear it. However, Ms Begum was not, at the relevant time, an adult. Nor were the other students to which the school's policy applied. Complicating the matter further, this was a school that was trying to foster a sense of community and harmony in the face of ethnic, cultural and religious diversity. In these circumstances, a uniform may give students from strict religious backgrounds space in which to decide for themselves what approach to take to the religious and social expectations placed on them by their parents or others. On the other hand, preventing students from complying with the genuinely held religious beliefs of their parents (or in the case of Ms Begum, her guardian, who was her brother) may have the consequence of driving religious communities away from public schooling, to the detriment of their children who may be sent to more strictly religious schools.

Faced with a situation of needing to accommodate religious expression in conditions of uncertainty as to what effect that accommodation may have, the school (which was a public authority under the *Human Rights Act*) had employed particular expertise: the makers of the school policy were themselves members of the community and closely familiar with the various forces at play in that community. A majority of the Board of Governors were Muslim, along with the headteacher, who was a Muslim woman. Roughly ten years prior to the incident giving rise to this case, the school appointed a working party to re-examine its dress code and how it would accommodate requests to wear Islamic dress. The governors consulted parents, students, staff and leaders of the three local mosques on providing three uniform options, one of which included the *shalwar kameez*. No objection was made to the *shalwar kameez*, and the governors approved a garment designed to ensure that it satisfied Islamic dress requirements. Following the working party report, the governors also approved the wearing of headscarves of a specified colour.

Following the complainant's insistence on wearing the *jilbab*, and refusal to comply with the school's dress code, there was further consideration by the school, and interaction with the complainant, which lasted over a year before she instituted her claim for judicial review of the school's decision. The school's consideration included seeking independent advice from local mosques as to whether the school's uniform policy violated Islamic requirements of modest dress, which stated that it did not. Attempts were made to find the complainant a place at another school which would allow her to wear the *jilbab*. The school met with the complainant and her guardian on repeated occasions. Finally, a committee of governors met to consider the issue and supported the decision of the headteacher to enforce the uniform policy. Ms Begum was told of two other schools where she could wear the *jilbab*, but she did not apply to them. All of this was conducted against the backdrop of the school's continuing reasons for having a uniform policy, which included fostering unity amongst a school community at risk of division on ethnic and religious lines (as had been experienced by the school in the past) and uncertainty regarding how making an exception for the complainant would affect that policy and other students. This included the concern that other girls would come under pressure to adopt more restrictive variants of Islamic dress, based on the reasoning that those students currently relied on the uniform policy to resist such pressure.

At first instance, the judge rejected Ms Begum's contention that the school had unjustifiably limited her Article 9 right. On appeal, the Court of Appeal held that the school had infringed Article 9. On further appeal to the House of Lords, the Court of Appeal decision was overturned and the Article 9 claim was rejected.

3.4.2 *Rejecting a Procedural Approach: The House of Lords*

Begum's claim raised two questions for judicial resolution: Was her Article 9 right to freedom of thought, conscience and religion subject to a limitation? If so, was the limitation proportionate to the need to protect the rights and freedoms of others?

Under a traditional approach to rights-based review, the task of a court is to determine the requirements of the relevant right – in this case, Article 9 of the ECHR. If those bounds have been transgressed, the action of the school is unlawful. If not, the complaint is to be dismissed. In particular, if the respondent seeks to justify its actions as necessary to protect the rights and freedoms of others, then this justification is to be decided on the evidence before the court, *whether or not* that evidence was available or considered by the school authority at the time. The court would be required to decide this substantive question irrespective of how the school reached its decision not to permit Ms Begum to attend school wearing a *jilbab*; it would not be relevant what inquiries or processes the school had undertaken if the school ultimately reached the wrong outcome and imposed on Begum a restriction on her Article 9 right that was disproportionate, and thereby illegal as a violation of Article 9.

The House of Lords unanimously espoused this traditional approach to human rights review. In fact, this approach was attributed to the ECtHR by Lord Bingham in his leading judgment:

> The focus at Strasbourg is not and has never been whether a challenged decision or action is the product of a defective decision-making process, but on whether, in the case under consideration, the applicant's Convention rights have been violated.[58]

Lord Bingham stated that it was 'the practical outcome, not the quality of the decision-making process that led to it' that was relevant to whether the school's decision complied with the Convention or not,[59] and warned against a 'retreat to procedure' by judges when faced with difficult questions of human rights compatibility.[60]

Yet, the court exercised judicial restraint when reaching its own decision that the claim be rejected. Lord Bingham stated, in reaching his conclusion:

> It would in my opinion be irresponsible of any court, lacking the experience, background and detailed knowledge of the head teacher, staff and governors, to overrule their judgment on a matter as sensitive as this.[61]

Moreover, there are suggestions in the reasoning of the various separate judgments that the 'immense pains' taken by the school in devising its uniform policy was a relevant factor to the decision that the school's actions were justified.[62]

Given Lord Bingham's reason for respecting the school's decision, a complete injunction on having regard to how a decision-maker has reached a decision seems out of step. It seems to follow from those reasons that it would be relevant if the decision-maker has become knowledgeable through undertaking consultation, or has drawn on background that was relevant to the particular issue under consideration.

[58] *Begum*, [29].

[59] *Begum*, [31]. To a similar effect, see Hoffman LJ at [68], and the agreement of Foscote LJ at [91].

[60] *Begum*, [30]. [61] *Begum*, [34].

[62] See Bingham LJ at [34], Hoffman LJ at [65], Foscote LJ at [77] and Hale LJ at [98]. All five judges agreed that the uniform policy was a justified interference with the complainant's Article 9 right, although three judges would have dismissed the complaint on the grounds that there was no interference with the complainant's Article 9 right because she was able to attend a different school, had she chosen to.

Lord Bingham's reasoning (and similar statements by Lords Hoffman and Foscote) appear to suggest that it is acceptable for a court to defer to an institution on the basis of its attributes, but not to inquire into how the decision was made to, say, identify those attributes or how those attributes were applied in the specific context. The strongly worded rejection of a procedural approach across the judgments in *Begum* is perhaps best understood as a reaction to the particular approach taken by the Court of Appeal, which had relied on the decision-making process of the school as the reason for finding that the school's actions were unlawful under Article 9.

The Court of Appeal had reasoned that, since the sincerity of the complainant's belief that she was required to wear the *jilbab* was not in question, her freedom to manifest her religion or belief in public was limited and it was for the school to justify this limitation within the terms of Article 9. It decided that the school had failed to justify its actions because it did not approach its decision-making in the proper way. The court set out what it considered to be the correct decision-making structure, namely:[63]

1) Has the claimant established that she has a relevant Convention right which qualifies for protection under Article 9(1)?
2) Subject to any justification that is established under Article 9(2), has that Convention right been violated?
3) Was the interference with her Convention right prescribed by law in the Convention sense of that expression?
4) Did the interference have a legitimate aim?
5) What are the considerations that need to be balanced against each other when determining whether the interference was necessary in a democratic society for the purpose of achieving that aim?
6) Was the interference justified under Article 9(2)?

The Court of Appeal concluded that 'because it approached the issues in this case from an entirely wrong direction and did not attribute to the claimant's beliefs the weight they deserved, the School is not entitled to resist the declarations'.[64] Moreover, the Court of Appeal left open the possibility that the outcome reached by the school *could* be justified if it approached the exercise in the manner that the Court had set out.

[63] *R (on the application of SB)* v. *Headteacher and Governors of Denbigh High School* ('*SB*') [2005] EWCA Civ 199; [2005] 1 WLR 3372, [75] per Brooke LJ (Mummery and Scott LJ agreeing).

[64] *SB*, [78].

It specified a series of matters, which it suggested that the school (and other schools in similar positions) have regard to, including whether the concerns expressed by other students ought to be taken into account and if so, what weight should be accorded to them.

The Court of Appeal expressly justified its decision as 'ensuring that schools will set out deciding issues of this kind in the manner now required of them by the Human Rights Act'.[65] In its view, the approach it had taken provided guidance for schools, if not other public authorities, to undertake human rights-based decision-making. In fact, the court went beyond incentivising public authorities by drawing a negative inference against the school: it stated that this structured form of decision-making was *required* of public authorities if they sought to justify a limitation on an individual's ECHR right.

The Court of Appeal's decision demonstrates a type of procedural review that is structured and prescriptive, with standards drawn from the process that a court would follow when assessing the justification of a limitation on an ECHR right.

As mentioned, this approach was strongly rejected by the House of Lords as wrongly applying an administrative law framework to a human rights claim. Setting aside the question of the correct approach under UK law, for our present purposes, the Court of Appeal's decision demonstrates some of the difficulties facing a court in developing decision-making standards to guide other bodies. Insofar as the Court of Appeal's decision provided guidance to schools on how to approach human rights issues, the House of Lords considered this guidance to be inappropriate, overly formalistic and to risk 'judicialising' administrative decision-making. In particular, the Court of Appeal was criticised for avoiding the substantive question before it by leaving it open for the school to maintain the same position on reconsideration in line with the Court of Appeal's guidance.

In identifying standards by which to assess the school's conduct, the Court of Appeal resorted to setting out the approach that a court would take. It also focused only on the process followed by the school once it was faced with Ms Begum's demand, and did not give any apparent weight to the process followed in developing the uniform policy in the first place. Nor did it give any weight to the various contextual factors – for example, the nature of the community – that would support consultation with the community being a relevant aspect of good decision-

[65] *SB*, [82].

making for a school to engage in. It simultaneously required an individualised decision-making process in relation to the complainant that was ill-fit to the capabilities of the school, and ignored the type of careful deliberation that the school *was* capable of engaging in.

In doing so, it highlighted the risk of judicialisation in formally broadening responsibility for human rights decision-making beyond courts (raised above in section 3.3), in which other institutions come to mimic courts and lose their distinctive, non-legal contributions to human rights debates. A procedural form of human rights review, were it to operate in this way, risks distorting deliberation away from the analysis suited to the institution and towards the type of analysis undertaken by lawyers and courts. At worst, this type of approach has been accused of inducing a 'box-ticking mentality' among decision-makers.[66]

However, the Court of Appeal's approach to procedural review is somewhat of a 'straw man'; easy to attack because its clear error in failing to decide the primary question of whether the school's actions were or were not ECHR-compatible, and for its rigid set of standards for deliberation applied in circumstances where the respondent had not acted carelessly. This helps to explain the resolute guidance (or warning) of the House of Lords to the lower courts to decide on the *outcome* of a decision, and not the procedure involved in reaching it.

Taking these facts, in the following section, I examine how the school's deliberation *could* have been treated by a court, to demonstrate a more tempered exercise of procedural review, where the school's deliberation is a secondary consideration, rather than a primary one.

3.4.3 *A Tempered Exercise of Procedural Review*

If we consider the decision-making process of the school to be a relevant consideration – departing from the wholly outcome-based focus of the House of Lords – then it could be argued in favour of the school authority's decision that it had followed a careful and consultative process in reaching a position on its uniform policy that took into account religious requirements, as well as other goals. The uniform policy was not devised or applied in a hasty or careless manner. Ultimately, a committee of governors of the school had weighed the complainant's demand against the headteacher's decision to avoid variants of uniforms that

[66] T. Poole, 'The Reformation of English Administrative Law' (2009) 68 *Cambridge Law Journal* 142, pp.154–155.

differentiated between students based on the strictness of their belief. It provided lengthy reasons to the complainant for its final decision.

The decision-maker in this case (a school board of governors and head teacher) did not have the democratic credentials of, say, the UK Parliament. This was not a general decision to ban the *jilbab* in legislation after full public debate.

However, there were grounds for exercising judicial restraint on the basis that the school was well-placed to make a decision on whether the application of the school uniform policy was a necessary and proportionate limitation on the complainant's freedom of religion. The school board and head teacher were familiar with the school and the local community, and were representative of that community. It can be expected that they were better placed than a court to understand the challenges in that community to both ensure cohesion within the school and serve the interests of other students who may have been under pressure to wear particular forms of religious dress. They had the benefit of hearing the views of other students. An important part of why they were well-placed to make this decision was because they had engaged a working party and consulted with parents and students about the issue over many years. Insofar as there was uncertainty as to the effect of an exception to the uniform, the school was likely better placed than a court to assess the risks.

I noted above that procedural review has been described mainly with reference to the proportionality analysis as to whether a limitation on rights is justified. But the anterior question is whether the decision or action under review interferes with the exercise of the right in all the circumstances. Here, there were questions over whether Ms Begum was required by her religion to wear the *jilbab* or not. This is a matter that courts understandably are wary to scrutinise,[67] particularly when it concerns the religious practices of a member of a minority group. As a consequence of the difficulty of a court engaging in debate internal to a religion, courts tend to defer to the genuinely held belief of the individual before the court (as both courts did).[68] However, the school board was better placed than a court to understand whether what the

[67] See discussion in R. Clayton and H. Tomlinson, *The Law of Human Rights* (2nd ed.) (Oxford: Oxford University Press, 2009), [14.94].

[68] In the House of Lords, Lord Bingham held that Article 9(1) was engaged on the ground of Ms Begum's sincere religious belief, even though he (along with a majority of judges in the House of Lords) did not consider the right had been interfered with, given that she chose to go to this particular school over others (see *Begum*, [21], [29]).

complainant – a minor – sought was in fact required for her to exercise her religion, and the severity of the imposition of a different Islamic dress to the *jilbab*. The school board was representative of its community and was in the position of having consulted a range of Islamic authorities to understand the religious needs that it had to accommodate amongst its student population, as well as specific consultation about Ms Begum's demand.

Therefore, there were attributes of the relevant decision-makers that provided grounds for a court to give some respect to the balance that the school had reached. The fact that the school had engaged in the deliberation described meant that it had *exercised* those attributes in making the relevant decision. The deliberative quality of the school's decision amplifies the reason for a court to exercise restraint before upsetting the balance struck by the school. By contrast, had the school board not in fact consulted the community in the development of its policy, or not included a diversity of members, or applied the policy to Ms Begum without considering her request diligently, this would have the opposite effect. It would have supported a court undertaking more searching scrutiny of the school's actions, even though a school would ordinarily be assumed to understand its local community better than a national court.

3.4.4 *Points of Distinction at the Supranational Level*

The above example is of a national court, and the problems with the Court of Appeal's attempt to apply standards for deliberation based on the proportionality inquiry undertaken by courts to a non-judicial decision-maker.

However, the situation would be different were such guidance as to the steps of reasoning being delivered to a lower court.[69] Scrutinising the process by which a lower court has reached its decision is entirely unremarkable for an appeal court, as is the exercise of providing guidance to lower courts about the proper structure of inquiry in relation to a certain legal issue.

Therefore, where a supranational human rights court, such as the ECtHR, is reviewing the procedures followed by national *courts*, the type of approach taken by the Court of Appeal would not appear to be problematic. While there is certainly diversity amongst courts across

[69] This was noted by Lord Bingham in *Begum* [31].

State parties to the ECHR, national courts are faced with the same task as the ECtHR insofar as they must decide an individual complaint based on the evidence before them. The strengths of national courts relative to the ECtHR lie in a better understanding of the national legal system, but this does not translate into a significantly different decision-making process, when applying the ECHR, from that undertaken by the ECtHR. Insofar as the ECtHR can guide and encourage national courts to engage in public reasoning, with reference to evidence, this will enhance the contribution of national judgments to deliberation within State parties and, on issues of common concern, across Europe.

The second distinction is that *Begum* did not concern a legislature. Yet, it would, for equivalent reasons to those set out above, be inappropriate to require a legislature to follow the same inquiry as a court when faced with human rights issues in legislation. The type of review proposed by the Court of Appeal in *Begum* has not been raised in relation to legislative decision-making by any UK court and, in the UK constitutional context, such scrutiny of legislative deliberation by the courts could not reasonably be expected.[70]

How then is a supranational court that faces different types of government agencies and legislatures to approach the formulation of procedural standards? As flagged above, one risk facing a supranational court engaging in procedural review in the human rights context is that the court may end up drawn into a supervision of national authorities that is outside the scope of its role as conferred by treaty. For some, this type of quasi-constitutional role for the ECtHR, which would align the democratic systems across Europe around a common set of deliberative principles, may be welcome as part of the Court's evolution beyond a treaty mechanism to a constitutional court for Europe. If this evolution were to be pursued, the starting point for a more ambitious procedural review, after providing guidance to national courts, would be to guide national legislatures as to the minimum standards of deliberation when rights-limiting legislation is passed.

[70] On which see Chapter 10 by Roger Masterman: 'Process and Substance in Judicial Review in the United Kingdom and at Strasbourg: Proportionality, Subsidiarity, Complementarity?' A more limited form of review of legislative decisions has been observed: A. Kavanagh, 'Proportionality and Parliamentary Debates: Exploring Forbidden Territory' (2014) 34 *Oxford Journal of Legal Studies*, p. 443. In this context, Kavanagh draws a similar conclusion as to the appropriateness (within the scheme of the UK's Human Rights Act) of a tempered form of procedural review (at pp. 470–472).

Still, the practical question of developing such standards – distinct from the type of reasoning that one expects of a court – remains. Such practices may be established through Europe-wide codes or legislation, but absent such a guide, the Court will need to develop its own standards. In contrast to reviewing the quality of reasoning in a national court judgment, it is not a straightforward task to systematically assess multi-participant deliberation on even the most basic deliberative criteria. The types of empirical models that social scientists might develop are not suited to a court reviewing procedure. For this reason – and without undertaking a detailed analysis of what standards may be available – it appears likely that, were procedural review of the variety I have focused on adopted in a regular manner by the ECtHR, the review of deliberation would be necessarily impressionistic, of the kind proposed in section 3.4.3 This is a practical limitation to judicially developed standards of good governance, implemented and incentivised through the decisions of a supranational court.

However, the more modest form of procedural review – where the deliberation undertaken by a particular institution in relation to a hard case is a factor in the Court deciding whether or not to exercise restraint – can proceed in an impressionistic way and still achieve a meaningful result. It can help avoid a situation where national authorities benefit from the margin of appreciation, despite not having acted with due care and deliberation. By having regard to how the national authority reached its decision, the Court can do a better job of deciding when to grant a wide margin of appreciation, and when to subject the national authority to a more demanding standard of justification. Having regard to deliberation at the national level can thereby provide a valuable discipline to the exercise of institutional restraint by the Court.

3.5 Adjusting Expectations: The Modest Promise of Courts Examining Deliberation

What I have set out in section 3.4 is an illustration of how procedural rights review may operate, with reference to a concrete case. Through this example, I have favoured a modest role for a decision-maker's deliberation within human rights review by a court. It can be summarised as follows: where a court is inclined to exercise restraint on the basis that the institution that made the decision is better placed to weigh up the issues raised by the human rights complaint, it is relevant whether the institution engaged in good deliberation. It is relevant both in terms of the democratic legitimacy of the decision, and the epistemic reasons for valuing the decision. A court will need to bear in mind the five touchstones of deliberation set out in section 3.3.3, but in the context of the particular institution and the type of processes of consideration, debate, information-gathering, representation and expertise that are appropriate to *that* institution. If the institution has not acted deliberatively, in this sense, then the court will not be justified in holding back from full and searching review. The court should not defer on an *assumption* that a decision has been carefully made such that the court should be hesitant to displace it.

This modest form of procedural review in the human rights context can be distinguished from a prescriptive procedural review, which systematically applies standards of decision-making, akin to domestic administrative law, to decisions challenged on human rights grounds. I have suggested above the general facets to a normatively grounded, but context-sensitive, evaluation of deliberation. Still, any such evaluation would necessarily be impressionistic. To develop a uniform set of standards that could be applied systematically to assess deliberation would be a significant exercise, beyond the scope of this chapter and, at least arguably, beyond what is feasible for a court to develop via case law alone.

A comment in relation to institutional comity: there is an obvious danger of drawing adverse inferences in terms of the need for institutional comity. The reason for a court to openly draw attention to the unsatisfactory nature of the deliberation is to incentivise better deliberation in future. However, a court that draws negative inferences on the basis of prescriptive standards of its own creation, not oriented in any binding legal instrument, opens itself to criticism for being overly interventionist.

While this is a careful line to tread, the modest approach I suggest does no more than interrogate assumptions that courts may otherwise rely upon in exercising restraint, so that they do so in the appropriate circumstances. It is within the court's discretion to undertake searching human rights review on the substantive question before it, or to exercise restraint – I am only proposing that a court exercising restraint does so on the basis of reality, and not unarticulated or unquestioned assumptions as to what institutions of government are good at, or worse, on the basis of a concern that the court is not sufficiently qualified. For if a particular human rights dilemma has not benefitted from careful deliberation elsewhere in the system of government, then the court may be the institution with responsibility to ensure that the State's answer to that dilemma – no matter how hard it is – is subject to public justification.

Indeed, none of the foregoing should neglect the fact that the process of human rights review has its own role to play in a deliberative democracy. By requiring public justification of rights-affecting decisions, by interrogating those reasons against evidence and by setting out the reasoned basis why certain public action is acceptable – or unacceptable – in a rights-respecting democracy, courts themselves enhance the deliberative character of the polity, and contribute to public discourse on human rights. This is a process available to any individual or minority group, including those who may not otherwise gain attention in the public sphere. A form of procedural review that neglects the substantive questions thrown up by human rights risks sacrificing this function of courts.

By taking steps in the direction of procedural review, the ECtHR and the other institutions discussed in this volume have embarked upon an experiment. There are reasons to favour this experiment, but as with all innovation, its success cannot be wholly predicted. If adopted by supranational courts with regularity, procedural review may support, over time, better deliberative outcomes and a healthy shared responsibility for fundamental rights protection across national and supranational institutions. Alternately, it may generate incentives for legalistic exercises in human rights consideration or symbolic parliamentary debates for the purposes of satisfying future fundamental rights review. It may do both, and this would be a valuable topic for future empirical research.

PART II

The (Potential) Value of Procedural Review for Supranational Courts Deciding Fundamental Rights Cases: Political Science Perspectives

4

Evidence-Based Lawmaking: Influences, Obstacles and the Role of the European Court of Human Rights

PATRICIA POPELIER

4.1 Introduction: Procedural Rationality Review – Deference or Intrusion?

Contemporary political systems experience an increasing pressure to adopt regulatory policy schemes, centred upon a set of regulatory tools such as impact assessments, consultation procedures, *ex post* monitoring and alternatives for regulation. Inspired by the US Administrative Procedure Act, which submits administrative rulemaking to public notice, hearings from interested persons and reason-giving paired with judicial review, procedural tools to improve legitimacy and efficiency of both administrative rules and parliamentary laws are being introduced in European democracies. The presidential system in the US explains why parliament is only interested in the establishment of procedural constraints combined with judicial review when delegating regulatory powers to the executive; in contrast, regulatory and primary lawmaking processes are more blurred in parliamentary systems, where parliaments, as a rule, enact laws prepared by the more skilled and resourceful administrations of the executive.[1] The distinction, however, reappears when courts come into play. Procedural review of executive acts is widespread and hardly contested. By contrast, procedural review of parliamentary acts is perceived as even more intrusive than substantive judicial review of these acts, as internal parliamentary procedures are considered sacrosanct.[2]

[1] S. Rose-Ackerman, S. Egidy and J. Fowkes, *Due Process of Lawmaking* (Cambridge University Press 2015) 13–16; 263–267.

[2] I. Bar-Siman-Tov, 'The Puzzling Resistance to Judicial Review of the Legislative Process' *Boston University Law Review*, 91 (2011), 1926; Rose-Ackerman, Egidy and Fowkes, *supra* note 1, at 186.

Nevertheless, simultaneously with the cross-national spread of regulatory policy programmes, a trend towards so-called procedural rationality review, or semi-procedural review, of both primary and secondary legislation is noted.[3] In its search for an evidentiary basis for justifications of government interference in fundamental rights, this type of review is linked to individual rights protection. Hence, scrutiny of the decision-making process serves to assess whether a law is justifiable in the light of substantive fundamental rights or constitutional values.[4] Courts seek the presence of substantive parliamentary debate, consultations, statistical evidence or expert advice to prove that an inclusive and informed balance of interests underpins the challenged measure. They do not prescribe detailed procedural requirements, but instead examine whether the procedure meets certain procedural quality standards.

Insofar as procedural rationality review leads courts to examine factual evidence for the assumptions that inspire legislative interference, it results in what is called an 'evidence-based judicial reflex'. According to Alemanno, the simultaneous rise of regulatory policy schemes and an evidence-based judicial reflex is no coincidence; the latter is 'directly related, and largely reflects' the diffusion of an evidence-based legislative policy model imposed on policy-makers across the world.[5] Evidence in support of this hypothesis would require elaborate comparative and empirical research. As yet, we can find indications in support of the hypothesis, as well as to the contrary (section 4.2). A further question, then, is whether the argument can be carried further, so as to stress a mutual influence. This would imply that evidence-based legislative policy programmes trigger procedural rationality review, and, conversely, procedural rationality review encourages evidence-based lawmaking (section 4.3).

In this contribution, a broader hypothesis is formulated, arguing that even if evidence-based legislative models and evidence-based judicial review mutually influence each other, several other determining factors come into play (section 4.4). This is where the paper links up with procedural review by the European Court of Human Rights (ECtHR), which is the subject of this edited volume. The hypothesis is presented in order to assess the Court's procedural rationality review of parliamentary

[3] For the term semi-procedural review: I. Bar-Siman-Tov, 'Semiprocedural Judicial Review', *Legisprudence*, 6 (2012), 271.

[4] Bar-Siman-Tov, *supra* note 3, 280.

[5] A. Alemanno, 'The Emergence of the Evidence-Based Judicial Reflex: A Response to Bar-Siman-Tov's Semiprocedural Review', *TPLeg*, 1 (2013), 333.

laws in particular, considering the tension with the procedural autonomy valued highly by national parliaments. In several cases, the Court turns to procedural aspects to underpin its substantive proportionality test and thereby imposes quality standards upon national legislators and encourages national courts to conduct their own procedural rationality review. It is argued in this paper that the ECtHR's increasing refuge to this type of review can be linked with the subsidiarity principle and a concern for a less intrusive practice, as expressed in the Brighton Declaration and Article 1 of Protocol 15 (section 4.5).

The research question, then, is how intensive such procedural inquiry can be with regard to parliamentary legislation, taking into account the (state-specific) factors that determine the presence or absence of evidence-based legislative policy models and/or procedural rationality review by the national courts. It is important for the ECtHR to take this into consideration for two reasons. First, it determines whether contracting parties will indeed perceive the Court's assessment as 'less intrusive' than traditional, purely substantive review. Second, it influences the effectiveness of procedural rationality review in so far as the Court would seek to change the style of policy-making so as to encourage the use of evidence.

4.2 Evidence-Based Legislative Policy as a Trigger for Procedural Rationality Review?

As mentioned, Alemanno introduces the hypotheses that the diffusion of an evidence-based legislative policy model triggers an 'evidence-based judicial reflex' in the Courts' practices. The author very consciously uses the term 'evidence-based judicial reflex' to stress that so-called procedural rationality review is not a separate type of review, but merely an inquiry to underpin the substantive assessment.[6] It is doubtful whether this suffices to counter legitimacy concerns, which the author brushes aside as being 'fundamentally misplaced'.[7] I will return to this point in section 4.4; for now, the main point is the link between the presence of evidence-based legislative policy models on the one hand, and, on the other hand, the trend to look for evidence in the decision-making process to substantiate justifications for government interference. As mentioned, in the absence of an in-depth comparative study into this link, we can

[6] Alemanno, *supra* note 5, 331. [7] Alemanno, *supra* note 5, 336.

merely estimate the probability of this hypothesis on the basis of indications.

We are indeed witnessing a widespread evidence-based policy diffusion, based on a blueprint promoted by the OECD and with economic competitiveness as a strong driver for the implementation of regulatory reform programmes.[8] Simultaneously, procedural rationality review is on the rise. In a comparative study, Rose-Ackerman et al. show that while courts in several jurisdictions are reluctant to review legislation against procedural requirements laid down in constitutional acts or rules of procedures, procedural inquiries tied to rights-based reviews are nevertheless emerging.[9] Alemanno's reasoning to link both phenomena boils down to three arguments. First, the argumentative space implied in fundamental rights adjudication and proportionality tests compels courts to look for evidence to substantiate their assessments. As Vandenbruwaene explains, the fear of judicial interference in political questions sometimes rests merely on methodological difficulties that can be remedied through evidence-seeking to underpin substantive scrutiny.[10] Second, Alemanno points to the availability of evidence as a result of 'rational policymaking'. According to the author, the 'rationality turn of policymaking' resulting from the introduction of regulatory reform programmes 'paves the way to an increased availability of ready-made materials' that courts can use to substantiate their assessment.[11] Third, there is not only the *possibility* for courts to turn to evidence in the law-making process, but also the public *expectation* that lawmakers respect procedural tools and requirements, whether they are laid down in formal rules or merely in guidelines or circulars available to the public, and that courts do justice to this expectation.[12]

The latter argument can be further elaborated in terms of judicial mandate. As unelected institutions, courts are reluctant to interfere in policy decisions. They will more easily scrutinise (both administrative and legislative) policy decisions if they have a strong constitutional mandate. Several factors determine how courts interpret the scope of

[8] For an overview of factors that explain policy diffusion, P. Popelier, 'The Role of Courts in Legislative Policy Diffusion and Convergence', *TPLeg*, 3 (2015), pp. 316–318.

[9] Rose-Ackerman, Egidy and Fowkes, *supra* note 1.

[10] W. Vandenbruwaene, 'The Judicial Enforcement of Subsidiarity', in P. Popelier, A. Mazmanyan and W. Vandenbruwaene (eds), *The Role of Constitutional Courts in Multilevel Governance* (Intersentia 2013) 139, pp. 146–162; W. Vandenbruwaene, 'Multi-Tiered Political Questions: The ECJ's Mandate in Enforcing Subsidiarity', *Legisprudence*, 6 (2012), pp. 336–343.

[11] Alemanno, *supra* note 5, 333.

[12] Alemanno, *supra* note 5, 337.

this mandate. Vanberg stresses in particular strategic considerations in the face of implementation problems: 'anticipations of reactions to their decisions may therefore shape their jurisprudence'.[13] He claims that courts will avoid exceeding the 'tolerance threshold of governing majorities' and take into account the larger political environment.[14] Consequently, procedural rationality review is more probable if it ties in with a political culture of rational policymaking – or the expectation thereof based on a framework of policy documents and administrative guidelines.

On the other hand, while the cross-national spread of evidence-based legislative policy programmes is undeniable, this does not result in policy convergence in practice:[15] large differences are noted across countries as to policy focus, scope and implementation.[16] This obfuscates somewhat the correlation between the rise of evidence-based legislative policy on the one hand and the emergence of procedural rationality review on the other. Moreover, a comparative overview makes clear that the implementation of an evidence-based policy programme and the intensity of procedural rationality review are not necessarily directly proportional. For example, while the United Kingdom has developed a comprehensive legislative and regulatory reform policy, courts are reluctant to conduct procedural inquiries when reviewing Acts of Parliament under the Human Rights Act.[17] By contrast, in Germany, where political commitment to and implementation of evidence-based better regulation programmes remain limited,[18] the Constitutional Court engages more aggressively in procedural rationality review.[19] Also, the emergence of procedural rationality

[13] G. Vanberg, *The Politics of Constitutional Review in Germany* (Cambridge University Press 2005) p. 12.

[14] Vanberg, *supra* note 13 at p. 14.

[15] C.M. Radaelli, 'Diffusion without Convergence: How Political Context Shapes the Adoption of Regulatory Impact Assessment', *Journal of European Public Policy*, 12 (2005), 924–943. The article is also included in C. Knill (ed) *Cross-National Policy Convergence* (Routledge 2006) pp. 161–177.

[16] Regulatory Policy Committee, *Indicators of Regulatory Management Systems* (OECD 2009) p. 21.

[17] See R. Masterman's chapter in this volume.

[18] K. Messerschmidt, 'The Race to Rationality Review and the Score of the German Federal Constitutional Court', 6 *Legisprudence*, 6 (2012), 359; S. Veit, 'National Experiences with General Forms of *Ex Ante* Evaluation of Legislation: The Cases of Germany and Sweden', in J. Verschuuren (ed), *The Impact of Legislation* (Martinus Nijhoff 2009) 182–184. Focus is rather on the reduction of red tape.

[19] K. Messerschmidt, 'The Good Shepherd of Karlsruhe. The "*Hartz* IV" Decision – A Good Example of Regulatory Review by the German Federal Constitutional Court?', in

review in the practice of the ECtHR is not backed by a legislating political system, let alone one that embraces an evidence-based legislative policy programme. According to Messerschmidt, then, procedural rationality review is rooted in the protection of fundamental freedoms, rather than better lawmaking agendas.[20] Obviously, neither factors – protection of fundamental freedoms or better law-making agendas – offer a sufficient explanation for the occurrence of procedural rationality review.

It appears from the above that a link between the diffusion of evidence-based legislative policy programmes and the rise of procedural rationality review is probable, but the presence of such policy programmes is clearly not the only or decisive factor to predict resource to this type of review. Moreover, the finding that courts may also turn to procedural inquiries aside of legislative policy programmes raises the question whether, conversely, procedural rationality review may encourage legislators to adopt an evidence-based policy style. The next section lingers on a little longer with this question, before turning to other factors that explain the introduction of both evidence-based legislative policies and procedural rationality review.

4.3 Procedural Rationality Review as a Trigger for Evidence-Based Legislative Policy?

It makes sense that courts conduct procedural inquiries to find evidence for the assumptions that justify government interference, if this ties in with a larger political environment that supports evidence-based policy-making. Conversely, the question rises whether this type of review may nevertheless give the legislator incentive for an intensified and transparent evidence-based approach. Such effect would link the Strasbourg Court's trend to turn to procedural rationality review with the diffusion of evidence-based legislative programmes after all.

Authors, commenting on procedural review trends, have suggested such a link. Messerschmidt concluded that 'procedural and methodological review of evidence-based lawmaking contribute to better regulation, not because of their intrinsic value, but as an incentive to improve impact assessment and the rationality of lawmaking by legislators who should be

Popelier, Mazmanyan and Vandenbruwaene, *supra* note 10 at pp. 237–246; Rose-Ackerman, Egidy and Fowkes, *supra* note 1, at pp. 175–189.

20 Messerschmidt, *supra* note 18 at pp. 360–361.

better prepared to launch smart regulation than any court'.[21] Rose-Ackerman et al., more cautiously, express the expectation that procedural inquiries by courts help to 'articulate transparently the trade-offs made to obtain passage'.[22] The courts' practices, then, might constitute one out of a variety of factors that explain both evidence-based legislative policy diffusion and divergence.[23]

The EU Smart Regulation programme provides an example in support of this expectation.[24] The European Court of Justice (ECJ)'s fundamental rights jurisprudence led to the introduction of a fundamental rights checklist to supplement the EU impact assessment tool in place. In its guidelines, the Commission pointed out that the new checklist is a response to the duty, as articulated and sanctioned by the ECJ, for the EU institutions 'to prove – in the light of the fundamental rights protected by the Charter – that they have carefully considered different policy options and have chosen the most proportionate response to a given problem'.[25] However, we lack further empirical evidence to more generally support the expectation that courts actually influence the legislator's policy style.

For want of empirical evidence, we turn to literature that examines the circumstances under which courts can secure the implementation of its decisions by the legislator. Vanberg pays particular attention to public support for the judiciary as an important factor that influences the implementation of judicial decisions, under the condition of transparency; citizens must be aware of the judicial decision, as well as the legislator's (non) response to it.[26] The ECtHR, however, is a judicial body external to the national political systems, and is therefore burdened with an additional legitimacy problem. The Court meets with implementation problems, in particular, in legal systems where public support for the Strasbourg Court is weak. This is most obviously the case in the United Kingdom; but in several other countries as well, criticism of the ECtHR is on the rise.[27] Hence, it needs the cooperation of national courts

[21] Messerschmidt, *supra* note 18 at p. 372.
[22] Rose-Ackerman, Egidy and Fowkes, *supra* note 1 at p. 275.
[23] I elaborated this idea in Popelier, *supra* note 8.
[24] See further Fay Kartner's and Anne Meuwese's Chapter 5: 'Responsiveness towards Fundamental Rights Impacts in the Preparation of EU Legislation'.
[25] Commission Staff Working Paper, *Operational Guidance on Taking Account of Fundamental Rights in Commission Impact Assessments*, SEC (2011) 567 final, 4 and 6.
[26] Vanberg *supra* note 13 at pp. 19–21.
[27] For an overview, see P. Popelier, S. Lambrecht and K. Lemmens, 'Introduction: Purpose and Structure, Categorization of States and Hypotheses', in P. Popelier, S. Lambrecht and K. Lemmens (eds), *Criticism of the European Court of Human Rights* (Intersentia 2016).

to strengthen incentives for a change in the legislature's policy style. This means that if the ECtHR aspires to change the national legislature's policy style, it should also encourage the national courts to turn to procedural rationality review. I return to this in section 4.5, where the Strasbourg Court's jurisprudence is examined.

4.4 Other Factors of Influence

In section 4.2, this paper has argued that courts will probably be more inclined to turn to procedural inquiries if the legislator is already committed to an evidence-based legislative policy programme. At the same time, it was claimed that this is not the only or decisive factor to explain process review. In this section, I look for other influential factors. I will first examine factors that influence the implementation of evidence-based legislative programmes, as these factors might also impact on the likelihood of procedural rationality review. I will then look for additional factors that hinder procedural rationality review, irrespective of whether an evidence-based legislative programme is already in place.

The success of evidence-based legislative policy programmes is explained by the emergence of the regulatory state, introducing new forms of legitimacy based on transparency and efficiency and with a focus on output parameters and monitoring of policy results.[28] Legislative policy programmes are strongly linked to efficiency goals, such as competitiveness and economic growth,[29] and international organisations such as the World Bank and the OECD promote Better Regulation programmes for that purpose. The OECD has in particular played an important role in the diffusion of a policy programme based on regulatory impact analysis, by providing a normative framework, benchmarking, training and recommendations.[30]

More interesting, however, is the finding, mentioned in section 4.2, that policy diffusion in practice did not result in policy convergence. The question then rises as to which factors explain either smooth or poor

[28] More at length: Popelier, *supra* note 8.

[29] OECD, *Guiding Principles for Regulatory Quality and Performance* (OECD 2005). See also Commission, 'Better Regulation for Growth and Jobs in the European Union' (Communication) COM (2005) 97 final. Critical: I. Lynch-Fannon, 'Legislative Policy, Law and Competitiveness: A Mysterious and Difficult Relationship in the EU', *European Law Journal*, 1 (2009), p. 98.

[30] See F. De Francesco, 'Diffusion of Regulatory Impact Analysis Among OECD and EU member states', *Comparative Political Studies*, 45 (2012), pp. 13, 14, 19, 21.

implementation of an evidence-based legislative programme. Here, legal and administrative culture, as well as political context, seem to play a role.[31] For example, regulatory impact analysis ties in better with common law systems with a more informal view on rulemaking[32] than with systems with a more formal-legalistic culture, such as France, Belgium or Finland. Evidence-based legislative policies are in particular incompatible with consociational practices typical for corporatist consensus democracies, such as Belgium and Finland. Consociational practices imply the making of compromises between established representatives from various social segments, but at the same time, result in partitocracy and opaque elitist decision-making.[33] This contrasts sharply with transparency and the use of studies, facts and figures central to evidence-based legislative policy programmes. Hence, the OECD criticised the Finnish political culture of consensus and corporatism for constituting an obstacle to transparency and the taking into account of the interests of all stakeholders,[34] and scholars pointed to the high level of partitocracy as an obstacle to the establishment of an effective evaluation policy in Belgium.[35] Transparent and rational lawmaking is perceived as a hindrance to complex negotiation processes that are necessary to find compromises between ideologically diverse coalition partners, across dividing language borders, and with social partners; exposure of the negotiating partners' position obstructs the willingness to compromise, and evaluators using naked facts and figures are easily perceived as additional veto players.[36] Courts will take these factors into account if they want their judgements to be effective. This is in particular the case where a particular legal, administrative or political culture is fundamental for the functioning of the political system. For example, in deeply divided heterogeneous societies such as Belgium, consociational practices can be vital to the stability of the state.[37]

[31] More at length: Popelier, *supra* note 8.

[32] R. Hoppe, '*Ex Ante* Evaluation of Legislation: Between Puzzling and Powering', in J Verschuuren (ed), *The Impact of Legislation* (Martinus Nijhoff 2009) p. 84.

[33] For Belgium: see B.G. Peters, 'Consociationalism, Corruption and Chocolate: Belgian Exceptionalism', (2006) *West EuropeanPolitics*, 29 (2006), pp. 1079–1092.

[34] OECD, *Regulatory Reform in Finland* (OECD 2003), pp. 6–7, 47; OECD, *Better Regulation in Europe. Finland* (OECD 2010), p. 56.

[35] F. Varone, S. Jacob and L. De Winter, 'Polity, Politics and Policy Evaluation in Belgium', *Evaluation Rev.*, 11 (2005), pp. 261–264.

[36] Varone, Jacob and De Winter, *supra* note 35, at p. 262.

[37] J. Andeweg, 'Consociational Democracy', *Annual Review of Political Science*, 3 (2000), p. 510.

Rose-Ackerman et al. also stress the importance of institutional design and constitutional values for the shaping of 'due process of lawmaking' in the legislative framework and the courts' practices, including pure as well as semi-procedural review.[38] They accentuate in particular the differences between presidential and parliamentary forms of government. However, while the first is more inclined to put procedural constraints on administrative rulemaking, both systems are reluctant to impose such constraints on parliamentary lawmaking. Here, values of separation of powers and democratic legitimacy come into play. The authors, in particular, alert to the sensitive nature of judicial interference in political processes. They claim that basing a decision on improper procedures is likely to be regarded as more, not less, intrusive than substantive review.[39] Hence, in legal systems where constitutional review by courts is contested, we can expect that process review raises even more controversy than substantive review. This may explain the public outcry in the UK against the *Hirst* judgment, where the ECtHR reproached the UK Parliament for not having 'sought to weigh the competing interests or to assess the proportionality of a blanket ban on the right of a convicted prisoner to vote', and, in particular, for not having carried out 'any substantive debate' in this respect.[40] A commentator pointed out that normative evaluations of parliamentary debates are 'a constitutional anathema in the domestic context'.[41]

4.5 The Practice of the European Court of Human Rights

So far, this paper came to the following conclusions. First, there is probably a mutual link between the rise of evidence-based legislative policy programmes on the one hand and the rise of procedural rationality review by courts. Secondly, this is not an exclusive link; legal, administrative and political culture, institutional design and constitutional values, come into play. When examining the practice of procedural rationality review by the ECtHR, the question, then, pops up whether this is able to influence the use of evidence-based decision-making by the national authorities and courts, taking into account all these factors.

[38] Rose-Ackerman, Egidy and Fowkes, *supra* note 1, p. 296.

[39] Rose-Ackerman, Egidy and Fowkes, *supra* note 1, at p. 185.

[40] *Hirst (No. 2)* v. *the United Kingdom* (App. No. 74025/01) ECHR 30 March 2005 and [GC] ECHR 2005-IX.

[41] S. Briant, 'Dialogue, Diplomacy and Defiance: Prisoners' Voting Rights at Home and in Strasbourg', *European Human Rights Law Review*, 3 (2011), pp. 248–250.

Another question is whether this is the Court's ambition anyway. The Court might have other intentions, such as proceeding with caution, especially towards Strasbourg-hostile Contracting Parties.

The ECtHR indeed shows an 'evidence-based judicial reflex', although this is not as yet a well-developed or coherent practice. Evidence thereof can be found in literature[42] and is given throughout this edited volume. Here, some examples suffice, focused on procedural rationality review of legislative, rather than administrative, decisions.

A milestone decision is *Hatton* v. *the United Kingdom*, regarding aircraft noise pollution, where the Court stressed that its subsidiary role in complex issues of environmental and economic policy did not prevent it from investigating the decision-making procedure. While the first chamber considered that the UK government had violated Article 8 of the Convention for not having made 'specific and complete studies' that allowed for the 'right' balance, the Grand Chamber was satisfied that the decision was based on 'appropriate' investigations and studies.[43]

In several cases, the Court criticised the defending party because no statistical or scientific evidence was produced to support the presumption that the contested interventions were necessary in order to safeguard the banking sector and economic activity in France;[44] to secure the fighting power and operational effectiveness of the armed forces in Russia;[45] or to protect the interests of children raised by same-sex couples in Austria.[46] Such evidence is required to convince the Court that the national authorities have based the interference on a careful balancing of rights and interests where the Court is not in a position to second-guess this balancing exercise. It does not solely rely on scientific evidence to that effect, but also values consultation processes and public debates.[47]

[42] P. Popelier, A. Mazmanyan and W. Vandenbruwaene (eds), *The Role of Constitutional Courts in Multilevel Governance* (Intersentia 2013), 249, at pp. 257–265. P. Popelier, 'The Court as Regulatory Watchdog: The Procedural Approach in the Case Law of the European Court of Human Rights' in P. Popelier, A. Mazmanyan and W. Vandenbruwaene (eds), *The Role of Constitutional Courts in Multilevel Governance* (Antwerp, Intersentia 2012) pp. 249–268.

[43] *Hatton* v. *the United Kingdom*, Decision of 2 October 2001 [App. No. 36022/97] and Grand Chamber decision of 8 July 2003 [2003] ECHR VIII.

[44] *Lecarpentier* v. *France*, Decision of 14 February 2006 [App. No. 67847/01], § 47.

[45] *Konstantin Markin* v. *Russia*, Grand Chamber Decision of 22 March 2012 [App. No. 30078/06], § 144.

[46] *X and Others* v. *Austria*, Decision of 19 February 2013 [App. No. 19010/07], § 142, 146.

[47] E.g. *Evans* v. *the United Kingdom*, Grand Chamber Decision of 10 April 2007 [App. No. 6339/05] *Reports* 2007-I, § 87–91; *A., B. and C.* v. *Ireland*, Grand Chamber decision of 16 December 2010, [App. No. 25579/05], § 241.

The Court specifically criticises the lack of a substantive debate in which competing interests are weighed – even if this implies attacking the functioning of the national Parliament – if this is not compensated by the possibility for the judge to carry out a balancing of interests in individual cases.[48] By contrast, in *Animal Defenders International*, the Court praised the quality of the national legislative, including the 'exceptional examination by parliamentary bodies' of the 'cultural, political and legal aspects' of the contested measure and stressed that the measure was deemed necessary by all specialist bodies and enacted with cross-party support. It consequently upheld a severe restriction of the freedom of public speech which, as a rule, falls within a narrow margin of appreciation.[49]

The question, then, is whether this approach may induce national authorities to favour an evidence-based legislative policy model. Again, this requires specific empirical investigation. However, given our finding that the adoption of or resistance against such policy model also depends on legal, administrative and political culture, as well as institutional design and constitutional values, we can expect that the Court's impact in this regard is relatively low. By contrast, legal systems that already have an evidence-based legislative policy programme in place benefit from procedural rationality review by the Strasbourg Court. As a result, in *Animal Defenders International*, the Court, with a narrow majority, upheld the legislative intervention, against all odds[50] and contrary to previous case law where similar cases were decided on their merits.[51] If the Court nevertheless finds fault with the way a particular decision was established, national authorities will not easily accept critique of an otherwise well-functioning legislative policy. This is especially so if the Court's grievances touch the very heart of constitutional values, such as the sovereignty of Parliament, as the UK reactions after the *Hirst* decision illustrate.[52]

[48] *Hirst (No. 2)* v. *the United Kingdom*, Grand Chamber Decision of 6 October 2005 [2005] ECHR 2005-IX; *Alajos Kiss* v. *Hungary*, Decision of 20 May 2010, [App. No. 38832/06].

[49] *Animal Defenders International* v. *the United Kingdom*, Grand Chamber decision of 22 April 2013 [App. No. 48876/08].

[50] In doctrine, expectations were that the Strasbourg Court would find a violation of Article 10 ECHR, see T. Lewis, 'Reasserting the Primacy of Broadcast Political Speech after Animal Defenders International? – *Rogaland Pensioners Party* v. *Norway*', *Journal of Media Law*, 1 (2009) p. 48.

[51] See in particular *VgT Verein gegen Tierfabriken* v. *Switzerland*, Decision of 28 June 2001, *Reports* 2001-VI.

[52] See *supra* notes 40 and 41.

Earlier in Chapter 1, it was argued that the Strasbourg Court, then, needs the cooperation of national courts and should encourage them to turn to procedural rationality review. The ECtHR seems conscious of this where it is more willing to accept measures that interfere with Convention rights if national courts have carefully scrutinised the measure in the light of the Convention and the Strasbourg case law.[53] In *Animal Defenders International* as well, the ECtHR not only praised the quality of the parliamentary process, but also the quality of the judicial decision-making process.[54] In *Kryvitska and Krivitskyy*, the Court explicitly required that judicial decisions affecting Convention rights are based on 'reasoning or an evidentiary basis'.[55] In legal systems where courts are reluctant to take an evidence-based approach because political context does not favour an overall evidence-based legislative, hints by the Strasbourg Court may lead to a more evidence-based approach in particular cases. For example, the Belgian Constitutional Court only hesitantly takes a procedural approach, which may be explained by the consociational nature of Belgian political decision-making. However, it does so more firmly if the ECtHR decided a similar matter with reference to the decision-making process. Hence, in a case concerning night flights, it explicitly quoted the *Hatton* judgment and judged that the measure was disproportional in so far as it was based on assumptions that were contradicted by the available scientific studies and reports.[56]

Yet, for courts to follow-up on Strasbourg case law in order to introduce procedural standards where political context does not favour this, the Strasbourg Court needs public support.[57] The *Konstantin Markin* case illustrates that the Strasbourg Court rapidly ventures on thin ice. The first chamber not only criticised the Russian legislature for interfering in Convention rights based on unfounded assumptions, but also reproached the Constitutional Court for going along with this assumption 'without attempting to probe its validity by checking it against statistical data or by weighing the conflicting interests' at stake.[58] This rather explicit instruction of national courts was repeated in *Kryvitska and Kryvitskyy*,[59] but it disappeared in the Grand Chamber's

[53] For example: *Sukhovetskyy* v. *Ukraine* (App. no. 13716/02) ECHR 2006-VI.
[54] *Animal Defenders International* v. *the United Kingdom*, Grand Chamber decision of 22 April 2013, [App. no. 48876/08].
[55] *Krivitska and Kryvitskyy* v. *Ukraine* (App. n.o 30856/03) ECHR 2 December 2010.
[56] Belgian Constitutional Court No. 51/2003, 30 April 2003. [57] See *supra* note 25.
[58] *Konstantin Markin* v. *Russia* (App. No. 30078/06) ECHR 7 October 2010.
[59] *Krivitska and Kryvitskyy* v. *Ukraine* (App. No. 30856/03) ECHR 2 December 2010.

Konstantin Markin judgment,[60] following the hostility with which this attack on the Russian Constitutional Court's functioning was greeted.[61]

The conclusion is that the Strasbourg Court may indeed stimulate an evidence-based approach by national courts and, in second order, national lawmaking authorities. This is especially the case where the national courts are reluctant to impose procedural standards as a general requirement, considering the political context, but take advantage of the Strasbourg's support in their particular political system to impose such standards in particular cases. Under different circumstances, the ECtHR's instructions are most probably not very effective and, as both the *Hirst* and the *Konstantin Markin* case illustrate, may even meet with severe resistance.

Possibly, however, the ECtHR is looking for a leeway between recent calls for deference and its supervisory role in fundamental rights protection, rather than a way to directly influence policy style. Following the Interlaeken and Brighton conferences in 2010 and 2012, the Court has been put under pressure to focus more strongly on the subsidiarity principle which is, most often, invoked as the opposite of legal control of legislative authority.[62] In the Court's view, however, subsidiarity and the margin of appreciation are about 'attributing responsibility' to national authorities, rather than 'waiving the power of review'.[63]

Elsewhere, I have developed the idea that procedural rationality review offers a balanced response to the recent calls for an intensified use of subsidiarity, but that the Court may also be tempted to use procedural rationality review as an escape way, to satisfy Strasbourg-hostile countries.[64] In this regard, the dissenting judges' opinions in *Animal Defenders International* are significant, where they criticise the use of double standards as well as the 'excessive importance attributed to the process generating the general measure', to the detriment of the protection of public debate.[65]

[60] *Konstantin Markin* v. *Russia*, Grand Chamber Decision of 22 March 2012 [App. No. 30078/06].

[61] See Chapter 7 by Angelika Nussberger in this volume: 'Procedural Review by the European Court of Human Rights: View from the Court'.

[62] M. Elliott, 'After Brighton: Between a Rock and a Hard Place', *Public Law* (2012) p. 627.

[63] D. Spielmann, 'Allowing the Right Margin: The European Court of Human Rights and the National Margin of Appreciation Doctrine: Waiver or Subsidiarity of European Review?', *Cambridge Yearbook of European Legal Studies*, 14 (2011–2012) p. 381.

[64] P. Popelier and C. Van De Heyning, 'Subsidiarity Post-Brighton: Procedural Rationality as Answer?', *Leiden Journal of International Law* (2017).

[65] *Animal Defenders International* v. *the United Kingdom*, Grand Chamber decision of 22 April 2013 [App. No. 48876/08], Dissenting opinions of judges Ziemele, Sajó, Kalaydjieva, Vučinić and De Gaetano, §§ 1, 3 and 9.

In this case, the Court turns to procedural rationality review even when the margin of appreciation is narrow, and, as criticised by dissenting opinions, took no notice of expert reports for rejecting less restrictive solutions.[66] According to the Court, the quality of the parliamentary and judicial decision-making process in assessing the necessity of a measure is of particular importance when general legislative measures are concerned.[67] This seems to indicate that when assessing Acts of Parliament, the Court will more easily turn to procedural rationality review with the purpose to loosen the proportionality analysis, even if a narrow margin of appreciation applies.[68]

Overall, the ECtHR seems to increasingly appreciate public support over substantial evidence. In *Anchugov and Gladkov*, the Court still cautions that even extensive public debate and a constitutional ground are insufficient, if there is no evidence that competing interests have actually been weighed.[69] But in *The National Union of RMT Workers*, the Court refers to an overwhelming 'democratic consensus' covering 'a broad spectrum of political opinion in the United Kingdom' to accept a ban on secondary action as justified.[70] In *Shindler* as well, extensive parliamentary debate was decisive for the Court to accept that a fair balance had been struck for regulating non-residents' voting rights.[71]

4.6 Conclusion

For want of specific empirical evidence, it is hard to tell how precisely evidence-based judicial review of government interference relates to the implementation of an evidence-based legislative policy. Nevertheless, we can find indications that they reinforce each other, but that other factors, such as legal, administrative and political context, as well as institutional

[66] Dissenting opinion of judge Tulkens, joined by judges Spielmann and Laffranque, § 16 and 17.

[67] *Animal Defenders International* v. *the United Kingdom*, Grand Chamber decision of 22 April 2013, [App. No. 48876/08], § 101. See also *The National Union of Rail, Maritime and Transport Workers* v. *United Kingdom*, Decision of 8 April 2014, [App. No. 31045/10], § 101, although reference is made to *Animal Defenders International* § 107 instead of 108.

[68] Dissenting judges opposed this new turn in the Court's case law: Dissenting opinions of judges Ziemele, Sajó, Kalaydjieva, Vučinić and De Gaetano, §§ 3.

[69] *Anchugov and Gladkov* v. *Russia*, Decision of 4 July 2013 [App. No. 11157/04 and 15162/05], § 108.

[70] *The National Union of Rail, Maritime and Transport Workers* v. *United Kingdom*, Decision of 8 April 2014, [App. No. 31045/10], § 99.

[71] *Shindler* v. *the United Kingdom*, Decision of 7 May 2013, [App. No. 19840/09], § 117.

design and constitutional values, either stimulate or discourage the adoption of such policy or the refuge to procedural rationality review.

In various cases, the ECtHR also takes an evidence-based approach, even if parliamentary legislation is at stake. The question is whether this may induce national authorities to adopt or reinforce an evidence-based legislative policy. The ECtHR will most probably be more effective if it appeals to national courts, and instructions to take an evidence-based approach must take into account political context and constitutional values. If political context does not favour the implementation of a comprehensive evidence-based legislative policy programme, then the interplay of procedural rationality review by the European and the national courts may at least create awareness when particular issues are concerned.

However, if procedural rationality review is to function as a compromise between deference and fundamental rights protection, the Court should be cautious not to use it as a way out and avoid substantive review of questionable measures. Hence, the Court should examine the quality of the decision-making process if a broad margin of appreciation applies, not as a reason in itself for deference regardless of the margin of appreciation.

5

Responsiveness towards Fundamental Rights Impacts in the Preparation of EU Legislation

FAY KARTNER AND ANNE MEUWESE

5.1 Introduction

The way in which courts look at the fundamental rights compatibility of rules is not set in stone, and the same goes for legislators. Procedural review has come into focus as an interesting way of mitigating the counter-majoritarian dilemma. With regard to the European Court of Human Rights (ECtHR), in Gerards' view, if legislation has been prepared in a proper way, this could allow the Court to 'take a step back', resulting in a sharper division of tasks and competences between the Court and states.[1] The ECtHR would then examine: 'whether the contested measure or decision has been prepared in a careful manner and if there have been sufficient remedies available to correct eventual mistakes or flaws in the decision-making process'. The focus would be on 'whether the decision-making process was such as to respect the various requirements of procedural justice, transparency, accountability and good governance'.[2] A procedural type of review (hereafter: 'procedural review') by the courts may work in two directions. Legislators that follow sound procedures and use effective tools for assessing the impact of their planned interventions may find themselves awarded – one might say 'rewarded by' – a larger margin of appreciation. Vice versa, if the procedures and tools are poor, the lack of consideration on the part of the legislator may contribute to the court's decision that there has been a violation of a fundamental right.

Fay Kartner contributed to this chapter as a junior lecturer in EU Law at Radboud University Nijmegen, The Netherlands. Since 16 January 2017, Fay works as a legal advisor (privacy law) at ICTRecht (Amsterdam).

[1] J. Gerards, 'The Prism of Fundamental Rights', (2012) 8 *European Constitutional Law Review*, pp. 173–202, at p. 196.

[2] Gerards (2012), p. 198.

The quality of the lawmaking process could be indicative of the quality of legislation and its compatibility with fundamental rights. The EU lawmaking process has been under reform and can be seen as an interesting test case for procedural review. Responsiveness towards fundamental rights impacts is linked to information collection during the regulatory process, the extent to which this information is debated and the extent to which the negative effects on fundamental rights are justified up by sound arguments.[3] Legitimacy of legislation and judicial decisions is attained in a different manner at the supranational level.[4] At the EU level, the European Parliament (EP) is the only directly elected institution, sharing legislative power with the Council and lacking a right of initiative.[5] Council and Commission decision-makers are only indirectly democratically accountable. Consensus seeking is common practice, with 'civil society participation' playing an even more important role than at the national level.[6]

Democracy, rights protection and effectiveness are closely related, and perhaps are preconditions for the success of each.[7] By 'responsiveness', we understand the extent to which a legislative process anticipates its (intended and unintended, direct and indirect) social, economic and fundamental rights consequences. In this contribution, we will focus on fundamental rights implications of legislative and regulatory proposals. 'Regulation' and 'rights' issues are often dealt with separately and the relationship between the two notions at first glance is tension-filled. Fundamental rights mechanisms can suffer from pressure due to globalisation and threats of terrorism. The concept of regulation is largely focused on effectiveness in combating societal problems.[8] The concept of

[3] This chapter will look at these elements, because they are also part of the characteristics of procedural review. See, for example, the chapters by Beijer, Gerards and Brems in this volume.

[4] J.L. Miller, 'A New "Democratic Life" for the European Union? Administrative lawmaking, democratic legitimacy and the Lisbon Treaty', (2011) 17 *Contemporary Politics*, pp. 321–334, at p. 323.

[5] In the ordinary legislative procedure. See also J. Greenwood, 'Organized Civil Society and Democratic Legitimacy in the European Union', (2007) 37 *British Journal of Political Science*, pp. 333–357, at p. 334.

[6] T. Persson, 'Democratizing European Chemicals Policy: Do Consultations Favour Civil Society Participation?', (2008) 3 *Journal of Civil Society*, pp. 223–238, at p. 225. See also Greenwood (2007), at p. 334.

[7] P. Popelier, 'Governance and Better Regulation: Dealing with the Legitimacy Paradox', 17 (2011) *European Public Law*, pp. 555–569, at p. 556.

[8] E. Darian-Smith and C. Scott, 'Regulation and Human Rights in Socio-Legal Scholarship', 31 (2009) *Law & Policy*, pp. 271–281, at pp. 271, 272.

fundamental rights emphasises universality, while the concept of regulation attaches more importance to the instrumental function of the law. The debate on regulation has focused on enforcement, compliance and implementation.[9] Both concepts, however, share a shift in focus from centralised state power to more attention for non-state actors as well.[10] In some circumstances, rights claims allow the state to act, and international regulatory bodies may constrain the state in its action.[11] Viewed in this way, rights and regulation are not strictly separated, but rather two sides of the same coin. They are both 'social practices articulating generalized claims upon the social order', an 'institutionalized response to a certain grievance'.[12] In this chapter, we will specify this special relationship between rights and regulation in the EU lawmaking context by exploring how the two concepts are dealt with in the 'Better Regulation' strategy, the European Commission's main generic policy for improving the overall quality of lawmaking. In particular, we will analyse the way impact assessment and scrutiny by the Regulatory Scrutiny Board are carried out. This will show how fundamental rights impacts can come to light in these procedures, and how this might affect judicial review.

The main question to be answered in this chapter is 'to what extent do various elements of EU legislative procedure contribute to responsiveness towards fundamental rights impacts?'.

As a practical indication of obstacles for fundamental rights responsiveness in the EU legislative process, we will highlight a single case: the Data Retention Directive.[13] Because of its disproportionate impact on privacy, this Directive was declared invalid by the Court of Justice of the EU (CJEU) in joined cases C-293/12 and C-594/12 (*Digital Rights Ireland and Seitlinger and others*).[14] The single case study, and a number of other examples, provide us with some valuable insights regarding the relationship between (due preparation of) legislation and regulation, fundamental rights and judicial review.

[9] Darian-Smith and Scott (2009), p. 274. [10] Darian-Smith and Scott (2009), p. 273.

[11] Darian-Smith and Scott (2009), p. 275.

[12] B. Morgan, 'The Intersection of Rights and Regulation: New Directions in Sociolegal Scholarship', in: B. Morgan (ed), *The Intersection of Rights and Regulation: New Directions in Socio-legal Scholarship. Markets and the Law*, (Ashgate, 2007); especially pp. 7–9.

[13] Directive 2006/24/EC of the European Parliament and of the Council of 15 March 2006 on the retention of data generated or processed in connection with the provision of publicly available electronic communications services or of public communications networks and amending Directive 2002/58/EC (OJ 2006 L 105, p. 54).

[14] CJEU 8 April 2014, Joined Cases C-293/12 and C-594/12, ECLI:EU:C:2014:238 (*Digital Rights Ireland*).

The chapter is structured as follows. In section 5.2 we discuss procedures that are intended to improve regulatory quality in the EU. Section 5.3 analyses to what extent these instruments can enhance the awareness of (intended and unintended) impacts on especially fundamental rights. We review the various procedures for moments in which fundamental rights impacts can come to light. Recent debates and examples from the literature are discussed to indicate whether the various instruments have in practice led to a better detection of possible fundamental rights impacts. Section 5.4 revisits the Data Retention case and discusses to what extent and in which ways information on possible fundamental rights impacts is used in practice. Section 5.5 identifies barriers to a fundamental rights-responsive legislative process: certain aspects of the legislative process can be identified that appear to hinder the effective collection of information on fundamental rights impacts, and the appropriate use of this data. Section 5.6 will briefly address the implications of these enhanced legislative procedural review tools for judicial review, in particular by the CJEU. Section 5.7 concludes.

5.2 Requirements of Regulatory Quality in the EU

Views differ greatly on what 'good legislation' is.[15] The European Union's recent history is rich in initiatives to further this, such as the White Paper on European Governance, the conclusions of the Laeken and Lisbon summits, the work of the Mandelkern group and the Better Lawmaking/ Better Regulation programmes.[16] The initiatives cover the legality principle, transparency, coordination between institutions, evidence-based decision-making, reason-giving, subsidiarity and proportionality. No excessive use should be made of implementing powers. Implementation should be monitored, evaluation should take place, and acts should be enforceable. Acts should be consistent, accessible and intelligible.[17]

In the 2015 Better Regulation package, the entire policy cycle is covered. The effectiveness and efficiency of legislation are assessed

[15] W.J.M. Voermans, 'Concern about the Quality of EU Legislation: What Kind of Problem, by What Kind of Standards?', (2009) 2 *Erasmus Law Review*, pp. 59–95, at 61.

[16] The Better Regulation Package of May 2015, as well as the newest Inter-Institutional Agreement on Better Lawmaking, can be found at www.ec.europa.eu/smart-regulation/better_regulation/key_docs_en.htm

[17] Voermans (2009), pp. 71–72; L.A.J. Senden, 'The Evolution of the Commission's REFIT Policy and the Interinstitutional Agreement on Better Lawmaking', speech at the symposium 'Better Regulation in the EU Revisited. Benefiting Business and Citizens', T.M.C. Asser Institute, The Hague, 23 April 2015.

through *ex ante* impact assessments, fitness checks in key areas, general policy evaluations, impact assessment (IA) and *ex post* evaluation.[18] Apart from this, the 2016 Inter-Institutional Agreement on Better Lawmaking is influential. This agreement repeats that legislation should be comprehensible and clear, include reporting, monitoring and evaluation requirements, avoid overregulation and unnecessary administrative burdens and be practical to implement. There is now a (slightly) stronger commitment on the part of the EP and Council to carry out their own IAs on 'substantial amendments', and to assess the potential impacts of implementing and delegated acts. These developments are important to the topic of the current chapter, since they change the ways in which impacts on fundamental rights can come to the attention of the legislature and the public.[19]

Impact assessment is prepared when a legislative proposal, non-legislative initiative or implementing/delegated act is expected to have significant impacts in the economic, social or environmental field. Impacts on fundamental rights are classified under social impacts.[20] The advantages and disadvantages of various options have to be clarified, ideally leading to a more rational and evidence-based choice as 'trade-offs' are being highlighted.[21] This requires openness to unintended effects as well. Implementation problems and enforcement difficulties may have fundamental rights implications.[22] For example, if strict requirements were imposed on the collection of personal data by companies, but in practice no fines would be imposed when these rules are breached, the rules would not be likely to protect privacy.

When drawing up an IA report, Commission officials take into account the 'Better Regulation Guidelines'. Officials carrying out an

[18] H. Xanthaki, 'European Union Legislative Quality after the Lisbon Treaty: The Challenges of Smart Regulation' (2013) 35 *Statute Law Review*, pp. 66–80, at p. 76. European Commission, 'Better Regulation for Better Results, An EU Agenda', COM (2015) 215 final. See also *Special Issue on the Better Regulation Package, European Journal of Risk Regulation* (3) 2015.

[19] Inter-Institutional Agreement on Better Lawmaking, 2015, to be found at: www.ec.europa.eu/smart-regulation/better_regulation/documents/20151215_iia_on_better_law_making_en.pdf

[20] Consultation document in preparation of the Better Regulation Guidelines 2015, to be found at: www.ec.europa.eu/smart-regulation/impact/docs/iag_pc_questionnaire_en.pdf. 43–46.

[21] See www.ec.europa.eu/smart-regulation/impact/index_en.htm

[22] Summary of the replies of the public consultation on the IA Guidelines review, p. 7. www.ec.europa.eu/smart-regulation/impact/docs/contributions/summary_replies_public_consultation_review_iag_2014_en.pdf

impact assessment are asked to assess how much the problem affects the daily life of individuals and enterprises and whose behaviour would have to change for the situation to improve. Commission officials should assess whether the problem addressed has transnational aspects which cannot be adequately addressed by action by member states and whether action at EU level would be beneficial given its scale. They should highlight any trade-off between policy goals. They should set out the criteria for comparing the different options. Monitoring and evaluation frameworks for the new rules should be set up. The widest range of alternatives should be considered, including the option of 'doing nothing', and both options that are likely to receive broad support and those that will probably not.[23] The following principles are seen as fundamental characteristics of a good IA: comprehensive, proportionate, evidence-based, open to stakeholders' views, unbiased, conducted in cooperation with other services, embedded in the policy cycle[24] and transparent.[25] For a long time, IA was 'nothing more than an internal procedure to aid decision-making and to bring about a culture change among Commission officials involved in the preparation of legislation.'[26] The question can be asked even today: Do IA reports have the potential of being more than an 'extended explanatory memorandum', of getting the legislature to switch from a 'justificatory mode' to a 'learning mode'?[27]

In order to get as close as possible to the situation described above, an internal quality control body for IAs was set up. In the recent 'Better Regulation package' the former Impact Assessment Board (IAB), which dated from 2007, was reinvented as a 'Regulatory Scrutiny Board' (RSB). The most important new feature of this board is three members from outside the Commission. The RSB scrutinises draft IA reports and makes recommendations to the relevant service.[28] Its opinion is 'negative' when

[23] Better Regulation Guidelines 2015, www.ec.europa.eu/smart-regulation/guidelines/docs/swd_br_guidelines_en.pdf. The previous Guidelines were adopted in 2009: Commission Impact Assessment Guidelines, 15 January 2009, SEC (2009)92, www.ec.europa.eu/smart-regulation/impact/commission_guidelines/docs/iag_2009_en.pdf

[24] This would also entail *ex post* evaluation, which we will however not deal with in this chapter.

[25] Consultation document in preparation of the Better Regulation Guidelines 2015, at p. 8.

[26] A.C.M. Meuwese and S. Gomtsian, 'Regulatory Scrutiny of Subsidiarity and Proportionality', (2015) 22 *Maastricht Journal of European and Comparative Law*, pp. 483–505, at p. 486.

[27] A.C.M. Meuwese and P. Popelier, 'Legal Implications of Better Regulation: A Special Issue', *European Public Law* 17 (2011), pp. 455–466, at, pp. 458–459.

[28] A. Alemanno, 'The Better Regulation Initiative at the Judicial Gate: A Trojan Horse within the Commission's Walls or the Way Forward?' (2009) 15 *European Law Journal* pp. 382–400, at p. 389.

'substantial improvements are needed on a number of significant issues'. The second opinion can also be positive or negative; only in very rare cases is the third opinion still negative. In principle, a positive opinion is needed to go ahead with a proposal.[29] Unlike the Office of Information and Regulatory Affairs (OIRA),[30] its US counterpart, the RSB cannot veto an IA report, since this would go against the principle of collegiality in the Commission. However, the Commission has pledged to not decide on any legislative proposals that do not carry a positive opinion from the RSB.[31] All members, so also those recruited from within the Commission, are expected to carry out their assessments independently, work full-time exclusively for the board and be selected transparently, on the basis of their expertise.[32] The RSB also carries out quality control of *ex post* analyses.[33] Although in the past IAB reports have (almost) never led to a legislative proposal not being adopted, they can lead to the Commission paying more attention to subsidiarity and proportionality concerns in IA reports, albeit in a very procedural manner.[34] Although institutionally speaking, the RSB is quite different from the IAB, there is no reason why this type of assessment should not remain. The RSB may be expected to look more substantively at impacts because it is set up less as a 'body of peers' (which might tell the drafters only to 'explain things better') and more as a college of experts.[35]

5.3 Improving the Preparation of Legislation?

Impact assessment reports require an analysis of the effects of various legislative options. When assessing these impacts, possible effects on fundamental rights can come to light. Smismans and Minto note that while fundamental rights impacts are dealt with in impact assessment as a negative criterion (preventing a too-large negative impact), they are still not used actively to define objectives of regulation to positively further these rights.[36] However, it is worthwhile to look at the way in which

[29] www.ec.europa.eu/smart-regulation/impact/key_docs/docs/iab_report_2013_en.pdf, pp. 1–2.
[30] See www.whitehouse.gov/omb/oira [31] Alemanno (2009), p. 390.
[32] For an overview of the current members of the Regulatory Scrutiny Board, see www.ec.europa.eu/smart-regulation/impact/iab/members_en.htm
[33] Meuwese and Gomtsian (2015), at p. 487. [34] Meuwese and Gomtsian (2015).
[35] A.C.M. Meuwese, 'Regulatory Scrutiny in Transition', (2015) 3 *European Journal of Risk Regulation*, p. 360.
[36] S. Smismans and R. Minto, 'Are Integrated Impact Assessments the Way Forward for Mainstreaming in the European Union?', 10 (2016) *Regulation & Governance*, forthcoming, pp. 13–15.

fundamental rights aspects are analysed into more detail and including the 'review stage' of the impact assessment process. The Regulatory Scrutiny Board (formerly the Impact Assessment Board) provides remarks on such reports, allowing their methodology to be improved. This can possibly lead to a more adequate justification for limitations on fundamental rights, a more rational choice between different options and better problem analyses in the first place. In the following section, we will point this out by means of examples. As Smismans and Minto also note, the way in which fundamental rights are dealt with varies from one Directorate-General to another.[37]

5.3.1 Better Problem Analyses

Often, IA reports fail to adequately describe why the current situation is problematic.[38] An example is the exchange of criminal record information between member states, as regards third country nationals and stateless people.[39] The impact assessment emphasises member state responsibility to implement the legislation in conformity with the right to privacy and data protection, and the legislation's conformity with the *Digital Rights Ireland* and *Schrems* judgments.[40] The IA report mentions that one of the goals of the measures is to protect children from the risk of abuse and exploitation[41] by enabling employers to verify whether someone has been banned from activities involving direct and regular contacts with children as a result of past criminal convictions.

[37] Smismans and Minto (2016), pp. 13–15.

[38] M. Souto-Otero, 'Is Better Regulation Possible? Formal and Substantive Quality in the Impact Assessments in Education and Culture of the European Commission', (2013) 9 *Evidence & Policy*, pp. 513–529. For conclusions regarding IA in earlier years, see A. Renda, *Impact Assessment in the EU. The State of the Art and the Art of the* State, 2006, Centre for European Policy Studies, www.ceps.eu/system/files/book/1291.pdf See also the evaluation by The Evaluation Partnership: www.ec.europa.eu/smart-regulation/impact/key_docs/docs/tep_eias_final_report.pdf

[39] www.ec.europa.eu/justice/criminal/files/ecris_tcn_commission_proposal_en.pdf

[40] M.-P. Granger and K. Irion, 'The Court of Justice and the Data Retention Directive in *Digital Rights Ireland*: Telling off the EU Legislator and Teaching a Lesson in Privacy and Data Protection', 39 (2014) *European Law Review*, pp. 835–850. CJEU 8 April 2014, Joined Cases C 293/12 and C 594/12, ECLI:EU:C:2014:238 (Digital Rights Ireland) CJEU 6 October 2015, Case C-362/14, ECLI:EU:C:2015:650 (Schrems).

[41] Proposal for a Directive of the European Parliament and of the Council amending Council Framework Decision 2009/315/JHA, as regards the exchange of information on third country nationals and as regards the European Criminal Records Information System (ECRIS), and replacing Council Decision 2009/316/JHA, COM (2016) 7 final, www.ec.europa.eu/justice/criminal/files/ecris_tcn_commission_proposal_en.pdf

The RSB did not find this reasoning sufficient; more explanation should be given on the scale of undetected recidivism, identification issues and fundamental rights issues. It should be better explained why other options, such as further automation of the current system, would not suffice.[42]

Many indirect impacts on fundamental rights come forward in the proposal for a Directive on the activities and supervision of institutions for occupational retirement provision. According to the IA report, the Directive will promote rights of the elderly to lead a life of dignity and independence. Positive effects on consumer protection and the freedom to conduct a business are named as well. The IA states shortly that the general objective justifies limitations on the freedom to conduct a business without further explanation.[43] The IAB report is again very critical; the options should be presented and assessed more elaborately and relevant stakeholder interests should be described and discussed more openly.[44] With regard to the right to legal aid in criminal proceedings and European Arrest Warrant procedures, the IA report should better explain why, in some member states, the ECHR legal aid requirements as regarded are not fulfilled. It should show a better analysis of enforcement power and a discussion of proportionality and subsidiarity. More precise monitoring and evaluation criteria should be provided for measuring the effectiveness and efficiency of the proposed EU measures.[45]

The examples show that the IA reports force the Commission to look at impacts, but that it still can fail in exactly describing the scale of the problem, which makes it harder to justify that the measure is proportionate. As regards Directives, the EU legislature often still wants to leave

[42] Impact assessment accompanying the proposal for a Directive amending Council Framework Decision 2009/315/JHA on the organisation and content of the exchange of information extracted from the criminal record between member states, as regards information on third country nationals and stateless people, www.ec.europa.eu/smart-regulation/impact/ia_carried_out/docs/ia_2016/sec_2016_0055_en.pdf

[43] Proposal for a Directive of the European Parliament and of the Council on the activities and supervision of institutions for occupational retirement provision (recast), COM/2014/0167 final, www.eur-lex.europa.eu/legal-content/EN/TXT/?uri=CELEX%3A52014PC0167

[44] IAB opinion on the proposal for a Directive of the European Parliament and of the Council on the activities and supervision of institutions for occupational retirement provision (recast), revised version of 16 October 2013, www.ec.europa.eu/smart-regulation/impact/ia_carried_out/docs/ia_2014/sec_2014_0208_en.pdf

[45] IAB opinion, SEC (2013) 616.

a large amount of discretion, and the responsibility that comes with it, to member states. Per situation, it is debatable whether this is a good thing.

5.3.2 *Preventing Unnecessary Action*

IA can also help the legislator to assess whether it is necessary to take action. An example is the proposal for a Directive on accessibility requirements for certain groups of products and services.[46] The IA report mentions freedom to conduct a business; it stresses that the proposal has a largely positive impact on rights such as freedom of movement and residence, human dignity, integrity of the person, access to employment and integration of persons with disabilities and rights of the elderly. If there are any restrictions, for example, on the right to conduct a business, then these would be justified and proportionate, because harmonisation would increase the potential for intra-EU trade.[47]

The IAB initially even issued a negative opinion. It was necessary to further explain how much fragmentation there actually is and why this is a problem, and to justify why self-regulation would not work. It was moreover not yet clear how the measures would work in practice.[48]

A comparable situation can be seen when looking at legislation on long-term shareholder engagement and the corporate governance statement.[49] There could be impacts on the freedom to conduct a business. The IA report shortly discusses that the measures do not go further than necessary for the goals of assessing the link between pay and performance, and for the facilitation of the exercise of shareholders' rights. The IAB report asks for a clear identification on the basis of empirical evidence of the actual

[46] Proposal for a Directive of the European Parliament and of the Council on the approximation of the laws, regulations and administrative provisions of the member states as regards the accessibility requirements for products and services, COM (2015) 615 final, www.eur-lex.europa.eu/legal-content/EN/TXT/?uri=CELEX:52015PC0615

[47] Impact Assessment accompanying the proposal for a Directive of the European Parliament and of the Council on the approximation of the laws, regulations and administrative provisions of the member states as regards accessibility requirements for products and services, SWD (2015) 264, www.ec.europa.eu/smart-regulation/impact/ia_carried_out/docs/ia_2015/swd_2015_0264_en.pdf

[48] IAB opinion (on the resubmitted draft version of 4 June 2013), www.ec.europa.eu/smart-regulation/impact/ia_carried_out/docs/ia_2015/sec_2015_0471_en.pdf

[49] Proposal for a Directive of the European Parliament and of the Council amending Directive 2007/36/EC as regards the encouragement of long-term shareholder engagement and Directive 2013/34/EU as regards certain elements of the corporate governance statement, COM (2014) 213 final, www.ec.europa.eu/internal_market/company/docs/modern/cgp/shrd/140409-shrd_en.pdf

problems to be addressed. The link between companies' management decisions, long-term shareholder engagement, should be better assessed.[50] The IAB does not directly mention fundamental rights concerns, but it becomes clear that the need for action needs to be more carefully assessed. Regarding the proposal for establishing the European Public Prosecutor's Office,[51] just emphasising the significant scale of fraud with EU financial means was, according to the IAB, not a sufficient intervention logic. The IAB required a better assessment of the precise effects on fundamental rights of the various options in order to scrutinise the cost-benefit analysis.

From the above, we can conclude that the IA and RSB not only try to look for undetected negative impacts on fundamental rights, but that they also try to prevent the EU legislator from making legislation to 'further' those rights when there are actually few problems.

5.3.3 *Providing the Decision-Makers with an Actual Choice*

Often, the RSB/IAB tells the IA drafters to better explain the need for the preferred option, and leave decision-makers an actual choice. An example is the proposal on a Directive on the cross-border supply of digital content.[52] This entails portability of rights to access to digital content; one then does not have to acquire rights to the content in different member states. There are two options available, leaving content providers with an opportunity to contractually restrict this portability right, or forbidding this. The IA report mentions possible impact on copyright and the freedom to conduct a business, but states that these restrictions are justified in the light of cross-border portability of online content; the large benefit enjoyed by consumers would strongly outweigh them.[53] The RSB again is critical; it thinks it should be explained better why the market itself cannot solve the problem (there was an industry pledge, 'Licences for Europe', which was not evaluated in detail in the IA). Moreover, the impacts on service providers and consumers need to be described better, as well as the balancing exercise between increased

50 IA report, SWD (2014) 127 final, www.eur-lex.europa.eu/legal-content/EN/TXT/PDF/?uri=CELEX:52014SC0127&from=EN

51 IAB opinion, SEC (2013) 422 and 1st IA Report on the proposal.

52 Proposal for a Directive of the European Parliament and of the Council on certain aspects concerning contracts for the supply of digital content, COM (2015) 634 final, www.ec.europa.eu/justice/contract/files/directive_-digital_content.pdf

53 IA report, SWD (2015) 274 final, www.ec.europa.eu/smart-regulation/impact/ia_carried_out/docs/ia_2015/swd_2015_0274_en.pdf

portability of rights and privacy risks (after all, the companies need to verify where the consumer is located).

The IAB thus emphasises the need to provide decision-makers with an actual choice, which can lead to an increased chance that fundamental rights concerns are adequately dealt with. Dealing with legislation on the presumption of innocence and the right to be present at trial in criminal proceedings, the IAB states that the causal links between the proposed measures and the strengthening of the presumption of innocence should be better explained, linked to the formulations of the ECtHR and fair trial rights. The report should substantiate better why the relevant rights are protected in an insufficient manner, why a more effective implementation of ECHR rules by member states would not be sufficient and why the existing appeal possibilities are not enough. The authors of the IA should take better care when assessing proportionality, subsidiarity and the effectiveness of the various options.[54]

With regard to the use of security scanners on airports, the IAB states that the IA report should integrate fundamental rights and human health concerns into the problem definition. The effectiveness and efficiency of various screening methods should have been assessed. Moreover, it should have been explained why the baseline scenario did not take technological development into account. Finally, trade-offs should be made clear between efficiency, security, health risk minimisation and privacy.[55] Not only intended fundamental rights effects catch the IAB's attention. It signals defects in enforcement and effectiveness, and asked the IA drafters to assess these. Indirectly, this could lead to the legislature paying more attention to these aspects. For example, on the General Data Protection Regulation, the IAB states that more evidence was needed on problems such as fragmentation and inconsistent enforcement of data protection rules and pleads for better reasons why the perceived lack of harmonisation is problematic and why current structures are not enough to ensure consistency.[56]

5.3.4 *Pitfalls When Addressing Fundamental Rights as Part of Regulatory Analysis*

Apart from several reports in which fundamental rights are rather central in the analysis or scrutiny, there are also those that mention rights as

[54] IAB opinion, SEC (2013) 617. [55] IAB opinion, SEC (2011) 1328.
[56] IAB opinion, SEC (2012) 74.

a 'side issue', without much specification. On the proposal on a European Platform to enhance cooperation in the prevention and deterrence of undeclared work,[57] the IA mentions that such a platform could contribute to the promotion of labour rights and social rights. The Commission backs this up by Fundamental Rights Agency research. The free movement of workers is discussed under 'fundamental rights impacts' as well.[58] The IAB is again critical. It does not give an opinion on the fundamental rights effects as such; however, the IA report should provide evidence of insufficient cooperation and the underlying incentives, and the added value of an EU initiative.[59]

To draw a preliminary conclusion, the analysis in this section demonstrates that IA and RSB reports have the potential to help the legislature assess better whether there is a fundamental rights problem in the first place, whether this requires action and what the implications of each described option are. However, this does not mean that each IA report extensively deals with the fundamental rights issues that are found. Admittedly, this is not always necessary. Sometimes the fundamental rights issues found are mere side-issues, issues can better be solved at the national level, or there is already other legislation that should deal with them (for example, privacy law). The RSB criticism does not always name fundamental rights as such, but its comments can ensure that the legislature gets a more complete picture of the effects of each option, including fundamental rights effects. IA reports should offer more than the legislator's justification for a certain piece of legislation. They require Commission and IAB officials to be genuinely open to all effects and also side-effects and unexpected effects, due to, for example, ineffective implementation or enforcement in member states.

5.4 Data Retention, Rights and Impacts: A Case Study

Under the Data Retention Directive, providers of communication services had to retain so-called 'metadata', details on the 'source,

[57] Proposal for a Decision of the European Parliament and of the Council on establishing a European Platform to enhance cooperation in the prevention and deterrence of undeclared work, COM/2014/0221 final, www.eur-lex.europa.eu/legal-content/EN/TXT/?uri=CELEX%3A52014PC0221

[58] SWD (2014) 137 final, www.eur-lex.europa.eu/legal-content/EN/TXT/PDF/?uri=CELEX:52014SC0137&from=EN

[59] IAB opinion, SEC (2014) 246, www.ec.europa.eu/smart-regulation/impact/ia_carried_out/docs/ia_2014/sec_2014_0246_en.pdf

destination, date, type, time' and (as regards mobile phones) location of communication.[60] There was no requirement of suspicion or intervention by a court.[61] The Data Retention Directive was declared invalid by the CJEU in joined cases C-293/12 and C-594/12 *Digital Rights Ireland and Seitlinger and others.*[62] The scheme was a disproportionate interference with the right to privacy.[63] The Court used to mostly defer to the EU legislator and state that it is a task for the member states to implement and apply EU legislation in a way that is in conformity with fundamental rights instruments. Now, it expressly stated that EU instruments *themselves* must contain sufficient safeguards for fundamental rights. EU institutions will need to evaluate even more carefully, support their legislation with convincing evidence and further minimise negative effects on fundamental rights. Detailed empirical questions asked by the Court, such as the effectiveness of the Directive and profiling, indicate for a stronger role of the EU legislature taking in safeguarding rights, apart from the member states.[64] It is however not clear how serious the interference with fundamental rights has to be to warrant strict scrutiny by the Court, and for which rights or objectives this is the case.[65] The Court may have marginalised the Directive's internal market objectives to leave open the possibility of review according to a different standard when internal market measures are concerned.[66] Moreover, the CJEU is said to be 'closing ranks with the ECtHR when it treats the collection and the use of the data as two separate instances of interference with the right to privacy'.[67]

Industry, data protection authorities and interest groups had brought forward an alternative scheme of data preservation; law enforcement authorities would then ask service providers to retain particular data on (a) specific person(s). The impact assessment stated that data

[60] E. Guild and S. Carrera, 'The Political and Judicial Life of Metadata: Digital Rights Ireland and the Trail of the Data Retention Directive', CEPS Paper in Liberty and Security in Europe No. 65, May 2014, www.ceps.eu/system/files/EG%20and%20SC%20Data%20retention.pdf, at p. 1.

[61] Guild and Carrera (2014), p. 2.

[62] CJEU 8 April 2014, Joined Cases C-293/12 and C-594/12, ECLI:EU:C:2014:238 (*Digital Rights Ireland*).

[63] Guild and Carrera (2014), p. 5.

[64] M.-P. Granger and K. Irion, 'The Court of Justice and the Data Retention Directive in *Digital Rights Ireland*: Telling off the EU Legislator and Teaching a Lesson in Privacy and Data Protection', 39 (2014) *European Law Review*, pp. 835–850, at p. 839.

[65] Granger and Irion (2014), p. 846. [66] Granger and Irion (2014), p. 847.

[67] Granger and Irion (2014), p. 849.

preservation alone would not be enough to fight serious crime and terrorism.[68] It also noted that a cost reimbursement scheme for companies would be needed to prevent market distortions.[69] The argument is sometimes made that retention of traffic data will not help law enforcement authorities. After all, criminals can, for example, access the internet on public computers in internet cafés or libraries; the impact assessment states that even then, their identities can be found out under a data retention scheme.[70] If their identities can be found out even if they use computers in public places, this is desirable with a view to combating criminality. However, it also contributes to a disproportionate interference with the right to privacy.

The next part of the impact assessment dealt with the most sensitive issue surrounding the Directive. The data can only be retained to prevent, detect or investigate serious crime. The categories of data which need to be retained are limited to what is necessary, and the periods of retention are limited. Moreover, the Directive is not applicable to the content of communications.[71] Individuals can access their data and can ask for it to be corrected or deleted, and can ask for compensation if their data has been handled in an unlawful way.[72] Many parties have been consulted: representatives of law enforcement authorities, the electronic communications industry and data protection experts. Public debate and debate in the EP have also been taken into account, the document states.[73] Therefore, the Commission concluded 'that the IA document was "convinced that its proposal can stand the test of compatibility with fundamental rights and freedoms. It is confident that the bodies mentioned will be able to revisit their position on the basis of the indications above"'.[74] The Court, however, ruled otherwise.

Two aspects of the impact assessment of the Data Retention Directive stand out as possibly linked to the failure to prevent a legislative breach of fundamental rights. The first is the brevity of the Commission's argumentation. The second is its focus on security. Time constraints caused the legislative procedure to be carried out in an accelerated form.[75] The IA only compared the situation to the results that would

[68] Commission staff working document – Annex to the proposal for a Directive of the European Parliament and of the Council on the retention of data processed in connection with the provision of public electronic communication services and amending Directive 2002/58/EC – Extended impact assessment, SEC (2005) 1131, 12.

[69] SEC (2005) 1131, 14. [70] SEC (2005) 1131, 17. [71] SEC (2005) 1131, 20.

[72] SEC (2005) 1131, 21. [73] SEC (2005) 1131, 23. [74] SEC (2005) 1131, 21.

[75] A.C.M. Meuwese, *Impact Assessment in EU Lawmaking*, Alphen aan den Rijn: Kluwer Law International (2008), p. 246.

arise if no action were taken.[76] This was in defiance of the IA guidelines, which stipulate that more options than 'doing nothing' and the 'preferred option' should always be considered.[77] The (then) MEP Cederschiöld[78] did not find the IA satisfactory and wanted to have an extra IA to be carried out, using outside expertise.[79] In particular, she was concerned with the emphasis on security.[80] Her requirements proved unviable, because this would cause too much delay.[81] Cederschiöld (also a member of the LIBE Committee and the shadow rapporteur for the IMCO Committee in these matters) had asked whether the extended IA had been carried out in accordance with the IA Guidelines.[82] The Commission answered that the Guidelines in force at the time were even less enforceable then.[83] Moreover, important issues (like the retention period, whether authorities should only be able to request specific data or entire databases of existing data, the scope of data retention and fundamental rights concerns) were discussed separately, instead of being part of a real integrated cost-benefit analysis.[84] The IA thus recognises that there are effects on fundamental rights, but it merely refers to the beneficial effects for criminal investigations. It is merely stated that the rules are proportionate, instead of a proper motivation. Even at the initial stage, there was a certain degree of awareness of possible negative effects on fundamental rights. However, these views were not seen as pressing enough to require further research into different policy options.[85]

The legislative proposal was modified afterwards. The first version featured a cost reimbursement scheme. In the amended proposal, this scheme was removed and the retention period was extended from 1 year to 2 years maximum.[86] The Commission did not apply IA again, despite several requests and despite a resolution requiring

[76] M.-H. Maras, 'The Economic Costs and Consequences of Mass Communications Data Retention: Is the Data Retention Directive a Proportionate Measure?', *European Journal of Law and Economics* 2012, at p. 450.

[77] Commission staff working document, Better Regulation Guidelines 2015, SWD (2015) 111 final.

[78] www.europarl.europa.eu/meps/en/2110/charlotte_cederschiold_home.html. She then was a member of the European Parliament for the European People's Party, dealing with, *inter alia*, the issue of data retention.

[79] Meuwese (2008), p. 246. [80] Meuwese (2008), p. 247. [81] Meuwese (2008), p. 246.

[82] Meuwese (2008), p. 247. [83] Meuwese (2008), p. 247.

[84] Meuwese (2008), pp. 247–248. [85] Meuwese (2008), p. 249.

[86] M.-H. Maras, 'The Economic Costs and Consequences of Mass Communications Data Retention: Is the Data Retention Directive a Proportionate Measure?' (2012) 33 *European Journal of Law and Economics*, pp. 447–452, at p. 450.

this.[87] The Directive required the processing and storage of data that had before not been retained for business purposes; moreover, this data would probably not even always be helpful in law enforcement.[88] The lack of a cost reimbursement scheme could be a heavy burden for companies.[89] Service providers might be forced to invest less in development of new technologies. Providers might store data outside the European Union to avoid data retention requirements, causing negative effects on law enforcement and the EU labour market.[90] Other commentators focused more on the fundamental right to privacy and data protection as such.[91] The comments reflect the consequences of not (properly) carrying out an IA on a legislative proposal that heavily affects fundamental rights. The first IA can be seen as not meeting the standards, and the amended version of the proposal did not even undergo IA. In conclusion, time constraints, and a political focus on security, seem to have reduced the safeguards that IA is designed to provide.

After the Directive was adopted, however, there was further activity. The Commission issued a report regarding the need to amend the Directive.[92] The report stressed the need to take into account the latest ICT developments. It focused on the scope of the data covered by the Directive and the length of the retention periods. The report also paid attention to the effects on fundamental rights. It stated that the Directive has not been entirely successful in harmonising data retention.[93] Various conferences and documents by stakeholders had been taken into account. The report refers to the *Digital Rights Ireland* case, which was pending at that time. The concerns of the EDPS are discussed, just like the Article 29 Working Party's comments.[94]

The report still supported data retention, but also urged the Commission to take proportionality and necessity concerns into account more properly. It noted that the Directive had not created a level playing field for operators and a cost reimbursement scheme should be installed.[95] The report had been drawn up to provide advice on which factors to take into account when improving the Directive. It named a few areas to be researched in a future impact assessment, and recommended

[87] Maras (2012), p. 450. [88] Maras (2012), p. 457. [89] Maras (2012), p. 461.
[90] Maras (2012), p. 466.
[91] E. Kosta and P. Valcke, 'Retaining the Data Retention Directive', *Computer Law & Security Report* 22 (2006), pp. 379–380.
[92] COM (2011) 225 final, p. 1. [93] COM (2011) 225 final, p. 1.
[94] COM (2011) 225 final, p. 29. [95] COM (2011) 225 final, pp. 26–27.

that a range of different options be assessed.[96] As required by the Directive, the Commission set up an experts group to advise on best practice in the implementation of the Data Retention Directive. As a result of the CJEU judgment, the group no longer exists. The Directive was annulled before the report could have any beneficial consequences.[97]

The further activities that were carried out show that fundamental rights debates continue even after legislation has been in place for some time. Clearly, the report itself asked for more concrete scientific analysis on a number of different points. Most importantly, it names the consistency of the purposes for which data retention may be used, the length of the data retention periods, independent supervision of requests for access, the group of people who can access the data, security measures, etc.[98] More attention could have been given to these aspects of the proposal (at the initial stage or after the legislation had been applied for a while). Then, the considerable extent of the negative effects on privacy would have become clearer.[99] It should be kept in mind that political factors always play a role when determining when a measure is proportionate. In the case of the Data Retention Directive, however, more research on the points mentioned above could have led to alternative schemes (which might have gained political support). It is imaginable that either the Commission would have come up with a more extensive motivation backed up by scientific evidence, or proposed a new scheme, less harmful to privacy.

The case exemplifies the link between the regulatory perspective and the fundamental rights perspective. It shows that fundamental rights impacts are not only discovered when explicitly looking for them. It shows that the safeguards that have been put in place via instruments such as Better Regulation do not always guarantee that fundamental rights are sufficiently respected.[100] Thus, IA reports need to be critically assessed. The RSB could play an important role in this. Nevertheless, it is important to maintain enough incentives for the Commission to conduct a proper IA in the first place, and use the results in an adequate and timely manner.[101]

[96] COM (2011) 225 final, pp. 32–33.

[97] www.ec.europa.eu/dgs/home-affairs/what-we-do/policies/police-cooperation/data-retention/index_en.htm

[98] COM (2011) p. 225 final. [99] See also Meuwese (2008).

[100] See also Granger and Irion (2014).

[101] On 21 December 2016, the CJEU (in Joined Cases C-203/15 and C-698/15 *Tele2 Sverige* and *Watson and others*) again ruled on the compatibility of data retention with EU law and fundamental rights. The e-Privacy Directive 2002/58, read in light of the Charter of Fundamental Rights, 'must be interpreted as precluding national legislation which, for the

5.5 Lessons in Responsiveness of the Legislative Process

This section identifies, on the basis of a review of the (fairly scattered) literature on Better Regulation and our findings in the context of the Data Retention case, how the EU legislator could take into account fundamental rights impacts in such a way that warrants a more procedural approach in judicial review.

5.5.1 *Openness of the Preparatory Process*

Critics view the system of consultation as 'bargaining between elites'.[102] Criticism is voiced, for example, about the European Anti-Poverty Network's relationship with DG EMP – is this 'lobby sponsorship'?[103] Civil society seems unable to 'threaten' the legislature, for example, by withholding votes. Even when Council and the EP would fear these threats, the Commission could prevent them from yielding.[104] Moreover, sometimes the Commission discusses with multinationals in order to gain power *vis-à-vis* the member states.[105] Business and industry interests may be expected to be more successful in the consultation than groups representing the environment, trade unions and consumers, and regional and transnational interests are not as well represented as national interests.[106] However, it can also be pointed out that the power of large industry is sufficiently countervailed in Brussels by NGO lobbying.[107] Good representation of large companies may be caused by their technical knowledge and the costs of lobbying.[108] The precise effects of consultation are thus uncertain, and probably depend on the policy field. According to Alemanno, trading more openness for increased legitimacy 'exposes the Commission to extra scrutiny during a phase that has historically been more informal and

purpose of fighting crime, provides for general and indiscriminate retention of all traffic and location data of all subscribers and registered users relating to all means of electronic communication.' It also precludes 'national legislation governing the protection and security of traffic and location data and, in particular, access of the competent national authorities to the retained data, where the objective pursued by that access, in the context of fighting crime, is not restricted solely to fighting serious crime, where access is not subject to prior review by a court or an independent administrative authority, and where there is no requirement that the data concerned should be retained within the European Union.'

102 Greenwood (2007), p. 339.

103 M. Bauer, 'Limitations to Agency Control in European Union Policy-Making: The Commission and the Poverty Programmes' (2002) 40 *Journal of Common Market Studies*, p. 389.

104 Miller (2011), p. 328. 105 Popelier (2011), p. 560. 106 Persson (2008), p. 235.

107 Meuwese (2008), pp. 187–190. 108 Popelier (2011), pp. 560.

confidential'.[109] There is a 'trade-off inherent in increasing transparency between increasing the potential for accountability, on the one hand, and decreasing negotiators' ability to reach compromise solutions due to their reputational concerns, on the other'.

Research indicates that more transparency can induce members of the legislature to take more extreme positions.[110] A high level of transparency is indeed often connected to a more polarised debate.[111] However, transparency remains an important instrument to bring possible negative impacts on fundamental rights to the attention of legislators.[112] The *Council/In 't Veld* judgment[113] can be seen as an important step in creating more openness in EU legislation. It is not the only important development, though. Commission Vice-President Timmermans announced plans[114] to make the Commission's working method more transparent.[115] Moreover, the European Ombudsman conducted an investigation on so-called 'trialogue' talks between the EP, Council and Commission for their lack of transparency.[116] A transparent legislative process is, after all, necessary to ensure a clear balancing of interests and standard of review.

5.5.2 Methods of IA

IA reports have been said to have important methodological shortcomings. The consultation on the new guidelines for the IA process offers an interesting overview.[117] Often, the desired output is determined from the

109 A. Alemanno, 'A Meeting of Minds on Impact Assessment–When *Ex Ante* Evaluation meets *Ex Post* Judicial Control' (2011) 17 *European Public Law*, pp. 485–505, at, p. 486.

110 Transparency includes: physical access to the decision-making process, recordings of meetings of legislative bodies, the intelligibility of the debates, the intelligibility of the voting results for non–experts in the field, and the clarity of the various groups that have an interesting connected to the issue at stake. See J.P. Cross, 'Striking a Pose: Transparency and Position Taking in the Council of the European Union', 52 (2013) *European Journal of Political Research*, pp. 291–315, at, pp. 293–294.

111 Cross (2013), p. 310.

112 P. Leino, 'Transparency, Participation and EU Institutional Practice: An Inquiry into the Limits of the 'Widest Possible', EUI Working Paper (2014), 17, www.cadmus.eui.eu/bitstream/handle/1814/30580/LAW_2014_03_Leino.pdf?sequence=1.

113 Case C-350/12 P, ECLI:EU:C:2014:2039 (*Council / In 't Veld*).

114 On the European Transparency Register, see www.europa.eu/rapid/press-release_MEX-16-1646_en.htm

115 www.ombudsman.europa.eu/cases/correspondence.faces/en/61589/html.bookmark

116 www.euractiv.com/sections/eu-priorities-2020/secretive-trialogue-talks-agree-eu-law-face-investigation-313936

117 Comments of the United States Government on the 2014 Revision of the European Commission Impact Assessment Guidelines Public Consultation Document September

outset and the Commission officials analyse how to minimise costs subsequently, rather than putting the focus on identifying the option for which the costs and benefits are balanced.[118] Some respondents ask for more guidance on how the principle of proportionality should be applied.[119] Some respondents wanted stakeholders to co-determine whether IA should be carried out in the first place and develop more useful criteria as to when IA should be carried out.[120] A number of stakeholders supported greater monetisation and a common methodology on cost-benefit analysis. Some NGOs favoured a more qualitative approach – in their view, current methods sometimes undervalue concerns such as the environment. What all agreed about is that analytical concepts should be clarified.[121] There were calls for more evidence-based problem definitions. Some respondents wanted political arguments to be avoided because the IA should be a completely analytical exercise.[122] The process of objective-setting should be more coherent. Consumer groups, trade unions and some NGOs are critical on the desirability of an emphasis on non-regulatory alternatives. A wider range of policy options should be considered in IA, not only the *status quo*, an extreme option and the preferred option. Stakeholders would also value more transparency on the actual choice of the preferred option and the justification for it; some think that political feasibility should not be a criterion of comparison.[123] Many stakeholders would value a better prioritisation of the questions asked in IA processes, but they disagree on which questions should be given more importance.[124] The IAs analysed by Souto-Otero named the causes of the problems to be solved, and the groups affected.[125] However, the problems were not quantified and often the need for public intervention was not sufficiently explained. The problem definition sections in the IAs reviewed 'reinforced the message that there is a right way to produce policy through a set of predefined procedures to be universally applied, even though the types of problems identified in the IAs were certainly heterogeneous'.[126] Similar problems can be seen in the Data Retention case.

30th, 2014. www.photos.state.gov/libraries/useu/231771/PDFs/USAresponseIA_final .pdf

118 US comments IA, p. 6.

119 Summary of the replies of the public consultation on the IA Guidelines review, p. 6.

120 Idem, p. 7. 121 Idem, p. 8. 122 Idem, p. 9. 123 Idem, p. 10. 124 Idem, p. 11.

125 The IAs concerned legislative proposals affecting education.

126 M. Souto-Otero, 'Is Better Regulation Possible? Formal and Substantive Quality in the Impact Assessments in Education and Culture of the European Commission', (2013) 9 *Evidence & Policy*, pp. 513–529, at p. 521.

5.5.3 *Interaction between the Different Instruments*

There are almost no formal links between impact assessment at the EU level and the national level.[127] Some member states do not apply IA when a rule is derived from EU law. Moreover, there is often not enough data on implementation and potential effects in the member states. Jacob *c.s.* suggests that national and EU IA systems be better streamlined, or that joint IAs be developed.[128] It could be beneficial to better coordinate the legality check by the Legal Service and the impact assessment. These two aspects of legislation, however, cannot be viewed separately from each other, and efficiency benefits can be achieved when they are coordinated.

Another crucial point is the coordination between the different phases of the policy cycle: a better coordination between IA and *ex post* evaluation. *Ex post* evaluation is still not carried out as often as *ex ante* IA. *Ex post* evaluations are also less heavily regulated than *ex ante* IA; however, the Commission is making efforts to create a better institutional framework for this.[129] It is therefore important to further investigate to what extent *ex ante* IA and *ex post* evaluation are, or should be, linked.[130] Better coordination is also advisable between legislative acts and delegated and implementing acts. The Lisbon Treaty changed the framework governing non-legislative acts. The White Paper on Governance stated that it should be clear who is responsible for these acts; the Commission should be the principal actor, and the Council and EP should be able to monitor it.[131] There are some political safeguards in the delegation process.[132] Initiatives are taken to further improve the 'rule of law' quality of delegated and implementing acts.[133]

[127] K. Jacob et al., Improving the Practice of IA–Policy Conclusions from EVIA (2008), p. 15.

[128] Jacob et al. (2008), p. 16.

[129] E. Mastenbroek, S. van Voorst and A. Meuwese, 'Closing the Regulatory Cycle? A Meta-Evaluation of *Ex Post* Legislative Evaluations by the European Commission', *Journal of European Public Policy*, 2015.

[130] Mastenbroek, Van Voorst and Meuwese (2015).

[131] R. Schütze, 'Delegated Legislation in the (New) European Union: A Constitutional Analysis' (2011), 74 *Modern Law Review*, pp. 661–693, at p. 681.

[132] See Schütze (2011), 684: the basic legislative acts can allow the EP or Council to revoke the delegation. It can also give these institutions the opportunity to veto delegated acts. This requires a majority of the component members of the EP and a qualified majority of the Council. The veto can be given on any ground, so no specific legal requirements are attached to this power.

[133] Summary of the replies of the public consultation on the IA Guidelines review, p. 6.

5.5.4 *Timing*

In a number of IAs, the social, economic and environmental impacts are only assessed for the preferred option, only listing the negative impacts of the other options.[134] The European Court of Auditors offers 'wrong timing' as a possible explanation for superficial treatment of alternative options. The decision whether or not to go ahead with a proposal is often taken before the IA is finalised or even started.[135] Was this perhaps also the case with Data Retention? After all, there was large political pressure to enact legislation to counter terrorism. Respondents to the public consultation on the new guidelines also confirm[136] that the public should be able to comment on draft impact assessment earlier, at a time when their opinion can still be taken into account. Opinions can regard supporting information, analysis, methodology, assumptions made, comparison of the different alternatives and the selection.[137] Broad consultation should also be used when there is already a draft regulatory text.[138] Some business groups stated that stakeholders should be able to report shortcomings of the IA directly to the RSB while an IA report is made.[139] One respondent even suggested appointing a neutral appeal committee, which could then take into account complaints by strongly affected parties, review and perhaps modify the IA. Alternatively, officials should give an explanation in case they reject stakeholder comments.[140] Most importantly, it is important to assess impacts sufficiently when amendments have been brought forward by the EP or Council – they have made a commitment to carry out assessments of significant amendments.[141] However, in practice, the different institutions do not coordinate their IA attempts. Moreover, EP

[134] Souto-Otero (2013), p. 523.

[135] He refers to: European Court of Auditors (2010) *Impact Assessments in the EU institutions: Do They Support Decision Making?*, Special report 3/2010, Luxembourg: Publications Office of the European Union (see p. 19 of this report). Souto-Otero (2013), p. 524.

[136] Summary of the replies of the public consultation on the IA Guidelines review, p. 5.

[137] Comments of the United States Government on the 2014 Revision of the European Commission Impact Assessment Guidelines, Public Consultation Document September 30th, 2014 www.photos.state.gov/libraries/useu/231771/PDFs/USAresponseIA_final.pdf (US comments IA), p. 3.

[138] US Comments IA, p. 11.

[139] Summary of the replies of the public consultation on the IA Guidelines review, p. 11.

[140] Summary of the replies of the public consultation on the IA Guidelines review, p. 11.

[141] See e.g. p. 12 of the 2009 IA Guidelines: www.ec.europa.eu/smart-regulation/impact/commission_guidelines/docs/iag_2009_en.pdf and the Inter-Institutional Common Approach for Impact Assessment, Council Doc. 14901/05 of 14.11.05, www.ec.europa.eu/smart-regulation/better_regulation/documents/ii_common_approach_to_ia_en.pdf

and Council do not always carry out IAs on amendments, which is problematic, since often these amendments entail significant changes.[142] The same can be seen with regard to Data Retention; this case therefore exemplifies the importance of assessing even amended versions carefully. Some effects may come to the attention only in this stage. Fortunately, the new Better Regulation package of 2015 offers more possibilities in this regard.

5.5.5 *Use of the Evidence Gathered*

IA reports should explain how evidence supports the proposed legislation, or what additional information is needed.[143] A problematic example is the Council Framework Decision on the use of PNR (Passenger Name Record) data for law enforcement purposes. Consultation was broad; however, strong criticism by the EDPS and the Article 29 Working Party (a cooperation body of national data protection authorities) was largely ignored.[144] Similarly, in the *Digital Rights Ireland* case, due to time constraints and political pressure, criticism was not dealt with adequately in the preparatory process. Other IA reports show similar problems, which could also be explained by political pressure. In the IA on the Visa Information system, 'significant concerns about the necessity for biometrics and the adequacy of controls that had emerged during consultation were brushed aside rather lightly', Toner notes.[145] In the Returns Directive IA, issues surrounding the use of detention, protection of minors and access to justice were not adequately dealt with. The IA report merely names the concerns and 'assumes rather than questions the starting point of an obligation to return' and 'fails to demonstrate in a convincing manner that the consultation and concerns expressed during it have any significant relevance in shaping the detailed content of the Directive'.[146] The Returns Directive provides 'an example of an IA which records concerns and commitments to act in accordance with fundamental rights but does far less to further this aim in concrete terms'.[147] Evidence is thus not always used in an adequate way. The US

[142] Toner (2006). [143] US Comments IA, p. 10.

[144] De Jesús Butler (2012), p. 402. IA report SEC (2011) 132 final.

[145] H. Toner, 'Impact Assessments: A Useful Tool for 'Better Lawmaking' in EU Migration Policy?', www.ru.nl/publish/pages/548953/cmr.28.11.1.pdf, p. 33. IA report SEC (2004) 1628.

[146] H. Toner, 'Impact Assessments: A Useful Tool for 'Better Lawmaking' in EU Migration Policy?', 33. IA report SEC (2004) 1628.

[147] Toner (2006), at p. 37.

recommendation can be followed that Commission staff should focus on the substance of the comments, not their sources or numbers.[148] Feedback should be focused and specific.[149] Respondents to the consultation on the new IA Guidelines highlight the importance of establishing quality standards for data collection and use. Analysts should be provided with guidance on how to deal with technical and scientific data; this could be attained via closer cooperation with stakeholders.[150] There used to be a Chief Scientific Adviser, and there is now a High Level Group of Scientific Advisors of the EC Scientific Advice Mechanism. Douwma has stated that sufficient attention should be paid to the methods of using scientific evidence in regulation to assess impacts.[151] Sometimes the information available is insufficient, but it is still considered appropriate to act. It will then need to be identified what additional information is needed and how to obtain it, according to the respondents.[152] Alemanno suggests a more extensive use of insights from behavioural sciences and concepts such as nudging.[153] Some stakeholders suggest making the IA and its procedural requirements legally binding.[154] A problem is that important stakeholders are often also the main experts in a certain technical field. This makes it all the more important to take a large variety of viewpoints into account (as regards scientific approach, types of expertise, institutional affiliations and fundamental assumptions).[155] It should thus be prevented that certain interests 'capture' the regulatory process, and to ensure objectivity. In the Data Retention case, all interests had their say, but the legislature let the interest of security prevail, likely because of the political climate.

148 Comments of the United States Government on the European Commission's Public Consultation Document for Stakeholder Consultation Guidelines 2014, September 30th, 2014, www.photos.state.gov/libraries/useu/231771/PDFs/USresponseConsultGuidelinesfinal.pdf at p. 15.

149 US comments consultation, p. 16.

150 Summary of the replies of the public consultation on the IA Guidelines review, p. 13.

151 W. Douwma, 'The Role of Science in Better Regulation', speech at the symposium 'Better Regulation in the EU Revisited Benefiting Business and Citizens', T.M.C. Asser Institute, The Hague, 23 April 2015.

152 Summary of the replies of the public consultation on the IA Guidelines review, p. 13.

153 A. Alemanno, 'Reconciling Alternative Approaches to Regulation with Democratic Principles: From Soft Law to Behavioural-Informed Interventions', speech at the symposium 'Better Regulation in the EU Revisited Benefiting Business and Citizens', T.M.C. Asser Institute, The Hague, 23 April 2015.

154 Summary of the replies of the public consultation on the IA Guidelines review, p. 12.

155 Popelier (2011), p. 563.

5.6 Better Regulation in Court

Although the focus of this paper is on responsiveness towards fundamental rights impacts and review within the legislative process, the issues raise some questions of a judicial nature as well. It is therefore useful to take look at the implications of Better Regulation for judicial review. On the ECtHR, Gerards notes that this court may attach great value to parliamentary deliberation and societal debate, especially in politically sensitive cases.[156] Although it does not completely let go of substantive checks, it may derive positive inferences from the existence of high-quality national procedures.[157]

The Luxembourg Court seems to have been inspired by similar ideas.[158] A degree of evidence-based lawmaking is crucial in certain cases in order for legislation to be upheld by the CJEU. Some of the IA requirements may become 'self-binding' on the legislature because of equal treatment and legitimate expectations.[159] In the *Vodafone* case, the CJEU expressly referred to the IA report when examining the proportionality of the roaming regulation. It may do so *sua sponte*, or under pressure of the parties. The CJEU took the IA in consideration before concluding disproportionality; Better Regulation instruments should be incentives for legislators to 'genuinely investigate alternative instruments and policies rather than be focused narrowly on justifying their chosen policy option'.[160] According to Lenaerts, the CJEU applied the principle of proportionality in a procedural fashion: 'instead of second-guessing the merits of the substantive choices made by the EU legislator', it 'preferred to make sure that law-makers had done their work properly', the legislator had to show that it had 'taken into consideration all the relevant interests at stake'.[161] The Court found the preparatory study by the Commission to be of great interest. In *Spain* v. *Council*,[162] the CJEU did not mention the absence of an IA as such. However, it held that the legislator must take into account all relevant factors and circumstances,

[156] J. Gerards, 'Procedural Review by the ECtHR: A Typology', (*current volume*).

[157] Chapter 6 of the current volume by Janneke Gerards: 'Procedural Review by the ECtHR: A Typology'.

[158] See also Chapter 8 of the current volume by Malu Beijer: 'Procedural Fundamental Rights Review by the Court of Justice of the European Union'.

[159] K. Lenaerts, 'The European Court of Justice and Process-Oriented Review', 31 (2012) *Yearbook of European Law*, pp. 3–16, at p. 3. See also the chapter by M. Beijer in this volume.

[160] Lenaerts (2012), p. 7. [161] Lenaerts (2012), p. 7.

[162] CJEU 7 September 2006, case C-310/04, ECLI:EU:C:2006:521 (*Spain* v. *Council*).

that certain relevant costs should have been taken into account, and that the regulation breached the proportionality principle. In the case of *Volker and Markus Schecke*,[163] the Court found that the Council and Commission should have examined whether the legitimate objective of the relevant acts could not be achieved by means less intrusive on privacy.[164] IA can thus facilitate judicial review.

Sometimes the Court cannot entirely rely on the IA report, for example, when amendments have been made by the Council and EP. In such a case, the Council and the EP are compelled by the Inter-Institutional Agreement on Better Lawmaking to carry out their own IA on the amendments. However, in *Afton Chemical*, the CJEU 'only' said that amendments should be based on scientific data.[165] This Court seems to be more willing to respect the legislature's motives for enacting a certain piece of legislation when the most relevant facts have been duly taken into account. According to Lenaerts, this method of judicial review may lead to more rational lawmaking.[166] He also points out that the Court looks at the question whether legislation is consistent in pursuing a certain goal.[167]

Keyaerts notes that the EU legislature is not trying to determine, instead of the legislature, whether a measure is effective of efficient. It leaves much discretion to the legislature. However, it does urge the legislature to provide a justification for its actions. This could lead to more output legitimacy. According to Keyaerts, the CJEU still misses some opportunities to use IA as an instrument to assess subsidiarity and the justification of the precise form of the measure. He notes that the Court needs to develop a coherent method of dealing with requirements of regulatory quality by more systematically discussing the justification for legislative action.[168] As the Data Retention case also exemplifies, the CJEU seems to require the legislator to legislate more and more on the basis of evidence, relevant expertise and scientific studies of sufficient quality.[169] This could mean that that at the European level, there is room for procedural review when legislation has been prepared properly. Does

[163] CJEU 9 November 2010, joined cases C-92/09 and C-93-09, ECLI:EU:C:2010:662 (*Volker and Markus Schecke*).

[164] Lenaerts (2012), pp. 10–12.

[165] CJEU 8 July 2010, C-343/09, ECLI:EU:C:2010:419 (*Afton Chemical*).

[166] Lenaerts (2012), p. 9. [167] Lenaerts (2012), p. 13.

[168] D. Keyaerts, 'De doorwerking van het wetgevingsbeleid in de rechtspraak van het Hof van Justitie. Het Hof van Justitie als bewaker van de wetgevingskwaliteit in de EU?', PhD thesis University of Antwerp, 2011, pp. 267–269.

[169] Popelier (2011), p. 566.

this mean that the EU legislature receives more trust, but also has a greater role when it comes to fundamental rights protection, as the events surrounding data retention exemplify?[170] It should also be taken into account that, as a result of Better Regulation, the CJEU has more substantial information on the effects as well. It could use this evidence to be more active in furthering the protection of fundamental rights. If the latter is the case, it could scrutinise the effects as such and not so much whether the quality and quantity of legislative debate has been sufficient.

5.7 Conclusion

The EU has brought forward many initiatives to improve the quality of legislation, and IA is one of the most important mechanisms. It can lead to openness to unintended effects as well, notably on fundamental rights. The RSB reviews IA reports. This can lead to a better intervention logic, more accurate problem definitions and an adequate amount of attention for each option, although the scrutiny exercise up until now has been fairly procedural in nature. The combination of IA and the RSB can lead to a more complete picture of possible effects on fundamental rights, although much is still to be gained.

Timing is crucial when gathering information to make a well-balanced legislative decision. The public should be able to comment on draft IAs at an early stage, when different options can still be taken into account. More transparency should be shown with regard to alternative options. When the Council and EP make amendments, a structural approach to assessing their impacts should be provided for. Methodological transparency could also be improved; IAs should explain how evidence and expert advice supports the key aspects of the proposal and, where necessary, extra research should be conducted. Consultation should be broad; indeed this requirement is mostly met in a formal sense, although many studies point to a disproportionate influence of corporate groups in practice.[171] Moreover, not all evidence is given the attention it deserves, perhaps because of biases, and the *Digital Rights Ireland* case confirms this. The same goes for the example of the Council Framework Decision on PNR data.[172] Better coordination is also crucial between the legal service opinions and IA, between member state and EU processes, and between legislative acts and delegated and implementing acts.

170 Granger and Irion (2014). 171 Souto-Otero (2013).
172 De Jesús Butler (2012), p. 402.

This chapter is concerned with clarifying the relationship between rights and regulation, combining two strands of the literature. From cases such as *Vodafone, Spain* v. *Council, Volker and Markus Schecke* and *Digital Rights Ireland*, we may infer that there is a link between regulation and fundamental rights and that the CJEU seems to be revisiting its orientation towards this.[173] A closer look at the processes through which regulation is being prepared in the EU shows some potential safeguards against rights abuses. By taking account of all possible consequences of a legislative proposal (not only obvious effects, but also side-effects and effects that could occur when legislation is not implemented properly), regulation and rights can be linked in an important way. When questions are dealt with that are politically sensitive, criticism is likely to arise. This is especially the case in sensitive areas like the area of freedom, security and justice. The Data Retention case is as an important illustration in this respect. Time constraints and political pressure can explain this. Of course, trade-offs between different interests are inevitable. A 'responsive' legislative process revolves around highlighting these trade-offs, though, in such a manner that accountability can be assigned more easily. Does this entail a greater role for the EU legislature with regard to safeguards for fundamental rights? Perhaps, in addition to this, the Court has more information, which it could use in a way that is more intrusive on the legislature's discretion. This remains slightly dangerous, however, since the information gathered during the preparation of legislation might not be entirely accurate or complete. The new Inter-Institutional Agreement on Better Lawmaking should contribute to sufficient quality and quantity of legislative debate, and serve as an important guideline to the Court in fine-tuning procedural review.

173 Lenaerts (2012).

PART III

Application of Procedural Review: Comparative Perspectives

6

Procedural Review by the ECtHR: A Typology

JANNEKE GERARDS

6.1 Introduction

The European Court of Human Rights (ECtHR) has often emphasised the importance of substantive reasonableness review of limitations of Convention rights. It has held that ' . . . inherent in the whole of the Convention is a search for a fair balance between the demands of the general interest of the community and the requirements of the protection of the individual's fundamental rights'.[1] Indeed, it can be seen that the Court often evaluates the substance of the arguments that have been exchanged before the national courts or in the national legislative process, and it assesses whether these arguments can serve to justify an interference with a Convention right. Regardless of the overriding importance of proportionality review and balancing to the Court's argumentation, it is equally clear that, over the past years, the Court increasingly has taken a procedural turn.[2] This is especially manifest in its case law related to positive obligations, which often are procedural in nature.[3] It is well-known, for example, that the Court has identified self-standing procedural

[1] *Soering* v. *the United Kingdom*, ECtHR 7 July 1988, no. 14038/88, para. 89.

[2] See more elaborately already e.g. O. De Schutter and F. Tulkens, 'Rights in Conflict: The European Court of Human Rights as a Pragmatic Institution', in E. Brems, *Conflicts between Fundamental Rights* (Antwerp, Intersentia 2008) pp. 169–216 at p. 208ff; P. Popelier, 'The Court as Regulatory Watchdog: The Procedural Approach in the Case Law of the European Court of Human Rights', in P. Popelier et al (eds), *The Role of Constitutional Courts in Multilevel Governance* (Antwerp, Intersentia 2012) pp. 249–268; P. Popelier and C. Van de Heyning, 'Procedural Rationality: Giving Teeth to the Proportionality Analysis', 9 *European Constitutional Law Review* (2013) pp. 230–262; J.H. Gerards, 'The European Court of Human Rights and the National Courts–Giving Shape to the Notion of 'Shared Responsibility', in J.H. Gerards and J.W.A. Fleuren (eds), *Implementation of the European Convention on Human Rights and of the Judgments of the ECtHR in National Case Law. A Comparative Analysis* (Antwerp, Intersentia) pp. 13–94; A. Kavanagh, 'Proportionality and Parliamentary Debates: Exploring Some Forbidden Territory', 34 *Oxford Journal of Legal Studies* (2014) pp. 443–479.

[3] See in more detail hereafter, section 6.2.

obligations in relation to Articles 2 and 3 of the Convention, compelling the States to conduct prompt, adequate and effective investigations into alleged cases of ill-treatment or suspicious deaths. The Court has found a wide range of procedural obligations in relation to other Convention articles, too, varying from obligations to protect against arbitrariness in house searches to obligations to provide for careful national review of restrictions of use of property.

Next to the development of procedural positive obligations, another development in the Court's approach can be noted that discloses a stronger emphasis on procedural aspects. It can be seen in various cases that the Court is no longer only looking at the reasonableness of the balance struck by the national authorities, but instead (or in addition to this) focuses on the fairness and due care taken in the national procedures leading up to a limitation.[4] In relation to cases concerning conflicts between the right to respect for one's private life and the freedom of expression, the Court even has expressly mentioned that 'where the balancing exercise has been undertaken by the national authorities in conformity with the criteria laid down in the Court's case law, the Court would require strong reasons to substitute its view for that of the domestic courts'.[5] In these cases, the Court does not intend to 're-balance' the interests at stake to arrive at a conclusion of its own on the reasonableness of a certain limitation of a fundamental right.[6] Instead, it mainly reviews whether the national courts have sufficiently carefully applied the Convention standards and if they have made an adequate effort to identify and balance all relevant interests. If so, the Court can relatively easily accept the decision the national court has made without paying much attention to its contents and the substance of its justification.[7]

Although it is widely agreed that elements of procedural review are increasingly common in the Court's case law,[8] and the Court itself has

[4] For further analyses of these developments, see the sources mentioned *supra*, n. 2.

[5] *Von Hannover (No. 2)* v. *Germany*, ECtHR 7 February 2012, nos. 40660/08 and 60641/08, para. 107.

[6] Cf. Popelier 2012, *supra* n. 2, p. 252 and 257; Gerards, *supra* n. 2, pp. 52ff.

[7] Indeed, in a background document prepared for the opening of the judicial year 2015, a few judges of the ECtHR have expressly mentioned this approach; see *Seminar to Mark the Opening of the Judicial Year 2015–Subsidiarity: A Two-Sided Coin?*, Background paper prepared by the organising committee, www.echr.coe.int/Documents/Seminar_background_paper_2015_ENG.pdf, paras. 34ff.

[8] See the various sources mentioned in Chapter 1 of this volume and see Chapter 2 by Eva Brems ('The "Logics" of Procedural-Type Review by the European Court of Human

stressed the importance of this,[9] as yet, there is not much clarity as regards the types of procedural review it conducts and the function of procedural review for its substantive examination of limitations.[10] Is this limited to the drawing of positive or negative inferences from national procedures? Or can 'procedural review' be defined more broadly?

Against that background, this chapter aims to provide for a typology of procedural review as it can currently be found in the case law of the ECtHR.[11] The typology presented is based on a distinction between two main aspects of the Court's 'procedural turn', i.e. (1) setting positive obligations of a procedural nature or improving the legitimacy of national procedures; and (2) relying on the quality of national decision-making in the review of justifications for interferences with Convention rights. It is submitted that these two aspects are closely connected, to the extent that procedural review of the second type, i.e. review that takes account of the quality of the national decision-making process, is often based on the degree to which states have acted in conformity with their procedural positive obligations. Because of this interconnectedness, this chapter first presents a brief review of different types of procedural positive obligations the Court has developed in its case law, with the objective of clarifying the benchmark of procedural requirements that need to be taken into account by national legislators and by administrative and judicial bodies (section 6.2). Subsequently, the chapter looks into the ways in which the Court has woven procedural elements into its substantive reasonableness review. Here, attention is paid to the Court's tendency to pay attention to the quality of national legislative debates underlying limitations to the exercise of Convention rights (section 6.3). An endeavour is made to identify different situation types in

Rights') and Chapter 7 by Angelika Nussberger ('Procedural Review by the European Court of Human Rights: View from the Court').

9 See *Contribution of the Court to the Brussels Conference*, 26 January 2015 (www.echr.coe.int/Documents/2015_Brussels_Conference_Contribution_Court_ENG.pdf), para. 6 and cf. R. Spano, 'Universality or Diversity of Human Rights? Strasbourg in the Age of Subsidiarity', 14 *Human Rights Law Review* (2014) pp. 487–502 at p. 498.

10 Although some analyses have been made in scholarly literature (see *supra* n. 2), they are far from comprehensive and mainly aim at giving examples as a basis for criticising or embracing the Court's procedural approach.

11 Different typologies from the one presented here are, of course, conceivable. Popelier, for instance, has categorised the case law according to the type of regulative instruments and the nature of the debates the Court takes into account (2012, *supra* n. 2, pp. 258ff), but she focuses on review of legislation only. Since the present chapter also analyses case law on national judicial and administrative decision-making, it seemed less suitable to follow-up on this particular typology.

which the Court relies on this argument in its case law, as well as to provide some clarity as to the actual impact of this type of argument on the Court's reasoning. The Court's review of the procedural fairness and quality of national judicial procedures is discussed next (section 6.4). Again, the objective is to investigate in which types of cases and to what effect the Court uses elements of procedural review. The typology presented in these two sections is based on an analysis of judgments and decisions of the Court's Chambers and Grand Chamber in the period 1 January 2012 up until 1 January 2015. The sample of judgments is based on their 'importance level' (selecting mainly level 1 and 2 cases)[12] and on their potential for a certain degree of procedural review.[13]

The final section of this chapter (section 6.5) aims to distil some common principles from the typology and analysis presented in sections 6.2–6.4. After summarising the current function of procedural review for the Court's case law, it discusses whether the use of procedural elements is consistent and it highlights some challenges for the future. By doing so, this section aims to provide a baseline for further development of techniques of procedural review by the Court, as well as for further debate on the legitimacy and acceptability of these techniques.

6.2 Procedural Requirements under the Convention

6.2.1 Introduction

The Court's procedural obligations case law has been analysed extensively in legal scholarship. In particular, important reviews have been provided of the various obligations developed in relation to the different articles of the Convention.[14] This chapter does not intend to duplicate such analyses, but it aims to build on them by identifying some general

[12] The 'importance level' system is explained in the Court's HUDOC database, www.hudoc.echr.coe.int; see also e.g. Annual Report 2012, *Short Survey of the Main Judgments and Decisions Delivered by the Court in 2012*, www.echr.coe.int/Documents/Short_Survey_2012_ENG.pdf, footnote 2.

[13] The selection of cases is on file with the author.

[14] See in particular E. Brems, 'Procedural Protection: An Examination of Procedural Safeguards Read into Substantive Convention Rights', in E. Brems and J.H. Gerards (eds), *Shaping Rights in the ECHR. The Role of the European Court of Human Rights in Determining the Scope of Human Rights* (Cambridge, Cambridge University Press 2014) pp. 137–161; E. Brems and L. Lavrysen, 'Procedural Justice in Human Rights Adjudication: The European Court of Human Rights', 35 *Human Rights Quarterly* (2013) pp. 176–200; C. Dröge, *Positive Verpflichtungen der Staaten in der Europäischen Menschenrechtskonvention* [Positive Obligations of the States in the European Convention of Human Rights] (Berlin, Springer

requirements for national legislation, national decision-making and national judicial procedures. This section thereby focuses on the procedural requirements that are of direct relevance to the second aspect of the Court's procedural turn, i.e. its tendency to pay attention to the fairness and quality of national decision-making procedures in its review of the reasonableness of limitations. It is important to stress that a rather wide understanding of 'procedural' positive obligations is used here, in the sense that also obligations related to the overall legitimacy of the legislative process are considered, such as obligations which directly contribute to deliberation and participation in legislative debates.

6.2.2 Legislation

The Court has been reluctant to define strict requirements to be met by national legislative processes. Legislation is the domain of national constitutional law and the Court, reasoning from its subsidiary position as a supranational court, does not regard it as its task to set specific obviously constitutional obligations for the States.[15] Moreover, the Court has generally refrained from formulating very clear and specific obligations related to the quality of legislation which are closely related to theories of 'better regulation'.[16] Although sometimes the Court has reproached national legislatures for not having taken sufficient care in preparing legislation, or rather commended them for the quality of their work (as will be discussed in section 6.3), it has not (yet) translated this into clear and concrete positive obligations to be met by all the States Parties.[17] Nevertheless, it has defined a number of more general requirements based on the principles of democracy, pluralism and the rule of law

2003); D. Xenos, *The Positive Obligations of the State under the European Convention of Human Rights* (London, Routledge 2012).

15 Cf. e.g. *McGonnell* v. *the United Kingdom*, ECtHR 8 February 2000, no. 28488/95, para. 51; *Kleyn and Others* v. *the Netherlands*, ECtHR (GC) 6 May 2003, nos. 39343/98 et al., para. 193; *Sindicatul 'Pastorul Cel Bun'* v. *Romania*, ECtHR (GC) 9 July 2013, no. 2330/09, paras. 156-157. See also, more elaborately, D. Kosař, 'Policing Separation of Powers: A New Role for the European Court of Human Rights?', 8 *European Constitutional Law Review* (2012) pp. 33–62 and H.M. ten Napel, 'The European Court of Human Rights and Political Rights: The Need for More Guidance', 5 *European Constitutional Law Review* (2009) pp. 464–480. Cf. further Popelier 2012, *supra* n. 2, p. 257.

16 See in more detail Chapter 4 in this volume by Patricia Popelier: *Evidence-Based Lawmaking: Influences, Obstacles and the Role of the European Court of Human Rights.*

17 It is not unlikely that this will happen in the future, given that in a recent policy document, the Court itself has stressed the importance of 'national parliaments to give careful consideration to the human rights issues that arise in the course of adopting legislation'

that may be seen to relate to the legitimacy and quality of the legislative process.[18] These requirements are closely connected to notions of deliberative democracy and they aim to incentivise the deliberative process in national legal orders.[19]

Generally, for example, the Court has embraced the general notion of rule of law and it has translated this into some concrete obligations and requirements for the States.[20] It may be recalled, for example, that the Court has formulated a number of rather detailed requirements related to legal certainty, such as requirements of forseeability and accessibility of legislation.[21] In other judgments, it has expressed that there is a need for safeguards to avoid arbitrariness and enhance transparency and predictability.[22]

The Court has also formulated a number of general requirements related to the quality of the underlying processes of and procedures for parliamentary deliberation and societal debate.[23] For example, the Court has defined a number of requirements in relation to Article 3 of Protocol No. 1 to the Convention relating to the openness and quality of parliamentary elections.[24] In this context, the Court has held, *inter alia*, that fair and equal participation in elections must be guaranteed in order to ensure good representation in legislative bodies.[25] More generally, the

(Contribution of the Court to the Brussels Conference, 26 January 2015, www.echr.coe .int/Documents/2015_Brussels_Conference_Contribution_Court_ENG.pdf).

[18] See expressly *Golder* v. *the United Kingdom*, ECtHR 21 February 1975, no. 4451/70, para. 34.

[19] On the relevance and importance of deliberative democracy for procedural review, see further Chapter 3 by Aruna Sathanapally in this volume: *The Modest Promise of 'Procedural Review' in Fundamental Rights Cases.*

[20] E.g. *McGonnell* v. *the United Kingdom*, ECtHR 8 February 2000, no. 28488/95; *Stafford* v. *the United Kingdom*, ECtHR 28 May 2002, no. 46295/99, para. 78; *Benjamin and Wilson* v. *the United Kingdom*, ECtHR 26 September 2002, no. 28212/95, para. 36; cf. also Kosař, *supra* n. 15.

[21] Classically in *Sunday Times* v. *the United Kingdom*, ECtHR 26 April 1979, no. 6538/74, para. 49. For the need to provide for clear legislation, see also e.g. *Gross* v. *Switzerland*, ECtHR 14 May 2013, no. 67810/10.

[22] E.g. *Malone* v. *the United Kingdom*, ECtHR 2 August 1984, no. 8691/79, para. 68; *P.G. and J.H.* v. *the United Kingdom*, ECtHR 25 September 2001, no. 44787/98, para. 63; *Assanidze* v. *Georgia*, ECtHR (GC) 8 April 2004, no. 71503/01 paras. 173 and 175; *Golovan* v. *Ukraine*, ECtHR 5 July 2012, no. 41716/06; *L.H.* v. *Latvia*, ECtHR 29 April 2014, no. 52019/07. See also Popelier 2012, *supra* n. 2, p. 253.

[23] See also Popelier 2012, *supra* n. 2, p. 256.

[24] On the general principles and obligations following from Article 3 P1, see e.g. *Hirst (No. 2)* v. *the United Kingdom*, ECtHR (GC) 6 October 2005, no. 74025/01.

[25] See e.g. *Mathieu Mohin and Clerfayt* v. *Belgium*, ECtHR 2 March 1987, no. 9267/81; *Yumak and Sadak* v. *Turkey*, ECtHR (GC) 8 July 2008, no. 10226/03; *Tanase* v. *Moldova*,

Court has emphasised the obligation of the States Parties to safeguard free exchange of ideas and to create an atmosphere in which there is room for public debate on topics of general interest. It is the States' task to guarantee media pluralism and to make sure everyone has adequate access to information.[26] The Court has also emphasised that freedom of expression is especially important for elected representatives of the people.[27] Parliamentarians must be able to draw attention to the people's preoccupations and defend their interests, and more generally, parliaments or comparable bodies are considered to constitute essential fora for political debate.[28] The Court highly values the existence of actual and explicit debate in the legislative bodies, as well as in general society, and it deems it crucial that there is sufficient openness to discuss all relevant issues and present all thinkable arguments and information.[29]

The States must further guarantee that no groups or minorities are unwarrantedly excluded from the process of decision-making and legislation, either *de iure* or *de facto*.[30] If certain groups historically have been placed in a disadvantageous position and their voice remains unheard because of negative stereotyping and stigmatisation, special attention must be paid to their representation and participation in the public debate.[31] More generally, the equality of all human beings before the law must be respected as a basic principle of the rule of law.[32]

Finally, it may be mentioned that it is considered unacceptable if legislation is overbroad or over-inclusive, excluding a large and indeterminate group from exercising a fundamental right,[33] or strongly

ECtHR (GC), 27 April 2010, no. 7/08; *Sitaropoulos and Giakomopoulos* v. *Greece*, ECtHR (GC) 15 March 2012, no. 42202/07.

26 E.g. *Manole and Others* v. *Moldova*, ECtHR 17 September 2009, no. 13936/02, paras. 100 and 107; *Frasila and Ciocirlan* v. *Romenia*, ECtHR 10 May 2012, no. 25329/03; *Centro Europa 7 S.r.l. and Di Stefano* v. *Italy*, ECtHR 7 June 2012, no. 38433/09.

27 *Karácsony and Others* v. *Hungary*, ECtHR 16 September 2014, no. 42461/13, para. 66.

28 Ibid.

29 This is particularly clear from the prisoners' voting rights cases; see especially *Hirst (No. 2)* v. *the United Kingdom*, ECtHR (GC) 6 October 2005, no. 74025/01. See also Popelier 2012, *supra* n. 2.

30 Cf. Popelier 2012, *supra* n. 2, pp. 255 and 264ff.

31 *Alajos Kiss* v. *Hungary*, ECtHR 20 May 2010, no. 38832/06.

32 *Refah Partisi* v. *Turkey*, ECtHR 31 July 2001, no. 41340/98, para. 43.

33 See also A. Stone Sweet, 'The European Convention on Human Rights and National Constitutional Reordering', 33 *Cardozo Law Review* (2012) pp. 1859–1868 at p. 1863. For a few examples, see *Dickson* v. *the United Kingdom*, ECtHR (GC) 4 December 2007, no. 44362/04; *Kubaszewski* v. *Poland*, ECtHR 2 February 2010, no. 571/04; *M.D. and others* v. *Malta*, ECtHR 17 July 2012, no. 64791/10; *Godelli* v. *Italy*, ECtHR 25 September 2012, no. 33783/09.

restricting the possibilities for individualised application or review.[34,35] The flipside of this is that there is a general presumption or even a requirement that there should always be room for individualised (judicial) decision-making.[36] In particular, in some cases regarding the exclusion of prisoners from the right to vote, the Court for some time appeared to require individual court judgments in each and every case of prisoner disenfranchisement, rather than the application of a general rule, even if such a general rule differentiated between groups of prisoners according to the type of offence or the duration of their sentences.[37] Also in the area of family law,[38] the Court has stressed time and again that legislative presumptions are problematic and should be replaced by particularised judicial decision-making.[39] Similarly, a system of lifetime sentences without possibility of interim review of the reasons for continued detention cannot be squared with the obligations under Article 3 ECHR,[40] and the same goes for 'blanket and indiscriminate' limitations of the freedom of movement.[41] Nevertheless, it is important to put this case law into perspective, since the Court does not always require individualisation and may be inclined to accept general measures and blanket bans.[42] Exceptions to this general presumption are visible mainly in those cases where moral issues are at stake and legal certainty would seem to prevail over individual justice,[43] as well as in cases concerning social

[34] E.g. *Ricci* v. *Italy*, ECtHR 8 October 2013, no. 30210/06; *Nusret Kaya and Others* v. *Turkey*, ECtHR 22 April 2014, nos. 43750/06 et al; *Paulet* v. *the United Kingdom*, ECtHR 13 May 2014, no. 6219/08; *Gablishvili* v. *Russia*, ECtHR 26 June 2014, no. 39428/12.

[35] Or both, see e.g. *Söyler* v. *Turkey*, ECtHR 17 September 2013, no. 29411/07. See also Popelier 2012, *supra* n. 2, p. 256 and Gerards, *supra* n. 2.

[36] Or rather, as Sales and Hooper have held, 'fact sensitive' laws are preferred over 'fact insensitive laws'; P. Sales and B. Hooper, 'Proportionality and the Form of Law', 119 *Law Quarterly Review* (2003) pp. 426–454, p. 429.

[37] E.g. *Frödl* v. *Austria*, ECtHR 8 April 2010, no. 20201/04, paras. 33-34; see also *Anchugov and Gladkov* v. *Russia*, ECtHR 4 July 2013, nos. 11157/04 and 15162/05.

[38] But certainly not limited to that; see e.g. *Bjedov* v. *Croatia*, ECtHR 29 May 2012, no. 42150/09, concerning the occupation of a social tenancy flat.

[39] E.g. *Ādamsons* v. *Latvia*, ECtHR 24 June 2008, no. 3669/03; *Schneider* v. *Germany*, ECtHR 15 September 2011, no. 17080/07, para. 100; *C.A.S. and C.S.* v. *Romania*, ECtHR 20 March 2012, no. 26692/05; *M.D. and Others* v. *Malta*, ECtHR 17 July 2012, no. 64791/10; *Godelli* v. *Italy*, ECtHR 25 September 2012, no. 33783/09.

[40] See in particular *Vinter* v. *the United Kingdom*, ECtHR (GC) 9 July 2012, nos. 66069/09, 130/10 and 3896/10, paras. 119-122.

[41] E.g. *Stamose* v. *Bulgaria*, ECtHR 27 November 2012, no. 29713/05, para. 34.

[42] See more elaborately Sales and Hooper, *supra* n. 36, p. 440 and Gerards, *supra* n. 2, pp. 59ff.

[43] See e.g. *Evans* v. *the United Kingdom*, ECtHR (GC) 10 April 2007, no. 6339/05; in this case, it turned out that all decisions that could be taken in an individual cases would harm the interests of another individual, making general legislation just as arbitrary as individual

security and planning issues.[44] Also in one of the voting rights cases, the Court's Grand Chamber has mentioned in general terms that the intervention of a judge is not always necessary, holding that 'the Contracting States may decide either to leave it to the courts to determine the proportionality of a measure restricting convicted prisoners' voting rights, or to incorporate provisions into their laws defining the circumstances in which such a measure should be applied. In this latter case, it will be for the legislature itself to balance the competing interests in order to avoid any general, automatic and indiscriminate restriction'.[45] In a more recent judgment in *Animal Defenders International* v. *the United Kingdom*, the Court's Grand Chamber confirmed this position and further elaborated on it.[46] In particular, it defined some criteria to determine whether general measures are acceptable or further individualisation can be required.[47] Clearly, thus, the Court accepts that there may be good reason to adopt a blanket rule that does not allow for (much) individualisation, especially from a perspective of legal certainty.[48] In the light of this chapter's aims, it is important to note, however, that in one breath, the Grand Chamber also stressed the importance of diligent parliamentary preparation of such general measures.[49] Moreover, it is clear in many cases the Court still requires a possibility of

decision-making, but more certain and predictable nonetheless; for a similar example, see *S.H. and Others* v. *Austria*, ECtHR (GC) 3 November 2011, no. 57813/00; on this, see also Sales and Hooper, *supra* n. 36, p. 434; J. Bomhoff and L. Zucca, 'The Tragedy of Ms Evans: Conflicts and Incommensurability of Rights', 2 *European Constitutional Law Review* (2006) p. 424 at pp. 429–430. However, the case law is not entirely consistent here; see e.g. *Dickson* v. *the United Kingdom*, ECtHR (GC) 4 December 2007, no. 44362/04.

44 See e.g. *Twizell* v. *the United Kingdom*, ECtHR 20 May 2008, no. 25379/02; *Maggio and Others* v. *Italy*, ECtHR 31 May 2011, no. 46286/09 et al. Cf. also already Sales and Hooper, *supra* n. 36, pp. 432-433.

45 *Scoppola (No. 3)* v. *Italy*, ECtHR (GC) 22 May 2012, no. 126/05, para. 102. See similarly *Shindler* v. *the United Kingdom*, ECtHR 7 May 2013, no. 19840/09 and, outside the context of voting rights of prisoners, *Hristozov and Others* v. *Bulgaria*, ECtHR 13 November 2012, nos. 47039/11 and 358/12, para. 126. Nevertheless, regardless of this nuance, clearly overbroad legislation is not accepted; see e.g. *Söyler* v. *Turkey*, ECtHR 17 September 2013, no. 29411/07.

46 *Animal Defenders International* v. *the United Kingdom*, ECtHR (GC) 22 April 2013, no. 48876/08.

47 See paras. 108–110.

48 See also *The National Union of Rail, Maritime and Transport Workers* v. *the United Kingdom*, ECtHR 8 April 2014, no. 31045/10, para. 101–104.

49 See also *The National Union of Rail, Maritime and Transport Workers* v. *the United Kingdom*, ECtHR 8 April 2014, no. 31045/10. For a critical note on this approach, see T. Lewis, '*Animal Defenders International* v. *United Kingdom*: Sensible Dialogue or a Bad Case of Strasbourg Jitters?', 77 *Modern Law Review* (2014) pp. 460–492 at p. 468.

individualisation, and it continues to reject automatically and indiscriminately applied legislation.[50]

6.2.3 *Judicial Procedures and Administrative Decision-Making*

6.2.3.1 General Overview of Procedural Obligations

Much has been written on positive obligations and requirements following from the Convention regarding the availability of national judicial remedies and the quality and fairness of national judicial procedures.[51] Such obligations either follow from dedicated Convention provisions (Article 6 on the right to a fair trial and Article 13 on the right to an effective remedy) or, increasingly, from substantive rights provisions, such as Article 2 (the right to life) or Article 8 (the right to private and family life). In relation to all rights laid down in the Convention, individuals need to be provided with effective access to a judicial remedy to enable them to complain about a lack of protection of their (Convention) rights and interests.[52] National procedures must be designed so as to guarantee procedural fairness. This does not only mean the obvious, such as guaranteeing that tribunals are established by law,[53] that judges are independent and impartial,[54] that proceedings are conducted within a reasonable time,[55] that adversarial proceedings respecting equality of arms are guaranteed,[56] that the legislature should not unduly intervene with judicial proceedings[57] and that final

[50] E.g. *Ricci* v. *Italy*, ECtHR 8 October 2013, appl. no. 30210/06 and *Brunet* v. *France*, ECtHR 18 September 2014, appl. no. 21010/10.

[51] See the sources mentioned *supra*, n. 14.

[52] Of course, this even is an express requirement laid down in Article 13 of the Convention. See in particular also e.g. *Silver and Others* v. *the United Kingdom*, ECtHR 25 March 1983, nos. 5947/72 et al, para. 90; *Brogan and Others* v. *the United Kingdom*, ECtHR 29 November 1988, nos. 11209/84 et al, para. 58; *Huvig* v. *France*, ECtHR 24 April 1990, no. 11105/84, para. 31; *Conka* v. *Belgium*, ECtHR 5 February 2002, no. 51564/99, para. 83.

[53] E.g. *Kress* v. *France*, ECtHR 7 June 2001, no. 39594/98, para. 69; *Lavents* v. *Latvia*, ECtHR 28 November 2001, no. 58442/00, para. 81.

[54] E.g. *Le Compte, Van Leuven and De Meyere* v. *Belgium*, ECtHR 23 June 1981, nos. 6878/75 and 7238/75, para. 55; *Kleyn and Others* v. *the Netherlands*, ECtHR (GC) 6 May 2003, nos. 39343/98 et al; *Kyprianou* v. *Cyprus*, ECtHR (GC) 15 December 2005, no. 73797/01.

[55] E.g. *Ferrari* v. *Italy*, ECtHR (GC) 26 July 1999, no. 33440/96.

[56] E.g. *Dombo Beheer* v. *the Netherlands*, ECtHR 27 October 1993, no. 14448/88, para. 33; *Steel and Morris* v. *the United Kingdom*, ECtHR 15 February 2005, no. 68416/01, paras. 59 and 62; *Krcmar and Others* v. *the Czech Republic*, ECtHR 3 March 2000, no. 35376/97, para. 40.

[57] E.g. *Stran Greek Refineries* v. *Greece*, ECtHR 9 December 1994, no. 13427/87, para. 49.

judgments are executed promptly and with due care.[58,59] With a great degree of detail and refinement, the Court has also held that national judgments ought to be adequately reasoned and sufficiently predictable,[60] that individuals should be granted access to (free or subsidised) legal assistance,[61] that the parties should be given sufficient time to study the files and to bring evidence, that judges should not blindly rely on the quality of expert opinions,[62] that solutions should be found to harmonise problematically inconsistent lines of case law[63] and so on. In addition, as a corollary of the requirement of individualised application discussed in section 6.2.2, the Court may require national courts to review the reasonableness of application of general legislation to the concrete case at hand.[64]

The Court has defined a similar variety of obligations of procedural fairness and procedural due care in relation to administrative decision-making. First and foremost, guarantees must be adopted to ascertain that administrative powers are not used in an arbitrary fashion.[65] Moreover, States have to abide by their own rules, which means that administrative authorities need to apply such rules consistently.[66] In addition to this, the Court has accepted a variety of more specific procedural positive obligations, which are closely geared to specific situation types. Decisions related to medical treatment, for example, must be reasoned and must

[58] E.g. *Hornsby* v. *Greece*, ECtHR 19 March 2007, no. 18357/91, para. 40; *Brumarescu* v. *Romania*, ECtHR (GC) 28 October 1999, no. 28342/95, para. 61.

[59] These requirements generally also follow from Article 6 ECHR; the interrelationship between the procedural positive obligations following from substantive provisions and the requirements following from Article 6 ECHR is a complicated one, however; see e.g. *Zagrebačka banka d.d.* v. *Croatia*, ECtHR 12 December 2013, no. 39544/05.

[60] E.g. *Beian* v. *Romania*, ECtHR 6 December 2007, no. 30658/05, para. 39; *Garcia Ruiz* v. *Spain*, ECtHR (GC) 21 January 1999, no. 30544/96, para. 26.

[61] Classically in *Airey* v. *Ireland*, ECtHR 9 October 1979, no. 6289/73.

[62] E.g. *Plesó* v. *Hungary*, ECtHR 2 October 2012, no. 41242/08.

[63] *Sahin and Sahin* v. *Turkey*, ECtHR (GC) 20 October 2011, appl. no. 13279/05.

[64] See more elaborately below, section 6.4.2; for one example out of many, see *Gablishvili* v. *Russia*, ECtHR 26 June 2014, no. 39428/12.

[65] E.g. *Malone* v. *the United Kingdom*, ECtHR 2 August 1984, no. 8691/79, para. 68; *Goranova-Karanaeva* v. *Bulgaria*, ECtHR 8 March 2011, no. 12739/05, para. 48; *Gillan and Quinton* v. *the United Kingdom*, ECtHR 12 January 2010, no. 4158/05, paras. 85-87; *Weber and Saravia* v. *Germany*, ECtHR 29 June 2006 (dec.), no. 54934/00, para. 95; *Telegraaf Media Nederland Landelijke Media B.V. and Others* v. *the Netherlands*, ECtHR 22 November 2013, no. 39315/06, para. 98. Indeed, administrative decisions disclosing arbitrariness always violate the Convention; see e.g. *Fatullayev* v. *Azerbaijan*, paras. 123-124; *Ternovszky* v. *Hungary*, ECtHR 14 December 2010, no. 67545/09, para. 26; *East/West Alliance Limited* v. *Ukraine*, ECtHR 23 January 2014, no. 19336/04, para. 167.

[66] E.g. *M.S.S.* v. *Belgium and Greece*, ECtHR (GC) 21 January 2011, no. 30696/09, para. 250.

be based on informed consent.[67] The informed consent requirement means, *inter alia*, that the individual must be given access to diagnostic facilities and, if so desired, a second opinion, and there must be a possibility for complaint and eventually judicial review.[68] Similarly intricate administrative, regulative and judicial obligations have been formulated in relation to other issues, varying from abortion[69] and assisted suicide[70] to protection of journalistic sources[71] and child abduction,[72] and from decision-making in relation to hazardous industrial installations[73] to prevention of human trafficking and exploitation,[74] domestic violence[75] and child abuse.[76]

6.2.3.2 Taking Convention Standards into Account

This chapter does not aim to map out all different obligations following from the Convention that are related to national judicial and administrative procedures. It is clear from the above examples that this would be too great an exercise, since detailed sets of obligations have been developed in relation to a wide number of fundamental rights issues. It is important to note, however, that such obligations have considerable impact on national judicial and administrative decision-making. Perhaps most interesting for the purposes of the current chapter, and therefore warranting more detailed attention, is the Court's requirement that national courts (as well as national administrative bodies) take due account of the standards for review developed in the Court's case law. On the one hand, the Court has held that the Convention does not impose a certain constitutional structure on the States and it does not

[67] E.g. *Codarcea* v. *Romania*, ECtHR 2 June 2009, no. 31675/04, paras. 102ff; *Csoma* v. *Romania*, ECtHR 15 January 2013, no. 8759/05, paras. 42ff.

[68] E.g. *Tysiac* v. *Poland*, ECtHR 20 March 2007, no. 5410/03; *R.R.* v. *Poland*, ECtHR 26 May 2011, no. 27617/04; *Assunção Chaves* v. *Portugal*, ECtHR 31 January 2012, no. 61226/08.

[69] E.g. *A., B. and C.* v. *Ireland*, ECtHR (GC) 16 December 2010, no. 25579/05, paras. 249 and 267.

[70] E.g. *Gross* v. *Switzerland*, ECtHR 14 May 2013, no. 67810/10.

[71] E.g. *Sanoma* v. *the Netherlands*, ECtHR (GC) 14 September 2010, no. 38224/03, paras. 88, 90-92.

[72] E.g. *X.* v. *Latvia*, ECtHR (GC) 26 November 2013, no. 27853/09, para. 107.

[73] E.g. *Öneryildiz* v. *Turkey*, ECtHR (GC) 30 November 2004, no. 48939/99, para. 90.

[74] E.g. *Rantsev* v. *Cyprus and Turkey*, ECtHR 7 January 2010, no. 25965/04; *C.N.* v. *the United Kingdom*, ECtHR 13 November 2012, no. 4239/08.

[75] E.g. *Opuz* v. *Turkey*, ECtHR 9 June 2009, no. 33401/02; *Busuioc* v. *Moldava*, ECtHR 16 July 2013, no. 61382/09.

[76] E.g. *O'Keeffe* v. *Ireland*, ECtHR (GC) 28 January 2014, no. 35810/09, para. 148.

require that the states make the Convention directly enforceable through the national courts.[77] The States remain free to decide how they want to meet their obligations under the Convention, although the Court generally requires the State to organise its internal structure in such a manner as to be able to meet its Convention obligations.[78] In line with this, the Court never expressly held that national courts (or, for that matter, any other national organs, institutions or administrative bodies) should have certain competences or be able to adopt certain approaches. Nevertheless, the Court may condemn a State if a violation of the Convention results from a lack of competence to disapply or nullify legislation that is contrary to the Convention.[79] In fact, thus, the national courts need to have avail of certain competences and procedural instruments in order to be able to comply with their obligations under the Convention. Furthermore, the States are not completely free in meeting their overall obligation to respect the Convention. In particular, it follows from cases such as *Pla and Puncernau* v. *Andorra* that the domestic courts are obliged to take the Convention into account in interpreting national law and even national contracts.[80] It is clear from this ruling that the States can be held responsible for interpretations and judgments of the national courts, and that the national courts have to copy the Court's approach to comply with the minimum standards of the Convention.[81] Moreover, in the case of *Fabris* v. *France*, the Court found that the domestic courts are obliged 'to ensure, in conformity with their

[77] *Swedish Engine Drivers' Union* v. *Sweden*, ECtHR 6 February 1976, no. 5614/72, para. 50; *James and Others* v. *UK*, ECtHR 21 February 1986, no. 8793/79, para. 85.

[78] Cf. E. Klein, 'Should the Binding Effect of the Judgments of the European Court of Human Rights Be Extended?', in P. Mahoney (ed), *Protecting Human Rights: the European Perspective* (Köln: Heymanns 2000) pp. 705–713, at p. 709; see also *Assanidze* v. *Georgia*, ECtHR 8 April 2004, no. 71503/01, para. 146.

[79] Cf. *Losonci Rose and Rose* v. *Switzerland*, ECtHR 9 November 2010, no. 664/06, para. 50.

[80] *Pla and Puncernau* v. *Andorra*, ECtHR 13 July 2004, no. 69498/01. In similar vein, see *Khurshid Mustafa and Tarzibachi* v. *Sweden*, ECtHR 16 December 2008, no. 23883/06. See also, outside the sphere of contractual obligations, *Paulić* v. *Croatia*, ECtHR 22 October 2009, no, 3572/06, para. 42 ('no legal provision of domestic law should be interpreted and applied in a manner incompatible with Croatia's obligations under the Convention') and, rather more implicitly, *X.* v. *Latvia*, ECtHR (GC) 26 November 2013, no. 27853/09, para. 107.

[81] See e.g. E. Bjorge, 'National Supreme Courts and the Development of ECHR Rights', 9 *International Journal of Constitutional Law* (2011) pp. 5–31, giving more examples of cases from which it appears that national courts must apply the principle of evolutive interpretation; see also L. Garlicki, 'Contrôle de constitutionnalité et contrôle de conventionalité. Sur le dialogue des juges', in *La conscience des droits. Mélanges en l'honneur de Jean-Paul Costa* (Paris, Dalloz 2011) pp. 271–280 at pp. 274–275.

constitutional order and having regard to the principle of legal certainty, the full effect of the Convention standards, as interpreted by the Court'.[82] Consequently, when domestic courts are confronted with legislative provisions that can be interpreted in different ways, they should use their competence to ensure that their interpretations are in conformity with the standards formulated by the ECtHR. One may even read the case as implying that national courts should set aside legislation that clearly conflicts with ECHR provisions as interpreted by the ECtHR.[83]

This line of case law evidences that relatively high demands are placed on the national authorities. The legislature must make sure that courts and administrative bodies can dispose of clear and well-prepared legislative standards that they can apply in an individualised manner to concrete cases. Moreover, administrative and judicial authorities have an important task of their own to make sure individual decisions and judgments are in conformity with the Convention standards as defined by the Court.

6.3 Procedural Review of Legislation

6.3.1 Introduction

As mentioned in section 6.1, many judgments of the Court focus on the quality and transparency of the national procedures and judicial remedies that have been used in relation to the disputed decision or rule. Arguably, there is a procedural aspect in those cases where the Court finds that domestic legislation offers insufficient guarantees against arbitrary application.[84] In those cases, the Court will usually hold that the legislation does not comply with the requirement of 'legality', or that the interference is not 'prescribed by law', as required by the Convention. For example, if there are no sufficient procedural guarantees to protect against arbitrary application of discretionary powers, or if legislation does not provide for sufficient clarity and forseeability, the Court usually will find a violation of the Convention, without even looking into the substantive reasonableness of an interference.[85] The current section will

[82] *Fabris* v. *France*, ECtHR (GC) 7 February 2013, no. 16574/08, para. 75.

[83] See further on this reading the case-note by Gerards to the case in *European Human Rights Cases* 2013/88 (in Dutch).

[84] See the examples mentioned in section 6.2.2 above; for one example out of many, see *Golovan* v. *Ukraine*, ECtHR 5 July 2012, no. 41716/06.

[85] See the case law discussed above, section 6.2.3.1; for some representative examples of application in different situation types, see *M.M.* v. *the United Kingdom*, ECtHR

not focus on such 'prescribed by law' judgments, however. It is rather more interested to see how procedural-type arguments are used in relation to the review of the reasonableness or proportionality of the legislative measures at stake. It is there, after all, that procedural arguments can supplement or even be an alternative to substantive reasonableness review.

The analysis of the case law reveals a difference between two types of procedural review of legislation in the context of proportionality issues, i.e., review in which positive inferences are made and cases in which such inferences are negative.[86] This section further explains this distinction, as well as the differences apparent from the Court's case law as to the nature and effects of these inferences (section 6.3.2). Subsequently, a further typology is made of different categories of cases in which the Court is most likely to rely on procedural-type arguments in relation to review of legislation (section 6.3.3). Review of judgments by domestic courts or of individualised administrative decisions is discussed in section 6.4.

6.3.2 'Positive' and 'Negative' Procedural Review of Legislation

6.3.2.1 Positive Procedural Review of Legislation

In a few cases, the Court seems to have attached positive value to the fact that a decision or rule is prepared and adopted with the greatest care and after extensive deliberation, in an open and transparent decision-making process. In these cases, thus, the Court's approach seems to be closely connected with the positive obligations discussed in section 6.2.2. A very clear example of this is the somewhat older case *Maurice* v. *France*,[87] which related to the very sensitive and complex issue of compensation in cases of wrongful birth.[88] The applicants argued that the relevant legislation violated their rights under Article 8 of the Convention because it offered a generally lower level of compensation than they could have obtained under the former case law of the French courts. In its judgment in the case, the Court paid close attention to the quality of the process that

13 November 2012, no. 24029/07; *Casuneanu* v. *Romania*, ECtHR 16 April 2013, no. 22018/10; *Petrova* v. *Latvia*, ECtHR 24 June 2014, no. 4605/05. In some cases, the Court does review the application of the legislation, but again it may do so in a rather procedural manner; see e.g. *Topcic-Rosenberg* v. *Croatia*, ECtHR 14 November 2013, no. 19391/11.

[86] Cf. also Kavanagh 2014, *supra* n. 2, p. 473.

[87] *Maurice* v. *France*, ECtHR (GC) 6 October 2005, no. 11810/03.

[88] See Gerards, *supra* n. 2, section 6.3.3.

had led to the adoption of the legislation. It stressed that there had been a 'stormy nation-wide debate' on the issue, in which politicians, interest groups and individuals had participated, and that close attention had been paid to all relevant legal, ethical and social considerations. It concluded that 'there is no serious reason for the Court to declare contrary to Article 8 . . . the way in which the French legislature dealt with the problem or the content of the specific measures taken to that end'.[89] The Court thus did not address the substantive issues of reasonableness and proportionality of the interference, restricting its review to procedural matters. In later cases, too, the Court has expressly mentioned the quality and extensiveness of parliamentary debates underlying legislation that restricts the exercise of Convention rights and it has considered this an important reason for holding the outcome of the decision-making process to be compatible with the Convention.[90]

The procedural arguments discernible in the case law discussed above relate to the quality of the process and deliberations underlying a certain piece of legislation, but positive procedural review also may take a different form. For example, the Court may expressly take into consideration that legislation allows for further concretisation and individualisation, thus offering a possibility to administrative authorities and courts to apply full reasonableness and proportionality review.[91] The same is true if national legislation generally provides for an intricate and well-considered set of remedies to prevent fundamental rights violations, which may help the domestic authorities to comply with positive obligations following from the Convention.[92] Such possibilities for procedural fairness and procedural due care may positively influence the outcome of the case.

It must be noted, however, that the Court does not always rely on this procedural approach to the same degree. This can be illustrated by the case of *Lindheim* v. *Norway*, which concerned Norwegian legislation on

[89] *Maurice* v. *France*, ECtHR (GC) 6 October 2005, no. 11810/03, para. 124.

[90] E.g. *Animal Defenders International* v. *the United Kingdom*, ECtHR (GC) 22 April 2013, no. 48876/08, paras. 113–116; *Shindler* v. *the United Kingdom*, ECtHR 7 May 2013, no. 19840/09; *The National Union of Rail, Maritime and Transport Workers* v. *the United Kingdom*, ECtHR 8 April 2014, no. 31045/10.

[91] E.g. *Schilder* v. *the Netherlands*, ECtHR 16 October 2012 (dec.), no. 2158/12; *Lohuis and Others* v. *the Netherlands*, ECtHR 30 April 2013 (dec.), no. 37265/10; *Peruzzo and Martens* v. *Germany*, ECtHR 4 June 2013 (dec.), nos. 7841/08 and 57900/12.

[92] E.g. *Wilson* v. *the United Kingdom*, ECtHR 23 October 2012 (dec.), no. 10601/09; however, it is also clear that such legislation must be applied in a proper manner, see e.g. *E.M.* v. *Romania*, ECtHR 30 October 2012, no. 43994/05.

ground lease contracts and which revolved around the balance the national legislature had struck between the social and financial burdens for lessors and lessees.[93] The Court paid considerable attention to the legislative process and it accepted that the Norwegian Parliament had carefully considered all relevant interests and had balanced them in a way that seemed reasonable to it. In addition, it expressly 'appreciated' the way the Norwegian Supreme Court had applied the Convention standards in reviewing the legislation.[94] Given the approach discussed above, this might lead one to expect the Court to embrace the outcome reached by the Norwegian Parliament and the Norwegian Supreme Court, even more so because the case concerned a difficult socio-economic policy issue. The Court did not do so, however. Instead, it substituted the national 'fair balance' for one its own, finding that the national authorities had taken insufficient account of certain aspects that it itself considered of importance to the balance to be struck.[95] This example may go to show that the Court's procedural review is not (yet) consistently applied.

6.3.2.2 Negative Procedural Review of Legislation

While in the case law discussed above, the Court draws positive inferences from the quality of the national legislative process, procedural arguments also may play a 'negative' role. A well-known example can be seen in the case of *Hirst* v. *the United Kingdom*,[96] where the Court found it problematic that the British Parliament had never expressly and extensively deliberated on the choice to exclude all prisoners (regardless of the duration of their sentence or the nature of the crimes committed) from the right to vote. It seemed that, regardless of the substantive reasons for and against such a complete, blanket prohibition, the Court would not have accepted the legislation for the lack of procedural safeguards surrounding its adoption.[97] Thus, the Court (at least partly) avoided a substantive assessment of the reasonableness of the exclusion

93 *Lindheim and Others* v. *Norway*, ECtHR 12 June 2006, nos. 13221/08 and 2139/10.

94 *Lindheim*, para. 135; see also Kavanagh, *supra* n. 2, p. 473.

95 For a similar example, see *Biao* v. *Denmark*, ECtHR 25 March 2014, no. 38590/10, paras. 79–103; interestingly, although the Court on substantive grounds clearly disagreed with the Danish legislature and the Danish Supreme Court in the case and expressly doubted the Convention compatibility of the limitations contained in the legislation, it did not find a violation of the Convention because it accepted that there was a sufficient justification in the concrete circumstances of the case.

96 *Hirst (No. 2)* v. *the United Kingdom*, ECtHR (GC) 6 October 2005, no. 74025/01.

97 *Hirst*, paras. 79–80.

of prisoners by relying on procedural arguments. In other cases, too, the Court has given attention to a lack of sound parliamentary debate on interferences with fundamental rights, although in most cases, this is combined with more substantive reasons for finding a violation.[98]

Another variant of negative review of legislation tunes in with the obligation to provide for a possibility of individualised review, which was discussed in section 6.2.2. In the *Hirst* case, the Court clearly also regarded it as problematic that the legislation did not provide for further individualisation and for concrete review of proportionality by a court. In other cases, too, the Court has held it against the State that it only provided for general and indiscriminate legislation, since this would stand in the way of concrete and substantive proportionality review by the courts.[99] Moreover, in several cases, such as cases concerning abortion and euthanasia, the Court has found a violation of the Convention because the State had not complied with its positive obligation to ensure sufficiently clear and foreseeable legislation.[100]

6.3.2.3 Importance of 'Procedural-Type' Arguments for the Court's Reasoning

It is clear, thus, that there are two main types of procedural review of legislation. The first is a 'negative' type of procedural review, in which the Court may find a violation due to the lack of sound preparation of legislation or due to procedural flaws. The second is a 'positive' type, in which the Court may commend the national authorities for the quality of the legislative process.

Interestingly, there appears to be a difference between the two types of review as to the degree to which the procedural aspect determines the outcome of the Court's reasonableness review.[101] In the 'positive' examples mentioned above, the argument played an important role, but the Court also looked at more substantive aspects related to the

[98] E.g. *Anchugov and Gladkov* v. *Russia*, ECtHR 4 July 2013, nos. 11157/04 and 15162/05, para. 108; *Dubská and Krejzová* v. *the Czech Republic*, ECtHR 11 December 2014, nos. 28859/11 and 28473/12. For some other examples and a further analysis, see Popelier and Van de Heyning, *supra* n. 2, p. 254.

[99] E.g. *Godelli* v. *Italy*, ECtHR 25 September 2012, no. 33783/09; *Ricci* v. *Italy*, ECtHR 8 October 2013, no. 30210/06.

[100] E.g. *A., B. and C.* v. *Ireland*, ECtHR (GC) 16 December 2010, no. 25579/05; *Gross* v. *Switzerland*, ECtHR 14 May 2013, no. 67810/10.

[101] See also Kavanagh, *supra* n. 2, p. 473, although she mainly notes that there is a difference in frequency of the use of both types of argument (positive-type review occurring more often than negative-type review).

proportionality of the interference, and the existence or lack of a certain European consensus on its acceptability, even if it did do so rather superficially. In fact, in none of the 'positive' procedural review cases analysed for the purposes of this chapter, the Court paid solely attention to the quality of the legislative debate. Even in cases in which the Court really seemed to find that the legislature had fully considered all relevant arguments and there was no reason to deviate from its findings, it appears that the existence of a lack of consensus or substantive reasonableness arguments played an important role in supporting the Court's findings.[102] In some cases, the Court even did not at all seem to give real weight to the existence of an elaborate national debate. The case of *S.A.S.* v. *France*, for example, concerned the delicate issue of a prohibition of wearing a full face veil in public places.[103] The relevant legislation had been the product of a lengthy and intensive national debate in France, which was conducted both inside and outside parliament, and which was carefully mapped out by the Court. Rather than attaching any positive value to the existence of such debate as such, however, as might be expected based on the reasoning in cases such as *Maurice*,[104] the Court in this judgment evaluated all different arguments advanced in the debate on their merits and for their persuasiveness. Although on some points, it agreed with the government and the national legislature, such agreement was based on substantive grounds, rather than on a presumption of fairness of the outcomes of a sound legislative procedure. Hence, although the existence of procedurally sound legislative procedures can constitute an important argument supporting the conclusions the Court wants to arrive at, it is clear that it is hardly ever decisive for the Court's findings.[105]

By contrast, procedural-type arguments appear to be more important in 'negative' cases of review. This is particularly so in the most common cases of procedural defects, i.e. cases where legislation did not provide for sufficient procedural guarantees as such (e.g. due to a lack of clarity or a lack of guarantees against arbitrariness), or where legislation did not allow for individualisation. In many such cases, the finding of a lack of procedural due care may immediately result in a finding of a violation of the Convention. By contrast, however, if the procedural shortcoming

[102] *Shindler* v. *the United Kingdom*, ECtHR 7 May 2013, no. 19840/09, para. 115; *Animal Defenders International* v. *the United Kingdom*, ECtHR (GC) 22 April 2013, no. 48876/08, paras. 118-124.

[103] *S.A.S.* v. *France*, ECtHR (GC) 1 July 2014, no. 43835/11.

[104] See *supra* n. 87.

[105] Cf. also Kavanagh, *supra* n. 2, p. 475; Popelier 2012, *supra* n. 2, p. 266.

mainly is a lack of procedural due care in the preparation or drafting of legislation, as in the *Hirst* case, it seems that it is merely one reason or argument for the Court to be taken into account in its overall substantive assessment of the reasonableness of the resulting legislation, rather than an argument that is decisive of its own. Such procedural review then, again, is flanked by a number of arguments of a more substantive nature. In the prisoners' voting rights cases, for example, the Court also stressed the overall importance of the right to vote within a democratic society and it mentioned the legitimacy of the aims pursued by the limitation of the right to vote for prisoners.[106]

6.3.3 *Types of Cases in Which Procedural Review is Applied*

Regardless of whether negative or positive inferences are drawn from the Court's procedural review, it appears that the Court is most inclined to attach value to the quality of the legislative process in hard cases with a high degree of sensitivity. Closer analysis of the cases discussed in section 6.3.2 discloses that procedural review is mainly applied in two types of sensitive cases, i.e. cases relating to complex choices in socio-economic policy fields, and 'dilemma-cases'. In addition, procedural review appears to be closely connected to the width of the margin of appreciation that is granted to the states.[107]

In cases concerning socio-economic rights, the Court generally provides the States with a wide margin of appreciation, in particular because national authorities are better placed than the Court itself is to make assessments of facts and make well-balanced choices.[108] In these cases, the Court often limits its substantive assessment of the

[106] E.g. *Hirst (No. 2)* v. *the United Kingdom*, ECtHR (GC) 6 October 2005, no. 74025/01 and *Anchugov and Gladkov* v. *Russia*, ECtHR 4 July 2013, nos. 11157/04 and 15162/05.

[107] On the interrelationship between the margin of appreciation doctrine and procedural review, see also O.M. Arnardóttir, 'Organised Retreat? The Move from "Substantive" to "Procedural" Review in the ECtHR's Case Law on the Margin of Appreciation', *European Society of International Law 2015 Annual Conference*, www.ssrn.com/abstract=2709669.

[108] See in more detail e.g. J.H. Gerards, 'The ECtHR's Response to Fundamental Rights Issues Related to Financial and Economic Difficulties – The Problem of Compartmentalisation', 33 *Netherlands Quarterly of Human Rights* 2015 (3) pp. 274–292; A.E.M. Leijten, 'Defining the Scope of Economic and Social Guarantees in the Case Law of the ECtHR' in E. Brems and J. Gerards (eds) *Shaping Rights in the ECHR. The Role of the European Court of Human Rights in Determining the Scope of Human Rights* (Cambridge, CUP 2014) pp. 109–136; E. Palmer, 'Protecting Socio-Economic Rights through the European Convention of Human Rights: Trends and Development in the European Court of Human Rights' (2009) 2 *Erasmus Law Review*, p. 408.

reasonableness of the resulting interferences to a test of manifest unreasonableness or a test of 'individual and excessive burden'.[109] At the same time, it is important for the Court to uphold Convention standards and exercise its supervisory task. It is not surprising, therefore, that the Court has chosen to support its very deferential reasonableness review by elements of procedural review.[110] After all, if the legislation itself is not to be looked at too closely, it is all the more important to ensure that such legislation is adopted through a fair decision-making process.[111] Indeed, the very 'better-placed argument' is based on the presupposition the national authorities pay due attention to all relevant interests and conduct a sound balancing exercise.[112] It is then of importance for the Court to check whether the national legislative and administrative bodies actually have done so and whether they have complied with the relevant standards in the field.

The second category of 'sensitive' cases is that involving ethical or moral dilemmas. The Court is frequently confronted with such cases, which may of course relate to abortion or euthanasia,[113] to choices closely related to personal autonomy (such as the choice to become a genetic parent),[114] or to the rights of same-sex partners,[115] but also to more societal dilemmas, such as how to deal with religious expressions in the public sphere,[116] or to what extent to respect and guarantee fundamental rights of prisoners, such as the right to vote[117]. Just as for cases in the socio-economic sphere, it is not surprising that positive arguments of a procedural nature surface in particular in this category of 'dilemma-cases'. Unavoidably, they are hard cases, in which conflicting rights and interests play a role and in which it is very difficult to arrive at one rational or legal conclusion.[118] Cases involving moral dilemmas inherently ask for value judgments to be made, and the

[109] Ibid.

[110] See e.g. *Hatton and Others* v. *the United Kingdom*, ECtHR (GC) 8 July 2003, no. 36022/97 and cf. Popelier and Van de Heyning, *supra* n. 2, p. 252.

[111] Cf. also Kavanagh, *supra* n. 2; Popelier 2012, *supra* n. 2.

[112] See further Gerards, *supra* n. 2 and Popelier and Van de Heyning, *supra* n. 2, p. 251.

[113] E.g. *A., B. and C.* v. *Ireland*, ECtHR (GC) 16 December 2010, no. 25579/05; *Gross* v. *Switzerland*, ECtHR 14 May 2013, no. 67810/10.

[114] E.g. *Dickson* v. *the United Kingdom*, ECtHR (GC) 4 December 2007, no. 44362/04.

[115] E.g. *X. and Others* v. *Austria*, ECtHR (GC) 19 February 2013, no. 19010/07.

[116] E.g. *S.A.S.* v. *France*, ECtHR (GC) 1 July 2014, no. 43835/11.

[117] See the various cases discussed above, in particular *Hirst (No. 2)* v. *the United Kingdom*, ECtHR (GC) 6 October 2005, no. 74025/01.

[118] Next to the cases expressly discussed here, see e.g. *Evans* v. *the United Kingdom*, ECtHR (GC) 10 April 2007, no. 6339/05, para. 89 and *Söderman* v. *Sweden*, ECtHR (GC) 12 November 2013, no. 5786/08.

Court usually does not regard it as its task to replace national value judgments for its own. For that reason, it tends to leave a very wide margin of appreciation to the States in these cases. Again, however, probably because of the importance of what is at stake in these cases, the Court may pay special attention to the care taken at the national level to arrive at certain choices.[119] Especially in dilemma-cases, it is apparent that the Court places great value on the existence of societal and legislative debates, which preferably involve a large number of stakeholders and are very open in nature, and only after due deliberation in Parliament lead to the adoption of legislation. As was demonstrated above, the existence of such a wide and deep national debate makes it easier for the Court to accept the reasonableness of the outcomes of that decision-making process.

Indeed, in cases of this type, the Court has rendered hardly any judgments in which it deviated from the outcomes of the national legislative process in dilemma-cases if it considers that underlying deliberations and debates have been sufficiently inclusive and comprehensive. Although even in these cases, the Court always provides for a substantive check of the reasonableness of the legislation of its own, this check usually is a very deferential one and it is still of a relatively procedural nature, to the extent that the Court mainly checks whether the national authorities have identified all relevant interests and whether the balance they have struck is not manifestly unreasonable.

Nevertheless, there are some clear dilemma-cases in which the Court does not at all apply a procedural approach. An example is the case of *X. and Others* v. *Austria*, which concerned a difference in treatment between unmarried different-sex couples and same-sex couples in respect of adoption.[120] Although this obviously was a hard case in which sensitive issues were at stake, the Court chose to apply a rather strict and clearly substantive proportionality review, carefully examining the various arguments adduced by the government for their reasonableness and persuasiveness. The quality of the national decision-making procedure did not play a role at all and the Court found, in clear deviation from the national legislature's view, that the difference in treatment could not be condoned. It is difficult to explain this deviation from the Court's usual approach, and the Court's judgment mainly seems to reveal that its procedural review case law is not (yet) fully consistent.

[119] Cf. also Kavanagh, *supra* n. 2; Popelier 2012, *supra* n. 2; Popelier and Van de Heyning, *supra* n. 2, p. 253.

[120] *X. and Others* v. *Austria*, ECtHR (GC) 19 February 2013, no. 19010/07.

6.3.4 *Conclusion*

In sum, in relation to the assessment of reasonableness of legislation, the Court often relies on arguments of procedural quality in cases presenting a dilemma or in cases involving difficult socio-economic choices. In both types of cases, this can be understood from the Court's subsidiary position and its view that national authorities are usually better placed to make political and value choices, as well as from the Court's desire to make sure that these choices have been made in a sound and equitable manner. The argument from procedure may be used in these cases in both a negative and a positive manner, to the extent that a lack of procedural quality may contribute to the finding of a violation, while a sound and careful preparation of legislation may contribute to the acceptance of the interference as reasonable and justifiable. In both types of cases, the Court mainly seems to regard the procedural arguments as supportive, i.e. as part of the overall set of arguments to be taken into account in building a 'narrative' leading up to a certain decision, although, especially in some 'negative' cases, the impact may be stronger.[121] Indeed, this seems to be in line with the Court's overall argumentative approach.[122] The Court is not likely to hold on to a strict canon of argumentation that requires it to first look at procedural arguments and, if it can build its conclusion on those arguments alone, stop there. Rather the Court tends to rely on a discursive approach, mentioning a wide number of different arguments in its judgments, including procedural arguments, none of which are apparently more important or decisive than another.[123] It is only the set of arguments taken together and read in their interrelationship that can support the final outcome.

6.4 Procedural Review of National Judicial Decision-Making

6.4.1 *Introduction*

The second main type of cases in which the Court relies on arguments of procedural fairness and procedural quality is that in which it reviews

[121] For the typical narrative structure of the Court's judgments, see further J.H. Gerards, 'European Court of Human Rights', in: A. Jákab, A. Dyevre and G. Itzcovich (eds), *Comparative Constitutional Reasoning* (Cambridge, Cambridge University Press, forthcoming). See also S. Smet, *Resolving Conflicts between Human Rights: A Legal Theoretical Analysis in the Context of the ECHR* (Dissertation Ghent University 2014), speaking of a 'net' of arguments.

[122] Ibid. [123] Ibid.

judicial decision-making.[124] In relation to this second type of cases, the interconnectedness between (procedural) positive obligations and procedural review is particularly strong. The Court greatly values its partnership and dialogue with the national courts, which it regards as important to ensure the protection of the Convention on the domestic level.[125] It is for that reason that the Court requires that the national courts take due account of the Convention standards and criteria in their case law.[126]

The implicit notion of 'partnership' in these cases also has found a translation into the Court's procedural review. Just as in cases concerning national legislation, the Court may pay attention to the quality of the national judicial proceedings and it may find support in its findings for reaching a certain outcome. Again, these findings may lead to either positive or negative inferences, as is further discussed in sections 6.4.2 and 6.4.3. In addition, there is a third category to be distinguished, which includes judgments in which the Court does not pay express attention to procedural requirements or compliance with Convention standards. This category is described in section 6.4.4.

6.4.2 *'Positive' Procedural Review of National Judicial Decisions*

In a large number of cases, the Court has paid 'positive' attention to national judicial decision-making by accepting that if the national courts have expressly taken account of the Court's case law and they have dutifully applied the substantive standards developed by the Court, there is not much need or room for the Court to deviate from their conclusions. Indeed, the Court has held that 'where the balancing exercise has been undertaken by the national authorities in conformity with the criteria laid down in the Court's case law, the Court would require strong reasons to substitute its view for that of the domestic courts'.[127]

[124] There are also cases concerning the procedural quality of administrative decision-making, but because they are rather similar to cases concerning judicial decision-making they are not discussed here separately; for some representative examples demonstrating the similarity of the Court's approach in administrative decision-making cases, see e.g. *C.N.* v. *the United Kingdom*, ECtHR 13 November 2012, no. 4239/08; *Maksymenko and Gerasymenko* v. *Ukraine*, ECtHR 16 May 2013, no. 49317/07; *Lavida and Others* v. *Greece*, ECtHR 30 May 2013, no. 7973/10; *Winterstein and Others* v. *France*, ECtHR 17 October 2013, no. 27013/07; *East/West Alliance Limited* v. *Ukraine*, ECtHR 23 January 2014, no. 19336/04.

[125] See section 6.2.3. [126] See in more detail Gerards, *supra* n. 2.

[127] *Von Hannover (No. 2)* v. *Germany*, ECtHR 7 February 2012, nos. 40660/08 and 60641/08, para. 107. See earlier also *MGN Limited* v. *the United Kingdom*, ECtHR 12 June 2012,

Clearly the Court can rely on this approach in relation to issues for which it has developed a strong and substantive body of case law identifying a set of standards and criteria that can be readily applied by national courts. For example, in relation to cases concerning the intended expulsion of immigrants, the Court has distinguished a variety of situation types in its case law, for each of which it has provided for an extensive 'catalogue' of relevant factors and criteria.[128] Similarly, for cases on the freedom of expression, such as cases on the publication of photographs of the private lives of famous people or cases on defamation by the press, the Court has created a list of 'general principles' to be taken into account in deciding on the reasonableness of limitations.[129] Although the Court seems to have devised such criteria and standards mainly for its own decision-making, they can just as well be used by national courts, and the Court often expresses its approval if they have done so. In many cases, the Court mainly looks into whether the national courts have actually relied on these factors and criteria and have duly taken them into account in their decision-making.[130] If so, it will not likely find a violation of the Convention. Such positive procedural reasoning in particular can be seen in private- and family law-related cases, such as cases concerning custody, guardianship, adoption or establishment of paternity,[131] some cases

no. 39401/04, paras. 150 and 155 and more recently e.g. *Aksu* v. *Turkey*, ECtHR (GC) 15 March 2012, nos. 4149/04 and 41029/04, para. 67; *Blaja News Sp. Z O.O.* v. *Poland*, ECtHR 26 November 2013, no. 59545/10. For a slightly different, though still similar approach, see *Eternit* v. *France*, ECtHR 27 March 2012 (dec.), no. 20041/10.

128 See in particular e.g. *Üner* v. *the Netherlands*, ECtHR (GC) 18 October 2006, no. 46410/99 and *Maslov* v. *Austria*, ECtHR (GC) 23 June 2006, no. 1638/03.

129 For a summary of these requirements, see e.g. *Von Hannover (No. 2)* v. *Germany*, ECtHR 7 February 2012, nos. 40660/08 and 60641/08. For some applications, see e.g. *Mouvement raëlien Suisse* v. *Switzerland*, ECtHR (GC) 13 July 2012, no. 16354/06; *Peta Deutschland* v. *Germany*, ECtHR 8 November 2012, no. 43481/09; *Remuszenko* v. *Poland*, ECtHR 16 July 2013, no. 1562/10; *Ojala and Etukeno Oy* v. *Finland*, ECtHR 14 January 2014, no. 69939/10; *Lillo-Stenberg and Sæther* v. *Norway*, ECtHR 16 January 2014, no. 13258/09; *Matúz* v. *Hungary*, ECtHR 21 October 2014, no. 73571/10; *Von Hannover (No. 3)* v. *Germany*, ECtHR 19 September 2013, appl. no. 8772/10. See similarly some cases relating to political parties; e.g. *Eusko Abertzale Ekintza-Accion Nacionalista Vasca (EAE-ANV)* v. *Spain (No. 2)*, ECtHR 15 January 2013, no. 40959/09.

130 See the cases mentioned *supra*, n. 127.

131 E.g. *Krisztián Barnabás Tóth* v. *Hungary*, ECtHR 12 February 2013, no. 48494/06; *Dmitriy Ryabov* v. *Russia*, ECtHR 1 August 2013, no. 33774/08; *A.L.* v. *Poland*, ECtHR 18 February 2014, no. 28609/08; *Z.J.* v. *Lithuania*, ECtHR 29 April 2014, no. 60092/12; *Buchs* v. *Switzerland*, ECtHR 27 May 2014, no. 9929/12; *I.S.* v. *Germany*, ECtHR 5 June 2014, no. 31021/08. For an interesting case in which the Court expressly embraced the criteria adopted by the national court, rather than reviewing whether the national

concerning domestic violence[132] and cases concerning moral dilemmas[133] or human dignity and personal autonomy.[134,135] In these cases, the Court often concludes that there is no violation of the Convention if it finds it established that the national procedures have been fair and the national courts have applied the Court's case law standards, as well as respected their procedural positive obligations. A similar approach is applied in relation to cases about the state's obligations to protect individuals against hazardous situations, such as natural disasters, life-threatening disease or serious environmental pollution. In this area, too, the Court has developed an elaborate case law, setting clear positive obligations to be met by decision-making authorities, such as obligations to provide for clear legislation and create special and transparent decision-making procedures, to provide for sufficient information, to safeguard involvement of interested parties, to provide for effective judicial remedies and so on.[136] In many of these cases, the Court mainly assesses whether these positive obligations have been complied with. If so, there is hardly any need for it to question the reasonableness of the decision reached, and it may instead only scrutinise the case to see if it discloses any 'manifest error of appreciation'.[137]

For the purposes of this chapter, it is important to emphasise that the Court appears to apply procedural-type review mainly in cases in which it has provided for elaborate lists of factors and standards to be taken into account.[138] Another commonality of the cases mentioned above is that they are strongly fact-based and they require a valuation of conflicting interests or of socio-economic factors. In that respect, they are similar to the types of cases about legislation in which the Court relies on

court applied the Convention standards, see *Harroudj* v. *France*, ECtHR 4 October 2012, no. 43631/09.

[132] E.g. *Wilson* v. *the United Kingdom*, ECtHR 23 October 2012 (dec.), no. 10601/09.

[133] See in particular *Stübing* v. *Germany*, ECtHR 12 April 2012, no. 43547/08.

[134] E.g. *McDonald* v. *the United Kingdom*, ECtHR 20 May 2014, no. 4241/12.

[135] See also *De la Flor Cabrera* v. *Spain*, ECtHR 27 May 2014, no. 10764/09.

[136] See already e.g. *Öneryildiz* v. *Turkey*, ECtHR (GC) 30 November 2004, no. 48939/99, para. 90; more recently, see e.g. *Martínez Martínez and Pino Manzano* v. *Spain*, ECtHR 3 July 2012, no. 61654/08; *Vilnes and Others* v. *Norway*, ECtHR 5 December 2013, nos. 52806/09 and 22703/10, para. 235; *Brincat and Others* v. *Malta*, ECtHR 24 July 2014, nos. 60908/11 et al.

[137] E.g. *Hardy and Maile* v. *the United Kingdom*, ECtHR 14 February 2012, no. 31965/07.

[138] A rare exception is *Julin* v. *Estonia*, ECtHR 29 May 2012, nos. 16563/08 et al, in which the Court applied positive procedural review to a case concerning the level of court fees under Article 6 ECHR. This is not normally a situation type in which a catalogue of factors is applied, so it is not entirely clear why the Court chose to rely on this approach.

procedural arguments and that were discussed in section 6.3.3. Here, too, the cases in which procedural review is applied appear to be either 'dilemma-cases', in which conflicting interests of rather similar weight are at stake or which relate to moral issues,[139] or cases in which the national authorities are particularly well-placed to make decisions because socio-economic interests or national resources or capacity play a role or, more generally, because 'the national authorities have the benefit of direct contact with all the persons concerned'.[140]

Interestingly, however, in hardly any of the cases in which this 'positive' type of procedural review is used, the Court takes its procedural approach to the fullest logical consequence, which would be that it would not at all look into the substance of the decision complained about. Surely, in some cases, the Court restricts itself to seeing whether the national court has taken sufficient heed of the various standards and positive obligations developed in the Court's case law and whether it has carefully applied the relevant criteria to the case at hand.[141] Those cases come closest to a purely procedural-type review.[142] In many other cases, however, while the Court expressly mentions that it will rely on a procedural approach or it accepts that the national authorities have carefully assessed the case, it still includes a number of more substantive arguments, complementing or comparing the national evaluation with one of its own.[143] In none of these cases is it very clear why the Court

[139] E.g. *Mouvement raëlien Suisse* v. *Switzerland*, ECtHR (GC) 13 July 2012, no. 16354/06; *Koch* v. *Germany*, ECtHR 19 July 2012, no. 497/09; *Peta Deutschland* v. *Germany*, ECtHR 8 November 2012, no. 43481/09.

[140] E.g. *Ahrens* v. *Germany*, ECtHR 22 March 2012, no. 45071/09, para. 64.

[141] See e.g. *Von Hannover (No. 2)* v. *Germany*, ECtHR 7 February 2012, nos. 40660/08 and 60641/08; *Aksu* v. *Turkey*, ECtHR 15 March 2012, nos. 4149/04 and 41029/04; *Mouvement raëlien Suisse* v. *Switzerland*, ECtHR (GC) 13 July 2012, no. 16354/06, paras. 67-75; *Spyra and Kranczkowski* v. *Poland*, ECtHR 25 September 2012, no. 19764/07; *Peta Deutschland* v. *Germany*, ECtHR 8 November 2012, no. 43481/09; *Remuszenko* v. *Poland*, ECtHR 16 July 2013, no. 1562/10; *Von Hannover (No. 3)* v. *Germany*, ECtHR 19 September 2013, no. 8772/10; *A.L.* v. *Poland*, ECtHR 18 February 2014, no. 28609/08.

[142] E.g. *Spyra and Kranczkowski* v. *Poland*, ECtHR 25 September 2012, no. 19764/07; *Krisztián Barnabás Tóth* v. *Hungary*, ECtHR 12 February 2013, no. 48494/06.

[143] E.g. *Axel Springer AG* v. *Germany*, ECtHR (GC) 7 February 2012, no. 39954/08 (the five dissenting judges in this case indeed disagreed with the majority judgment for this reason); *Samsonnikov* v. *Estonia*, ECtHR 3 July 2012, no. 52178/10; *Küchl* v. *Austria*, ECtHR 4 December 2012, no. 51151/06; *Cichopek and Others* v. *Poland*, ECtHR 14 May 2013 (dec.), no. 15189/10; *Ojala and Etukeno Oy* v. *Finland*, ECtHR 14 January 2014, no. 69939/10; *Lillo-Stenberg and Sæther* v. *Norway*, ECtHR 16 January 2014, no. 13258/09; *Ciesielczyk* v. *Poland*, ECtHR 26 June 2012, no. 12484/05; *Brincat and Others* v. *Malta*, ECtHR 24 July 2014, appl. nos. 60908/11 et al.

makes one or the other choice for a particular argumentative approach, especially since the Court does not provide any reasons for this. It can be concluded, therefore, just as in regard to national legislative decision-making, that procedural review may play a certain role, but the Court does not regard it as a full alternative to substantive review.

6.4.3 'Negative' Procedural Review of National Judicial Decisions

In addition to the positive form of procedural review of judicial decision-making, there is a 'negative' type of review. In negative-type procedural review cases, the Court is dismissive of a national judicial decision because the national court has paid insufficient heed to the fundamental rights aspects of a case or to the standards developed by the Court, the national judgment was inadequately reasoned or unduly formalistic, the national judicial proceedings were unfair, there has been no real review of the individual case and so on.[144] Similarly, in cases where the Court has set elaborate procedural positive obligations, such as in relation to hazardous situations or infringements of physical or mental integrity, the Court may find a violation of the Convention if these obligations have not been complied with, even without really looking into the substantive arguments presented by the government.[145] The same is true in many private- and family law-related cases, such as those relating to establishment of paternity, adoption or care orders,[146] cases concerning child

[144] E.g. *Hirsi Jamaa and Others* v. *Italy*, ECtHR 23 February 2012, no. 27765/09; *Waldemar Nowakowski* v. *Poland*, ECtHR 24 July 2012, no. 55167/11; *Jucha and Żak* v. *Poland*, ECtHR 23 October 2012, no. 19127/06; *E.M.* v. *Romania*, ECtHR 30 October 2012, no. 43994/05; *OOO Ivpress and Others* v. *Russia*, EHRM 22 January 2013, nos. 33501/04 et al.; *Bugan* v. *Romania*, ECtHR 12 February 2013, no. 13824/06; *Rousk* v. *Sweden*, ECtHR 25 July 2013, no. 27183/04; *R.M.S.* v. *Spain*, ECtHR 18 June 2013, no. 28775/12; *Cumhuriyet Vakfi and Others* v. *Turkey*, ECtHR 8 October 2013, no. 28255/07; *Ringier Axel Springer Slovakia A.S.* v. *Slovakia (No. 2)*, ECtHR 7 January 2014, no. 21666/09; *İhsan Ay* v. *Turkey*, ECtHR 21 January 2014, no. 34288/04; *Mugenzi* v. *France*, ECtHR 10 July 2014, no. 52701/09; *Matúz* v. *Hungary*, ECtHR 21 October 2014, no. 73571/10.

[145] E.g. *Kolyadenko and Others* v. *Russia*, ECtHR 28 February 2012, nos. 17423/05 et al; *P. and S.* v. *Poland*, ECtHR 30 October 2012, no. 57375/08; *Vilnes and Others* v. *Norway*, ECtHR 5 December 2013, nos. 52806/09 and 22703/10; *Oruk* v. *Turkey*, ECtHR 4 February 2014, no. 33647/04.

[146] E.g. *K.A.B.* v. *Spain*, ECtHR 10 April 2012, no. 59819/08; *Santos Nunes* v. *Portugal*, ECtHR 22 May 2012, no. 61173/08; *M.D. and Others* v. *Malta*, ECtHR 17 July 2012, no. 64791/10; *A.K. and L.* v. *Croatia*, ECtHR 8 January 2013, no. 37956/11; *Ageyevy* v. *Russia*, ECtHR 18 April 2013, no. 7075/10; *R.M.S.* v. *Spain*, ECtHR 18 June 2013, no. 28775/12; *Antonyuk* v. *Russia*, ECtHR 1 August 2013, no. 47721/10; *Zhou* v. *Italy*, ECtHR 21 January 2014, no. 33773/11.

abduction[147] or cases about personal autonomy and informed consent.[148] In these cases, the Court may conclude that national courts have taken insufficient care to comply with the procedural requirements formulated in the Court's case law. Similarly, in conformity with the requirement of individual decision-making rather than indiscriminate application of legislation, the Court has held it against the national courts if they have omitted to apply proportionality review in the concrete case at hand.[149]

The lack of procedural care in these cases often constitutes an important or even decisive reason for the Court to find a violation of the Convention. This forms an interesting contrast with the cases in which procedural carefulness and quality play a positive role, and where such procedural care usually is merely one argument considered next to a set of more substantive considerations. Nonetheless, even in the 'negative' cases, the Court sometimes pays attention to the substance of the case and the way in which the balance ought to have been struck, if only because some substantive review is necessary to establish if the authorities have taken insufficient care in deciding upon a certain matter.[150] Perhaps it does do so to enable the national courts to improve their reasoning in subsequent, similar cases, or perhaps it does do so because it seems too 'empty' to base a judgment on procedural reasons alone. Regardless of the explanation, however, these cases clearly illustrate that the presence of procedural-type arguments is seldom decisive.

6.4.4 *No Procedural Review*

Although procedural arguments play at least some role in many of the recent cases decided by the Court, it is equally clear that the Court does not always rely on these arguments. Although there are some cases on expulsion or reputation in which the Court expressly mentions its reliance on procedural review, there still are far more cases in which

[147] E.g. *X.* v. *Latvia*, ECtHR (GC) 26 November 2013, no. 27853/09.

[148] E.g. *A.K.* v. *Latvia*, ECtHR 24 June 2014, no. 33011/08.

[149] E.g. *Bjedov* v. *Croatia*, ECtHR 29 May 2012, no. 42150/09; *Godelli* v. *Italy*, ECtHR 25 September 2012, no. 33783/09; *Henry Kismoun* v. *France*, ECtHR 5 December 2013, no. 32265/10; *Paulet* v. *the United Kingdom*, ECtHR 13 May 2014, no. 6219/08; *Gablishvili* v. *Russia*, ECtHR 26 June 2014, no. 39428/12.

[150] E.g. *Waldemar Nowakowski* v. *Poland*, ECtHR 24 July 2012, no. 55167/11; *Czaja* v. *Poland*, ECtHR 2 October 2012, no. 5744/05; *Plesó* v. *Hungary*, ECtHR 2 October 2012, no. 41242/08; *Brezec* v. *Kroatia*, ECtHR 18 July 2013, no. 7177/10; *Jelševar and Others* v. *Slovenia*, ECtHR 11 March 2014 (dec.), no. 47318/07.

the Court embarks on its own review of reasonableness, re-balances all interests involved and arrives at a substantive conclusion without (elaborately) referring to the national decision-making process.

Logically, such a substantive, or at least hybrid, approach is visible in cases involving a legal or factual element which has not yet surfaced in the Court's case law or which concerns a rather special factual situation.[151] These elements may require new standard-setting, a re-shuffling of existing standards of review, or at the least an adaptation of the standards to the special facts of the case. It is rather obvious that the Court in these cases refrains from relying on the national decision-making process, but chooses to (re-)define and apply its set of general principles. In the same vein, the Court will not rely on procedural arguments in cases where its own standards are in need of further clarification.[152]

Perhaps more surprising is that there are also cases in which the Court does not rely on procedural arguments, whereas the case itself, to all outside appearance, does not disclose any new elements. Many cases on freedom of expression, migration and deprivation of property, as well as some family law cases, are fully reviewed on substantive grounds, without the Court making (much) reference to procedural requirements, to the quality of the national judicial procedure or to the national court's review.[153] Even in cases in which it would be relatively easy to apply

151 E.g. *Popov* v. *France*, ECtHR 19 January 2012, nos. 39472/07 and 39474/07; *Vejdeland and Others* v. *Sweden*, ECtHR 9 February 2012, no. 1813/07; *Antwi and Others* v. *Norway*, ECtHR 14 February 2012, no. 26940/10; *Babar Ahmad and Others* v. *the United Kingdom*, ECtHR 10 April 2012, nos. 24027/07 et al; *S.F. and Others* v. *Sweden*, ECtHR 15 May 2012, no. 52077/10; *Tatar and Faber* v. *Hungary*, ECtHR 12 June 2012, nos. 26005/08 and 26160/08; *Schweizerische Radio- und Fernsehgesellschaft SRG* v. *Switzerland*, ECtHR 21 June 2012, no. 34124/06; *Fáber* v. *Hungary*, ECtHR 24 July 2012, no. 40721/08; *Alkaya* v. *Turkey*, ECtHR 9 October 2012, no. 42811/06; *Szima* v. *Hungary*, ECtHR 9 October 2012, no. 29723/11; *Bucur and Toma* v. *Romania*, ECtHR 8 January 2013, no. 40238/02; *Neij and Sunde Kolmisoppi* v. *Sweden*, ECtHR 19 February 2013 (dec.), no. 40397/12; *Eon* v. *France*, ECtHR 14 March 2013, no. 26118/10; *K.A.B.* v. *Sweden*, ECtHR 5 September 2013, no. 886/11; *I.B.* v. *Greece*, ECtHR 3 October 2013, no. 552/10; *Tierbefreier e.V.* v. *Germany*, ECtHR 16 January 2014, no. 45192/09; *Perikäinen* v. *Finland*, ECtHR 4 February 2014, no. 11882/10; *Mustafa Erdogan and Others* v. *Turkey*, ECtHR 27 May 2014, nos. 346/04 and 39779/04; *Erdoğan Gökçe* v. *Turkey*, ECtHR 14 October 2014, no. 31736/04; *Murat Vural* v. *Turkey*, ECtHR 21 October 2014, no. 9540/07; *Gough* v. *the United Kingdom*, ECtHR 28 October 2014, no. 49327/11.

152 This may explain the reliance on substantive argumentative methods in cases such as *B.* v. *the United Kingdom*, ECtHR 14 February 2012, no. 36571/06 and *Jeunesse* v. *the Netherlands*, ECtHR (GC) 3 October 2014, no. 12738/10.

153 For migration and expulsion cases, see e.g. *Balogun* v. *the United Kingdom*, ECtHR 10 April 2012, no. 60286/09; *Nacic and Others* v. *Sweden*, ECtHR 15 May 2012, no. 16567/10; *A.A. and Others* v. *Sweden*, ECtHR 28 June2012, no. 14499/09; *Kissiwa*

the negative or positive procedural review forms discussed above, the Court usually applies a rather full reasonableness review.[154] Equally remarkable is that procedural review is hardly ever visible in cases concerning, for example, the freedom of assembly and demonstration and the freedom of religion.

Even a close analysis does not disclose any good explanation for the Court's non-reliance on procedural arguments in these cases. Perhaps such an explanation must be looked for in the Court's overall argumentative approach, which is not very dogmatic, but rather discursive.[155] In each case, the Court appears to provide for a number of arguments which, taken together, offer sufficiently persuasive reasoning to support its findings. Put differently, even if the Court's reliance on procedural arguments seems to disclose a degree of inconsistency, the Court itself

Koffi v. *Switzerland*, ECtHR 15 November 2012, no. 38005/07; *Shala* v. *Switzerland*, ECtHR 15 November 2012, no. 52873/09; *Hamidovic* v. *Italy*, ECtHR 4 December 2012, no. 31956/05; *Butt* v. *Norway*, ECtHR 4 December 2012, no. 47017/09; *Udeh* v. *Switzerland*, ECtHR 16 April 2013, no. 12020/09, *Hasanbasic* v. *Switzerland*, ECtHR 11 June 2013, no. 52166/09; *Vasquez* v. *Switzerland*, ECtHR 26 November 2013, no. 1785/08; *Biao* v. *Denmark*, ECtHR 25 March 2014, no. 38590/10; *M.P.E.V. and Others* v. *Switzerland*, ECtHR 8 July 2014, no. 3910/13. For freedom of expression, see e.g. *Martin and Others* v. *France*, ECtHR 12 April 2012, no. 30002/08; *Tanasoaica* v. *Romania*, ECtHR 19 June 2012, no. 3490/03; *Krone Verlag GmbH* v. *Austria*, ECtHR 19 June 2012, no. 27306/07; *Martin Kostov* v. *Bulgaria*, ECtHR 24 July 2012, no. 13801/07; *Łopuch* v. *Poland*, ECtHR 24 July 2012, no. 43587/09; *Falter Zeitschriften GmbH* v. *Austria (No. 2)*, ECtHR 18 September 2012, no. 3084/07; *Smolorz* v. *Poland*, ECtHR 16 October 2012, no. 17446/07; *Karpetas* v. *Greece*, ECtHR 30 October 2012, no. 6086/10; *Novaya Gazeta and Borodyanskiy* v. *Russia*, ECtHR 28 March 2013, no. 14087/08; *Reznik* v. *Russia*, ECtHR 4 April 2013, no. 4977/05; *Saint-Paul Luxembourg S.A.* v. *Luxemburg*, ECtHR 18 April 2013, no. 26419/10; *OOO 'Vesti' and Udkhov* v. *Russia*, ECtHR 30 May 2013, no. 21724/03; *Morice* v. *France*, ECtHR 11 July 2013, no. 29369/10; *Stojanovic* v. *Croatia*, ECtHR 19 September 2013, no. 23160/09; *Belpietro* v. *Italy*, ECtHR 24 September 2013, no. 43612/10; *Print Zeitungsverlag GmbH* v. *Austria*, ECtHR 10 October 2013, no. 26547/07; *Ristamäki and Korvola* v. *Finland*, ECtHR 29 October 2013, no. 66456/09; *De Lesquen du Plessis-Casso* v. *France (No. 2)*, ECtHR 30 January 2014, no. 34400/10; *Dilipak and Karakaya* v. *Turkey*, ECtHR 4 March 2014, nos. 7942/05 and 24838/05; *Brosa* v. *Germany*, ECtHR 17 April 2014, no. 5709/09; *A.B.* v. *Switzerland*, ECtHR 1 July 2014, no. 56925/08; *Erla Hlynsdottir* v. *Iceland (No. 2)*, ECtHR 21 October 2014, no. 54125/10. For property cases, see e.g. *Dimitru and Others* v. *Romania*, ECtHR 4 September 2012 (dec.), no. 57265/08; *Pyrantiene* v. *Lithuania*, ECtHR 12 November 2013, no. 45092/07; *Vikentijevik* v. *FYR Macedonia*, ECtHR 6 February 2014, no. 27853/09. For family law cases, see e.g. *B.* v. *Belgium*, ECtHR 10 July 2012, no. 4320/11.

[154] See e.g. *Karabadze and Others* v. *Georgia*, ECtHR 2 October 2012, no. 1484/07; *Gün and Others* v. *Turkey*, ECtHR 18 June 2013, no. 8029/07; *Kudrevecius and Others* v. *Lithuania*, ECtHR 26 November 2013, no. 37553/05.

[155] See Gerards, *supra* n. 121 and Smet, *supra* n. 121.

may not regard this as problematic, since what counts is whether the conclusion of each particular judgment is sufficiently underpinned by the arguments provided. Whether these arguments are procedural or substantive in nature may depend on coincidence or preference, rather than on a well-considered policy of judicial argumentation.[156]

6.5 Conclusions

The analysis of the Court's case law presented in this chapter clearly witnesses to the importance of procedural elements and procedural review for its case law. The Court often attaches value to procedural fairness in relation to both the legislative process and judicial and administrative decision-making on the domestic level. It has set a variety of procedural requirements, the disobedience of which may give rise to the finding of a Convention violation of its own. Particularly interesting to the procedural turn taken in the Court's case law are the obligations to allow for individualised decision-making and for the domestic courts to apply the standards and criteria developed in the Court's case law. Also of importance is the value the Court attaches to the quality of national legislative procedures, where equal representation and participation, transparency and deliberation play an important role, and national stakeholders and civil society must be involved in fundamental rights debates.

In parallel with the case law establishing these requirements, the Court has developed several lines of case law in which it draws the consequences from the national authorities' compliance with these requirements. It has been shown that procedural-type review is visible both in relation to legislation and in relation to administrative and judicial decisions. Especially in cases concerning moral dilemmas, conflicts of rights and socio-economic matters, the Court tends to attach importance to the quality of the national decision-making, both in relation to legislation and in relation to national judgments. Where national judicial and administrative decisions are concerned, the Court mainly relies on procedural arguments in standard cases for which it has already developed easy-to-use standards and criteria for review. In these situation types, the Court may attach both negative and positive value to the quality of the decision-making process. To this extent, thus, a typology indeed can be provided for.

[156] Ibid.

Importantly, the analysis also reveals that in hardly any of these cases are the arguments from procedure decisive. Mostly they are only supportive, and they form part of a 'net' of arguments that, taken in their entirety, support the outcome reached by the Court.[157] The main variation seems to be in whether the Court takes procedural arguments into account at all, and how much supportive value the argument has. It seems impossible to find a rational explanation for the Court's choice to either rely on procedural arguments, to a greater or lesser degree, or to leave them completely out of consideration. Sometimes the reason for not considering procedural arguments can be that the Court wants to redefine its substantive standards for review; then, indeed, procedural arguments have no real place in the Court's reasoning. In other cases, it may be that it has not obtained sufficient information by the parties about the national procedures in order to allow it to base its judgment on procedural arguments. And in yet other cases, it may simply be that the judges prefer a substantive approach over a more procedural one for reasons of their own.

In by far the most cases, thus, it seems that the Court relies on a 'pick and choose' approach, selecting those arguments that it considers useful in reasoning its judgment. These arguments may be of a procedural nature, for instance, if a procedural flaw or quality is particularly striking, but just as easily, they may not. These conclusions may not come as a surprise for close observers of the Court's case law. A 'bric-a-brac' approach is typical for the Court's argumentative style and, in fact, it is hardly to be expected that the Court would suddenly start relying on a highly structured and dogmatic argumentative approach that would clearly stipulate in which types of cases it will rely on procedural arguments and which value it will attach to such arguments.

Yet, the Court may be criticised for the lack of clarity and consistency that is disclosed by its use of procedural arguments in its reasonable review. National authorities are offered little guidance by this case law, as they can hardly know in advance how the Court will go about reviewing decisions taken by the legislature or by national courts. For that reason, it may be useful for the Court to build on the potential and possibilities offered by its case law on procedural review, applying the review more consistently in the types of cases set out above and drawing clearer consequences from procedural findings. Of course, such a more consistent approach can be hazardous, given the type of criticism that is

[157] Smet, *supra* n. 121.

possible of procedural review, and which is set out more clearly in other chapters of the current volume.[158] Nonetheless, building on techniques and possibilities developed in other legal systems and in theoretical literature, as also further examined in this volume, it must certainly be possible to improve the Court's use of procedural arguments and to enable for finding a more fully developed typology in the future.

158 See in particular Chapter 7 of this volume by Angelika Nussberger: 'Procedural Review by the European Court of Human Rights: View from the Court'.

7

Procedural Review by the ECHR: View from the Court

ANGELIKA NUSSBERGER

7.1 Introductory Remarks

7.1.1 *Procedure as a Key Element on the Way to Justice*

Procedure matters. This is well-expressed in the dissenting opinion of Judge Jackson and Judge Frankfurter to a judgment of the US Supreme Court:

> Indeed, if put to the choice, one might well prefer to live under Soviet substantive law applied in good faith by our common-law procedures than under our substantive law enforced by Soviet procedural practices.[1]

This idea was expressed at a point in time when the European Convention of Human Rights had just entered into force while the European Court of Human Rights (ECtHR) had not yet been established, at a time when the world was still divided into two ideologically different blocks. The message remains nevertheless true; the value of procedural safeguards cannot be underestimated.

This does not mean, however, that a shift from a substantive to a procedural review of human rights violations is to be *per se* welcomed. On the contrary, the ECtHR has been given the task of controlling the violation of substantive rights, some of which are even existential. It also has to guarantee 'fair trial'; but this is not a substitute, but an add-on to the control of substantive violations. Thus, the starting point for the Court's task of reviewing the member States' actions or inaction is quite clear.

This text expresses exclusively the author's opinion and does not bind the Court in any way.

[1] Dissenting opinion US Supreme Court (Jackson, Frankfurter), 1953, US Supreme Court, *Shaughnessy* v. *Mezei*, 345 US 206, S. 224.

7.1.2 Critique on Procedural Deficiencies: A Risky Game

Procedural review might seem to be 'softer' than substantive control. This is, however, not confirmed by the reactions from outside. One of the most famous examples is the debate on the judgment *Konstantin Markin* v. *Russia*,[2] in which the Chamber found quite harsh words for the judicial review that had taken place in Russia.

The Court first outlined the main argument of the Russian Constitutional Court justifying a different treatment of men and women in the military and then continued:

> The Court finds that argument unconvincing. It notes the lack of concrete evidence to substantiate the alleged damage to national security. There is no indication that any expert study or statistical research was made to assess the number of servicemen who would be in a position to take three years' parental leave at any given time and would be willing to do so. There is accordingly no evidentiary basis for the assertion that the number of servicemen simultaneously taking parental leave would be so significant as to undermine the fighting capacity of the army. It follows that the Constitutional Court based its decision on a pure assumption, without attempting to probe its validity by checking it against statistical data or by weighing the conflicting interests of maintaining the operational effectiveness of the army, on the one hand, and of protecting servicemen against discrimination in the sphere of family life and promoting the best interests of their children, on the other.[3]

The Court thus not only assesses and criticises the contents of the argumentation, but also procedural aspects. This has caused a vehement reaction from the President of the Russian Constitutional Court, Valeri Zorkin, and led to a crisis in the relationship between Russia and the Court.[4] The case was sent to the Grand Chamber, which came to the same result as the Chamber, but without directly criticising the deficiencies of the procedure before the Russian Constitutional Court. It only mentioned:

> There is no indication that any expert study or statistical research was ever made by the Russian authorities.[5]

Similarly, it seems that one of the many reasons for the heated debate on the judgment in the case *Hirst* v. *United Kingdom (No. 2)* is the explicit

[2] ECtHR 7 October 2010, *Konstantin Markin* v. *Russian Federation*, App. No. 30078/06.
[3] ECtHR 7 October 2010, *Konstantin Markin* v. *Russian Federation*, App. No. 30078/06, para. 57.
[4] *Valerij Zorkin, Rossijskaja gazeta*, 29 October 2010, No. 5325 (246).
[5] ECtHR 22 March 2012, *Konstantin Markin* v. *Russian Federation*, App. No. 30078/06, para. 144.

critique of the lack of a 'substantive debate by members of the legislature on the continued justification in light of modern-day penal policy and of current human rights standards'.[6] Thus, Lady Arden explained that 'the criticism did not reflect the reality how Parliamentary business is conducted'.[7]

This shows that a procedural turn does not necessarily smoothen the relationship between the Strasbourg Court and the national authorities. On the contrary, it may cause tensions in the so-called dialogue of judges, either because national judges feel personally offended or because they are of the opinion that the national system has not been understood and the Court has intruded into something which should be outside its reach.

7.1.3 Explicit and Implicit Procedural Review

Janneke Gerards has argued that the Court has a varied approach in its reasoning based on procedural aspects. Thus, it did not pay the same attention to the existence of an elaborate nationwide debate in the case *S.A.S.* v. *France*,[8] as in the case *Maurice* v. *France*.[9] On the surface, this observation is correct, as the Court has indeed taken up all the pros and cons of the prohibition of wearing the burka in public and entered into an in-depth debate of all the arguments advanced by the French government. At the same time, the main message of the judgment is that the blanket ban of wearing a burka in public is justifiable as a 'choice of society'.[10] It can be understood that the Court is satisfied that this choice had been made consciously and deliberately and that the democratic process lived up to what might be called 'European standards'. This has been spelt out clearly, even if the Court has not focused on the procedural aspects of the legislative process:

> the Court has a duty to exercise a degree of restraint in its review of Convention compliance, since such review will lead it to assess a balance that has been struck by means of a democratic process within the society in question.[11]

[6] ECtHR (Grand Chamber) 6 October 2005, *Hirst* v. *United Kingdom*, App. No. 74025/01, *(No. 2)* para. 79.
[7] Lady Arden, *An English Judge in Europe*, available at: https://www.judiciary.gov.uk/wp-content/uploads/JCO/Documents/Speeches/lj-arden-an-english-judge-in-europe.pdf.
[8] ECtHR 1 July 2014, *S.A.S.* v. *France*, Grand Chamber, App. No. 43835/11.
[9] ECtHR 6 October 2005, *Maurice* v. *France*, App. No. 11810/03.
[10] ECtHR (Grand Chamber) 1 July 2014, *S.A.S.* v. *France*, App. No. 43835/11, para. 157.
[11] ECtHR (Grand Chamber) 1 July 2014, *S.A.S.* v. *France*, App. No. 43835/11, para. 154.

Thus, (legislative) procedure, which was extensively described in the first parts of the judgment,[12] did not only matter, but was a dominant aspect of the case. In this sense, it may be argued that there is not only an explicit, but also an implicit procedural review. Whenever the Court accepts the 'choice of society' based on a democratic decision-making process, it can be assumed that in the Court's view, the procedure which led to this decision fulfilled all the requirements.

This implicit procedural review can also be illustrated in the judgment *A, B and C* v. *Ireland* on abortion and inhuman treatment.[13] Contrary to the government, the Court argued that there was a European consensus for allowing abortion, at least under specific circumstances, and that Ireland could therefore not be granted a wide margin of appreciation. Nevertheless, the Court accepted the choice of the Irish society to prohibit abortion, which had been expressed in three consecutive referenda. Without explicitly analysing the procedural aspects in detail, the Court accepted the 'profound moral values concerning the nature of life which were reflected in the stance of the majority of the Irish people against abortion during the 1983 referendum'.[14] The only procedural aspect explicitly mentioned was that the referendum had been adopted 'by a substantial majority'.[15]

It is most interesting to analyse under which circumstances the Court prefers to stress procedural arguments and under which circumstances it rather takes the procedural analysis for granted on the basis of the 'choice-of-society-argument' and refers to it only implicitly. This could be a subject for further research.

7.1.4 Parallel Developments in National Law

It is worth mentioning that proceduralisation is not only characteristic of human rights jurisprudence on the European level, but also generally of judicial control on the national level.

Reasons may be found in the complexity of the problems courts are nowadays confronted with, in the impact of expert knowledge in finding

[12] ECtHR (Grand Chamber) 1 July 2014, *S.A.S.* v. *France*, App. No. 43835/11, para. 15–27.

[13] ECtHR (Grand Chamber) 16 December 2010, *A, B and C* v. *Ireland*, App. No. 25579/05.

[14] ECtHR (Grand Chamber) 16 December 2010, *A, B and C* v. *Ireland*, App. No. 25579/05, para. 222.

[15] ECtHR (Grand Chamber) 16 December 2010, *A, B and C* v. *Ireland*, App. No. 25579/05, para. 224.

solutions and in the principle of subsidiarity developed in order to cope with the multiplication of levels of judicial decision-making.

Complex matters such as permissions for major industrial projects tend to end up before courts which usually do not have the necessary expert knowledge to foresee all the consequences and thus make an informed decision on the substantive question. The focus on procedural aspects, such as transparency and participation of all concerned, allows for judicial decision-making in a more 'neutral' and 'distant' manner. The same can be true in international human rights cases such as, for instance, child abduction cases in which the Court is unable to decide what solution is in the best interest of the child, as it lacks the direct contact to all those involved. This has been clearly spelled out in the case *X.* v. *Latvia*:

> Specifically, in the context of this examination, the Court reiterates that it does not propose to substitute its own assessment for that of the domestic courts ... Nevertheless, it must satisfy itself that the decision-making process leading to the adoption of the impugned measures by the domestic courts was fair and allowed those concerned to present their case fully, and that the best interests of the child were defended.[16]

In controversial cases on the national level, it is often the rule, rather than the exception, that claims are brought to the very top of the pyramid. In this context, proceduralisation serves as a means of avoiding conflicts of competence, especially between the Constitutional Court and ordinary courts. While the specialised ordinary courts are called upon to decide on the substance, Constitutional Courts tend to focus on procedural aspects and reduce substantive review to the control of arbitrariness.[17]

7.2 Risks of the Proceduralisation of Human Rights Protection

Proceduralisation of human rights jurisprudence can be motivated by many different reasons[18] and can have many different facets. While, to a certain extent, it can be seen as a positive – and even necessary – development, the shift of perspective is risky for the Court. The judgments might lead to unsatisfactory results for those protesting

[16] ECtHR (Grand Chamber) 26 November 2013, *X.* v. *Latvia*, App. No. 27853/09, para. 102.

[17] This is the doctrinal approach the German Federal Constitutional Court has explicitly taken in conflicts in which the right to freedom of expression coincides with the protection of private life.

[18] See Eva Brems' chapter in the current volume (Chapter 2: 'The "Logics" of Procedural-Type Review by the European Court of Human Rights').

against the violation of their rights. At the same time, they might be criticised by the member states as not in accordance with the Convention.

7.2.1 Procedural Justice in the Perspective of the Applicants

In the aftermath of the reunification in Germany, one of the leading dissidents, Bärbel Bohley, criticised that what they longed for was 'justice' and what they got was 'the Rechtsstaat':

> Wir wollten Gerechtigkeit und bekamen den Rechtsstaat.

This famous quotation illustrates quite well one of the main problems linked to a proceduralisation of human rights protection. What matters for the 'Humiliated and Insulted', in the sense of Fyodor Dostoyevsky, are the results. It is not sufficient that justice is seen to be done, but that it is done. Therefore, the finding of a procedural violation of a Convention right is often unsatisfactory for the applicant. The case *Schüth* v. *Germany* offers a good illustration for this kind of frustrated expectations.[19] The applicant, an organist and choirmaster in a Catholic parish, was dismissed for adultery after he got divorced and married for the second time. The Court found a violation of Article 8 of the Convention, not because of the dismissal, but because of the brevity of the labour courts' reasoning, which had failed to thoroughly weigh all the rights involved. In the ensuing procedure on pecuniary and non-pecuniary damage, the applicant claimed almost a million euro for lost income and lost pension rights. The Court, however, argued that it had never decided on the substantive violation of the Convention, but only on the procedural aspect:

> La Cour considère dès lors que la seule base à retenir pour l'octroi d'une satisfaction équitable réside en l'espèce dans le fait que les juridictions du travail n'ont pas suffisamment pris en considération tous les éléments pertinents lors de la mise en balance des intérêts du requérant et ceux de l'Eglise employeur et n'ont pas suffisamment exposé leur raisonnement. Elle rappelle qu'il ne lui appartient pas de spéculer sur les conclusions auxquelles les juridictions du travail allemandes auraient abouti si elles avaient procédé à une mise en balance conforme à la Convention.[20]

[19] ECtHR 23 September 2010, *Schüth* v. *Germany*, App. No. 1620/03.

[20] ECtHR 28 June 2012 (Just Satisfaction), *Schüth* v. *Germany*, Fifth Section, App. No. 1620/03, para. 23 ('The Court therefore considers that in the present case an award of just satisfaction can only be based on the fact that the employment tribunals did not take

Therefore, the Court accorded only a fraction of the amount claimed by the applicant.

7.2.2 *Deficient Protection of Minority Rights*

While there might be a presumption that an unfair procedure leads to an unfair result, there is no guarantee that sound procedures result in fair outcomes. Majority votes, even if based on a transparent exchange of views, tend to suppress minorities' rights, especially if the minorities are small. The case *S.A.S.* v. *France*, which has been mentioned before, is exemplary in this context. The same may be said for decision-making on subjects such as prisoners' rights.[21] The very function of human rights review is to counterbalance majority decisions. This cannot be done by reviewing the procedure only.

7.2.3 *Difficulties in Evaluating Decision-Making Procedures on the National Level*

Another problem is the difficulty in evaluating the quality of the national parliamentary debate and other national non-judicial decision-making procedures. While the Convention provides with Article 6 a yardstick for judicial procedures, it is silent on how to assess and evaluate other forms of (political) decision-making processes.

In practice, the Court's approaches vary. It can check if the concrete human rights issues involved in (new) legislation have been duly evaluated and discussed, as it did in the aforementioned *Hirst* case. It is also possible to go further and assess if the discussion on a human rights problem was based on sufficient and reliable statistical material, as it did in the *Konstantin Markin* case. Or the procedure can be evaluated on the basis of abstract concepts such as transparency or inclusiveness.

It is, however, doubtful if these approaches are satisfactory and lead to convincing results.

sufficient account of all the relevant aspects when weighing the applicant's interests against those of the employing Church and did not sufficiently explain their reasons. It observes that it is not its task to speculate as to what conclusions the German employment tribunals would have reached had they carried a balancing exercise complying with the Convention' (author's translation).

21 E.g. ECtHR 4 December 2007 (Grand Chamber), *Dickson* v. *United Kingdom*, App. No. 44362/04.

Parliamentary debate is shaped by tradition and national experience and is deeply embedded in the relevant cultural setting. Even if some forms of best practice can be identified,[22] the Court is not a master in this field. It is true that the Court has always stressed that democracy is the only model under which the values of the Convention can be implemented:

> As has been stated many times in the Court's judgments, not only is democracy a fundamental feature of the European public order but the Convention was designed to promote and maintain the ideals and values of a democratic society. Democracy, the Court has stressed, is the only political model contemplated in the Convention and the only one compatible with it.[23]

At the same time, it has avoided the slippery slope of giving definitions for basic concepts:

> The Court emphasises that the notion of the separation of powers between the political organs of government and the judiciary has assumed growing importance in its case-law . . . At the same time, neither Article 6 nor any other provision of the Convention requires States to comply with any theoretical constitutional concepts regarding the permissible limits of the powers' interaction.[24]

It might be a temptation to judge outside appearances. But a thorough debate can take place behind closed doors without leaving clear traces for outsiders. Inclusiveness, participation and transparency can be guaranteed in many ways. A unanimous result in the votes cast in Parliament may be interpreted in two ways, either as a consequence of the lack of inclusiveness in the democratic process and a suppression of the views of the opposition, or as a realistic mirror of the wishes and attitudes held in a certain society.

The wide spectrum of constitutional arrangements cannot be judged in the abstract. In some States, for example, referenda on human rights issues are possible, and in others they are not. While the Court can take the results of referenda into account, it cannot draw any inferences from the lack of such a referendum in evaluating the democratic process. The same is true for differentiations between constitutional provisions. Some constitutions contain 'eternal clauses', and others do not. Such

[22] This is basically the work of the Venice Commission, which tries to identify European standards in constitutional law.

[23] ECtHR 3 May 2007, *Bączkowski and Others* v. *Poland*, App. No. 1543/06, para. 61.

[24] ECtHR 9 January 2013, *Oleksandr Volkov* v. *Ukraine*, App. No. 21722/11, para. 103.

mechanisms of securing rights and anticipating the results of a balancing process between different rights are not universal. It is not possible to draw any conclusions from them.

Time is also an important factor in this context. Restrictions on human rights may be based on laws adopted at a time when the understanding of the essential elements of a good decision-making process was different. Old laws can be applied to new challenges. This generally accepted legal technique excludes an *ex ante* balancing of the specific interests involved.

Last but not least, there may be differences between what is usually called 'old democracies' and 'new democracies', i.e. those States where democracy had to be rebuilt after the communist era. It would undermine a uniform approach to human rights if such differences were taken into account.

Evaluating the quality of the national parliamentary debate is therefore a sensitive issue and does not fall into the Court's competence. Such matters rather belong to the '*domaine reservé*' of national Constitutional Courts. Questions of style may be misunderstood as questions of quality; systemic differences may be over-interpreted. Nevertheless, transparency and open debate matter. As this should be self-evident, only extreme (positive and negative) divergences from what is considered as 'standard' are worth mentioning in judgments of the Court.

7.2.4 *Dangers of Advocating 'Micro-Justice'*

It is true that the Court's procedural critique often concentrates on the lack of individual justice, especially if individual problems cannot be sufficiently taken into account because of legal presumptions or regulations not allowing for exceptions.[25] The Court's perspective is shaped by its task of reviewing human rights violations in individual concrete cases. Nevertheless, it also has to accept arguments that are relevant in a holistic perspective. This is well illustrated by the case *Pretty* v. *United Kingdom*, in which the applicant wished to be able to control how and when she died and be spared the suffering and indignity of the final stages of her disease by allowing her husband to assist her in committing suicide.[26] The Court accepted that the blanket ban on assisted suicide was 'designed to safeguard life by protecting the weak and vulnerable and especially those who are not in a condition to take informed decisions against acts

[25] See Chapter 6 by Janneke Gerards: 'Procedural Review by the ECtHR: A Typology'.

[26] ECtHR 29 April 2002, *Pretty* v. *United Kingdom*, Fourth Section, App. No. 2346/02.

intended to end life or to assist in ending life'.[27] The refusal of the British authorities to grant an exception in Mrs Pretty's case and to give an advance undertaking that no prosecution would be brought against her husband was deemed to be proportionate. In this context, the Court held:

> The more serious the harm involved the more heavily will weigh in the balance considerations of public health and safety against the countervailing principle of personal autonomy.[28]

That means that effective protection can require strict provisions not allowing for any exceptions.

'Micro-justice' in the form of laws that are tailor-made for all potential situations and allow for a case-by-case study and decisions based on the concrete circumstances of the case are, as a rule, compatible with human rights protection. But in advocating individual justice, issues of legal security and equality should not be underestimated. The more exceptions and the more discretion in deciding concrete cases, the less the results are foreseeable, the more they depend on those called upon to decide. For the Court, it is hardly recommendable to favour one model of justice over another one, especially when questions of separation of powers and definition of competences are involved.

The Court's jurisprudence itself oscillates between the two poles, demanding general solutions based on clear-cut and strict criteria and demanding individual solutions where different criteria have to be evaluated on a case-by-case basis. A famous example is the shift in the Court's jurisprudence on hearsay evidence in *Al Khawaja and Tahery* v. *United Kingdom*.[29] While the Chamber judgment followed a strict approach and found a violation, whatever the reasons for the condemnation based exclusively on hearsay evidence, the Grand Chamber developed a more nuanced approach where the different factors have to be carefully weighed. Experience shows that the black-and-white solution enhanced legal certainty, but led to unconvincing results in individual cases, while the more nuanced approach has raised a lot of questions as to the correct application of the criteria elaborated in the jurisprudence.

[27] ECtHR 29 April 2002, *Pretty* v. *United Kingdom*, Fourth Section, App. No. 2346/02, para. 74.

[28] ECtHR 29 April 2002, *Pretty* v. *United Kingdom*, Fourth Section, App. No. 2346/02, para. 74.

[29] ECtHR (Grand Chamber) 15 December 2011, *Al Khawaja and Tahery* v. *United Kingdom*, App. Nos. 26766/05 and 22228/06, paras. 129–142.

7.2.5 Overlap in the Interpretation of the Convention Provisions

Last but not least, procedural review developed on the basis of substantive rights may render an analysis under Article 6 and Article 13 redundant if there are no separate issues left. This has, however, to be clarified on a case-by-case basis. If, for example, a complaint under Article 13 would be confined to a restatement of the actual deficiencies of the Article 3 investigation, the finding of a violation would add nothing to the case. If, however, the deficiencies in the investigation were such that the applicant was denied the possibility of bringing a civil action for compensation, that allegation should be examined separately under Article 13 and cannot be taken to have already been sufficiently addressed in the finding of a breach of the procedural limb of Article 3.[30]

Furthermore, it is unclear how far the principles developed in the case law on Article 6 and 13 apply without any modifications to the procedural review under Article 2 and 3. It is necessary to avoid any inconsistencies in the jurisprudence, but nevertheless, the perspective of the analysis can be a different one. This is, for example, the reason why the case *Tunç* v. *Turkey* was referred to the Grand Chamber:

> Having regard to the Chamber's findings, the reasons given in the Government's request for referral and the parties' submissions, the Court nevertheless considers it useful to provide some clarification concerning the requirement that the investigation be independent for the purposes of Article 2, and particularly as to whether the investigative authorities in the broad sense must meet similar criteria of independence as those which prevail under Article 6 of the Convention.[31]

The Court explained that the safeguards provided under Article 2 and Article 6 are not necessarily to be assessed in the same manner:

> Article 6 requires that the court called upon to determine the merits of a charge be independent of the legislature and the executive, and of the parties. Compliance with this requirement is assessed, in particular, on the basis of statutory criteria, such as the manner of appointment of its members and the duration of their term of office, or the existence of sufficient safeguards against the risk of outside pressures. The question whether the body presents an appearance of independence is also of relevance.

[30] See e.g. ECtHR 13 July 2010, *Karagöz and Others* v. *Turkey*, App. Nos. 14352/05, 38484/05 and 38513/05, para. 59; ECtHR 15 March 2011, *Serdar Güzel* v. *Turkey*, App. No. 39414/06, para. 50.

[31] ECtHR (Grand Chamber) 14 April 2015, *Mustafa Tunç and Fecire Tunç* v. *Turkey*, App. No. 24014/05, para. 219.

> For their part, the requirements of Article 2 call for a concrete examination of the independence of the investigation in its entirety, rather than an abstract assessment.[32]

Contrary to the Chamber, the Court therefore did not find a violation in the case.

This shows that the procedural duties under Articles 2 and 3 have to be distinguished from the procedural duties under Articles 6 and 13. The Court is called upon to develop its jurisprudence in this context with great diligence.

7.3 Context of the Procedural Turn in the Court's Case Law

There are many elements in the Court's case law which support the thesis that there has been a procedural turn in the Court's recent jurisprudence. Insofar as the procedural focus can lead to a less intense control, it can be linked to the 'Brighton-philosophy', which puts much emphasis on subsidiarity.[33]

At the same time, scrutinising the procedure on the national level can also be seen as a way of intensifying what is criticised as 'micromanagement' of national legal systems and thus as 'anti-Brighton'. Therefore, it is not surprising that in the Court's recent jurisprudence, examples can be found where the Court has 'softened' or 'diluted' requirements concerning the procedure to be followed on the national level.

One example of a marked change in the Court's jurisprudence is the case *X.* v. *Latvia* in comparison to *Neulinger and Shuruk* v. *Switzerland*. Both cases concern international child abduction and the application of the Hague Convention on International Child Abduction in the light of Article 8 of the Convention. In *Neulinger and Shuruk* v. *Switzerland*, the Court had specified a very far-reaching procedural duty for the national courts and required them to conduct an 'in-depth examination of the entire family situation' when deciding on the request to return the abducted child.[34] This approach was seen to conflict with the Hague Convention. Therefore, the Court was

[32] ECtHR (Grand Chamber) 14 April 2015, *Mustafa Tunç and Fecire Tunç* v. *Turkey*, App. No. 24014/05, paras. 221, 222.

[33] A high-level Conference on the future of the Court was organised by the United Kingdom in Brighton on 18–20 April 2012, during which the so-called Brighton declaration was adopted; cf. www.echr.coe.int/Documents/2012_Brighton_FinalDeclaration_ENG.pdf. It is a very important document defining, among many other things, the interaction between the Court and the national courts.

[34] ECtHR (Grand Chamber) 6 July 2010, *Neulinger and Shuruk* v. *Switzerland*, App. No. 41615/07, para. 139.

asked to 'set limits on the examination of the family situation by the court deciding on an application for a child's return',[35] i.e. to redefine the procedural duty of the national courts under the Convention. The Court accepted to 'clarify' its earlier finding in *Neulinger and Shuruk* v. *Switzerland* and promoted a more restrictive approach in *X.* v. *Latvia.*[36]

Similarly, a certain softening of procedural duties can also be seen in the judgment *Scoppola (No. 3)* v. *Italy*, which gives up the approach followed in *Frödl* v. *Austria*. While the Chamber in *Frödl* v. *Austria* required that 'the decision on disenfranchisement should be taken by a judge, taking into account the particular circumstances' and 'specific reasoning [should be] given in an individual decision explaining why in the circumstances of the specific case disenfranchisement was necessary',[37] the Grand Chamber in *Scoppola* v. *Italy (No. 3)* held that 'the circumstances in which the right to vote is forfeited may be detailed in the law, making its application conditional on such factors as the nature or the gravity of the offence committed'.[38]

These examples are, however, linked to specific situations and cannot be seen to indicate a trend against proceduralisation. Nevertheless, they also have to be taken into consideration.

7.4 Link between Proceduralisation and Margin of Appreciation

In Janneke Gerards' chapter in the present volume, it has been shown that procedural aspects tend to be emphasised in cases which concern moral dilemmas or socio-economic rights.[39] A third group may be added, i.e. cases in which the Court has to balance rights equally protected under the Convention, such as Article 8 and Article 10[40] or Article

[35] ECtHR (Grand Chamber) 26 November 2013, *X.* v. *Latvia*, App. No. 27853/09, para. 103.

[36] ECtHR (Grand Chamber) 26 November 2013, *X.* v. *Latvia*, App. No. 27853/09, para. 106: 'Firstly, the factors capable of constituting an exception to the child's immediate return in application of Articles 12, 13 and 20 of the said Convention, particularly where they are raised by one of the parties to the proceedings, must genuinely be taken into account by the requested court. That court must then make a decision that is sufficiently reasoned on this point, in order to enable the Court to verify that those questions have been effectively examined. Secondly, these factors must be evaluated in the light of Article 8 of the Convention.'

[37] ECtHR 8 April 2010, *Frödl* v. *Austria*, App. No. 20201/04, paras. 34 and 35.

[38] ECtHR (Grand Chamber) 22 May 2012, *Scoppola* v. *Italy (No. 3)*, App. No. 126/05, para. 99.

[39] Chapter 6: 'Procedural Review by the ECtHR: A Typology'.

[40] See the jurisprudence in the cases ECtHR, *Von Hannover* v. *Germany (No. 1, 2 and 3)*, App. Nos. 59320/00, 40660/08 and 60641/08, 8772/10.

9 and Article 11.[41] All these categories of cases have in common that the Court usually grants a wide or even a very wide margin of appreciation. Therefore, it can be argued that there is a direct link between the degree of proceduralisation of the Court's review and margin of appreciation. When States are free to decide a case in different ways without violating the Convention, the inclusiveness and transparency of the decision-making process is the most relevant element for the Court to control. It is true, however, that even in such cases, procedural control cannot replace substantive control. Dissenting opinions show that there is no consensus among the judges how far the substantive control in such cases should go.[42]

In order to enhance the foreseeability of its jurisprudence, the Court has elaborated for some recurring problems lists of factors to be weighed for arriving at a balanced decision. This is true for conflicts between the individual's right to respect for his or her private life and publishing companies' right to freedom of expression,[43] as well as for the protection of foreigners in cases of deportation following series of criminal convictions.[44] In these cases, the review of the decision-making process on the national level could take a specific form. It could be confined to analysing whether the national courts have taken into account all the factors defined to be relevant by the Court and, if this is the case, limit substantive control to the control of arbitrariness. The advantage of such an approach would be to reduce the 'subjective factor' inherent in weighing different criteria, which is evidenced by the zig-zag of decision-making in such cases. Just by way of an example, in the case von *Hannover (No. 3)* v. *Germany*, 27 German judges had decided on the case; different conclusions were reached on almost all the different levels of jurisdiction.[45] On the other hand, as the Court has to exert 'European control', it will usually also want to have a say on the weighing of the different factors and the result of the balancing procedure. The question of when the Court should limit itself to the finding of a procedural violation and when it

[41] See ECtHR (Grand Chamber) 9 July 2013, *Sindicatul 'Păstorul cel Bun'* v. *Romania*, App. No. 2330/09, para. 160.

[42] See for a detailed analysis A. Nussberger, *Subsidiarity in the Control of Decisions Based on Proportionality: An Analysis of the Basis of the Implementation of ECtHR Judgments into German Law*, in: A. Seibert-Fohr and M. Villiger (eds), *Judgments of the European Court of Human Rights–Effects and Implementation* (Baden-Baden, 2014) pp. 165–186.

[43] ECtHR (Grand Chamber) 7 February 2012, *Von Hannover* v. *Germany (No. 2)*, 40660/08 and 60641/08, paras. 108 et seq.

[44] ECtHR 23 June 2008 (Grand Chamber), *Maslov* v. *Austra*, App. No. 1638/03, paras. 71–76.

[45] Nussberger, *supra* n. 42.

should enter into the substance of the issue is therefore highly controversial, as is shown by the quantity of dissenting opinions in such cases, as well as by the fact that it is not rare that they are sent to the Grand Chamber.[46]

7.5 Auxiliary Character of Procedural Arguments

Procedural arguments outside the scope of Article 6 and Article 13 usually have an auxiliary function. The 'creation' of procedural violations is meant to render effective the protection against a substantive violation. This has been clearly expressed in *McCann*:

> The Court confines itself to noting, like the Commission, that a general legal prohibition of arbitrary killing by the agents of the State would be ineffective, in practice, if there existed no procedure for reviewing the lawfulness of the use of lethal force by State authorities. The obligation to protect the right to life under this provision, read in conjunction with the State's general duty under Article 1 of the Convention to "secure to everyone within their jurisdiction the rights and freedoms defined in [the] Convention", requires by implication that there should be some form of effective official investigation when individuals have been killed as a result of the use of force by, *inter alios*, agents of the State.[47]

The idea of reviewing the investigation procedures is thus 'to secure the effective implementation of the domestic laws which protect the right to life'.[48]

Procedural violations are also auxiliary in the sense that they make it possible for the Court to attribute responsibility to the State in cases in which it would otherwise escape responsibility because the high standard of proof cannot be reached. Not conducting a thorough investigation could otherwise help the State avoiding responsibility. This would be a perverse effect. One of the early famous cases in this regard is *Assenov and Others* v. *Bulgaria*, in which the Court found it impossible to establish on the basis of the evidence before it whether or not the applicant's injuries were caused by the police as alleged, but it could compensate this negative result by criticising the lack of a thorough and effective investigation.[49]

[46] See, e.g. ECtHR 12 June 2014, *Couderc and Hachette Filipacchi Associés* v. *France*, App. No. 40454/07.

[47] ECtHR (Grand Chamber), *McCann and Others* v. *United Kingdom*, App. No. 18984/91, 27 September 1995, para. 161.

[48] ECtHR 13 June 2002, *Anguelova and Others* v. *Bulgaria*, App. No. 38361/97, para. 137.

[49] ECtHR 28 October 1998, *Assenov and Others* v. *Bulgaria*, App. No. 38361/97, paras. 100, 106.

The recourse to procedural arguments in assessing the 'necessity' of an interference with a right protected by the Convention can also be regarded as auxiliary or secondary. The interpretation of what is 'necessary in a democratic society' does not per se require taking into account procedural aspects as long as the emphasis is laid on 'necessity'. If, however, the emphasis is laid on 'democratic society', procedural review will be considered as an indispensable element.

It is evident that the Court uses procedural arguments more often if it finds some 'deviation from normality', i.e. if the procedure is either especially elaborate or on the contrary shows obvious deficiencies. In controversial cases, the 'procedural check-up' might also help to find a compromise solution among judges. Another factor that might explain a somewhat flexible approach to the inclusion or exclusion of procedural arguments is the argumentation provided by the parties. If they insist on procedural deficiencies or positive aspects of effective scrutiny of the human rights involved, the Court will include this aspect in its legal evaluation. Seen on this background, it is no surprise that 'it seems impossible to find a logical and rational explanation for the Court's choice to either rely on procedural arguments, to a greater or lesser degree, or to leave them even completely out of consideration.'[50]

Nevertheless, the lesson learnt for national authorities should be that procedure matters even if this aspect is not explicitly used in the Court's argumentation.

[50] See the chapter by Janneke Gerards (Chapter 6: 'Procedural Review by the ECtHR: A Typology').

8

Procedural Fundamental Rights Review by the Court of Justice of the European Union

MALU BEIJER

8.1 Introduction

At the supranational level, the Court of Justice of the European Union (CJEU) has made quite some effort to develop procedural standards to ensure the protection of EU law. Its case law especially reveals some extensive judicial and administrative standards which national authorities must comply with to ensure the protection of EU law as national law.[1] It has also been noticed by scholars that the CJEU has attached importance to the fulfilment of procedural standards in its review of EU legislation in light of fundamental rights.[2] The CJEU has, in fact, been willing to declare EU legislation either valid or invalid based on the quality of the decision-making process.[3] To what extent can this interest of the CJEU for procedures, specifically in fundamental rights cases, also be related to a notion of procedural review? This type of review would mean that the CJEU takes the quality of the legislative, administrative and judicial procedures into account to be able to decide about the

The author wishes to thank the editors, as well as Leonie Huijbers and Sybe de Vries, for their helpful comments.

[1] S. Prechal and R. Widdershoven, 'Redefining the Relationship between "Rewe-effectiveness" and Effective Judicial Protection', (2011) 4 *Review of European Administrative Law* 2011, pp. 31–50.

[2] K. Lenaerts, 'The European Court of Justice and Process-Oriented Review', Research Paper in Law European Legal Studies 01/2012; O. de Schutter, 'The Implementation of the Charter by the Institutions of the European Union', in S. Peers, T. Harvey, J. Kenner, and A. Ward (eds), *The EU Charter of Fundamental Rights* (Oxford: Hart Publishing, 2014), p. 1644; and S. de Vries, 'Balancing Fundamental Rights with Economic Freedoms According to the European Court of Justice', (2013) 9 *Utrecht Law Review*, p. 174.

[3] See in particular Joined Cases C-92/09 and C-93/09, *Volker und Markus Schecke*, 9 November 2010; Case C-236/09, *Test-Achats*, 1 March 2011; Case C-356/12, *Glatzel*, 22 May 2014. Other cases will be mentioned in section 8.3.3 of this chapter.

reasonableness of interferences with fundamental rights in situations falling within the scope of EU law.[4]

This chapter aims to explore the answer to that question by further analysing a set of fundamental rights cases of the CJEU that contain various procedural arguments. The CJEU is increasingly required to make very difficult and sensitive decisions when judging the (legislative) decisions taken by the EU institutions, as well as in answering the questions of national courts on the interpretation of EU law under the preliminary reference procedure in fundamental rights cases.[5] This chapter will further analyse such cases to see what type of procedural arguments the CJEU uses, and to find out whether they are part of a procedural review. Before doing so, this chapter first presents some reasons why the CJEU in particular may want to opt for a procedural type of review, both more generally and also more specifically in the area of fundamental rights (section 8.2). After that, the case law analysis is presented (section 8.3), which will be followed by an evaluation of the benefits and drawbacks of this type of review (section 8.4). The conclusion brings forth some insights as to how the CJEU (could) make(s) use of a procedural type of review (section 8.5). In this chapter, it will be argued that the specific position of the CJEU towards the EU institutions and the member states can provide a sound reason for the CJEU to use procedural arguments in its review. It will be explained that it is also of great interest that the CJEU contributes to strengthening the procedural quality of decisions because of the difficult character of the decision-making procedures within the EU. Specifically, in respect of the decisions being taken by the EU institutions in the field of fundamental rights, it will be held that the CJEU should not only watch over the (quality of the) decision-making procedure. It is further necessary for the CJEU to also develop the substantive standards of fundamental rights that need to be complied with in relation to the actions falling within the scope of EU law.

[4] This chapter aims to rely on the notion of procedural review as explained by Gerards in relation to the case law of the ECtHR; see Gerards's Chapter 6 to this volume 'Procedural Review by the ECtHR: A Typology'.

[5] For statistical information on the fundamental rights cases which have been brought to the CJEU from 2009 onwards, see European Commission, Staff Working Document on the Application of the EU Charter of Fundamental Rights in 2015, SWD (2016) 158 final, pp. 8–10.

8.2 Deference, Subsidiarity and Attention for Decision-Making Processes within the EU

Lenaerts in particular has explained why paying attention to the fulfilment of procedural standards would be an effective method for the CJEU in reviewing EU legislation.[6] According to Lenaerts, by examining the procedures that have been followed by the EU legislature to reach its decisions, the CJEU could find out whether there is no arbitrariness in the decision-making of the EU, and it could further encourage the rationality of the decision-making process. By drawing its conclusions on the basis of procedural arguments, the CJEU could stay away from second-guessing the substantive decisions of the EU institutions, and still give teeth to its review if there are clear shortcomings.[7] Lenaerts sees the judgments in the *Volker und Markus Schecke* and *Test-Achats* cases as good examples of such a procedural strategy. In these cases, which were both concerned with the protection of fundamental rights, the CJEU mostly used procedural arguments as a basis for its finding that the respective instruments of EU legislation were invalid.[8] According to Lenaerts, it could generally be held that 'the ECJ is more respectful of the prerogatives of the political institutions of the EU if it rules that, when adopting the contested act, those institutions failed to take into consideration all the relevant interests at stake, than if it questions their policy choices by reference to its own view of the issues involved'.[9]

The subsidiary function of courts and their specific position *vis-à-vis* the other branches of government are indeed considered to form important motivations to engage in a procedural type of review.[10] This would also seem to hold true in respect of the CJEU. In the specific context of EU law, there often can be very complex socio-economic and technical internal market questions that need to be solved. Further, the decisions being made in the area of freedom, security and justice on the (procedural) cooperation between the member states in areas of criminal law and of asylum law, could give rise to some deeply sensitive questions.[11] In relation to both areas, fundamental rights are increasingly invoked by the national courts and by the CJEU as principles that need to be taken

[6] Lenaerts, 'The European Court of Justice and Process-Oriented Review, *supra* n. 2.

[7] Ibid. p. 15. [8] See further section 8.3.3 of this chapter.

[9] Lenaerts, 'The European Court of Justice and Process-Oriented Review', *supra* n. 2, p. 16.

[10] See further Chapter 1 (Janneke Gerards and Eva Brems: Introduction) and Chapter 2 (Eva Brems: 'The 'Logics' of Procedural-Type Review by the European Court of Human Rights') of this volume.

[11] E. Muir, 'The Fundamental Rights Implications of EU Legislation: Some Constitutional Challenges', (2014) 51 *Common Market Law Review*, pp. 220–221.

into account.[12] It could be argued that the political authorities in those contexts are better placed to decide about the reasonableness of the decisions that are taken in those areas. Moreover, supranational courts are said to be positioned at too great a distance to be able to form a good judgment over the decisions which have been taken at the national level. The CJEU might in that respect find itself in a similar position as the ECtHR.[13] National authorities can be expected to be able to be in a better position to decide about societal interests than such supranational courts are. The CJEU might therefore, just like the ECtHR, be seeking ways to reconcile its subsidiary position with the effective protection of the rights it aims to guarantee.[14] In relation to decisions and measures taken by the EU institutions, by contrast, the CJEU may want to opt for deferential review, as the EU institutions have better knowledge and stronger legitimacy to decide on the kind of complex socio-economic matters these decisions and measures often are about.[15] Further, Popelier has held, more generally, that the balancing of interests should not be undertaken by courts themselves, because the balancing of the 'national, subnational, supranational, and private interests [is] of a political nature'.[16]

There also is a more general reason to keep an eye open for the procedural rationality of the decisions that are taken on the basis of EU law. The legitimacy of those decisions can be challenged because of the (potential) democratic deficiencies of the EU's legal order, as well the multilevel setting of the decision-making processes.[17] These aspects

[12] See further European Commission, Staff Working Document on the Application of the EU Charter of Fundamental Rights in 2015, SWD (2016) 158 final, pp. 7–8; and cf. S. Bartolini and A. Bondi, 'Life as Human Rights Court: Challenges and Developments in EU Courts Activity in 2014' (2016) 22 *European Public Law*, pp. 3–23.

[13] Cf. Gerards's Chapter 6 to the current volume: 'Procedural Review by the ECtHR: A Typology'.

[14] For the differences and similarities between the supranational position of the ECtHR and the CJEU, see S. Besson, 'European Human Rights, Supranational Judicial Review and Democracy: Thinking outside the Judicial Box', in P. Popelier, C. Van de Heijning and P. Van Nuffel (eds), *Human rights protection in the European legal order: the interaction between the European and the national courts* (Cambridge: Intersentia, 2011), pp. 97–145.

[15] The CJEU has, for example, held so in relation to its review of a Commission decision on state aid, see Case C-525/04 P, *Spain* v. *Leipzig*, 22 November 2007; Cf. further for arguments on a deferential type of review by the CJEU in the field of fundamental rights, J. Gerards, 'Pluralism, Deference and the Margin of Appreciation Doctrine' (2011) 17 *European Law Journal*, pp. 85–87.

[16] P. Popelier, 'Governance and Better Regulation: Dealing with Legitimacy Paradox' (2011) 17 *European Public Law*, pp. 565–566.

[17] See in particular P. Popelier, 'The Court as Regulatory Watchdog. The Procedural Approach in the Case Law of the European Court of Human Rights', in P. Popelier,

could cast doubt on whether all interests are duly taken into account at the different national, regional and local levels, as they may not be directly represented in the parliamentary decision-making process. This could ultimately be reflected in the quality of the outcome of European decision-making. In the particular field of fundamental rights protection by the EU, there may especially be fears as to whether these rights have specifically been taken into account at the different levels on which decisions are being made. The fundamental rights of minorities are, for example, especially prone to be excluded in (majoritarian) decision-making procedures.[18] Within the EU's complex legal order, minorities could possibly face an even bigger risk of such exclusion, because of the democratic deficiencies.[19] Also, the protection of fundamental rights still is, to some extent, a novel feature of the decision-making process of the EU authorities. Fundamental rights have only really become very visible within the EU when the Charter was made binding in 2009, and it has proven necessary to 'remind' the EU legislatures of their obligation to take fundamental rights into account by means of the adoption of checklists.[20] Thus, in the field of fundamental rights protection by the EU in particular, there may even be stronger arguments for the CJEU to watch over the decision-making process and to strengthen it where possible. Therefore, extra care needs to be paid to the quality of the input as well as the output of the decision-making process within the EU. Aside from efforts that evidently need to be undertaken by the political institutions themselves, the CJEU could stimulate them to face these challenges by checking whether institutional and procedural safeguards have been respected, and if necessary, develop procedural

A. Mamanyan and W. Vandenbruwane (eds), *The Role of Constitutional Courts in Multilevel Governance* (Cambridge: Intersentia, 2013), p. 251; and Popelier, 'Goverance and Better Regulation: Dealing with Legitimacy Paradox, *supra* n. 16, pp. 555–556.

[18] See Gerards's Chapter 6 to the current volume: 'Procedural Review by the ECtHR: A Typology'; and Besson, 'European Human Rights, Supranational Review and Democracy', *supra* n. 14, p. 124.

[19] See Besson, 'European Human Rights, Supranational Review and Democracy', *supra* n. 14, pp. 124–125 and 128.

[20] See J. Morijn, 'Kissing Awake a Sleeping Beauty? The Charter of Fundamental Rights in EU and Member States' Policy Practice', in V. Kosta, N. Skoutaris and V. Tzevelekos (eds), *The EU Accession to the ECHR* (Oxford: Hart Publishing, 2014), pp. 123–139. See further for the usefulness of such an approach Meuwese and Kartner's Chapter 5: 'Responsiveness towards Fundamental Rights Impacts in the Preparation of EU Legislation' in this volume. Morijn has, however, warned (at p. 130) against the use and reliance on the fundamental rights checklists that have been drawn up by the EU institutions: ' … they could result in raising "CFR alerts" in the wrong way, to the wrong people at the wrong time in the EU policy-making process'.

requirements of their own.[21] To this end, the CJEU may in particular contribute to the success of the programmes that have been set up to improve the quality of EU regulation. 'Better regulation' or 'smart regulation' programmes have been initiated with the aim of providing clearer and more effective rules primarily to increase the economic efficiency of EU regulation. This seeks to improve the participation of stakeholders in the decision-making process and may also require the examination of alternative measures and the study of their effects to be documented in such instruments as impact assessments. Some scholars have suggested that the CJEU could rely on such instruments in its assessment of the validity of EU (legislative) decisions to check the quality of the decision-making process, and it has been shown that, in a few cases, the CJEU has indeed done so.[22]

It would thus appear worthwhile for the CJEU to pay attention to the quality of the procedures that lead to the (legislative) decisions which it may be requested to review, taking into consideration the position of the CJEU towards the EU institutions and towards the member states, as well as the difficulties arising out of the decision-making procedures within the EU. Such considerations are also of particular relevance in the context of fundamental rights protection, as discussed above.

8.3 The Scope for Procedural Review in the Case Law of the CJEU

A distinction can be made between three types of fundamental rights cases in which the CJEU uses procedural arguments.[23] Firstly, procedural arguments can be found in the judgments of the CJEU which it delivers under the preliminary reference and in which national courts ask questions on EU law in relation to the decisions being made at national level. Secondly, it can be seen that quite some attention for the quality of procedures is paid by the CJEU in its case law on the so-called sanction

[21] Popelier, 'The Court as Regulatory Watchdog', *supra* n. 17, p. 566.

[22] Case C-58/08, *Vodafone Ltd*, 8 June 2015, para. 55; and Case C-176/09, *Luxemburg* v. *Parliament and Council*, 12 May 2012, para. 65. See further D. Keyaerts, 'Courts as Regulatory Watchdogs. Does the European Court of Justice Bark or Bite?', in P. Popelier, A. Mamanyan and W. Vandenbruwane (eds), *The Role of Constitutional Courts in Multilevel Governance*, (Cambridge: Intersentia, 2013), pp. 269–289; and Lenaerts, 'The European Court of Justice and Process-Oriented Review', *supra* n. 2.

[23] For the various kinds of procedural arguments and types of procedural review, see Gerards's Chapter 6 to the current volume: 'Procedural Review by the ECtHR: A Typology'. This chapter relies on the typologies defined in that chapter.

decisions. This is where the fundamental rights of individuals or organisations are restricted *inter alia* because of their alleged involvement with terrorist activities. Thirdly, a variety of procedural arguments can be found in several judgments of the CJEU in which it reviews EU legislation in light of fundamental rights. These three categories of cases will be analysed separately to determine how procedural arguments are used and indeed to what extent the CJEU exercises procedural review in such cases.

8.3.1 *Review of Actions Taken by the National Authorities*

8.3.1.1 Procedural Obligations

In its case law, the CJEU has often dealt with questions which have been referred by the national courts on the procedural protection that needs to be offered by the national administrative and judicial authorities on the basis of EU law. In response to the questions of the national courts, the CJEU has been willing to develop a strong set of requirements that the national authorities need to comply with.[24] The CJEU has requested that judicial remedies are provided to allow individuals to challenge infringements of EU law at national level, as well as set obligations for national courts to interpret national law in conformity with rights that are protected under EU law.[25] On the basis of the case law of the CJEU, national courts must even set national laws aside if they conflict with EU law,[26] and they may be obliged to order interim measures under certain conditions.[27] In relation to the decisions taken by national administrative authorities based on EU law, the CJEU has furthermore clarified that such decisions must be well reasoned and individuals whose interests may be affected by those decisions must be heard.[28] The CJEU has always found the rationale for imposing such requirements in the objective of assuring the effectiveness of community and

[24] Cf. Prechal and Widdershoven, 'Redefining the Relationship between Rewe-effectiveness and Effective Judicial Protection', *supra* n. 1.

[25] Case C-305/05, *Ordre des barreaux francophone and germanophone and Others*, 26 June 2007, para. 28; and Case C-275/06, *Promusicae*, 29 January 2008, paras 68 and 70.

[26] Case C-6/90, *Francovich*, 19 November 1991, paras 31–37; and Case C-182/10, 16 February 2012, *Solvay*, para. 49. On horizontal disputes, see Case C-144/04, *Mangold*, 22 November 2005, para. 77; Case C-555/07, *Kücükdeveci*, 19 January 2010, para. 51; and Case C-208/90, *Emmott*, 25 July 1991, paras. 21–23.

[27] Case C-213/89, *Factortame*, 19 June 1990, paras. 18–22; Case C-432/05 *Unibet*, 13 March 2007, para. 67; and Case C-562/13, *Abdida*, 18 December 2014, para. 50.

[28] Case C-222/84, *Johnston*, 15 May 1986, paras. 17–19 (right to equal treatment); Case C-222/86, *Heylens*, 15 October 1987 (free movement of workers), para. 14.

later EU law.[29] Increasingly, the CJEU (also) bases such procedural obligations on the need to respect the fundamental rights provisions as laid down in the Charter.[30] Presently, there is a particularly clear basis for procedural obligations in Article 41 of the Charter, which guarantees the right to good administration, and in Article 47 of the Charter, which guarantees the right to effective judicial protection.[31] In addition, the procedural obligations which the CJEU has developed as part of the general principles of EU law, including the rights of defence and the principle of effective judicial protection, provide relevant bases to take into account.[32]

Hence, there exists a quite strong set of procedural requirements under EU law, especially on the basis of the Charter, which the national courts need to comply with in areas of EU law where the protection of material fundamental rights interests can be at stake.[33] There are (only) a few judgments in which the CJEU developed further procedural obligations and safeguards for the national level to secure that the responsible authorities take (certain) material fundamental rights interests into account when making their decisions. In fact, it has only done so in cases where such obligations do not clearly and unambiguously follow from secondary legislation. The case of *ZZ* provides an example of one occasion in which the CJEU imposed such more detailed obligations.[34]

[29] Cf. Case C-33/76, *Rewe*, 16 December 1976, para. 5.

[30] Cf. Prechal and Widdershoven, 'Redefining the Relationship between 'Rewe-effectiveness' and Effective Judicial Protection', *supra* n. 1.

[31] In fact, the right to an effective remedy and the right to good administration rank among the first rights which are referred to most of the rights of the Charter by the CJEU in 2015; see European Commission, Staff Working Document on the Application of the EU Charter of Fundamental Rights in 2015, SWD (2016) 158 final, pp. 9–10.

[32] The CJEU has explained that the right to good administration under Article 41 of the Charter does not apply to the national authorities, because the provision is textually restricted to the EU institutions. However, the CJEU protects a right to good administration on the basis of the general principles of EU law, see Case C-141/12ECJ 17 July 2014, C-141/12, *YS and Others*, 17 July 2014, para. 67; Case C-277/11, *M.*, 22 November 2012, paras 81 ff.; and Case C-166/13, *Mukarubega*, 5 November 2014, paras 43 ff. Also cf. H. Hofman and B. Mihaescu, 'The Relation between the Charter's Fundamental Rights and the Unwritten General Principles of EU Law: Good Administration as the Test Case' (2013) 9 *European Constitutional Law Review*, pp. 73–101.

[33] For example, in the case of *Mangold*, it is noticeable that the CJEU also requires national courts to exercise the power to set aside national legislation where it conflicted with EU law and the principle of non-discrimination on grounds of age, see Case C-144/04, *Mangold*, 22 November 2005. Also it has recognised rights to be heard in cases concerned with asylum applications, see e.g. Case C-277/11, *M.*, 22 November 2012.

[34] Case C-300/11, *ZZ*, 4 June 2013.

This case concerned a decision on the expulsion of an EU citizen on grounds of public security. In its judgment, the CJEU clarified that 'the court with jurisdiction in the member state concerned must have at its disposal and apply techniques and rules of procedural law which accommodate, on the one hand, legitimate state security considerations regarding the nature and sources of the information taken into account in the adoption of such a decision and, on the other hand, the need to ensure sufficient compliance with the person's procedural rights, such as the right to be heard and the adversarial principle'.[35]

The development of more concrete procedural obligations can, to some extent, also be noticed in the case of *UPC Telekabel Wien*.[36] This case concerned a national court's order containing an obligation for an internet service provider to block the access of its users to websites to ensure protection of intellectual property rights. The referring court sought guidance from the CJEU in respect of the complex and technical balancing assessment which it had to make and which required it to take into account intellectual property rights, the freedom to conduct a business and the freedom of information.[37] In view of the protection of the freedom of information, the CJEU established that 'national procedural rules must provide a possibility for internet users to assert their rights before the court once the implementing measures taken by the internet service provider are known'.[38]

Thus, the CJEU is developing procedural obligations for the national courts in some of its fundamental rights cases. These procedural obligations could be used at the national level to secure that better outcomes on fundamental rights decisions are reached, while the fulfilment of such procedural obligations could also be valued in itself.

8.3.1.2 Proportionality and Procedural Review

In relation to the preliminary reference procedure, it is important to keep in mind that national courts are, in principle, responsible for ensuring

[35] Case C-300/11, *ZZ*, 4 June 2013, para. 57. Cf. ECtHR, *Al-Nashif* v. *Bulgaria*, 20 June 2002, Application no. 509639/99, para. 123; and see E. Brems and L. Lavrysen, 'Procedural justice in human rights adjudication: the European Court of Human Rights' (2013) 35 *Human Rights Quarterly*, pp. 198–199.

[36] Case C-314/12, *UPC Telekabel Wien*, 27 March 2014.

[37] *Ibid.*, para. 47.

[38] *Ibid.*, para. 57.

that EU law is applied correctly at national level.[39] If the national courts need guidance on how EU law must be interpreted and/or if they have questions about the validity of EU law, they can, and sometimes must, make a preliminary reference to the CJEU.[40] Therefore, it is in principle up to the national courts to decide on the reasonableness of national measures, including those with an EU dimension.[41] In this respect, the role of acting as a regulatory watchdog is then attributed to the national courts.[42] Indeed, national courts may have an important role to play in ensuring that the decisions taken by national authorities, which fall within the scope of EU law, comply with fundamental rights.[43]

At the same time, when certain interests of EU law are at stake and in cases on certain areas of EU law, it can be seen that the CJEU does take a much closer look at the reasonableness of decisions or measures that have been taken at the national level. Sometimes, the CJEU can also specifically be invited by the national courts to provide further substantive guidance. For example, in the specific context of a collision of the EU free movement rights and the protection of fundamental rights, the CJEU has been invited on different occasions by national courts to give guidance on deciding over the reasonableness of the decisions reached by the national authorities. Such situations provide particularly difficult

[39] Moreover, as Besson points out with regard to the specific characteristics of the fundamental rights review of the CJEU 'it is rare for the ECJ to face a conflict between national law and EU fundamental rights only, most cases will be cases in which EU law (e.g. fundamental freedoms) conflicts with national fundamental rights and hence also with EU fundamental rights, thus giving a balance of interests. This balance of interests is a matter of fact often in the end left to the member states, which have a positive duty to interpret domestic law in conformity with EU fundamental rights'. See Besson, 'European Human Rights, Supranational Judicial Review and Democracy', *supra* n. 14, p. 116.

[40] The room for discretion for national courts, as well as restrictions placed thereon under the preliminary reference procedure, has been further explained in Case C-283/81, *CILFIT*, 6 October 1982, paras 7–20; and more recently in Case C-160/14, *Ferreira da Silva*, 9 September 2015, paras. 38–45; and Joined Cases C-72/15 and C-197/14, *X. and T.A. van Dijk*, 9 September 2015, paras 54–62.

[41] The CJEU has held that 'it is not for the Court, in the context for a reference of a preliminary ruling, to give a ruling on the interpretation of provisions of national law or to decide whether the interpretation given by the national court of those provisions is correct' see e.g. Case C-58/98, *Corsten*, 3 October 2000, para. 24.

[42] See Keyaerts, 'Court as Regulatory Watchdog', *supra* n. 22, pp. 269–289.

[43] The CJEU has e.g. stressed that national courts need to ensure that the individual circumstances have been taken into account of a third-country national who is deported because of the risk to public policy, or whose residence permits are revoked because they no longer fulfil the conditions for receiving refugee status. See respectively Case C-554/13, *Z.Zh. and O.*, 11 June 2015, paras 48–49 and 53; and Case C-373/13, *H.T.*, 24 June 2015, paras 89–90.

challenges for the CJEU, as it must decide over rights which in, the Court's view, are all 'fundamental' under EU law.[44] In the case of *Schmidberger*, the CJEU chose to undertake a substantive assessment of the proportionality of the measure that was adopted by a national authority. However, it has also shown, for example, in the case of *Omega* to be willing to exercise a much more deferential review as regards substantive proportionality issues.[45] By contrast, in the *Dynamic Medien* case, the CJEU decided to try a different approach, which is much more procedural in nature.[46] This procedural approach has been applied more often by the CJEU in cases on the restrictions of the free movement provisions by the member states.[47]

The preliminary reference that was made in the *Dynamic Medien* case followed from a dispute on the import by a company of Japanese cartoons, known as 'anime', on DVDs and videocassettes. The import took place by mail order from the United Kingdom to Germany. The British Board of Film Classification had classified the image storage media as 'suitable only for 15 years and older'. Dynamic Medien, a competitor on the relevant market, claimed that the sale by mail order of image storage media should have been prohibited on the basis of German law, as the competent authority in Germany should also have decided to restrict the sale on the basis of the German laws on the protection of young persons. The German court decided to refer questions to the CJEU concerning the compatibility of the German rules in view *inter alia* of the protection of the free movement of goods. In the examination of the justification of those rules, the CJEU accepted that member states may take into account the protection of the rights of the child, as it is recognised by various international human rights instruments and by Article 24 of the Charter in particular.[48] Measures such as the one that was at issue must be

[44] Case C-112/00, *Schmidberger*, 12 June 2003, para. 51; and see A. Biondi, 'Free Trade, a Mountain Road and the Right to Protest: European Economic Freedoms and Fundamental Individual Rights', (2004) 9 *European Human Rights Law Review*, p. 54; and De Vries, 'Balancing Fundamental Rights with Economic Freedoms According to the European Court of Justice', *supra* n. 2.

[45] Case C-112/00, *Schmidberger*, 12 June 2003; and Case C-36/02, *Omega*, 14 October 2014.

[46] Case C-244/06, *Dynamic Medien*, 14 February 2008. See further De Vries, 'Balancing Fundamental Rights with Economic Freedoms According to the European Court of Justice', *supra* n. 2, p. 174.

[47] See S. Prechal, 'Topic One: National Applications of the Proportionality Principle – Free Movement and Procedural Requirements: Proportionality Reconsidered' (2008) 35 *Legal Issues of Economic Integration*, pp. 201–216.

[48] Case C-244/06, *Dynamic Medien*, 14 February 2008, paras. 39–41.

suitable for securing the attainment of their objective, however, and they may not go beyond what is necessary in order to attain it.[49] The CJEU clarified that member states have a 'definite margin of discretion' as to the conception of the protection of the rights of the child considering that the conception varies from one member state to another.[50] At the same time, the CJEU also held 'that discretion must be exercised in conformity with the obligations arising under Community law'.[51] According to the CJEU, the national court specifically had to ascertain whether the examination procedure established by the national legislature 'is readily accessible, can be completed within a reasonable period, and, if it leads to a refusal, the decision of a refusal must be open to challenge before the courts'.[52] Here, the CJEU clearly steered the national court into looking at whether there were sufficient procedural safeguards at national level to prevent the arbitrary use of powers. It seems that the CJEU thereby complemented a deferential review of substantive proportionality with a more procedural element. This appeared suitable in view of the idea of subsidiarity and the discretion which the member states enjoy in respect of the measures which they take to protect the rights of the child. The specific benefits and drawbacks of this approach will, as announced, be discussed further in section 8.4.

All in all, while there is indeed attention in the case law of the CJEU on the development of procedural obligations and standards at national level, it is only in some cases that clear procedural review is adopted by the CJEU. In this specific context, the CJEU then specifically relies on the substantive reasonableness review that can be undertaken by the national courts themselves.

8.3.2 Review of the EU's Sanction Decisions

In the specific context of the EU's sanction decisions, the CJEU has paid particular efforts to develop several procedural obligations and standards which the competent EU authorities must comply with when placing individuals or entities on sanctions lists. Placement on such sanction lists can result in individuals' assets being frozen, travel and visa bans being imposed and other restrictive measures being taken. The CJEU has famously made clear in the *Kadi* cases that to respect the right to effective judicial protection and the rights of defence, the competent EU authorities must communicate the grounds for the imposition of restrictive

[49] Ibid. para. 42. [50] Ibid. para. 44. [51] Ibid. para. 45. [52] Ibid. para. 50.

measures to the person or entity concerned, so far as possible, and as swiftly as possible after the decision has been taken.[53] Also, to ensure respect for the right to be heard, the EU Courts must apply techniques to reconcile the interests of maintaining the security of the information that is provided for by the state, and the interests of providing procedural justice to the individual involved.[54] These and other procedural standards and obligations have been further developed in its case law related to sanction decisions, such as in cases related to counteracting terrorism and preventing nuclear proliferation in Iran, and also in cases about the EU's autonomous sanctions decisions.[55]

Looking somewhat closer at the approach of the CJEU in the *Kadi* case, the CJEU actually appears to have placed much focus on procedural arguments. In the greatest part of its judgments, the CJEU explained that there was a serious lack of procedural protection provided by the competent authorities, and that they thereby failed to pay sufficient respect to the principles of the rights of defence and of effective judicial protection on the basis of EU law. Interestingly, in its examination of the justification that could be provided for the restriction of the right to property, the CJEU also primarily used a procedural argument to come to its conclusion.[56] The CJEU held that no guarantee was provided for an individual to put a case to the competent authorities, while the restriction of the right to property could be regarded as significant.[57] It thereupon concluded that the right to property was also violated.

In the *Kadi* cases, the CJEU explained the importance of the development of procedural obligations and standards on the basis of the principle of the rule of law.[58] Although the CJEU did not further elaborate on that point, it would seem that it considered the procedural safeguards of importance to prevent arbitrary interferences by public authorities in individuals' lives. Nevertheless, even though the CJEU thus paid great attention to the procedural shortcomings in relation to the sanction decisions, the CJEU has shown that it is still willing to engage in

[53] Joined Cases C-402/05 P and C-41/05 P, *Kadi and Al Barakaat*, 3 September 2008, paras 336–337; and Case C-584/10 P, *Commission and Others* v. *Kadi*, 18 July 2013, paras 111–115.

[54] *Kadi and Al Barakaat*, para. 344; and *Commission and Others* v. *Kadi*, para. 125.

[55] Cf. C. Eckes, 'EU Restrictive Measures against Natural and Legal Persons: From Counterterrorist to Third Country Sanctions' (2014) 51 *Common Market Law Review*, pp. 869–906; and M. Wimmer, 'Inward- and Outward-Looking Rationales behind Kadi II' (2014) 21 *Maastricht Journal of European and Comparative Law*, pp. 676–703.

[56] *Kadi and Al Barakaat*, paras. 369–370. [57] *Ibid.*, paras. 368–370.

[58] *Commission and Others* v. *Kadi*, para. 66.

a substantive assessment of the sanction decision. In the *Kadi II* case, which concerned the Commission's decision to relist Kadi, the CJEU also reviewed the substantive grounds for the relisting decision, which the CJEU did not find sufficient to justify the restrictive measures that had been taken.[59]

In this particular context of sanction decisions, arguments of a procedural nature thus play an important role in the judgments of the CJEU. It is rather difficult, however, to find out to what degree the findings on the (lack of) procedural quality ultimately played a role in reaching conclusions about the reasonableness of the sanction decisions itself. As explained, the CJEU further reached its conclusions as to the validity of the decisions by assessing the substantive grounds for relisting a particular individual. Moreover, it must be realised that the development of procedural standards in this particular area was of great importance by itself, as such standards had so far clearly been lacking.[60]

8.3.3 Review of Legislative Actions of the EU Institutions

By now, quite some cases have been brought to the CJEU under the preliminary reference procedure contesting the validity of EU legislation because of an incompatibility with fundamental rights, especially after the Charter was made binding.[61] On a few occasions, the CJEU has been willing to declare such legislation void (*Volker und Markus Schecke, Test-Achats, Digital Rights Ireland* and *Schrems*), whereas it has affirmed the validity of EU legislation in other cases (*Sky Österreich, Schwarz* and *Glatzel*). In these cases, it has sometimes relied heavily on procedural

59 *Ibid.* paras. 151–165.

60 By scrutinising the sanction decisions, the CJEU has received much criticism from an international law perspective. Some of the sanctions lists originated from the UN Security Council and were implemented directly by the EU on the basis of Regulations. Thus, the active development by the CJEU of the (procedural) standards in this context and its judicial review of such measures is precarious in view of the EU's relationship to the UN legal order; see e.g. G. de Búrca, 'The European Court of Justice and the International Legal Order after *Kadi*' (2010) 51 *Harvard International Law Journal*, pp. 1–49. It also raises complexities, because national authorities are now faced with conflicting obligations under EU and UN law respectively; see Wimmer, 'Inward- and Outward-Looking Rationales behind Kadi II', *supra* n. 55.

61 The more recent cases of *Neptune Distribution* and *J.N* may also be mentioned in this regard, which were not, however, included in the analysis; see Case C-157/14, *Neptune Distribution*, 17 December 2015; and C-601/15, *J.N.*, 15 February 2016.

arguments, but in other cases it has also, or instead, included substantive arguments. This section aims to analyse and categorise the different choices that the CJEU has made in these cases, to enable a better understanding of when and why the CJEU resorts to procedural arguments, and also of when it decides to focus on substantive arguments (instead). To allow a further debate about the use of procedural arguments, the different types of procedural arguments that can be found in these cases are presented first (section 8.3.3.1). Secondly, an analysis is provided of the types of conclusions which the CJEU reaches in response to the procedural arguments, and of the extent to which also a substantive review of EU legislation in light of fundamental rights is given (section 8.3.3.2). Thirdly, and lastly, as part of an overall evaluation of the use of procedural arguments by the CJEU in the three different types of cases that are examined in this chapter, it is further discussed for what reasons the CJEU seems to engage in a procedural review instead of, or alongside, a substantive review (section 8.4).

8.3.3.1 Procedural Arguments

The following subsections will reveal three types of procedural arguments which the CJEU has taken account of in its review of EU legislation. The CJEU has looked at the quality of the legislative process, the foreseeability and accessibility of the legislation and the availability of judicial review. Elsewhere in this volume, Gerards has explained that these requirements, which are also to be found in the case law of the ECtHR, arguably all relate to procedural arguments and they are concerned with the quality of the legislation.[62]

Quality of the Legislative Process The CJEU has discussed specific aspects relating to the quality of the legislative process in the cases of *Volker und Markus Schecke, Glatzel* and *Test-Achats.* Firstly, in the case of *Volker und Markus Schecke*, the CJEU was asked to examine the validity of a provision laid down in an EU Regulation which required member states to publish information on the beneficiaries of European agricultural funds.[63] This included the publication of the amounts received by those beneficiaries, the names of the natural or the legal persons and their municipality and, if available, the postal code of

62 See Gerards's Chapter 6 to the current volume: 'Procedural Review by the ECtHR: A Typology'.

63 Joined Cases C-92/09 and C-93/09, *Volker und Markus Schecke*, 9 November 2010.

residence. In reviewing the proportionality of this measure, the CJEU noted that '[t]here is nothing to show that, when adopting [the contested provision], the Council and the Commission sought to strike such a balance between the European Union's interest in guaranteeing the transparency of its acts and ensuring the best use of public funds, on the one hand, and the fundamental rights enshrined in Articles 7 and 8 of the Charter, on the other hand.'[64] The CJEU thus expressed some criticism, in a rather general way, on the effort that was made by the EU legislature to include the different interests in the decision-making process.

Secondly, in the case of *Glatzel*, the CJEU looked at the establishment of a specific minimum standard by the EU legislature relating to the physical fitness for visual acuity for driving a motor vehicle, which was laid down in an annex of an EU Directive on driving licenses.[65] The case was brought before a German court by a person who suffered from a vision disability and therefore had lost his driving license. This gave rise to questions concerning the validity of the minimum standard under EU law in light of the principle of non-discrimination on grounds of disability, which were referred to the CJEU. In examining whether there was an objective justification for the resulting difference in treatment within the meaning of Article 21 of the Charter, the CJEU took into account the care that was taken by the EU legislature to include scientific and technical studies in the legislative process.[66] The CJEU noted that the EU legislature had previously amended the minimum level of visual acuity in the Regulation in response to a report that had been drawn up by an 'eyesight working group' that was established under the same Regulation. This group had concluded that the ability to drive a vehicle was of great fundamental social and economic importance and that there was no scientific data that could justify the choice for the earlier value of visual acuity. The CJEU held that 'it appears that the EU legislature amended that annex in the light of that knowledge and attempted to limit as much as possible any interference with the rights of persons suffering from visual defects'.[67] In this case, the CJEU was thus rather appreciative of the quality of the legislative process.

Thirdly, in *Test-Achats*, the CJEU was asked to examine the validity of a specific provision that was laid down in the EU Directive on equal treatment of men and women in the access to and supply of goods and

[64] *Ibid.*, paras. 80–81. [65] Case C-356/12, *Glatzel*, 22 May 2014. [66] *Ibid.*, paras. 59–62.
[67] *Ibid.*, para. 62.

services.[68] The specific provision allowed for a distinction to be made on the basis of gender in the assessment of an individual's premiums and benefits in insurance and other financial services based on relevant and accurate actuarial data without any temporal limitation. In examining the compatibility of this provision with the prohibition of discrimination on the grounds of gender and the equality between men and women as guaranteed by Articles 21 and 23 of the Charter, the CJEU reasoned that when the EU legislature decides to adopt measures, 'it must contribute, in a coherent manner to the achievement of the intended objective, without prejudice to the possibility of providing for transitional periods or derogations of limited scope'.[69] The CJEU then noted that the principle of equal treatment requires comparable situations not to be treated differently, and different situations not to be treated the same, unless an objective justification can be provided.[70] Based on the Directive, the situations of men and women with regard to insurance premiums and benefits contracted by them was to be treated alike. In the absence of any temporal limitation for member states, the CJEU concluded that there was a risk that differences in treatment would continue to exist indefinitely and would actually work against the achievement of the Directive's objective of equal treatment between men and women.[71]

Thus, in all three cases, the CJEU clearly expressed its concern about, or its appreciation of, the quality of the legislative process. As it formed part of its examination of the reasonableness of the interferences with the respective fundamental rights, these cases showed examples of procedural review. The effects of the use of these procedural arguments for the conclusions about the (in)validity of EU legislation, as well as the scope of a more substantive reasonableness review by the CJEU in these cases, will be further discussed in section 8.3.3.2 below.

Foreseeability and Accessibility of Legislation In the judgments in the cases of *Digital Rights Ireland, Schwarz, Sky Österreich* and *Schrems*, the CJEU has looked at whether procedural safeguards were provided for in specific legislative instruments of the EU that could avoid arbitrariness and enhance the transparency and predictability of the legislation. Such requirements can be considered to relate to the foreseeability and accessibility of legislation, which form procedural arguments that the ECtHR

[68] Case C-236/09, *Test-Achats*, 1 March 2011. [69] *Ibid.*, para. 21. [70] *Ibid.*, para. 28.
[71] *Ibid.*, paras. 30–32.

has also particularly used in its case law, as Gerards discussed in her chapter elsewhere in this volume.

The CJEU has especially drawn attention to the degree to which the said safeguards were provided for, in the case of *Digital Rights Ireland*.[72] In this case, the national court had referred questions about the validity of the Data Retention Directive in light of the right to the protection of privacy, and, more specifically, personal data as guaranteed under Articles 7 and 8 of the Charter. The Data Retention Directive required telephone communication service providers to store certain data of its users for at least six months and for a maximum of two years. This allowed national authorities to have access to such data in relation to crime investigation and prevention. In its judgment, the CJEU found that these measures clearly interfered with Articles 7 and 8 of the Charter.[73] In examining whether these fundamental rights were not restricted by the Directive any further than was strictly necessary, it held that 'EU legislation ... must lay down clear and precise rules governing the scope and application of the measure in question and imposing minimum safeguards so that the persons in question whose data have been retained have sufficient guarantees to effectively protect their personal data against the risk of abuse and against any unlawful access and use of that data'.[74] The CJEU noted *inter alia* that the Directive allowed data to be retained without any differentiation, limitation or exception for specific individuals, data or type of communication.[75] The Directive also did not establish any objective criteria which were to be complied with by the member states in so far as it allowed the use of the data by the competent authorities.

Later in the *Schrems* case, the CJEU referred to several of the principles which it had established in the *Digital Rights Ireland* case with regard to the availability of safeguards to prevent arbitrary interferences with the rights to privacy and the protection of personal data.[76] This case was about a challenge that had been brought regarding the transfer of personal data by companies established in Europe to companies in the United States, where such data could be stored. The legal basis for the transfer of

[72] Joined Cases C-293/12 and C-594/12, *Digital Rights Ireland*, 8 April 2014.

[73] *Ibid.*, paras. 32–37.

[74] *Ibid.*, para. 54. In this regard, the CJEU also specifically referred to similar safeguards which the ECtHR has established in its judgment in *S. and Marper*, see ECtHR, *S. and Marper* v. *the United Kingdom*, Application nos. 30562/04 and 30566/04, 4 December 2008, para. 102.

[75] *Digital Rights Ireland*, paras 54 ff.

[76] Case C-362/14, *Schrems*, 6 October 2015.

these data was provided by a decision taken by the European Commission, which established that the use of the safe harbour principles by companies in the United States would ensure an equivalent level of protection to allow the transfer of such data. In its judgment, the CJEU again explained that sufficient safeguards needed to be established in relation to the transfer of such data to the United States, as well as in relation to the use of such data by the intelligence services in that country.[77]

The cases of *Schwarz* and *Sky Österreich* also show the importance of safeguards or limitations that must be provided for by EU legislation when it allows for a restriction of certain fundamental rights. The case of *Schwarz* was concerned with an EU Regulation that required fingerprints to be taken and stored on passports of citizens of the EU member states.[78] The CJEU examined whether the interferences with the right to privacy was limited to what was necessary to achieve its aim, and again held that specific guarantees needed to be provided to prevent misuse and abuse in the processing of information.[79] The CJEU highlighted, as part of this examination, that the regulation specifically limited the use of personal data (i.e., the fingerprints) to verify the authenticity of the passport and the identification of the holder, and that the regulation obliged that the data must be kept in a highly secured storage medium in the passport of the person concerned.[80] In the *Sky Österreich* case, the CJEU also indicated that several limitations were to be found in the Audiovisual Media Directive to ensure that the interferences with several fundamental rights were restricted only in so far as was necessary (the freedom to conduct a business and the right to property).[81] This Directive required member states to ensure that broadcasters of short news reports would be allowed access to the signal of the broadcasters which held the exclusive broadcasting rights to events of high interest. The compensation that could be requested for such access to the signal needed to be limited to certain costs, which were in effect very marginal. In the examination made by the CJEU of the proportionality of this measure, the CJEU noted *inter alia* that in accordance with the Directive, access to the signal could only be granted for a limited type of programme.[82] Also, member states were required by the Directive to define the modalities and the conditions of

[77] *Ibid.*, paras. 91–94. [78] Case C-299/12, *Schwarz*, 17 October 2013.
[79] *Ibid.*, paras. 54–63. [80] *Ibid.*, paras. 56–57.
[81] Case C-283/11, *Sky Österreich*, 22 January 2013. [82] *Ibid.*, para. 62.

the obligation to provide extracts of the signal.[83] The CJEU concluded that '[b]y establishing requirements relating to the use of extracts from the signal, the European legislature had ensured that the extent of the interference with the freedom to conduct a business and the possible economic benefit which broadcasters may draw from making short news reports are confined within precise limits'.[84]

In all these four cases, it can be seen that the procedural argument of the accessibility and foreseeability of EU legislation form important arguments which are used by the CJEU in its assessment. It could therefore again be concluded that this forms part of a procedural strategy by the CJEU to decide about the interferences with the respective fundamental rights. At the same time, it may be argued that in the cases of *Digital Rights Ireland* and *Schrems*, the CJEU (also) aimed to contribute to the setting of (procedural) fundamental rights standards as such, which was greatly needed in the particular area that was under review (see further section 8.3.3.2).

Availability of Judicial Review The cases of *Digital Rights Ireland* and *Schrems*, which have been discussed in the previous section already, also contain another type of procedural argument, that is, the availability of judicial review. In *Digital Rights Ireland*, the CJEU noted that the access of the national authorities to the data retained was not made dependent on prior review that could be carried out by a court or an independent administrative body, which could ensure the limited use of such data for what was strictly necessary to attain the objective that was pursued.[85] Such limits were not to be found in the Directive itself, nor was a requirement to that effect imposed by the Directive on the member states.

In the proportionality assessment the CJEU undertook in the case of *Schrems*, there is even further emphasis to be found on the importance of the availability of judicial review. Here, the CJEU particularly noted that 'legislation permitting the public authorities to have access on a generalised basis to the content of electronic communications must be regarded as compromising the essence of the fundamental right to respect for private life, as guaranteed by Article 7 of the Charter'.[86] The CJEU continued by stating that 'legislation not providing for any possibility for an individual to pursue legal remedies in order to have

[83] *Ibid.*, paras. 61–65. [84] *Ibid.*, para. 61. [85] *Digital Rights Ireland*, para. 62.
[86] *Schrems*, para. 95.

access to personal data relating to him, or to obtain the rectification or erasure of such data, does not respect the essence of the fundamental right to effective judicial protection, as enshrined in Article 47 of the Charter'.[87]

Thus, in *Digital Rights Ireland*, as well as in *Schrems*, the CJEU made use of the argument of the availability of judicial review to determine the proportionality of the interferences that could be made on the basis of the Directive and the Decision respectively. This would ultimately allow for individuals to seek redress, and perhaps to have a certain individualised application of the rules established by EU legislation.

8.3.3.2 Effects of Procedural Arguments and Substantive Reasonableness Review

This section aims to take a further look at the role procedural arguments have played in reaching the conclusions on the validity of EU legislation in the cases discussed in the previous section. It will also discuss to what extent the CJEU has undertaken a substantive examination of fundamental rights protection. It appears that there are three choices which the CJEU may take in this regard. The CJEU firstly may base its conclusions on the (in)validity of legislation purely on the basis of procedural arguments. Secondly, it may draw its conclusions on the basis of substantive and procedural arguments combined. Thirdly, the CJEU may decide to undertake a full substantive review of the legislation in light of fundamental rights, and lay less emphasis on procedural arguments.

The cases of *Test-Achats* and *Glatzel* provide the clearest examples of judgments where procedural arguments formed the main basis for the CJEU to support its findings regarding the (in)validity of the EU legislation.[88] In *Test-Achats*, the CJEU expressed criticism on the quality of the EU legislative process and it did not really take up any further arguments to finally find the invalidity of the legislation.[89] This shows a negative procedural review, which means that the CJEU reaches a negative conclusion based on a clear procedural shortcoming.[90] In the *Glatzel* case, the CJEU reached the opposite decision, given the care that was taken by the EU legislature to include scientific data in its

[87] *Ibid.*, paras. 96–97.

[88] Cf. Gerards's Chapter 6 to the current volume: 'Procedural Review by the ECtHR: A Typology'.

[89] Cf. *Test-Achats*, paras. 27–32.

[90] Gerards distinguishes between negative and positive procedural review; see Gerards's Chapter 6 to the current volume: 'Procedural Review by the ECtHR: A Typology'.

decision-making process. This case thus shows what may be termed positive procedural review. In both of these cases, the CJEU did not further engage in any meaningful substantive assessment of the extent to which the restrictions of the fundamental rights that were at stake could be justified.[91] In the case of *Glatzel*, the CJEU was asked to examine the compliance of the legislation with Article 26 of the Charter on the integration of persons with disabilities. However, the CJEU in its judgment showed a quite deferential review of the compliance with this provision. Article 26 of the Charter was held to comprise a 'principle' within the meaning of Article 52(5) of the Charter and therefore has a more limited justiciability.[92]

Next, it can be seen that procedural arguments were of importance in the cases of *Volker und Markus Schecke, Digital Rights Ireland, Schrems* and *Schwarz*, but the CJEU was also willing to undertake a somewhat more substantive assessment of the fundamental rights which were restricted by the respective instruments of EU legislation. In the *Volker und Markus Schecke* case, the CJEU noted alternative measures which could be taken by the EU legislature that would interfere less with the right to privacy and the protection of personal data.[93] Such measures could, according to the CJEU, entail a limitation of the publication of data according to the period for which the beneficiaries of the subsidies received the aid or according to the frequency or the nature and the amount of the aid. The CJEU did not, however, fully rebalance the interests which the EU legislature should have taken into account.[94] In *Digital Rights Ireland*, the CJEU drew some negative inferences from the procedural defects in its examination of the respect for fundamental rights. A substantial portion of its judgment is indeed composed of spelling out the procedural requirements which must be complied with to ensure the foreseeability and accessibility of the legislation. In *Digital Rights Ireland*, the CJEU also did, to some extent, seem willing to undertake a stricter assessment of proportionality. The EU legislature failed to comply with some of the standards formulated by the CJEU to ensure the protection of the right to privacy and the protection of personal data, such as that the retention of data must be restricted to a clear time period and to a circle of persons involved in serious crimes.[95] The CJEU thereby gave some clear and substantive guidance towards the EU legislature, but

[91] Cf. *Glatzel*, paras. 41–86. [92] *Ibid.*, paras. 74–79.
[93] *Volker und Markus Schecke*, paras. 79–87. [94] *Ibid.*, paras. 65–89.
[95] Digital Rights Ireland, paras. 57–59.

it still allowed room for the EU legislature to make its own autonomous choices. The CJEU undertook a similar approach in the case of *Schrems*.[96] Here, the CJEU placed perhaps even more emphasis on the importance of the substantive assessment which the Commission should have made in relation to the protection of fundamental rights, and the CJEU specifically required the Commission to explain in its own decisions how it aimed to ensure compliance with fundamental rights. The CJEU indicated in its judgment that the contested Commission decision itself did not provide any clarity over the rules which exist in the United States to limit interferences with the rights to privacy and of personal data, and to provide effective legal protection against such interferences.[97] In this regard, the CJEU even pointed out the findings of the European Commission that are laid down in its impact assessment as to the lack of procedural safeguards that were provided by US law.[98] It finally explained that (in its next decision) the Commission must duly state its reasons when taking the decision about the adequacy of the protection of fundamental rights in a third country.[99] By doing so, the CJEU seemed to send a clear signal to the Commission that it must undertake a thorough assessment of its own.

In *Schwarz*, next to some procedural arguments, the CJEU also allowed room for a rather more substantive assessment of the proportionality of the restriction of the rights to privacy and protection of personal data. It held in respect of the use of iris scans that it regarded such a measure as being not as effective as the use of finger prints on the basis of the high costs of iris scans and the fact that the technology is not yet as advanced as that of finger prints.[100] Overall, however, the substantive reasoning of the CJEU in this judgment was very terse and limited to a few paragraphs, and it cannot be held that the CJEU fully substantively rebalanced all the interests which the EU legislature was required to take into account.

Lastly, in the case of *Sky Österreich*, despite paying considerable attention to the procedure, the CJEU also showed itself willing to undertake a fully substantive examination of the proportionality of the measure. In fact, the procedural arguments mentioned by the Court did not seem to constitute the main reason why it considered the particular Directive valid in light of EU law. Whether the procedural arguments thus had an effect on reaching a conclusion, and thus whether the case really presents an example of procedural review, is therefore unclear.

[96] *Schrems*, paras. 93 ff. [97] *Ibid.*, paras. 88–89. [98] *Ibid.*, para. 90.
[99] *Ibid.*, para. 96. [100] *Ibid.*, para. 52.

In the *Sky Österreich* case, the CJEU examined quite extensively whether the requirements of the proportionality test under Article 52(1) of the Charter had been satisfied by the EU legislature.[101] The CJEU carefully examined the alternative measures that could have been chosen by the EU legislature to interfere less with the freedom to conduct a business. It suggested that compensation could be provided to the broadcasters holding exclusive (and valuable) rights to broadcast events of high interest to the public, taking into account the costs they made to acquire such exclusive rights or the financial capacities of the broadcasters seeking access to the signal.[102] On the basis thereof, the CJEU finally concluded that such alternative measures would not achieve the objective of ensuring access of the general public to information as effectively as in the situation under the Directive, where a much more restricted amount of compensation would be imposed.[103]

8.4 Evaluating the Procedural Approach of the CJEU

The following two subsections further discuss what specific reasons the CJEU might have had in the cases that have been studied to opt for procedural review and it is explained what benefits and drawbacks are related to such an approach. Since the case law of the CJEU with respect to the decisions being taken at the national level clearly differs from the case law on the decisions being taken at EU level, the different aspects are discussed separately.

8.4.1 *Procedural Review* vis-à-vis *the National Authorities*

As has been explained in relation to the review of decisions that are taken at the national level, although the CJEU generally attaches much value in its case law to procedural standards, which especially national courts should comply with, most cases do not reveal how those procedures relate to the substantive assessments that need to be made of fundamental rights restrictions. In *Dynamic Medien*, the CJEU exceptionally did steer

[101] In most of the other cases, the CJEU pointed out the separate requirements which need to be taken into account in relation to interferences with fundamental rights under the proportionality test, which has been laid down in Article 52(1) of the Charter, see *Volker und Markus Schecke*, para. 65; *Sky Österreich*, para. 47; *Schwarz*, para. 34; *Glatzel*, para. 42; and *Digital Rights Ireland*, para. 38. No reference was made to this provision, however, in the case of *Test-Achats*.

[102] *Sky Österreich*, paras. 30–68. [103] *Ibid.*, para. 55.

the national court into adopting a procedural approach, however, and refrained from imposing a very clear view on the substantive assessment which the national court could make. From a subsidiary perspective towards the national authorities, the CJEU may rather decide to let the national court check whether fundamental rights are substantively complied with. In comparison to the CJEU, national courts could be considered better placed than the CJEU, as well as more experienced or specialised, to deal with (certain) fundamental rights. By adding a procedural flavour to its approach, the CJEU could encourage the establishment of a sound decision-making process at the national level to prevent arbitrary decisions being taken on the basis of EU law, as well as help secure that fundamental rights are taken into account in the decision-making procedures at the national level.

That said, national courts may still want the CJEU to provide for further clarification of the reasonableness of the decisions taken at the national level, and may send some detailed questions concerning the justification of certain national policies or decisions in light of EU law.[104] Evidently, the CJEU may also want to undertake a more substantive assessment of decisions taken by the national authorities on the basis of EU law if particular interests of EU law are at stake or if the uniformity and effectiveness of EU law must be secured.[105] It would therefore not necessarily be expected that the CJEU would (entirely) substitute a substantive review by a procedural review.

The CJEU further needs to be careful not to meddle too much in the particular procedural standards that must be provided at national level. The extensive development of procedural standards by the CJEU has been considered problematic from the point of view of the member states' autonomous powers, and on that account does not seem to comply with the subsidiarity principle.[106] Also, the development of procedural requirements by the CJEU under the proportionality test has been criticised because the proportionality test itself does not include any

[104] Also, scholars such as *Kühling* encourage the CJEU generally to develop its own substantive doctrines regarding the restrictions of fundamental rights and the justifications thereof; see J. Kühling, 'Fundamental Rights', in A. von Bogdandy and J. Bast (eds.), *Principles of European Constitutional Law* (Oxford: Hart Publishing, 2009), pp. 502 ff.

[105] See Case C-399/11, *Melloni*, 26 February 2013, para. 60. Recently the ECJ again held in *Opinion 2/13*, 18 December 2014, paras. 188–189 that 'the application of national standards of protection of fundamental rights must not compromise the level of protection provided for by the Charter or the primacy, unity and effectiveness of EU law.'

[106] Prechal and Widdershoven, 'Redefining the Relationship between 'Rewe-effectiveness' and Effective Judicial Protection', *supra* n. 1.

procedural requirements and therefore does not provide a very clear legal basis.[107] It could also be argued that the CJEU is not well-placed to determine which procedural requirements must be lived up to at the national level.[108] In the development of procedural requirements, the CJEU could consider making use of the requirements laid down in the Charter, as well as resorting to the procedural standards which have been developed in the case law of the ECtHR.[109] This could provide a way of further justifying its procedural approach.

The CJEU thus has many different interests and concerns to take into account when it comes to the review of decisions being taken at the national level. A procedural approach could provide an intermediate solution which helps the CJEU to avoid being criticised for applying too detailed guidance over the substantive reasonableness of the measures adopted by national authorities while still ensuring an effective protection of EU law at national level. The CJEU would have to look closely at the specific circumstances of a case, and the specific questions that have been asked by the national court, to decide about applying a more procedural or a more substantive assessment.

8.4.2 *Procedural Review* vis-à-vis *the EU Institutions*

Sections 8.3.2. and 8.3.3 have shown that the CJEU uses procedural arguments to review the acts of the EU institutions in light of fundamental rights in different cases. It has been shown that procedural arguments can provide very important reasons for the CJEU to reach conclusions about to the reasonableness of the (legislative) decisions taken by the EU institutions. Most judgments do not show a very elaborate examination by the CJEU as to the substantive compliance with fundamental rights standards. Only in the *Kadi* cases, the CJEU looked at the substantive grounds for placing an individual on a sanction list. In that context, the CJEU finds it of great importance that full, and

[107] Prechal, 'Topic One: National Applications of the Proportionality Principle – Free Movement and Procedural Requirements: Proportionality Reconsidered', *supra* n. 47, p. 214.

[108] Cf. P. Popelier, 'Preliminary Comments on the Role of Courts as Regulatory Watchdogs', (2012) 6 *Legisprudence*, pp. 261–262.

[109] See E. Brems, 'Procedural Protection: An Examination of Procedural Safeguards Read into Substantive Convention Rights', in E Brems and J.H. Gerards (eds), *Shaping Rights in the ECHR* (Cambridge: Cambridge University Press, 2013), pp. 137–161.

thus substantive, judicial review takes place to ensure effective judicial protection.[110]

Scholars have often argued, especially in the past, that the CJEU has not been willing to undertake an elaborate or full substantive assessment of EU legislation.[111] The CJEU itself does not provide for very structured or illuminating reasoning as to its approach and to its choice for the level of intensity of its (substantive) review.[112] The cases that have been studied in this chapter show that the CJEU generally aims to stay close to the choices that have already been made by the EU legislature. In the *Volker und Markus Schecke* case, for example, although the CJEU seemed to make its own substantive assessments here and there (e.g. concerning the question whether the publication of data on subsidies would contribute to achieving the objective of transparency), it preferred to rely, where it could, on the normative choices and clarifications which had already been laid down in the treaty provisions (e.g. to confirm the legitimacy of the objective of transparency).[113] It has been argued that the CJEU could have made a stricter assessment of the suitability of the retention of data as a method to combat crime, however.[114] Also, in *Test-Achats*, it can be seen that the CJEU reached its conclusion that men and women are in a comparable position with regard to insurance premiums and benefits primarily on the basis of the set-up and wording of the Directive.[115] The difference between men and women in the calculation of insurance premiums was construed in the Directive, as the CJEU explained, as an exception to the fundamental principle of gender equality. The CJEU did not further assess to what extent and based on which substantive considerations such an exception could be justified. It rather concluded that the Directive was invalid on the basis of the absence of a temporal limitation in relation to (potential) restrictions of the principle of unequal treatment.[116]

The focus of the CJEU on procedural arguments in its case law may be inspired by the same deferential position towards the EU institutions.

[110] See C-402/05, *Kadi and Al Barakaat International Foundation* v. *Council and Commission*, 3 September 2008, para. 326.

[111] Cf. G. de Búrca, 'The Principle of Proportionality and Its Application in EC Law', (1993) 13 *Yearbook of European Law*, p. 146.

[112] Gerards, 'Pluralism, Deference and the Margin of Appreciation Doctrine', *supra* n. 15, p. 101.

[113] *Volker und Markus Schecke*, paras. 71 and 83.

[114] *Digital Rights Ireland*, para. 49. Cf. O. Lynskey, 'The Data Retention Directive Is incompatible with the Rights to Privacy and Data Protection and Its Invalidity in Its Entirety: *Digital Rights Ireland*', (2014) 51 *Common Market Law Review*, pp. 1789–1811.

[115] *Test-Achats*, para. 30. [116] *Ibid.*, paras. 30–32.

In the case of *Test-Achats*, for example, the CJEU specifically mentioned that 'in the progressive achievement of that equality, it is the EU legislature which, in the light of the task conferred on the European Union by the second sub-paragraph of Article 3(3) TEU and Article 8 TFEU, determines when it will take action, having regard to the development of economic and social conditions within the European Union'.[117] Also in the case of *Glatzel*, which was concerned with the establishment of certain standards of visual acuity, the CJEU noted that the EU legislature had a wide margin of discretion and that its own analysis had to be limited to reviewing 'whether there has been a manifest error of assessment or a misuse of powers, or whether the legislature has manifestly exceeded the limits of its discretion'.[118] Thus, the CJEU clearly considered that the EU legislature was better placed to make assessments relating to economic, social or technical decisions. In the particular judgment in the case of *Glatzel*, the CJEU further made explicit that it had insufficient information about the specific circumstances of the case to be able to decide whether there was in fact a 'disability' within the meaning of Article 21(1) of the Charter.[119] This proves that the CJEU may not have felt sufficiently well-placed to be able to decide about the concrete circumstances of a case due to its supranational position.[120] For that reason, the CJEU may have been inspired to mainly focus on procedural arguments in its review.

The use of procedural arguments by the CJEU may, however, also depend on the evidence that is brought to the table by the parties to a case on certain shortcomings or rather the good quality of the decision-making process. Interestingly, for example, in the case of *Volker und Markus Schecke*, it seemed that the CJEU was able to find out that there had been shortcomings in the legislative process on the basis of the written and/or oral submissions by the responsible EU institutions.[121] The case of *Schrems* further shows that the CJEU also can take into account the impact assessments which are undertaken by the Commission in relation to its decisions.[122] If these reports accurately show the reasoning behind certain legislative decisions, the CJEU could

117 *Ibid.*, para. 20. 118 *Glatzel*, para. 52. 119 *Ibid.*, para. 47.

120 In the case of *Schwarz*, it can even be seen that the CJEU reasoned on the basis of assertions, which it regarded as 'common knowledge', rather than on fact-based information, see *Schwarz*, para. 52.

121 Cf. the account of the Advocate General on these hearings, Opinion of A-G Sharpston in *Volker und Markus Schecke*, Joined Cases C-92/09 and C-93/09, paras. 114–118.

122 *Schrems*, paras. 88–90.

decide to make use of such reports in its own substantive review. Conversely, it could point out certain weaknesses in the procedure that could appear from such reports, or that the reports have not sufficiently been taken into account in establishing the eventual legislation.

In any case, it seems quite worthwhile for the CJEU to check the procedural rationality of the decisions being made by the EU institutions in fundamental rights cases. Several judgments of the CJEU have brought to light that there can be (serious) shortcomings in the remedies that allow individuals to challenge their fundamental rights under EU law, which especially the *Kadi* cases have demonstrated. Further shortcomings have appeared in the safeguards that were provided in EU legislation to prevent arbitrariness of the actions of public authorities (the *Digital Rights Ireland* and *Schrems* case), and in the account taken by the EU legislature of the interests of fundamental rights in the lawmaking process (the *Volker und Markus Schecke* and *Test-Achats*).

Interestingly, the development of procedural safeguards in the case law of the CJEU can have effects beyond the legislative processes at the EU level. The judgment of the CJEU in the *Digital Rights Ireland* case leads the member states to bring their own laws in line with the procedural standards which the CJEU had formulated effectively to annul the legislation that member states had so far been required to implement. This could be of importance due to the concerns over the multilevel setting in which the EU norms are adopted and subsequently executed. The establishment of certain procedural (as well as substantive) standards of fundamental rights could also, however, have been of particular importance for the CJEU, because there is a certain need for uniform standards to secure the effective application of EU law in this particular area privacy law. From both perspectives, the example of *Digital Rights Ireland* shows that the CJEU can strengthen the development of procedural safeguards both in EU legislation and in legislation of the member states in relation to the protection of fundamental rights.

That said, while a procedural review would seem to provide an effective strategy for the CJEU to strike down EU legislation (such as in *Volker Markus and Schecke* and in *Test-Achats*), it could be valuable if the CJEU would also choose to further guide the EU institutions in their substantive review of the reasonableness of decisions. In many cases, the EU institutions, as well as the national authorities, still appear in need of guidance on how to deal with the fundamental rights that are to be protected under EU law. As compared to the case law of the ECtHR, the case law of the CJEU does not yet contain elaborate standards with regard to the protection of fundamental rights that are to be guaranteed under EU law. A proportionality test is laid down in Article 52(1) of the Charter, but the specific tailoring of this test depends on the specific fundamental right at issue and the specific context of the case at hand. It therefore would make sense for the CJEU to provide more concrete guidance on that provision, as well as on the provisions laying down substantive fundamental rights in the Charter, and make sure that fundamental rights are indeed sufficiently protected. Basing its case law solely on procedural review could therefore be ill-suited in these cases.

A substantive assessment of proportionality in cases such as *Sky Österreich* thus is to be welcomed. Article 16 of the Charter on the freedom to conduct a business, for example, is quite a novel fundamental right that is still in need of further clarification, which may perhaps explain, but certainly also justify, why the CJEU undertook an elaborate examination of proportionality in *Sky Österreich*. Such an extensive assessment of the proportionality of national measures might also set an example for the national courts on how to review the national measures in other cases in light of the EU standards of fundamental rights.

Lastly, it can be noted that the case law of the CJEU includes one 'bad' example of procedural review. In the case of *Glatzel*, the CJEU clearly paid attention to the quality of the legislative procedure. The CJEU's judgment revealed that the report which was relied upon by the EU legislature showed some very clear weaknesses.[123] The report neither provided any scientific evidence to back up the particular minimum standard for visual acuity that was chosen by the EU legislature, nor did it as such demonstrate that the interests of fundamental rights protection had actually been taken into account by the experts or by the EU legislature. Moreover, quite some time had elapsed since the report had been published (in the year 2005) and the adoption of the legislation.[124] These shortcomings did not provide very strong grounds for concluding that sufficient attention was paid by the EU legislature to securing the protection of Article 21(1) of the Charter. The arguments of the CJEU rather unveiled that relevant fundamental rights had not been

[123] See also for critical remarks on the CJEU's approach C. O'Brien, 'Driving Down Disability Equality?', (2014) 21 *Maastricht Journal of European and Comparative Law*, pp. 723–738.

[124] Moreover, the CJEU could also have considered whether there was a possibility for an individualised approach for those not fulfilling the exact minimum standards, as it had been shown that such an exceptional assessment could have been made for drivers falling within another category of visual impairments; see *Glatzel*, para. 80.

taken into account in the legislative process. It could have been expected that the CJEU would draw a negative inference about the quality of the legislative process, contrary to the positive conclusions which it did reach in this case.

8.5 Conclusion

This chapter has shown different ways in which the CJEU seems to have made use of procedural review in fundamental rights cases. The CJEU shows in its review of EU legislation that it attaches value to the quality of the legislative process, the accessibility and foreseeability of legislation and/or the availability of judicial review. The quality of the legislative process actually provides an important ground for the CJEU to reach conclusions on the reasonableness of the restrictions of fundamental rights under EU law. There can be good arguments for the CJEU to use procedural review in such cases. Especially in respect of the complex socio-economic or technical decisions which the EU legislature must make, the CJEU is expected to show some deference towards the EU legislature. Indeed, in practice, the CJEU seems inclined to use procedural arguments in order to provide meaningful assessment of the restrictions that are placed on fundamental rights.

In relation to decisions taken at the national level, there are much fewer occasions in which the use of procedural arguments by the CJEU can clearly be linked to a notion of procedural review. The CJEU has, however, developed strong standards of procedural protection which must be applied at the national level, especially by the national courts, so as to ensure the protection of fundamental rights in situations falling within the scope of EU law. The CJEU could decide to refrain from undertaking a detailed substantive assessment of restrictions of fundamental rights on its own, because the CJEU is placed too far away to be able to judge well over such decisions. The CJEU could then decide to further encourage the national courts in watching over the procedural rationality of decisions being taken at the national level. The procedural provisions of the Charter, as well as the case law of the CJEU on general principles of procedural fundamental rights, can provide a strong basis for imposing procedural standards which national authorities must comply with when acting within the scope of EU law.

At the same time, an examination on the merits by the CJEU in many cases is much-needed, because guidance from the CJEU is still required for the EU institutions, as well as the national institutions, with regard to dealing with the protection of fundamental rights laid down in the Charter. The Charter is a relatively new instrument. National courts may therefore still need substantive guidance on the interpretation of the rights contained in it, and the uniformity of EU law and the principle of effective protection of EU law could require the CJEU to give such guidance. Also in relation to the EU legislature, the CJEU can be expected to play an important role in checking whether fundamental rights have been sufficiently taken into account in the legislative choices which they make. Therefore, only in exceptional circumstances should the CJEU give decisive weight to the process of decision-making in fundamental rights cases.

If the CJEU were to make procedural review more central to its decision-making, it would generally have to make its choices somewhat more explicit, in order to prevent it of being accused of applying too much deference to the political institutions, which it has been criticised of in its relations with the EU institutions. Also, it is important that the CJEU draws the right conclusions when the legislative procedures appear to show some serious shortcomings in relation to the assessment that has been made by the EU legislature fully relevant fundamental rights.

9

Procedural Review in WTO Law

ISABELLE VAN DAMME

9.1 Introduction

This chapter examines the function of the principle of procedural fairness, and its specific expressions, in World Trade Organization (WTO) law and the case law of the WTO dispute settlement bodies, that is to say, panels and the Appellate Body. Many contributions in this volume concern practical and theoretical perspectives on the use by, in particular, the European Courts of the principle of procedural fairness and of process-based considerations in reviewing the reasonableness or proportionality of interferences with fundamental rights. Others focus on how, outside the context of such types of process-based review, procedural fairness considerations are taken into account in formulating and adopting legislation or in reviewing compliance with procedural treaty obligations under the European Convention on Human Rights (ECHR) or the European Union (EU) Treaties.

In examining the relevance and function of procedural fairness in WTO law, all of those perspectives are relevant. That is so because the WTO agreements themselves lay down detailed obligations as regards, *inter alia*, the preparation, adoption, publication, implementation, and the administrative and judicial review of WTO Members' legislation and other measures falling within the scope of those agreements. Those treaty obligations are the primary basis for procedural review by WTO

Isabelle van Damme is Référendaire, Chambers of Advocate General Sharpston, Court of Justice of the European Union; and Visiting Lecturer, Université Catholique de Louvain. This chapter is written in the author's personal capacity. The author is grateful to all participants in a seminar (Ghent, 21 and 22 May 2015) organised by the editors of this volume for their useful comments.

Members themselves, by the WTO as an international organisation in relation to its Members and by the dispute settlement system in resolving disputes between WTO Members. Thus, treaty obligations are the foremost guarantee for the quality of WTO Members' legislation, decision-making and administration. That feature of WTO law may suggest that the WTO can serve as a model for developing primary and secondary norms in other treaty-based legal orders studied in this volume. In addition, in interpreting other types of obligation, some form of procedural or process-based review is visible in the reports of panels and the Appellate Body. That occurs in relation to obligations that are not primarily aimed at protecting procedural fairness values (in particular in the context of so-called exception clauses), though the distinction between the character of each type of obligation is ultimately a matter of interpretation. This process-based review is related more closely to the main thrust of most chapters in this volume, despite the fact that any comparison with similar types of review under EU law and the ECHR is necessarily incomplete. However, due to the fact that the WTO agreements lay down a core set of procedural obligations and that, in principle, WTO law does not as such grant directly rights to individuals,[1] there might be fewer instances in which it would be appropriate for WTO panels and the Appellate Body to adopt a similar process-based review as that which appears to be so clearly visible in the case law of, in particular, the European Court of Human Rights (ECtHR; and as attested by many contributions in this volume). At the same time, where such type of review is applied, the reliance on the treaty obligations reflecting the principle of procedural fairness results in an interaction between process-based review in the context of justifications of otherwise WTO-inconsistent measures and those treaty obligations.

In the WTO, process-based review and review of compliance with procedural treaty obligations may occur in different fora. On the one hand, review of individual WTO Members' trade policies and practices takes place in the context of the trade policy review mechanism and, depending on the content and objectives of those policies and practices, in specific committees or working parties and various councils monitoring compliance with specific agreements.[2] On the other hand, review may

[1] See for example Panel Report, *United States – Sections 301–310 of the Trade Act of 1974*, WT/DS152/R, adopted 27 January 2000, DSR 2000:II, 815, para. 7.72.

[2] See, for example, review of customs unions and free trade areas pursuant to paragraph 7 of the Understanding on the Interpretation of Article XXIV of the General Agreement on Tariffs and Trade 1994 ('GATT 1994'); consultations and the periodic review of all

result from the initiation of dispute settlement procedures pursuant to the Understanding on Rules and Procedures Governing the Settlement of Disputes ('DSU'). Only WTO Members have standing in this type of proceeding and no requirement of exhaustion of remedies applies. Review may pertain to either an 'as such' challenge of a measure or the challenge of a measure 'as applied'.[3] An 'as such' claim challenges laws, regulations or other instruments that have general and prospective application, and are directed against a Member's conduct not only in a particular instance, but as well in future situations and which is allegedly necessarily inconsistent with that Member's WTO obligations.[4] By contrast, an 'as applied' claim presupposes that there has been an assessment of an individual case.

The thesis developed in this chapter is that WTO law relevant to the protection of procedural fairness, when studied in isolation, is detailed, fragmented and incomplete. However, reading and applying those treaty provisions against the background of a growing body of case law of WTO panels and the Appellate Body[5] show the importance of the WTO procedural fairness obligations in the day-to-day practice of trade and their transformative effect on national laws, the administration of those laws and more broadly the rule of law in, especially, newly acceded WTO

restrictions applied for balance of payment purposes by the Balance-of-Payments ('BoP') committee pursuant to paragraph 7 of the Understanding on Balance-of-Payments Provisions of the General Agreement on Tariffs and Trade 1994 ('BoP Understanding'); review of agricultural measures pursuant to Article 18 of the Agreement on Agriculture; review of technical barriers to trade ('TBT') measures pursuant to Articles 15.2 to 15.4 of the Agreement on Technical Barriers to Trade ('TBT Agreement'); consultations, negotiations, monitoring and review in the Sanitary and Phytosanitary ('SPS') Committee pursuant to Article 12 of the Agreement on the Application of Sanitary and Phytosanitary Measures ('SPS Agreement'); Article 23 of the Agreement on Implementation of Article VII of the General Agreement on Tariffs and Trade 1994 ('Customs Valuation Agreement'); Article 6 of the Agreement on Rules of Origin; Article 32.7 of the Agreement on Subsidies and Countervailing Measures ('SCM Agreement'); Article 13 of the Agreement on Safeguards.

[3] See further N. Lockhart and E. Shearhold, 'In Search of Relevant Discretion: The Role of the Mandatory/Discretionary Distinction in WTO Law' *Journal of International Economic Law*, 13(2) (2011) p. 379.

[4] See for example Appellate Body Report, *United States – Sunset Reviews of Anti-Dumping Measures on Oil Country Tubular Goods from Argentina* ('*US – Oil Country Tubular Goods Sunset Reviews*'), WT/DS268/AB/R, adopted 17 December 2004, DSR 2004:VII, 3257, para. 172.

[5] On that growing body of case law, see for example P. Ala'i, 'From the Periphery to the Center? The Evolving WTO Jurisprudence on Transparency and Good Governance', *Journal of International Economic Law*, 11(4) (2008), p. 779 (showing that, despite being considered as subsidiary, Article X of the GATT 1994 now forms part of a good governance mandate).

Members (China being the most visible example thereof[6]). At the same time, when studied in a broader perspective, it appears that WTO law may be a useful (and even progressive) model for developing in other parts of international law primary treaty obligations reflecting different dimensions of the principle of procedural fairness, studying how such treaty obligations may affect process-based review under exceptions clauses and evaluating the significance of using treaty obligations as compared to judicial techniques.

In order to develop this thesis in a manner that provides a useful basis for comparison with the application of standards of procedural fairness by, in particular, the ECHR, this chapter focuses on expressions of procedural fairness in WTO treaty provisions disciplining the use of trade instruments by WTO Members and affecting more directly the application and administration of trade instruments in relation to individual traders. It explores core applications and features of the function of the principle of procedural fairness in WTO law, rather than to offer an exhaustive study of each and every obligation in each of the WTO agreements expressing that principle. Before doing so, this chapter first addresses a few preliminary matters forming an essential background for understanding the relevance and function of the principle of procedural fairness in WTO law. These matters concern typology, terminology and the structure and content of the WTO agreements and other normatively relevant instruments.

9.2 Typology, Terminology and Sources of WTO Law

The vocabulary used in WTO law to articulate the principle of procedural fairness is rich and somewhat undisciplined. Common terms found in both the WTO agreements and the case law include: due process, non-arbitrary, reasonable, transparent, foreseeable, in good faith, equitable, impartial, uniform, equal, neutral, fair and proportionate. However, the term 'procedural fairness' itself does not appear in the text of any WTO agreement (though it was mentioned in the 2001 Doha Declaration, in

[6] See for example C.-H. Wu, 'How Does TRIPS Transform Chinese Administrative Law?; *Global Jurist*, 8(1) (2013): Article 6; G. Wang, 'Radiating Impact of WTO on Its Members' Legal System: The Chinese Perspective (Volume 349)' *Collected Courses of the Hague Academy of International Law*, The Hague Academy of International Law, Brill Online, 2015 (www.referenceworks.brillonline.com/entries/the-hague-academy-collected-courses/radiating-impact-of-wto-on-its-members-legal-system-the-chinese-perspective-volume-349-ej.9789004185180.277_536).

the context of future work on the relation between trade and competition policy).[7] The WTO secretariat's explanation is that relevant provisions in the WTO agreements 'have been negotiated in order to respond to the specific needs of individual agreements and subject-matters, rather than as part of any common overall design or pattern'.[8]

Many WTO treaty obligations expressing the principle of procedural fairness relate to the protection of the rights of parties facing adverse decisions, the right of access to review, the right to information (mostly through publication and notification, including during the adoption of an instrument or decision), the rights of defence, the right to proper administration and the right to protection of confidential information. Many of these treaty-based rights (and corresponding obligations) are relative and need to be balanced and weighed against competing legitimate concerns, which may include other expressions of procedural fairness.[9]

The function and application of procedural fairness in WTO law and case law must be understood against the background of the evolving landscape of the sources of WTO law, meaning here the sources of law constituting the applicable law in resolving disputes arising between WTO Members and forming the basis for a claim upon which the WTO dispute settlement bodies are competent to hear and decide.

WTO law is primarily treaty law. The WTO 'treaties' consist of the Marrakesh Agreement Establishing the World Trade Organization (or 'WTO Agreement') and 'agreements and associated legal instruments' attached in the form of four annexes to the WTO Agreement. All of those agreements and certain other legal instruments are considered to be an integral part of the WTO Agreement and binding on all WTO Members

[7] WTO Doha Ministerial Declaration, adopted on 14 November 2001, WT/MIN(01)/DEC/1, para. 25. In the context of that work programme, the Secretariat has produced studies on procedural fairness, including: WTO, Working Group on the Interaction between Trade and Competition Policy, *Core Principles, Including Transparency, Non-Discrimination and Procedural Fairness–Background Note by the Secretariat*, WT/WGTCP/W/209 (19 September 2002); WTO, Working Group on the Interaction between Trade and Competition Policy, *Provisions on Procedural Fairness in Existing WTO Agreements–Background Note by the Secretariat*, WT/WGTCP/W/231 (22 May 2003).

[8] *Provisions on Procedural Fairness in Existing WTO Agreements – Background Note by the Secretariat*, cited at note 7 above, para. 5.

[9] See also A. Mitchell, 'Fair Crack of the Whip: Examining Procedural Fairness in WTO Disputes Using an Australian Administrative Law Framework' in WTO Trade Law Branch, DFAT (eds), *Ten Years of WTO Dispute Settlement: Australian Perspectives* (Canberra: DFAT, 2006), p. 45.

(with the exception of Annex 4, discussed below).[10] In principle, WTO membership is conditional upon acceptance to be bound by all of those treaties and other instruments. Annexes 2 and 3 contain, respectively, the DSU and the Trade Policy Review Mechanism. Annex 1, by contrast, is further divided into three parts dealing with trade in goods (the GATT 1994), trade in services (the General Agreement on Trade in Services, or the GATS) and trade-related aspects of intellectual property rights (the Agreement on Trade-Related Aspects of Intellectual Property Rights, or the TRIPs Agreement). The first part of the first annex (so-called Annex 1a agreements), containing multilateral agreements on trade in goods further consists of a set of separate treaties, such as the TBT Agreement, the SPS Agreement and the Agreement on Implementation of Article VI of the General Agreement on Tariffs and Trade 1994 (Anti-Dumping Agreement). In addition, some of those agreements need to be read together with, for example, the schedules of concessions and commitments (for each WTO Member) attached to them, protocols and certifications relating to tariff concessions, annexes containing notes and supplementary provisions, decisions on waivers, GATT decisions forming part of the WTO agreements,[11] so-called 'Understandings', etc. For new Members, accession protocols and working party reports typically lay down obligations that apply together with and in addition to those obligations in the other agreements which apply to all WTO Members. A fourth annex contains agreements and associated legal instruments that are 'part' of the WTO Agreement, but only for those WTO Members that have accepted them (the so-called plurilateral agreements).[12] Many of those treaty provisions include obligations reflecting procedural fairness.

Despite difficulties in concluding the Doha Development Round (which is intended to result in a series of amendments and additional obligations), progress has been achieved in some areas, notably in the area of trade facilitation. In December 2013, WTO Members concluded negotiations on the Agreement on Trade Facilitation, which is intended

[10] Article II:2 of the WTO Agreement.

[11] For example, the Enabling Clause or Decision of 28 November 1979 on Differential and More Favourable Treatment, Reciprocity and Fuller Participation of Developing Countries (L/4903). That GATT decision is part of the GATT 1994 on the basis of paragraph 1(b)(iv) of Annex 1A of the WTO Agreement. See also Appellate Body Report, *European Communities – Conditions for the Granting of Tariff Preferences to Developing Countries* ('*EC–Tariff Preferences*'), WT/DS246/AB/R, adopted 20 April 2004, DSR 2004:III, 925, para. 90, footnote 192.

[12] Article II:3 of the WTO Agreement.

to be inserted in Annex 1a of the WTO Agreement.[13] In this agreement, WTO Members agreed on a series of detail (mostly procedural) obligations in order to improve, in particular, the movement, release and clearance of goods and thus to clarify and improve aspects of Articles V, VIII and X of the GATT 1994. Such obligations relate to, for example, publication (in a non-discriminatory and easily accessible manner) of procedures for importation, exportation and transit; required forms and documents, laws, regulations and administrative rulings of general application relating to rules of origin; procedures for appeal or review; the making available (and the need to update in so far as possible and appropriate) of a description of procedures for importation and exportation and transit and information about enquiry points to answer reasonable enquiries of governments, traders and other interested parties; notification; providing opportunities to traders and other interested parties to comment on the proposed introduction or amendment of relevant laws and regulations of general application.

With respect to measures falling within the scope of the GATT 1994 (measures on trade in goods), the key generally applicable disciplines on procedural fairness are set out in Article X of the GATT 1994. Other similarly broad standards can be found in, for example, Articles III and VI of the GATS and Articles 41.2–4 and 63 of the TRIPs Agreement. Whilst this chapter focuses on core disciplines in the GATT 1994, many Annex 1a agreements, as well as the GATS and the TRIPs Agreement (which, unlike the text of the GATT 1994, lay down new obligations as compared to the older GATT 1947 obligations), often contain more detailed provisions on transparency, participation, administration and review applicable to measures falling within their respective scope. Those obligations in agreements resulting from the Uruguay Round negotiations reflect Members' recognition of the increased relevance of the need to regulate processes and require procedural fairness. For example, the SPS Agreement sets out elaborate rules for developing, adopting and enforcing a certain category of measures of which the objective corresponds with that laid down in Article XX(b) of the GATT 1994 ('sanitary or phytosanitary measures' or 'SPS measures'), that is, measures 'necessary for the protection of human, animal or plant life or health'. Those rules relate mostly to process and procedural fairness. Panels and the Appellate Body have also injected, through interpretation,

[13] WTO, Preparatory Committee on Trade Facilitation, Agreement on Trade Facilitation (WTO/L/931).

forms of process-based review in the standards which the SPS Agreement articulates. As a result, that agreement appears somewhere at the intersection of the two perspectives from which this chapter studies the function of procedural fairness in WTO law.

The general principle governing the relationship between the GATT 1994 and the more specific agreements annexed to it is that, in the event of a conflict between provisions of those agreements, the provision of the latter shall prevail.[14] Some Annex 1a agreements also specify the relationship between them (such as the relationship of mutual exclusivity between the TBT Agreement and the SPS Agreement[15]). In any event, the content of the obligations under the GATT 1994 and the Annex 1a agreements may overlap and the latter may simply confirm or further develop the obligations under the GATT 1994. As a result, as regards certain obligations, cross-fertilisation of the case law regarding one agreement in the context of a dispute regarding another agreement is visible.

Whilst it might be true that the jurisdiction of panels and the Appellate Body is limited to the WTO agreements, the scope of the law which they may apply, in resolving disputes, is less clear.[16] Case law has none the less shown that effective resolution of WTO disputes can impossibly depend only on the WTO agreements which are like most, if not all, treaty texts incomplete. Procedural silences and some substantive silences have been addressed by relying on general principles of law and, assuming such a distinction exists, general principles of international law. Moreover, panels and especially the Appellate Body have used also rules of customary international law and general principles of (international) law in interpreting the WTO agreements.

The WTO Agreement does not explicitly provide for general powers of various WTO committees and other bodies to adopt binding decisions having legal authority similar to one or another form of EU secondary law. At the same time, many of those committees and bodies increasingly produce different forms of instruments which are undoubtedly of some normative relevance and cannot easily be ignored in subsequent interpretations and applications of the WTO agreements to which they

[14] GATT 1994, General Interpretative Note to Annex 1A.

[15] See Article 1.5 of the TBT Agreement and Article 1.4 of the SPS Agreement.

[16] See for example I. Van Damme, 'The Function of Interpretation in the WTO', *European Journal of International Law*, 21(3) (2010), p. 605; I. Van Damme, 'Interpretation, Jurisdiction, and Applicable Law' in D. Bethlehem, D. McRae, R. Neufeld, and I. Van Damme (eds), *The Oxford Handbook of International Trade Law* (Oxford University Press, 2009), at p. 298 (and the debates about this question described therein).

relate.[17] Moreover, some of those instruments are aimed at increasing participation and transparency in developing and understanding WTO law. This evolution is visible also in the case law. For example, the Appellate Body in *US – Tuna II (Mexico)* accepted that a TBT Committee Decision on Principles for the Development of International Standards, Guides and Recommendation[18] was a subsequent agreement between the parties regarding the interpretation of the TBT Agreement. Therefore, it could, based on Article 31(3)(a) of the Vienna Convention on the Law of Treaties (concerning subsequent agreements),[19] be used to interpret Article 2.4 of that agreement.[20] That committee decision was in fact prepared so as to increase the legitimacy, accountability and fairness in deferring, under the TBT Agreement, to standards developed by other international bodies. It thus had a procedural fairness objective. Other normative activity in WTO committees sometimes pursues a similar objective.

Against that background, this chapter now discusses WTO treaty obligations reflecting the principle of procedural fairness before turning to process-based review in the context of the substantive disciplines governing the justification (under Article XX of the GATT 1994) of an otherwise GATT 1994-inconsistent measure.

9.3 Compliance with WTO Obligations Aimed at Ensuring Procedural Fairness

9.3.1 *Introduction*

Obligations aimed at ensuring procedural fairness are included in the WTO agreements because of WTO Members' concern about the need to reduce or

[17] See for example A. Lang and J. Scott, 'The Hidden World of WTO Governance', *European Journal of International Law*, 20(3) (2009), p. 575.

[18] Decision of the Committee on Principles for the Development of International Standards, Guides and Recommendations with relation to Articles 2, 5 and Annex 3 of the Agreement, in WTO document G/TBT/1/Rev.9, Decisions and Recommendations adopted by the WTO Committee on Technical Barriers to Trade since 1 January 1995, 8 September 2008, pp. 37–39; and WTO document G/TBT/1/Rev.10, 9 June 2011, pp. 46–48. A more recent version dates from 21 January 2015: G.TBT/1/Rev.12.

[19] United Nations Treaty Series, Vol. 1155, p. 331 ('the VCLT').

[20] Appellate Body Report, *United States – Measures Concerning the Importation, Marketing and Sale of Tuna and Tuna Products* ('*US – Tuna II*'), WT/DS381/AB/R, adopted 13 June 2012, paras. 371 to 379. Article 2.4 lays down the obligation, subject to some conditions, for Members, where technical regulations are required and relevant international standards exist or their completion is imminent, to use them, or the relevant parts of them, as a basis for their technical regulations.

avoid obstacles to trade. That concern has also led to finding an agreement on new WTO disciplines whereas such agreement has not been possible in other areas.[21] WTO law in essence regulates WTO Members' use of trade instruments in the exercise of their inherent right to regulate. Some of those instruments are outright prohibited (though their use may be justified based on legitimate objectives), while others are permissible subject to certain conditions (of which the most important is probably the non-discrimination principle and its different emanations in the form of the national treatment principle and the most favoured nation principle). However, the lack of transparency, fairness and legal certainty can in itself constitute an obstacle to trade. The WTO agreements therefore contain a broad set of disciplines aimed at guaranteeing protection against such obstacles. Depending on the type of measure and thus applicable WTO agreement, those disciplines may apply to the entire lifespan of such a measure: their preparation, adoption, entry into force, publication, implementation, notification, administration and (administrative and judicial) review.

It is not the purpose of the analysis here to be exhaustive of the different contexts in which the WTO agreements seek to guarantee procedural fairness. Rather, this chapter seeks to sketch the broad landscape of such obligations. The core obligations as regards trade in goods are laid down in Article X of the GATT 1994.[22] Other agreements set out similar or more detailed obligations. The relevant disciplines in the GATT 1994 apply mostly to generally applicable measures governing trade in goods, whereas the specific agreements set forth disciplines that more often apply also to individual measures, such as anti-dumping measures and the processes of their adoption and review. Those obligations have been described as constituting 'what is probably the most highly developed and profoundly transformative administrative law programme of any global regime'.[23]

9.3.2 Transparency

Market access presupposes access to information. The WTO agreements ensure that WTO Members, traders and other interested parties are

[21] See the example of the Trade Facilitation Agreement (discussed at p. 214).

[22] See on the history of that provision P. Ala'i, 'From the Periphery to the Center? The Evolving WTO Jurisprudence on Transparency and Good Governance', cited at note 5 above, at p. 779.

[23] R.B. Stewart and M. Ratton Sanchez Badin, 'The World Trade Organization and Global Administrative Law', *New York University School of Law Public Law & Legal Theory Research Paper Series* Working Paper No. 09-71 (December 2009), at p. 13.

informed of measures that (might) concern them. Most typically, this is to be done through prompt publication of national measures that are to come into force and through notification to relevant WTO bodies of the introduction, application, maintenance of and changes to measures (on an *ad hoc* basis[24] and in consolidated form[25]). However, with respect to some types of measure, Members must also provide information upon request. That is the case for (proposals for) measures falling within the scope of the TBT and SPS Agreements, which both provide for enquiry as another means to achieve transparency. Moreover, apart from provisions applicable to specific types of measure, a separate agreement (contained in Annex 3 to the WTO Agreement and thus not annexed to the GATT 1994) has as its main objective achieving greater transparency in (the understanding of) the trade policies and practices of? WTO Members. The Trade Policy Review Mechanism provides for periodic review of such policies and practices and requires each Member to report regularly to the Trade Policy Review Body ('TPRB') (and the reported information should, to the greatest extent possible, be coordinated with information that is to be notified pursuant to other WTO agreements). Following the review, the reports filed and those prepared by the Secretariat, as well as the minutes of the TPRB meetings, are to be published promptly. In paragraph D of that agreement, WTO Members also confirm the inherent value of domestic transparency of government decision-making on trade policy matters for both Members' economies and the multilateral trading system. They further commit to encourage and promote greater transparency within their own systems.

In all these circumstances, the purpose of those obligations is to enable, depending on the provision at issue, other Members and/or individual (domestic and foreign) traders to become acquainted with (soon to be) applicable measures falling within the scope of the WTO agreements.[26]

Article X:1 of the GATT 1994 requires publication of a very wide set of measures falling within the scope of different other provisions of the

[24] See Articles 5(7), 12.1(b) and 18.1 and 2 Agreement on Agriculture; Article 7 of the SPS Agreement; Articles 2.1 and 2.15, 3, 6.1, 7.2 Agreement on Textiles and Clothing.

[25] See for example paragraph 9 of the BoP Understanding.

[26] As regards Article X:1, see for example Panel Reports, *European Communities and its member States – Tariff Treatment of Certain Information Technology Products* ('*EC – IT Products*'), WT/DS375/R/WT/DS376/R/WT/DS377/R, adopted 21 September 2010, DSR 2010:III, DSR 2010:IV, 1567, para. 7.1015; Panel Report, *Thailand – Customs and Fiscal Measures on Cigarettes from the Philippines* ('*Thailand – Cigarettes (Philippines)*'), WT/DS371/R, adopted 15 July 2011, as modified by Appellate Body Report WT/DS371/AB/R, para. 7.787.

GATT 1994 (relevant to the substantive content of such measures).[27] However, no WTO Member can be required 'to disclose confidential information which would impede law enforcement or otherwise be contrary to the public interest or would prejudice the legitimate commercial interests of particular enterprises, public or private'. Article X:2 of the GATT 1994 prevents Members from enforcing certain measures of general application before their official publication. Other WTO obligations may require forms of publication of either more specific measures[28] or more broadly described conduct[29] and be laid down in greater detail[30] or confirm the obligations set out in Article X.[31]

Initially, the draft proposal for Article X:1 provided for both publication and a form of notification to what was to become (but was never established as) the International Trade Organization (ITO).[32] That distinction was not maintained in the final version of the provision. Instead, specific provisions of Annex 1a agreements provide for notification and a separate agreement, which applies together with the GATT 1994 and the annexes, provides for (periodic) notification mechanisms.

Whilst Article X:1 has been invoked more often than Article X:2,[33] some of the case law involving both provisions is relevant to

[27] Namely '[l]aws, regulations, judicial decisions and administrative rulings of general application, made effective by any contracting party, pertaining to the classification or the valuation of products for customs purposes, or to rates of duty, taxes or other charges, or to requirements, restrictions or prohibitions on imports or exports or on the transfer of payments therefor, or affecting their sale, distribution, transportation, insurance, warehousing inspection, exhibition, processing, mixing or other use'.

[28] See, for example, paragraph 1 of the BoP Understanding (committing Members to public announcement, as soon as possible, of time schedules to remove restrictive import measures taken for BoP purposes); prompt publication of all SPS regulations (that is to say SPS measures such as laws, decrees or ordinances that apply generally) pursuant to paragraph 1 and 2 of Annex B to the SPS Agreement; prompt publication of technical regulations pursuant to Article 2.11 of the TBT Agreement.

[29] See for example Article 2.5 of the Agreement on Preshipment Inspection (on the need to ensure that preshipment inspection activities are conducted in a transparent manner).

[30] For example, compare Article X:2 of the GATT 1994 with paragraph 2 of Annex B to the SPS Agreement requiring that, except for urgent circumstances, Members allow for a reasonable interval between the publication of an SPS regulation and its entry into force (see similarly Article 2.12 TBT Agreement).

[31] See for example Article 6.1 of the TRIMS Agreement; Article 12 of the Customs Valuation Agreement; Article 3.2 of the Agreement on Preshipment Inspection; Article 2(g) of the Agreement on Rules of Origin; Article 3.1 of the Agreement on Safeguards.

[32] See EPCT/C.II/W.41, EPCT/C.II/54/Rev.1, p. 29.

[33] For recent case law on Article X:2, see Appellate Body Report, *United States – Countervailing and Anti-Dumping Measures on Certain Products from China* ('*US – Countervailing and Anti-Dumping Measures (China)*'), WT/DS449/AB/R, adopted 22 July 2014.

understanding the scope of each. Thus, it is equally relevant to Article X:1 that the Appellate Body has explained that Article X:2 embodies the fundamental principle of transparency according to which full disclosure of governmental acts affecting Members and private persons and enterprises is to be promoted. The Appellate Body in essence recognised that, as a result of transparency, affected parties are to be given a reasonable opportunity to acquire authentic information about measures and accordingly to protect and adjust their activities or alternatively seek modification of such measures.[34]

Article X:1 applies to both border and internal measures.[35] In *EC – IT Products*, the panel found that the ordinary meaning of the measures covered by Article X:I 'range[s] from imperative rules of conduct to the exercise of influence or an authoritative pronouncement by certain authoritative bodies'.[36] According to that panel, the scope of Article X:1 extends to 'instruments with a degree of authoritativeness issued by certain legislative, administrative or judicial bodies', but is not limited to instruments which are binding under domestic law.[37] Consistent therewith, the panel in *Thailand – Cigarettes (Philippines)* accepted that a methodology for calculating maximum retail sales prices for imported and domestic cigarettes which applied prospectively and generally to all potential sales of cigarettes (and was set out only in the course of the panel proceedings) fell within the scope of Article X:1.[38] In an unappealed finding, the panel in *Dominican Republic – Import and Sale of Cigarettes* held that the establishment of a tax base is an administrative ruling of general application.[39] That panel also defined laws and regulations as 'general acts with a legal content issued by state authorities invested with normative powers' and judicial decisions as

[34] Appellate Body Report, *United States – Restrictions on Imports of Cotton and Man-Made Fibre Underwear* ('*US – Underwear*'), WT/DS24/AB/R, adopted 25 February 1997, DSR 1997:I, 11, p. 21. On Article X:2, see also Appellate Body Report, *US – Countervailing and Anti-Dumping Measures (China)*, paras. 4.53 to 4.94.

[35] Appellate Body Report, *European Communities – Regime for the Importation, Sale and Distribution of Bananas* ('*EC – Bananas*'), WT/DS27/AB/R, adopted 25 September 1997, DSR 1997:II, 591, para. 70.

[36] Panel Reports, *EC – IT Products*, para. 7.1027.

[37] Panel Reports, *EC – IT Products*, para. 7.1027.

[38] Panel Report, *Thailand – Cigarettes (Philippines)*, para. 7.779.

[39] Panel Report, *Dominican Republic – Measures Affecting the Importation and Internal Sale of Cigarettes* ('*Dominican Republic – Import and Sale of Cigarettes*'), WT/DS302/R, adopted 19 May 2005, as modified by Appellate Body Report WT/DS302/AB/R, DSR 2005:XV, 7425, para. 7.406.

'pronouncements with the force of *res judicata* issued by judicial authorities as a result of a legal process'.[40]

Article X:1 thus guarantees transparency with regard to a wide category of measures, provided these are measures of general application and thus affect an unidentified number of economic operators, including domestic and foreign producers.[41] As a result, they concern only instruments that apply to a range of situations or cases.[42] The scope of the obligation under Article X:2 depends on traders' expectations about the applicable measure; they must 'have a reasonable opportunity to acquire authentic information about . . . measures and accordingly to protect and adjust their activities or alternatively to seek modification of such measures'.[43] Unlike Article X:3, Article X:2 does not refer to the same category of measures as Article X:1. In fact, the obligation thereunder applies as regards any measure. It thus refers to a broader category of measures as compared to Article X:1.[44]

Article X:1 is limited in another manner. It does not apply to business decisions of individual traders or companies, or individual transactions.[45] That was the position of the Panel in *Thailand – Cigarettes (Philippines)* as regards the ex-factory price which was deemed to result from internal decision-making on a firm-by-firm basis.[46] Thus, despite

[40] Panel Report, *Dominican Republic – Import and Sale of Cigarettes*, para. 7.404.

[41] Appellate Body Report, *US – Underwear*, p. 21. One panel has interpreted this definition to mean that Article X:1 applies also to administrative rulings in individual cases where such rulings establish or revise principles or criteria applicable in future cases. Panel Report, *Japan – Measures Affecting Consumer Photographic Film and Paper* ('*Japan – Film*'), WT/DS44/R, adopted 22 April 1998, DSR 1998:IV, 1179, para. 10.388.

[42] Panel Report, *European Communities – Selected Customs Matters* ('*EC – Selected Customs Matters*'), WT/DS315/R, adopted 11 December 2006, as modified by Appellate Body Report WT/DS315/AB/R, DSR 2006:IX X, 3915, para. 7.116; Panel Report, *Argentina – Measures Affecting the Export of Bovine Hides and Import of Finished Leather* ('*Argentina – Hides and Leather*'), WT/DS155/R and Corr.1, adopted 16 February 2001, DSR 2001:V, 1779, para. 10.5; but see also Panel Report, *United States – Anti-Dumping Measures on Certain Hot-Rolled Steel Products from Japan* ('*US – Hot-Rolled Steel*'), WT/DS184/R, adopted 23 August 2001 modified by Appellate Body Report WT/DS184/AB/R, DSR 2001:X, 4769, para. 7.268.

[43] Appellate Body Report, *US – Underwear*, p. 21; Appellate Body Report, *United States – Definitive Anti-Dumping and Countervailing Duties on Certain Products from China* ('*US – Anti-Dumping and Countervailing Duties (China)*'), WT/DS379/AB/R, adopted 25 March 2011, para. 4.66.

[44] See also Panel Reports, *EC – IT Products*, para. 1.097.

[45] Appellate Body Report, *European Communities – Measures Affecting the Importation of Certain Poultry Products* ('*EC – Poultry*'), WT/DS69/AB/R, adopted 23 July 1998, DSR 1998:V, 2031, para. 113.

[46] Panel Report, *Thailand – Cigarettes (Philippines)*, para. 7.826.

the need to publish the outcome of such decision (in the form of a measure of general application), the decision itself need not be published. The position might none the less be different as regards administrative rulings in individual cases where such rulings establish or reverse principles or criteria applicable in future cases.[47] The same applies where a measure is addressed to a specific and named exporting Member, but does not try to become specific as to individual persons or entities which might be affected by it.[48]

In order to fall within the scope of Article X:1, instruments must have been 'made effective', meaning that they must have been brought into effect, made operative, in practice. It follows that the scope of Article X:1 is not limited to measures that are merely formally promulgated or have formally entered into force.[49]

What constitutes 'prompt' publication needs to be assessed on a case-by-case basis. It may involve determining the time span between the moment at which the measure was made effective and the time of its publication.[50] 'Prompt' publication is defined by reference to the function of publication, namely to enable governments and traders to become acquainted with whatever measures under examination are being published. Thus, a prompt publication has been found to mean publication that is quick and without delay.[51] Whilst Article X:1 does not prescribe a time limit or delay between publication and entry into force, GATT panels have found that publication of quotas covering a period that preceded the date of publication is inconsistent with Article X:1.[52]

The medium in which publication must occur will depend on the facts at issue; measures must be generally available through the appropriate medium. Official publication might not always be sufficient.[53] Unlike Article X:2, Article X:1 does not refer to measures having been 'officially published'. Thus, what is required is publication that gives power to or supplies governments and traders with knowledge of the particular measures and that is adequate so that they may become familiar with

[47] Panel Report, *Japan – Film*, paras. 10.383–10.401.

[48] Appellate Body Report, *US – Underwear*, p. 21.

[49] Panel Reports, *EC – IT Products*, para. 7.1048.

[50] See Panel Reports, *EC – IT Products*, para. 7.1074.

[51] Panel Report, *US – Countervailing and Anti-Dumping Measures (China)*, para. 7.89.

[52] See for example GATT Panel Report, *EEC – Restrictions on Imports of Dessert Apples, Complaint by Chile*, L/6491, adopted on 22 June 1989, paras. 12.1, 12.29; GATT Panel Report, *EEC – Restrictions on Imports of Apples, Complaint by the United States*, L/6531, adopted 22 June 1989, paras. 5. 20, 5.23.

[53] Panel Reports, *EC – IT Products*, para. 7.1077.

them or become known to them in a more or less complete way.[54] Thus, publication means making measures generally available through an appropriate medium, not simply making them publicly available.[55]

A difficulty in making a claim under Article X:1 occurs where the lack of transparency coexists with uncertainty about the existence of measures that otherwise fall within the scope of that provision. The latter might be inconsistent with other provisions of the GATT 1994 but, in principle, cannot be sanctioned under Article X:1. Put differently, a claim under Article X:1 typically presupposes knowledge by the complainant of the existence of a measure of general application. Yet, the lack of transparency might be the very cause of the absence of such knowledge. In *Thailand – Cigarettes (Philippines)*, that difficulty was resolved when Thailand explained its general methodology for setting maximum retail selling prices for cigarettes for the first time in the context of the panel proceedings.[56]

In practice, panels often exercise judicial economy with respect to claims under Article X:1 of the GATT 1994. That practice was already visible in GATT case law.[57] The explanation therefore is that, where a measure is found to be inconsistent with other (substantive) provisions of the GATT 1994, it is no longer relevant or necessary to consider the GATT-consistency of the measure's administration of which publication is just one aspect[58] (even if the Appellate Body has described Article X as concerning both the publication and administration of measures[59]). The Appellate Body appears to consider that due process requirements under Article X apply generally to measures that are otherwise in compliance

[54] Panel Reports, *EC – IT Products*, para. 7.1082; see also Panel Report, *Thailand – Cigarettes (Philippines)*, para. 7.860.

[55] Panel Reports, *EC – IT Products*, para. 7.1084.

[56] Panel Report, *Thailand – Cigarettes (Philippines)*, paras. 7.778 and 7.779.

[57] GATT Panel Report, *Japan – Trade in Semiconductors*, L/6309, adopted on 4 May 1988, 35S/116, 161, paras. 128–129; GATT Panel Report, *Japanese Measures on Imports of Leather*, L/5623, adopted on 15/16 May 1984, 31S/94, para. 57; GATT Panel Report, *Japan – Restrictions on Imports of Certain Agricultural Products*, L/6253, adopted on 2 February 1988, para. 5.4.2; GATT Panel Reports, *Republic of Korea – Restrictions on Imports of Beef, Complaints by Australia, New Zealand and the United States*, L/6504, L/6505, L/6503, adopted on 7 November 1989; GATT Panel Report, *Canada – Import Restrictions in Ice Cream and Yoghurt*, L/6568, adopted on 5 December 1989, para. 82; GATT Panel Report, *EEC – Regulation on Imports of Parts and Components*, L/6657, adopted on 16 May 1990, para. 5.27.

[58] See for example GATT Panel Report, *EEC – Restrictions on Imports of Apples, Complaint by the United States*, L/6531, adopted 22 June 1989, paras. 5.20 and 5.23.

[59] Appellate Body Report, *EC – Poultry*, para. 115.

with other WTO obligations.[60] Whilst that is undoubtedly a logical position, it none the less means that WTO Members sometimes escape being subject to findings under Article X. This may reduce incentives to increase transparency and modify administrative laws and processes.[61]

Notification and reporting in essence consist of the communication of information about measures falling within the scope of the WTO agreements to one or more organs of the WTO. The obligation to notify may arise in the context of the trade policy review mechanism or as a result of particular conduct (such as the introduction of a new or changed measure) for which a specific agreement lays down a notification obligation.[62] Notification may involve an ongoing obligation.[63] On the basis of, *inter alia*, that notified information,[64] WTO committees, working parties and other bodies (as relevant) then review the status of implementation of Members' obligations under the WTO agreements. That review typically results in recommendations, but certain agreements also foresee that a body or committee may make findings.[65]

For example, pursuant to Article 7 of the SPS Agreement, Members are to notify changes in their SPS measures and provide other information on those measures. In the circumstances set out in paragraph 5 of Annex B to the SPS Agreement (and except for situations where urgent problems of health protection arise or threaten to arise[66]), Members

[60] Appellate Body Report, *United States–Import Prohibition of Certain Shrimp and Shrimp Products* ('*US – Shrimp*'), WT/DS58/AB/R, adopted 6 November 1998, DSR 1998:VII, 2755, para. 182.

[61] See also Y. Ishikawa, 'Regulation the Administration of Trade or Customs Laws and Regulations: Reassessing the Role of Article X:3(a) of the GATT 1994' in W. Choi (ed), *The WTO at 20 and the Future of International Economic Law – The Asia-Pacific Perspectives* (Cambridge University Press, 2015).

[62] See Paragraphs 9 to 12 of the BoP Understanding; Articles 2 and 3 of the Agreement on Textiles and Clothing; Articles 3.2 and 15.2 of the TBT Agreement; Article 5.1 of the TRIMs Agreement; Articles 16.4, 16.5 and 18.5 of the Anti-Dumping Agreement; Article 5 of the Agreement on Preshipment Inspection; Article 5 of the Agreement on Rules of Origin; Article 5 of the Agreement on Import Licensing; Article 25 of the SCM Agreement; Article 12 of the Agreement on Safeguards; Article III:3 of the GATS.

[63] See also the ongoing obligation, pursuant to paragraph 11 of the Understanding on the Interpretation of Article XXIV of the GATT 1994, to report periodically to the Council for Trade in Goods on the operation of an agreement covered by Article XXIV of the GATT 1994; annual consultations in the Committee on Agriculture pursuant to Article 18.5 of the Agreement on Agriculture; Article 32.6 of the SCM Agreement.

[64] Such reviews may also be based on, for example, documentation prepared by the WTO Secretariat. See for example Article 18.2 of the Agreement on Agriculture and Article 7 of the Agreement on Import Licensing.

[65] See for example Articles 2.21 and 8 Agreement on Textiles and Clothing.

[66] See paragraph 6 of Annex B to the SPS Agreement.

must, at an early stage, publish a notice regarding the proposal to impose a particular SPS regulation, notify (when amendments can still be introduced and comments be taken into account) other Members (through the WTO Secretariat) of products to be covered with a brief indication of the objective and rationale of the proposed regulation. They must also, upon request, provide copies of the proposed regulation to other Members. That paragraph further requires other Members to be given a reasonable period of time to make comments in writing and for those comments to be discussed and taken into account. Article 2 of the TBT Agreement lays down similar obligations.

Whilst parties other than WTO Members may benefit indirectly from any reported or notified information, certain WTO agreements establish also notification and related obligations with regard to those parties. For example, Article 12.1 of the Anti-Dumping Agreement requires notification to the member(s) the products of which are subject to an anti-dumping investigation and to other interested parties known to the investigating authorities as having an interest in that investigation.[67] Under Article 16 of the Customs Valuation Agreement, an importer must be given, upon request, the right to a written explanation from the customs administration as to how the customs value of its goods was determined.[68]

Enquiry (and resulting explanation) is yet another instrument of achieving transparency. It may involve that a Member or WTO body asks another WTO Member for explanations[69] in the context of the WTO, or it may need to be foreseen in the form of (an) enquiry point(s) or information point(s) with responsibility to provide answers to (reasonable) questions from interested Members and relevant documents. The latter type of enquiry is used especially in the annexes to the GATT 1994, such as the SPS Agreement,[70] the TBT Agreement,[71] the Agreement on Preshipment Inspection[72] and the GATS.[73]

[67] See also Article 22 of the SCM Agreement; Article 3.1 of the Agreement on Safeguards.
[68] See also for example Articles 2.6 and 2.7 of the Agreement on Preshipment Inspection.
[69] See for example Article 12.4 SPS Agreement.
[70] See paragraph 3 of Annex B to the SPS Agreement.
[71] See Article 10 of the TBT Agreement.
[72] See Article 2.7 of the Agreement on Preshipment Inspection.
[73] See Article III:4 of the GATS.

9.3.3 *Administration of Measures*

The WTO consistency of a measure falling within the scope of one of the WTO agreements may depend not only on the character of the instrument and the reasons for its adoption, but also on its administration or application. At issue here is the latter category of disciplines under the GATT 1994, in particular the stand-alone disciplines governing the administration of generally applicable measures that are otherwise consistent with the GATT 1994. Other agreements may lay down more detailed (and additional) requirements as regards the administration of defined types of measure and the processes of examination, investigation and determination from which they result[74] and the treatment of evidence on which they are based.[75]

Article X:3 of the GATT 1994 lays down minimum standards for transparency and procedural fairness in the administration of trade regulation.[76] In applying that provision, one panel has signalled that it is necessary to balance between the traders' fundamental right to procedural fairness and the sovereign right afforded to WTO Members' governments in managing how they administer their laws and regulations.[77] As a result, some deference is to be given to WTO Members in administering their own laws.

Panels and the Appellate Body have set a high burden of proof for claims under Article X:3(a). They have required solid evidence and shown deference to safeguards which Members might have in place to avoid inappropriate administration. In part, this deference might be due to the diversity of the legal systems and cultures of WTO Members.[78]

It remains unclear whether a *de minimis* rule applies for finding a violation of those standards, meaning that a single instance of lack of uniformity, impartiality and reasonableness might not necessarily be sufficient. One panel has suggested that, in such a case, it is necessary to show that the actions have a significant impact on the overall administration of the law.[79] Another panel has taken the view that a

[74] See for example Articles 3, 5, 7 of the Anti-Dumping Agreement; Articles 1.3 and 2.2 of the Agreement on Import Licensing; Article 11 and 15 of the SCM Agreement.

[75] See for example Article 6 of the Anti-Dumping Agreement; Articles 11, 12, 15 of the SCM Agreement.

[76] Appellate Body Report, *US – Shrimp*, para. 183.

[77] Panel Report, *Thailand – Cigarettes (Philippines)*, para. 7.874.

[78] See in that regard, for example, WTO, Working Group on the Interaction between Trade and Competition Policy, *Provisions on Procedural Fairness in Existing WTO Agreements–Background Note by the Secretariat*, WT/WGTCP/W/231 (22 May 2003), para. 11.

[79] Panel Report, *US–Hot-Rolled Steel*, para. 7.268.

government's measure or act may be so egregiously flawed that the unfairness inherent in that measure or act may be sufficient to show impartial administration without the need to illustrate it by giving concrete examples.[80]

Under Article X:3(a), each member is to administer laws, regulations, decisions and rulings falling within the scope of Article X:1 in a 'uniform, impartial and reasonable manner'. Thus, the scope of Article X:3 depends in part on what measures must be published in conformity with Article X:1 of the GATT 1994. The requirements of uniformity, impartiality and reasonableness, which are legally independent and cumulative,[81] do not apply to the covered measures themselves. The administration (that is, their putting into practical effect[82]) of those measures is to be distinguished from their substantive content.[83] At the same time, administration within the meaning of Article X:3(a) also covers the substantive content of a legal instrument regulating the administration of legal instruments covered by Article X:1, though such type of instrument may only be found to be contrary to Article X:3(a) if it is proven that it necessarily leads to a lack of uniform, impartial or reasonable administration.[84] It follows that administrative law can be scrutinised also under Article X:3(a). Finally, Article X:3(a) applies to administrative processes, broadly understood as 'a series of steps, actions, or events that are taken or occur in relation to the making of an administrative decision'.[85] As a result, what can be challenged under Article X:3 is: the substantive content of a legal instrument that regulates the administration or implementation of a legal instrument of the kind described in Article X:1, the manner in which such legal

[80] Panel Report, *Thailand – Cigarettes (Philippines)*, para. 7.909.

[81] Panel Report, *Argentina – Hides and Leather*, para. 11.86.

[82] Appellate Body Report, *European Communities – Selected Customs Matters* ('*EC – Selected Customs Matters*'), WT/DS315/AB/R, adopted 11 December 2006, DSR 2006: IX, 3791, para. 224; see also Panel Reports, *United States – Certain Country of Origin Labelling (COOL) Requirements* ('*US – COOL*'), WT/DS384/R/ WT/DS386/R, adopted 23 July 2012, as modified by Appellate Body Reports WT/DS384/AB/R/ WT/DS386/AB/R, adopted 23 July 2012, DSR 2012:VI, p. 2745, para. 7.816.

[83] Appellate Body Report, *EC – Poultry*, para. 115; Appellate Body Report, *EC – Bananas*, para. 200. Similar requirements may apply also to the measures themselves: see for example Article 9.1 of the Agreement on Rules of Origin according to which rules of origin should be, *inter alia*, 'objective, understandable and predictable', 'administrable in a consistent, uniform, impartial and reasonable manner' and 'coherent'.

[84] Appellate Body Report, *EC – Selected Customs Matters*, para. 201.

[85] Appellate Body Report, *EC – Selected Customs Matters*, para. 224.

instruments are applied or implemented and administrative processes leading to administrative decisions.[86]

Whilst the case law on Article X:3 remains limited and focuses on particular patterns of behaviour (such as the potential involvement of industry interests in the administration of measures that affect competitors), panels and the Appellate Body increasingly interpret 'administration' more broadly and offer more precise guidance on what administration involves. At the same time, they have refrained from defining the legal standards of uniformity and impartiality, preferring to focus on their ordinary meanings found in dictionaries. That reluctance to explain how Article X:3(a) is to be implemented risks undermining the prescriptive value of that provision and its potential for transforming WTO Members' administrative laws and practices.

Uniform administration concerns the uniform treatment accorded by government authorities to individual traders similarly situated. In that sense, it is distinct from substantive non-discrimination standards found elsewhere in the GATT 1994 (which concern treatment between like products of WTO Members). The sole fact that there are differences in administrative processes or in instruments regulating the application or implementation of laws, regulations, decisions and administrative rulings does not necessarily show lack of uniformity.[87] Such differences may very well stem from the exercise of discretion in applying the law and the specific circumstances of the case.[88] Instead, the focus of the inquiry is to be on whether there are sufficient guarantees for avoiding the risk that traders in similar situations are treated differently and whether features of an administrative process necessarily lead to non-uniform administration of a legal instrument covered by Article X:1.[89] Thus, the requirement guarantees that 'every exporter should be able to expect treatment of the same kind, in the same manner, both over time and in different places, and with respect to other persons' and the consistent and predictable application of laws.[90] Whilst there must be uniform actual application of laws, uniform administrative processes need not be adopted throughout the territory of a member.[91]

[86] Panel Report, *Thailand – Cigarettes (Philippines)*, para. 7.873.
[87] Appellate Body Report, *EC – Selected Customs Matters*, paras. 211 and 224.
[88] Appellate Body Report, *EC – Selected Customs Matters*, paras. 213 and 216.
[89] Appellate Body Report, *EC – Selected Customs Matters*, para. 239.
[90] Panel Report, *Argentina – Hides and Leather*, para. 11.83.
[91] Appellate Body Report, *US – Countervailing and Anti-Dumping Measures (China)*, para. 4.82.

Impartial administration has been interpreted to mean fair, unbiased and unprejudiced application or implementation of covered measures.[92] So far, disputes have focused on whether the involvement of certain actors in administering such measures creates risks of partial administration and in essence conflicts of interest.[93] Panels have suggested that features of such an administrative process may be considered partial if it is shown that they necessarily lead to lack of impartial administration.[94] The likelihood of success of such a claim appears to depend on the availability and degree of safeguards in place which avoid this consequence.

Reasonable administration is administration that is not appropriate and/or sensible.[95] Other ordinary meanings given to the term 'reasonable' include 'in accordance with reason', 'not irrational or absurd', 'proportionate', 'having sound judgment', 'not asking for too much', 'within the limits of reason, not greatly less or more than might be thought likely or appropriate' and 'articulate'.[96] The reasonableness standard applies to different features of the administration of covered measures, including the time taken to complete administrative processes,[97] the application of a methodology to determine a tax base which is not supported by any particular rule in force at the relevant time and is different from the methodologies contained in the relevant legislation (which does not foresee discretion to the authorities in that regard) and uncertainties resulting from contradicting guidance on the administration of a measure falling within the scope of other substantive provisions.

9.3.4 *Administrative and Judicial Review*

Articles X:3(b) and (c) of the GATT 1994 require WTO Members to maintain or institute as soon as practicable, judicial, arbitral or

[92] Panel Report, *Thailand – Cigarettes (Philippines)*, para. 7.903.

[93] Certain other agreements contain separate and more detailed provisions on conflicts of interest: see for example Article 2.14 of the Agreement on Preshipment Inspection.

[94] See for example Panel Report, *Thailand – Cigarettes (Philippines)*, para. 7.898.

[95] Panel Report, *Thailand – Cigarettes (Philippines)*, para. 7.919.

[96] See for example Panel Report, *Dominican Republic – Import and Sale of Cigarettes*, para. 7.385; Panel Report, *US – COOL*, para. 7.850; Panel Report, *Thailand – Cigarettes (Philippines)*, para. 7.969.

[97] Some agreements articulate more specific standards of reasonable administration with respect to the time frame within which procedures are to be completed. See for example Article 41.2 of the TRIPS Agreements (enforcement procedures shall not entail unreasonable time-limits or unwarranted delays); Article 2.15 of the Agreement on Preshipment Inspection (need to avoid unreasonable delays in inspection of shipments); Articles 5.10 and 11.4 of the Anti-Dumping Agreement; Articles 11.11 and 21.4 of the SCM Agreement.

administrative tribunals or procedures, which are to be independent of the agencies entrusted with administrative enforcement, for the purposes of, *inter alia*, the prompt review and correction of administrative action relating to customs matters. An exception exists under Article X:3(a) where procedures already exist 'which in fact provide for an objective and impartial review of administrative action even though such procedures are not fully or formally independent of the agencies entrusted with administrative enforcement'. Certain other agreements reiterate this obligation with respect to certain types of measure (sometimes using different wording) and make the obligation more specific and possibly burdensome.[98] For example, under Article 11.1 of the Customs Valuation Agreement, each Member is to provide for the right to appeal the determination of customs value and make it available to the importer or any other person liable for payment of the duty. The appeal should be to a judicial authority, but legislation may provide for an initial right of appeal without penalty to an authority within the customs administration or to an independent body (Article 11.2). By contrast, Part III of the TRIPs Agreement lays down an altogether different and more detailed set of obligations on the enforcement of intellectual property rights.[99]

Due process underlies each of those provisions. Thus, the objective of Article X:3(b) is to ensure that a trader who has been adversely affected by a decision of an administrative agency may seek review of that decision.[100] This type of first instance review[101] must be done in a prompt manner, meaning that, taking into account the context and the particular circumstances, review and correction (meaning that the action is set right) of administrative actions is performed in a quick and effective manner without delay.[102] This review must be independent and thus free of control or influence from the administrative actors whose actions are the subject of the review.[103] This first instance review may take the form of different tribunals and procedures having different substantive or

[98] See for example Article 13 of the Anti-Dumping Agreement; Articles 2.21 and Article 4 of the Agreement on Preshipment Inspection; Article 2(j) of the Agreement on Rules of Origin; Articles 21 and 23 of the SCM Agreement.

[99] Those obligations concern, *inter alia*, fair and equitable procedures, evidence, injunctions, damages and other remedies, the right of information, indemnification of the defendant, provisional measures, specific requirements related to border measures and criminal procedures.

[100] Panel Report, *EC – Selected Customs Matters*, para. 7.536.

[101] Appellate Body Report, *EC – Selected Customs Matters*, para. 294.

[102] Appellate Body Report, *Thailand – Cigarettes (Philippines)*, paras. 203 to 205.

[103] Panel Report, *EC – Selected Customs Matters*, para. 7.520.

geographic areas of competence, or a member may establish first instance review tribunals and procedures governing the practice of all administrative agencies in their entire territory.[104] Thus, each WTO member has discretion to decide on the specific structure of its review mechanism[105] and whether decisions emanating from first instance review must govern the practice of all agencies entrusted with administrative enforcement throughout its territory of a particular WTO member.[106]

9.3.5 Conclusion

Article X of the GATT 1994, which is the main source of treaty obligations expressing the principle of procedural fairness as it applies to measures governing trade in goods, sets out different legal standards that apply to distinct parts of the life of a measure, broadly understood, falling within its scope. The body of case law on the meaning of this provision is growing. However, the Appellate Body has mostly focused on the ordinary meaning of those standards as found in dictionaries. As a result, the case law is clear on adjectives corresponding with terms such as reasonable and impartial and on specific applications of those standards. Uncertainty none the less remains on how far these standards reach. At the same time, the Appellate Body's case law on Article X suggests a high burden of proof for establishing a violation of the obligations assumed under that provision.

9.4 Process-Based Review in WTO Dispute Settlement

9.4.1 Introduction

Outside the context of disputes in which treaty obligations expressing procedural fairness are the subject of a claim and therefore require interpretation and application, the case law of panels and Appellate Body also shows signs of what has been coined elsewhere in this volume as a 'procedural turn', meaning a focus on process-based review of interferences in rights. In WTO law, such process-based review is gradually being developed in the context of, in particular, the interpretation of the general exceptions clause under Article XX of the GATT 1994,

104 Appellate Body Report, *EC – Selected Customs Matters*, para. 297.
105 Appellate Body Report, *EC – Selected Customs Matters*, para. 298.
106 Appellate Body Report, *EC – Selected Customs Matters*, para. 303.

with the potential of seeing that approach transposed to similar clauses in other WTO agreements.

Process-based review is visible in panels' and the Appellate Body's review of a defendant Member's alleged justification of an otherwise WTO-inconsistent measure, in particular with respect to the general exception clause in Article XX of the GATT 1994 and equivalent clauses in other agreements. The Appellate Body reports in *US – Shrimp* and *EC – Seals* illustrate this development well.

A measure which is found to be inconsistent with the obligations under the GATT 1994 may be justified, pursuant to Article XX of the GATT 1994, if it falls under one of the exceptions listed in the various sub-paragraphs of Article XX (which lists, in an exhaustive manner, legitimate objectives) and satisfies the requirements of the introductory paragraph (or so-called 'chapeau') of that provision. Assuming it has been shown that the objective of the measures corresponds with one of the legitimate objectives and that the measure has the required connection with that objective (because, for example, it relates to it or is necessary for achieving it), the measure is also subject to the requirement that it is '. . . not applied in a manner which would constitute a means of arbitrary or unjustifiable discrimination between countries where the same conditions prevail, or a disguised restriction on international trade'. Process-based review has been used with respect to both steps in the analysis under Article XX of the GATT 1994.

Under each sub-paragraph, a defendant Member needs to show that the measure at issue pursues the stated objective and has the required connection to that objective. However, panels and the Appellate Body are not to interfere with the level of protection set by a defendant.[107] The degree of deference shown to the Member concerned with respect to the evidence of the objective of the measure and the required connection appears to differ depending on the sub-paragraph which is invoked. In particular with respect to measures allegedly based on the need to protect public morals (under Article XX(a) of the GATT 1994), the Appellate

[107] See for example Panel Report, *United States – Measures Affecting the Cross Border Supply of Gambling and Betting Services* ('*US – Gambling*'), WT/DS285/R, adopted 20 April 2005, as modified by Appellate Body Report WT/DS285/AB/R, DSR 2005:XII, 5797, para. 6.461; Appellate Body Report, *Korea – Measures Affecting Imports of Fresh, Chilled and Frozen Beef* ('*Korea – Various Measures on Beef*'), WT/DS161/AB/R, WT/DS169/AB/R, adopted 10 January 2001, DSR 2001:I, 5, para. 176; and Appellate Body Report, *European Communities – Measures Affecting Asbestos and Asbestos Containing Products* ('*EC – Asbestos*'), WT/DS135/AB/R, adopted 5 April 2001, DSR 2001:VII, 3243, para. 168.

Body is careful not to second-guess the legitimacy of the objective pursued. In *EC – Seals*, one issue before the Appellate Body was whether the Panel had failed to establish that there was a risk to EU public morals consisting of concerns regarding animal welfare that are particular to seals or whether a successful defence under Article XX(a) requires only that it is shown that the measure is designed to protect public morals. The Appellate Body took the view that identification of such a risk was not required, relying especially on the consideration that scientific or other methods of inquiry might not be particularly useful or relevant in identifying and assessing public morals.[108] Moreover, it did not require that a panel identify the exact content of the public morals standard at issue.[109] Indeed, the panel in *EC – Seals* had focused in particular on the evidence showing the objective of the measure at issue, including the text of the measure, a broad understanding of its legislative history and, to a limited extent, public surveys without interfering with the choice of what are, as regards the subject of the measure at issue, the actual standards of right and wrong conduct maintained by, or on behalf of, a community or nation.[110]

The chapeau lays down two separate obligations: (i) a prohibition of the application of a measure in a manner which would constitute a means of arbitrary or unjustifiable discrimination (which itself contains two separate standards), and (ii) a prohibition of the application of a measure in a manner which would constitute a disguised restriction of trade. The Appellate Body has accepted that 'the actual contours and contents of these standards will vary as the kind of measure under examination varies'.[111] Moreover, the second prohibition in essence encapsulates also the first. The general purpose of the introductory paragraph has been described as preventing the abuse or the exceptions found in the sub-paragraphs of Article XX,[112] though that characterisation appears to apply mostly to the second prohibition. None the less, both types of prohibition reflect the general principle of (international) law of good

[108] Appellate Body Report, *European Communities – Measures Prohibiting the Importation and Marketing of Seal Products* ('*EC – Seals*'), WT/DS400/AB/R, WT/DS401/AB/R, adopted on 18 June 2014, para. 5.198.

[109] Appellate Body Report, *EC – Seals*, para. 5.199.

[110] Panel Report, *EC – Seals*, paras. 7.399 to 7.410.

[111] Appellate Body Report, *United States–Import Prohibition of Certain Shrimp and Shrimp Products* ('*US – Shrimp*'), WT/DS58/AB/R, adopted 6 November 1998, DSR 1998:VII, 2755, para. 120.

[112] Appellate Body Report, *United States – Standards for Reformulated and Conventional Gasoline* ('*US – Gasoline*'), WT/DS2/AB/R, adopted 20 May 1996, DSR 1996:I, 3, p. 22.

faith that controls the exercise of rights by States; the doctrine of abuse of rights is but one expression of that principle.[113] The Appellate Body has accepted that there may be abuse or misuse of an exception under Article XX if the detailed operational provisions of the measure prescribe arbitrary or unjustifiable activity and where a measure, otherwise fair and just, is actually applied in an arbitrary or unjustifiable manner.[114]

Initially, the standards in the chapeau were considered to apply mostly to the application of a measure, rather than to its specific contents.[115] However, more recent case law has cast doubt on that characterisation of the scope of the chapeau. Thus, in *EC – Seals*, the Appellate Body held that it is relevant, for the purposes of the chapeau, to consider 'the design, architecture, and revealing structure of a measure in order to establish whether the measure, in its actual or expected application, constitutes a means of arbitrary or unjustifiable discrimination between countries where the same conditions prevail'.[116] Even if a WTO member has the right to adopt a measure that is otherwise inconsistent with the GATT 1994, that right must be balanced against the legal rights of the other parties concerned.[117]

Despite the distinct prohibitions found in the chapeau, panels and the Appellate Body have not always been explicit in stating why features of the measure and its application are contrary to one or the other prohibition. Similar to case law on Article X:3(a) of the GATT 1994, the interpretation of the chapeau thus lacks precision and clarity. None the less, it is especially in interpreting and applying the first prohibition that the Appellate Body has shown that process-based review can be relevant to the justification of a measure under Article XX of the GATT 1994.

The first type of prohibition presumes that a difference in treatment exists between countries where the same conditions prevail. It does not as such prohibit measures that are applied in an arbitrarily or unjustifiable manner irrespective of comparative treatment. Some type of discrimination may thus be permitted. The analysis is to focus primarily on the cause or the rationale for the discrimination (and not exclusively on the effects of such discrimination[118]); where the cause or rationale relates or promotes

[113] Appellate Body Report, *US – Shrimp*, para. 158.

[114] Appellate Body Report, *US – Shrimp*, para. 160.

[115] Appellate Body Report, *US – Gasoline*, p. 22; Appellate Body Report, *US – Shrimp*, para. 150.

[116] Appellate Body Report, *EC – Seals*, para. 5.302.

[117] Appellate Body Report, *US – Gasoline*, p. 22; Appellate Body Report, *US – Shrimp*, paras. 157 and 158.

[118] Appellate Body Report, *EC – Seals*, para. 5.303.

the objective that was provisionally found to justify a measure under one of the sub-paragraphs of Article XX, the measure might be justified under the chapeau.[119] However, that will not be the case where the cause of the discrimination does not bear a relationship (that is, a rational connection) to the legitimate objective pursued and even undermines it.[120]

The impact of this first type of prohibition on the administrative laws and processes of WTO Members is well illustrated by the report in *US – Shrimp*. The measure at issue, which was accepted to be justified on the basis of Article XX(g) of the GATT 1994, was a US prohibition on the importation of certain shrimp and shrimp products harvested with commercial fishing technology which adversely affected sea turtles. However, the import ban did not apply to harvesting nations that were certified. Certification was to be granted to countries with a fishing environment which did not pose a threat of the incidental taking of sea turtles in the course of shrimp harvesting and to harvesting nations that provided documentary evidence of the adoption of a regulatory programme governing the incidental taking of sea turtles that was comparable to the US programme and where the average rate of incidental taking of sea turtles was comparable to that of US vessels. Under US law, all US shrimp trawl vessels were required to use approved Turtle Excluder Devices ('TEDs') or tow-time restrictions in areas where there was a significant mortality of sea turtles in shrimp harvesting. Certain limited exceptions applied. At the same time, US law foresaw that the US Secretary of State was to initiate as soon as possible negotiations on bilateral or multilateral agreements for the protection and conservation of sea turtles. The Appellate Body held that the measure, or at least its application, failed to satisfy the conditions under the chapeau. In particular, first, the measure constituted unjustifiable discrimination because, as applied, the import ban meant that all exporting Members were required to adopt the same policy and measures as those applied to the US domestic shrimp trawlers in order to obtain certification. The Appellate Body considered the operation of the measure in practice. It found that the actual application of the measure required other WTO Members to adopt a regulatory programme that was essentially the same as that applied to the US shrimp trawl vessels.[121] Administrators were not

[119] See Appellate Body Report, *Brazil–Measures Affecting Imports of Retreaded Tyres* ('*Brazil – Retreaded Tyres*'), WT/DS332/AB/R, adopted 17 December 2007, DSR 2007:IV, 1527, para. 213.

[120] Appellate Body Report, *Brazil–Retreaded Tyres*, para. 227.

[121] Appellate Body Report, *US – Shrimp*, para. 163.

taking into account the policies and measures in place by exporting Members for protecting and conserving sea turtles. Thus, it was contrary to the chapeau to apply the import ban in a manner that did not allow for any inquiry into the appropriateness of the regulatory programme for the conditions prevailing in exporting countries.[122] Other obstacles were the fact that the US was not sufficiently inclusive as regards its efforts to negotiate multilateral disciplines[123] and the exclusion of certain countries from the option to enjoy a phase-in period during which shrimp trawling sectors could adjust to the TED requirement.[124]

The application of the US measure also resulted in differential treatment that was arbitrary because exporting Members whose certification applications were rejected were denied basic fairness and due process.[125] That was so because the certification process showed rigidity and inflexibility and lacked transparency and predictability.[126] Nor was there a procedure for review and appeal from a decision rejecting an application.[127] The fact that there was no formal legal procedure for review of, or appeal from, a denial of an application, are all contrary to the spirit, if not the letter, of Article X:3 of the GATT 1994, which, according to the Appellate Body, '... establishes certain minimum standards for transparency and procedural fairness in the administration of trade regulations'.[128] As a matter of principle, the Appellate Body held that: 'Inasmuch as there are due process requirements generally for measures that are otherwise imposed in compliance with WTO obligations, it is only reasonable that rigorous compliance with the fundamental requirements of due process should be required in the application and administration of a measure which purports to be an exception to the treaty obligations of the Member imposing the measure and which

122 Appellate Body Report, *US – Shrimp*, para. 165.
123 Appellate Body Report, *US – Shrimp*, para. 172.
124 Appellate Body Report, *US – Shrimp*, para. 173. Compare with Appellate Body Report, *EC – Tariff Preferences*, paras. 182 to 188, where the Appellate Body found that the (then) EC's Drug Arrangements were contrary to the requirement of non-discrimination in footnote 3 of the Enabling Clause according to which identical tariff treatment must be available to all similarly situated GSP beneficiaries. That was so because: (i) there was a close list of beneficiaries and thus it could not be guaranteed that the preferences would be available to all GSP beneficiaries suffering from illicit drug production and trafficking and (ii) the EC measure at issue or any other measure did not contain criteria or standards providing a basis for distinguishing beneficiaries under the Drug Arrangements from other GSP beneficiaries.
125 Appellate Body Report, *US – Shrimp*, para. 181.
126 Appellate Body Report, *US – Shrimp*, paras. 177 and 180.
127 Appellate Body Report, *US – Shrimp*, para. 180.
128 Appellate Body Report, *US – Shrimp*, para. 183.

effectively results in a suspension *pro hac vice* of the treaty rights of other Members'.[129] The Appellate Body in *US – Shrimp* thus incorporated administrative law-type considerations in interpreting and applying the chapeau under Article XX of the GATT 1994. It did not base that reasoning on the text of Article XX of the GATT 1994; rather, it appeared to rely on Article X of the GATT 1994 and standards of due process that are not expressly stated in Article XX.[130] Comments on this part of the reasoning have suggested that '... the Appellate Body attempted to enhance the representation of affected foreign parties and thereby counter the national biases of domestic legislative and administrative bodies'.[131]

In *EC – Seals*, the Appellate Body expressed similar concerns regarding the process of administering the exceptions to the EU ban on marketing seals products. The ambiguity in the criteria for applying the exception for indigenous communities and the broad discretion of authorities competent to apply those criteria meant that, by its design, the EU seal regime could be applied in a manner contrary to the first prohibition under the chapeau; seal products derived from what should be properly characterised as commercial hunts could potentially enter the EU market under that exception.[132]

Whilst the standards under the chapeau thus differ from those found in Article X:3 of the GATT 1994, the Appellate Body has none the less considered that that provision is relevant to interpreting the chapeau of Article XX of the GATT 1994. It has suggested that, where standards of transparency and procedural fairness are not met, this goes against at least the spirit of Article X:3 and hence is contrary to the first prohibition under the introductory paragraph of Article XX.[133] Conversely, panels have relied on case law relating to the chapeau of Article XX in interpreting Article X:3(a) of the GATT 1994.[134] In any event, even if a measure is found to be justified under Article XX of the GATT 1994, its administration none

[129] Appellate Body Report, *US – Shrimp*, para. 182.

[130] See also A.D. Mitchell and E. Sheargold, 'Global Governance: The World Trade Organization's Contribution', *Alta. L. Rev.*, 46(4) (2008–2009), p. 1061, at p. 1069; A. D. Mitchell, *Legal Principles in WTO Disputes* (Cambridge University Press, 2008), at pp. 173–175.

[131] G. Schaffer and J. Trachtman, 'Interpretation and Institutional Choice at the WTO', *Virginia Journal of International Law*, 52(1) (2011), p. 103, at p. 150.

[132] Appellate Body Report, *EC – Seals*, para. 5.329.

[133] Appellate Body Report, *US – Shrimp*, para. 183.

[134] Appellate Body Report, *Thailand–Customs and Fiscal Measures on Cigarettes from the Philippines* ('*Thailand – Cigarettes (Philippines)*'), WT/DS371/AB/R, adopted 15 July 2011, para. 7.921.

the less must comply with Article X.[135] Whether that suggests that not all of standards of conduct laid down in Article X of the GATT 1994 are integrated in Article XX of the GATT 1994 is less certain.

Thus, what is visible in the case law is a form of cross-fertilisation between the case law interpreting and applying the treaty obligations directly aimed at procedural fairness and that in which panels and the Appellate Body have read exception clauses in the light of the principle of procedural fairness as expressed in substantive treaty obligations. But if different parts of Article X are indeed expressed in the chapeau of Article XX of the GATT 1994, that interpretation does not appear to preclude an applicant from bringing a separate claim under Article X of the GATT 1994 in addition to the claim under a provision with respect to which the defendant relies on Article XX of the GATT 1994. With respect to such a claim, it is for the complainant to establish a *prima facie* violation and thus to carry the (high) burden of proof. By comparison, in relation to the chapeau of Article XX of the GATT 1994, it is the defendant who has the initial burden of proof as regards the standards stated therein. Considerations relating to the principle of procedural fairness that might find expression also in Article X of the GATT 1994 are but one part of the analysis of whether a measure satisfies the conditions of the chapeau. It would then seem that the burden of proof with respect to such aspects of the measure is less intensive under the chapeau as compared to that which applies to a claim under Article X of the GATT 1994. The standard of review also is possibly less strict. But if it is the case that a measure that is in breach of the legal standard under Article X:3 of the GATT 1994 has considerable consequences for that measure's assessment under the chapeau in the context of a justification under Article XX of the GATT 1994, it remains unclear how a claim based on Article X:3 of the GATT 1994 is to be analysed together with the justification under Article XX of the GATT 1994 of that same measure (being administered) that is otherwise found to be inconsistent with another provision of the GATT 1994.

9.5 Conclusion

In WTO law, obligations reflecting procedural fairness are mostly treaty-based and thus the content of such obligations, in so far as they have been

[135] See Panel Reports, *China – Measures Related to the Exportation of Various Raw Materials* ('*China – Raw Materials*'), WT/DS394/R/ WT/DS395/R/ WT/DS398/R /and Corr.1, adopted 22 February 2012, as modified by Appellate Body Reports WT/DS394/AB/R/ WT/DS395/AB/R /WT/DS398/AB/R, paras. 7.635 and 7.636.

the subject of WTO dispute settlement, results from treaty interpretation. Whilst the Appellate Body's interpretive methods are sometimes characterised as excessively textual, its interpretive approach has in fact been more varied and balanced.[136] None the less, its case law regarding the provisions discussed in this chapter shows that, at least with regard to Article X of the GATT 1994 and the chapeau of Article XX of the GATT 1994, it is reluctant to define in great detail (as it often does with respect to substantive provisions) vague standards on the quality of administration and prefers to focus on the application of such standards.

The practice of process-based review in WTO law is probably insufficiently developed in order to draw firm conclusions on its function and importance. At present, it seems that a systematic application of process-based review is lacking. Whether such review occurs depends mostly on the character of the measure and the manner in which a justification has been argued. It none the less seems prudent to suggest that process-based review should not be used as an alternative to any other type of review. Rather, the challenge is how to integrate such a form of review in a more global method of reviewing the compliance of a measure with standards of conduct laid down in the WTO agreements. Put differently, it is a question of finding a methodology according to which process-based review can beneficially complement that method. It would appear that process-based review will be used more actively and purposively when there appear to be concerns about processes and methods. Such considerations may more often be used to find that the measure is WTO-inconsistent, rather than to uphold the WTO-consistency of the measure. If that is so, questions remain about when such type of review is sufficient to make a finding of inconsistency and whether it can justify avoiding to take a position on whether the substantive standards of conduct were in fact consistent with applicable obligations. In the context of US constitutional theory, it has been argued that process-based review is fundamentally incomplete and can exist only when its presuppositions are specified and its content is supplemented by a full theory of substantive rights or values.[137] Similarly, in the context of EU law, President Lenaerts has discussed how ' . . . "process review" is an interesting way of making sure that, in areas where the EU legislator enjoys broad discretion, the latter does not commit abuses and "increases

[136] See I. Van Damme, *Treaty Interpretation by the WTO Appellate Body* (Oxford University Press, 2009).

[137] See L.H. Tribe, 'The Puzzling Persistence of Process-Based Constitutional Theories', *Yale Law Journal* 89 (1980), p. 1063, at p. 1065.

judicial scrutiny over the decision making process of the EU institutions"'.[138] Similar conclusions apply to process-based review in WTO law.

In performing process-based review, panels and the Appellate Body can rely on a set of treaty standards governing transparency, administration and administrative and judicial review, in particular in Article X of the GATT 1994. In that manner, those standards are being integrated into other parts of the WTO agreements and, as regards the GATT 1994, especially in Article XX of the GATT 1994. In turn, that integration enhances the acceptability of engaging in process-based review.

The potential of Articles X:1, X:3(a) and the chapeau of Article XX of the GATT 1994 to transform administrative laws and practices of WTO Members is promising and has been shown in several dispute settlement reports. This is particularly so with regard to the definition of what constitutes the administration or application of a GATT measure. None the less, the prescriptive value of the obligations assumed under those provisions suffers from the vagueness of the standards expressed therein and the loose and sometimes confusing use of terms in interpreting those distinct standards. Indeed, especially the Appellate Body's interpretation of those standards (unlike its interpretation of the concept of administration) fails to offer certainty and predictability.

None the less, the Appellate Body has shown willingness to interpret the scope of these obligations widely so as to encompass the application and features of the administrative processes and laws governing the application of measures that are otherwise justified under other provisions of the GATT 1994.

[138] K. Lenaerts, 'The European Court of Justice and Process-Oriented Review' College of Europe Research Paper in Law 01/2012, at p. 15.

10

Process and Substance in Judicial Review in the United Kingdom and at Strasbourg: Proportionality, Subsidiarity, Complementarity?

ROGER MASTERMAN

10.1 Introduction

Recent decisions of the European Court of Human Rights (ECtHR) concerning the United Kingdom – and indeed other member states – suggest an approach to the assessment of proportionality that takes into account the adequacy of administrative and legislative (and adjudicative[1]) process at the domestic level. On the basis of this approach, national legislation and policy decisions which can demonstrate a firm evidential, as well as democratic, underpinning may be more likely to fall within a state's margin of appreciation, and therefore would be more likely to be regarded by the Strasbourg Court as being compliant with the Convention. Decisions adopted following 'extensive debate by the democratically elected representatives of the state',[2] which can be shown to be 'the culmination of . . . detailed examination of the social, ethical and legal implications of developments'[3] or which have proceeded following 'exacting and pertinent reviews, by both parliamentary and judicial bodies',[4] for instance, have been taken by the ECtHR to contribute to its assessment of compliance with the Convention standards.[5] As a result, consideration of

My thanks are due to Helen Fenwick, Ian Leigh, David Mead, Matthew Saul and Se-shauna Wheatle for their comments and suggestions on an earlier draft.

[1] Though this piece focuses on administrative and legislative process at the national level, it is clear that domestic judicial process may also be examined in the reasoning of the Strasbourg Court (see: *Von Hannover (No.2)* v. *Germany* (2012) 55 E.H.R.R. 15).

[2] *Friend* v. *United Kingdom* (2010) 50 E.H.R.R. 51, at [50].

[3] *Evans* v. *United Kingdom* (2008) 46 E.H.R.R. 34, at [60].

[4] *Animal Defenders International* v. *United Kingdom* (2013) 57 E.H.R.R. 21, at [116].

[5] On which see: J. Gerards, 'The European Court of Human Rights and the National Courts: Giving Shape to the Notion of "Shared Responsibility"' in J. Gerards and J. Fleuren (eds),

the depth and quality of the decision-making process at the national level will be weighed in the Court's assessment of the proportionality of a challenged measure. Affording a wide(r) margin of appreciation in recognition of systematic national decision-making emphasises the importance of domestic processes to Strasbourg adjudication and in so doing, illustrates but one of the mechanisms by which the European Court may give life to the notion of subsidiarity,[6] but it also runs the risk of dilution of the Convention's potency; procedural propriety cannot be a proxy for proportionality, nor for ultimately ensuring the maintenance of the Convention's minimum standards.[7]

Since the enactment of the Human Rights Act 1998 (hereafter HRA), the United Kingdom's jurisprudence on rights protection has been umbilically linked to the case law of the ECtHR. In spite of this, process review is at once orthodox and alien to UK constitutional law. Fair process lies at the heart of common law judicial review of administrative action; alongside illegality and irrationality, procedural impropriety provides one of the established grounds by which public authority decision-making might be challenged. Traditionally, by contrast, legislative judicial review has not been a feature of UK constitutional law and the courts have long regarded the propriety of legislative processes as lying within the exclusive domain of Parliament. Though the enactment of the HRA facilitates, and renders constitutionally permissible, a species of legislative review in the United Kingdom, additionally creating a statutory requirement that public authorities act compatibly with the Convention rights to which it gives further effect, the extent to which an effective translation of the Strasbourg jurisprudence engaging with process review has taken place is unclear.

In the first instance, there is uncertainty amongst the domestic judiciary as regards the place of process-based review in the case law of the Strasbourg Court. The sense that the ECtHR is largely focused on matters of substance, to the virtual exclusion of procedural review, has served to minimise the relevance of procedural review to HRA adjudication concerning executive (public authority)

Implementation of the European Convention on Human Rights and the Judgments of the ECtHR in National Case-Law (Cambridge: Intersentia, 2014), pp. 52–62.

[6] See also *Nicklinson and Lamb* v. *United Kingdom* (2015) 61 E.H.R.R. SE7, at [84].

[7] On the heightened scrutiny required by a proportionality, as opposed to reasonableness or rationality, inquiry, see: *R. (on the application of Daly)* v. *Secretary of State for the Home Department* [2001] UKHL 26; 2 A.C. 532, at [27]-[28].

decision-making.[8] Taking their lead from the supposed 'outcome orientated approach'[9] of the ECtHR, the House of Lords and UK Supreme Court have tended to place the focus of domestic proportionality analysis on 'the practical outcome, not the quality of the decision-making process that led to it.'[10] In doing so, the United Kingdom's apex court reveals a potential disconnect between the adjudicative approach to the Convention rights taken at the national and supranational levels and simultaneously appears to eschew one of the standard tenets of domestic judicial review.

The picture is complicated by the adjudicative differences between judicial (administrative) and legislative review at the domestic level; the former being primarily traditionally driven by concerns relating to procedural legitimacy,[11] the latter not only historically regarded as being incompatible with the doctrine of parliamentary sovereignty, but more broadly obstructed by the fact that parliamentary process has been long considered to be non-justiciable. While in its examinations of the Convention-compliance of primary legislation under the HRA the United Kingdom's apex court has stopped short of questioning the legitimacy of domestic legislative procedure, a closer engagement with legislative deliberative process than traditionally permitted has become evident, with courts taking the 'quality of the legislative decision-making process into account when assessing whether legislation is compatible with Convention rights';[12] prior to the implementation of the HRA, such an approach would have been regarded as being constitutionally illegitimate.

The extent to which techniques of procedural review have been adopted in domestic adjudication concerning the Convention rights therefore provides a lens through which the interplay between domestic and supranational judicial processes and reasoning can be examined, raising questions relating to the purpose of the HRA, subsidiarity and complementarity within the Convention system and the intensity of

[8] See: *R. (on the application of Nasseri)* v. *Secretary of State for the Home Department* [2010] 1 A.C. 1, at [12]-[14].

[9] T. Hickman, *Public Law after the Human Rights Act* (Oxford: Hart Publishing, 2010), p. 243.

[10] *R. (on the application of Begum)* v. *Governors of Denbigh High School* [2006] UKHL 15; [2007] 1 A.C. 100, at [31].

[11] The ground of 'unreasonableness' provides the exception to this general rule (see, originally, *Associated Provincial Picture Houses Ltd* v. *Wednesbury Corporation* [1948] 1 K.B. 223, esp. at 230).

[12] A. Kavanagh, 'Proportionality and Parliamentary Debates: Exploring some Forbidden Territory' (2014) 34 O.J.L.S. *443*, 478–479.

proportionality review as carried out by the Strasbourg and domestic courts.

10.2 Process and Substance in the European Court of Human Rights

In adjudication under the HRA, the ECtHR has frequently been portrayed as concerned only with the substance of a decision taken by national authorities. As Lord Bingham outlined in *R. (on the application of Begum)* v. *Governors of Denbigh High School*:

> the focus at Strasbourg is not and has never been on whether a challenged decision or action is the product of a defective decision-making process, but on whether, in the case under consideration, the applicant's Convention rights have been violated.[13]

As such, proportionality is viewed as 'a test...which the Court applies in order to structure its own decision-making rather than a decision-making structure that it seeks to impose on primary decision-makers'.[14] On the basis of this, so long as the outcome of a decision-making process achieves a proportionate balancing of rights and interests, compliance with the Convention might be anticipated. To say that the content of, or procedures adopted during, the decision-making processes of national authorities are irrelevant to the adjudicative processes of the ECtHR is, however, incorrect. For instance, the European Court clearly delineated two lines of inquiry in its decision in *Hatton* v. *United Kingdom*: (i) an assessment of the substantive merits of the decision, to ensure compatibility with the relevant right and (ii) scrutiny of relevant decision-making processes 'to ensure that due weight has been accorded to the interests of the individual'.[15]

While the primary focus of the European Court is to ensure that the substance of the Convention rights has been protected in practice – to use the language of the Court, in order to ensure that the protected rights are 'practical and effective', rather than 'theoretical and illusory'[16] – decision-making processes followed at the domestic level are often taken by the

[13] *R. (on the application of Begum)* v. *Governors of Denbigh High School* [2006] UKHL 15; [2007] 1 A.C. 100, at [29].

[14] T. Poole, 'Of Headscarves and Heresies: The Denbigh High School Case and Public Authority Decision Making under the Human Rights Act' [2005] P.L. 685, 690.

[15] *Hatton* v. *United Kingdom* (2003) 37 E.H.R.R. 28, at [99].

[16] *Artico* v. *Italy* (1981) 3 E.H.R.R. 1, at [33].

court to demonstrate the sufficiency (or otherwise) of the justifications proposed for the member state's actions in relation to the right in question. As the Strasbourg Court noted in *Martinez* v. *Spain*:

> the court cannot satisfactorily assess whether the reasons adduced by national authorities to justify their decisions were 'sufficient' for the purposes of Art 8(2) without at the same time determining whether the decision-making process, seen as a whole, provided the applicant with the requisite protection of his interests.[17]

Procedural review can therefore be seen to play a supplementary role within the European Court's overall assessment of compliance, contributing to the Court's examination of proportionality, rather than seeing it displaced.[18]

In addressing the domestic decision-making process, the European Court has placed emphasis on the adequacy of the evidence that the interests of the claimant(s) have been considered in sufficient depth.[19] This analysis may be used to affirm the domestic decision, or to demonstrate its deficiencies. The European Court, in its decision in *Hirst (No.2)*, made clear that 'negative inferences'[20] could be drawn from the failure of the UK Parliament to engage with the rights – implications of the denial of voting rights to convicted prisoners:

> [T]here [was] no evidence that Parliament had ever sought to weigh the competing interests or to assess the proportionality of a blanket ban on the right of a convicted prisoner to vote. . .it cannot be said that there was any substantive debate by members of the legislature on the continued justification in light of modern day penal policy and of current human rights standards for maintaining such a general restriction on the right of prisoners to vote.[21]

17 *Martinez* v. *Spain* (2015) 60 E.H.R.R. 3, at [147].

18 On which see Gerards (Chapter 6: 'Procedural Review by the ECtHR: A Typology') in this volume.

19 See e.g. *Brežec* v. *Croatia* [2014] H.L.R. 3, at [50]. Such an approach is, in one of the leading English texts on the Convention, outlined as one of the general principles by which the Court approaches qualification of the Convention rights: 'A limitation upon a right, or steps taken positively to protect or fulfil it, will not be proportionate, even allowing for a margin of appreciation, where there is no evidence that the state institutions have balanced the competing individual and public interests when deciding on the limitations or steps, or where the requirements to be met to avoid or benefit from its application in a particular case are so high as not to permit a meaningful balancing process (D.J. Harris, M. O'Boyle, E.P. Bates and C.M. Buckley, *Law of the European Convention on Human Rights* (2nd ed.) (Oxford: Oxford University Press, 2009), p. 11).

20 A. Kavanagh, 'Proportionality and Parliamentary Debates: Exploring some Forbidden Territory' (2014) 34 O.J.L.S. 443, 476.

21 *Hirst* v. *United Kingdom (No.2)* (2006) 42 E.H.R.R. 41, at [79].

Judicial review by the ECtHR is not therefore so outcome-centric as to be completely disassociated from the circumstances of the individual complaint giving rise to the application *and* the processes by which that decision was taken by national authorities.[22]

Nor does Strasbourg engagement with domestic decision-making processes necessarily demonstrate the Court making further inroads into the policy and legislative autonomy of domestic authorities. Process review is also in evidence and is arguably of greater prominence in those cases in which the court has deferred to the judgments and decision-making processes of national authorities.[23] As such, where a margin of appreciation is likely to be afforded to the national authorities, 'the Court has recognised the "special weight" to be accorded to the role of the domestic policy-maker in matters of general policy on which opinions within a democratic society may reasonably differ widely'.[24] In such instances, process review plays an affirmative role and can be regarded as an effective demonstration of the 'shared responsibility' of the European Court and national authorities for upholding the Convention's standards.[25] In those areas in which a wide margin may be affordable, process-based review also serves to (partially) counter the suggestion that the courts' indications that intervention will only occur where a domestic decision is 'manifestly unreasonable' or 'without legal foundation'[26] equate to a downgrading of the standard of review.[27]

[22] *National Union of Rail, Maritime and Transport Workers* v. *United Kingdom* (2015) 60 E.H.R.R. 10, at [98]. For further analysis of this point, see the chapters by Eva Brems (Chapter 2: 'The "Logics" of Procedural-Type Review by the European Court of Human Rights'), Janneke Gerards (Chapter 6: 'Procedural Review by the ECtHR – A Typology') and Angelika Nussberger (Chapter 7: 'Procedural Review by the European Court of Human Rights – View from the Court') in this volume.

[23] P. Popelier and C. Van De Heyning, 'Procedural rationality: Giving Teeth to the Proportionality Analysis' (2013) *European Constitutional Law Review* 230, 252.

[24] *National Union of Rail, Maritime and Transport Workers* v. *United Kingdom* (2015) 60 E.H.R.R. 10, at [99].

[25] *Nicklinson and Lamb* v. *United Kingdom* (2015) 61 E.H.R.R. SE7, at [84]: 'The contracting states are generally free to determine which of the three branches of government should be responsible for taking policy and legislative decisions which fall within their margin of appreciation and it is not for this Court to involve itself in their internal constitutional arrangements. However, when this Court concludes in any given case that an impugned legislative provision falls within the margin of appreciation, it will often be the case that the Court is, essentially, referring to Parliament's discretion to legislate as it sees fit in that particular area.'

[26] *National Union of Rail, Maritime and Transport Workers* v. *United Kingdom* (2015) 60 E.H.R.R. 10, at [99]. See also *James* v. *United Kingdom* (1986) 8 E.H.R.R. 123, at [43].

[27] P. Popelier and C. Van de Heyning, 'Procedural Rationality: Giving Teeth to the Proportionality Analysis' (2013) 9 *European Constitutional Law Review* 230, 243.

Equally, however, process review is by no means confined to those fields in which a wide margin of appreciation might be thought to apply. Thus, for example, in *Animal Defenders International*, a case concerned with political expression, and therefore typically an area in which any margin of appreciation would be relatively narrowly drawn,[28] the ECtHR found that national authorities were 'best-placed' to determine what should be regarded as a 'country specific and complex assessment' of the balance to be struck.[29] The court went on to thoroughly outline the process by which the challenged ban on political advertising had been enacted (and subsequently found to be compatible with the requirements of Article 10 in domestic adjudication[30]). The court noted that:

> The prohibition was . . . the culmination of an exceptional examination by Parliamentary bodies of the cultural, political and legal aspects of the prohibition as part of the broader regulatory system governing broadcasted public interest expression in the United Kingdom, and all bodies found the prohibition to have been a necessary interference with art. 10 rights . . .
>
> The proportionality of the prohibition was, nonetheless, debated in some detail before the High Court and the House of Lords . . . both levels endorsed the objective of the prohibition as well as the rationale of the legislative choices which defined its particular scope and each concluded that it was a necessary and proportionate interference with the applicant's rights under art. 10 of the Convention.
>
> The Court, for its part, attaches considerable weight to these exacting and pertinent reviews, by both parliamentary and judicial bodies, of the complex regulatory regime governing political broadcasting in the United Kingdom, and to their view that the general measure was necessary to prevent the distortion of crucial public interest debates and, thereby, the undermining of the democratic process.[31]

Affording weight to the considered judgment of a national legislature (and/or courts) could be said to illustrate in practice that '[s]ubsidiarity is at the very heart of the Convention' and is demonstrative that the European Court is 'intended to be subsidiary to the national systems'.[32] Critics of such an approach, however, argue that rather than off-setting

[28] See e.g. *Worm* v. *Austria* (1998) 25 E.H.R.R. 454.

[29] *Animal Defenders International* v. *United Kingdom* (2013) 57 E.H.R.R. 21, at [111].

[30] *R. (on the application of Animal Defenders International)* v. *Secretary of State for Culture, Media and Sport* [2008] UKHL 15; [2008] 1 A.C. 1312.

[31] *Animal Defenders International* v. *United Kingdom* (2013) 57 E.H.R.R. 21, at [114]-[116].

[32] *Austin* v. *United Kingdom* (2012) 55 E.H.R.R. 14, at [61]. And see: M. Saul, 'The European Court of Human Rights' Margin of Appreciation and the Processes of National Parliaments' (2015) H.R.L.R. 1.

a rather more modest rationality-style review, endorsement of a domestic process in review is used by the court in order to 'appease'[33] those member states in which the reach and influence of the Strasbourg court is the source of political controversy and scepticism.[34] But, just as an overly abstract approach to judicial review may see European Court decisions excessively divorced from the 'vital forces'[35] at play across the member states, a purely 'country specific'[36] approach to adjudication would undermine the Court's ability to shape common minimum standards between signatories to the Convention. While the term 'appeasement' connotes submission in the face of opposition, recourse to review which is critical of domestic decision-making process demonstrates that procedural review cannot be uniformly seen as such. Rather, procedural review is best encapsulated as one of a number of mechanisms at the disposal of the Court which *may* be utilised in order to emphasise the subsidiarity in the Convention system.

That process review is essentially a discretionary tool in the hands of the Court is, however, problematic. A lack of specificity as regards the circumstances in which the Court might invoke procedural techniques of review has prompted a degree of concern relating to the consistency of the Court's adjudicatory approach.[37] It is further acknowledged, and evidenced by the fine margin by which the *Animal Defenders International* case was decided,[38] that the Strasbourg Court itself is divided on the extent to which domestic processes should influence the standard of Strasbourg review.[39] Both factors can be seen to underpin, in

[33] See: H. Fenwick, 'Enhanced Subsidiarity and a Dialogic Approach – Or Appeasement in Recent Cases on Criminal Justice, Public Order, Counter-Terrorism at Strasbourg against the UK?' in K. Ziegler, E. Wicks and L. Hodson, *The UK and European Human Rights: A Strained Relationship?* (Oxford: Hart Publishing, 2015).

[34] For a perspective from the United Kingdom, see: R. Masterman, 'The United Kingdom: From Strasbourg Surrogacy towards a British Bill of Rights?' in S. Lambrecht, K. Lemmens and P. Popelier (eds), *Shifting the Convention System: Counter-Dynamics at the National Level* (Cambridge: Intersentia, 2016).

[35] *Handyside* v. *United Kingdom* (1979–1980) 1 E.H.R.R. 737, at [48].

[36] *Animal Defenders International* v. *United Kingdom* (2013) 57 E.H.R.R. 21, at [111].

[37] See: C. Barrow, '*RMT* v. *United Kingdom*: The European Court of Human Rights Intimidated into Timidity or Merely Consistent in Its Inconsistency?' [2015] E.H.R.L.R. 277 and generally M. Saul, 'The European Court of Human Rights' Margin of Appreciation and the Processes of National Parliaments' (2015) H.R.L.R. 1.

[38] The case was determined by a split in the Grand Chamber of the European Court of 9:8.

[39] Judge Spano, 'Universality or Diversity of Human Rights? Strasbourg in the Age of Subsidiarity' (2014) 14 H.R.L.R. 487, 497.

part at least, the uncertain domestic response to procedural human rights review pursuant to the HRA.

10.3 Procedural Judicial Review in the United Kingdom

Judicial review in the United Kingdom is bifurcated, with review of administrative action and of legislation regarded as being conceptually distinct. As regards the former, judicial review of administrative action remains a largely procedural guarantee; the common law of judicial review provides for a supervisory, rather than an appellate, jurisdiction which is focused on the legality of a decision (rather than its merits, or substance).[40] Judicial review of legislation, meanwhile, is a relatively recent addition to a constitutional system in which legislative process lay, and which substantially lies still, beyond the realms of justiciability. Legislative review is currently limited to scenarios in which domestic statute is alleged to be in contravention of European laws;[41] there exists no freestanding or common law power to review the constitutionality or legality of primary legislation enacted by the Westminster Parliament.[42] Implementation of the HRA has therefore legitimated judicial scrutiny of the compatibility of primary legislation with the

[40] The canonical articulation of the substantive grounds of judicial review at common law can be found in *Council of Civil Service Unions* v. *Minister for the Civil Service* [1985] A.C. 374, 410–411 (Lord Diplock): 'one can conveniently classify under three heads the grounds upon which administrative action is subject to control by judicial review. The first ground I would call "illegality," the second "irrationality" and the third "procedural impropriety." [...] By "illegality" as a ground for judicial review I mean that the decision-maker must understand correctly the law that regulates his decision-making power and must give effect to it. Whether he has or not is par excellence a justiciable question to be decided, in the event of dispute, by those persons, the judges, by whom the judicial power of the state is exercisable. By "irrationality" I mean what can by now be succinctly referred to as "Wednesbury unreasonableness" (*Associated Provincial Picture Houses Ltd.* v. *Wednesbury Corporation* [1948] 1 K.B. 223). It applies to a decision which is so outrageous in its defiance of logic or of accepted moral standards that no sensible person who had applied his mind to the question to be decided could have arrived at it...I have described the third head as "procedural impropriety" rather than failure to observe basic rules of natural justice or failure to act with procedural fairness towards the person who will be affected by the decision. This is because susceptibility to judicial review under this head covers also failure by an administrative tribunal to observe procedural rules that are expressly laid down in the legislative instrument by which its jurisdiction is conferred, even where such failure does not involve any denial of natural justice.'

[41] Pursuant to the provisions of the European Communities Act 1972 and Human Rights Act 1998.

[42] Cf. *R. (on the application of Jackson)* v. *Attorney General* [2005] UKHL 56; [2006] 1 A.C. 262, at [102] (Lord Steyn) and [159] (Baroness Hale).

Convention rights,[43] *and* introduced a statutory species of illegality to supplement the existing common law grounds of judicial review (introducing a further sub-division into the domestic law of judicial review in so doing[44]). The foundation of the latter can be found in Section 6 of the HRA, which renders it '*unlawful* for a public authority to act in a way which is incompatible with a Convention right'. As will be seen, this provision has also been interpreted as directing courts' analysis towards the substance of public body decision-making and away from the traditional procedural focus of judicial review at common law.

10.3.1 Judicial Review of Administrative/Executive Action

Fair process lies at the very heart of English administrative law:

> The teeth of public law are in process review. Most successful judicial review claims succeed on the basis that the decision-maker has done something in the wrong way, rather than the decision-maker has done something that is, all things considered, unjustifiable.[45]

Many of the central principles of the common law of judicial review of administrative action can therefore be seen to highlight procedural flaws or defects in executive decision-making. As such, decisions might be challenged and might be demonstrated to fail to meet the standards required under the head of procedural fairness on the grounds that the relevant decision-maker was biased,[46] that the claimant was denied a fair hearing[47] or that the claimant enjoyed a reasonable expectation which

[43] Section 3(1) HRA provides: 'So far as it is possible to do so, primary legislation and subordinate legislation must be read and given effect in a way which is compatible with the Convention rights' (s.4 permits that legislation which cannot be rendered compatible with the Convention rights via interpretative means may be subject to a judicial declaration of incompatibility).

[44] With proportionality review (in HRA adjudication) co-existing, occasionally uneasily, alongside *Wednesbury* (reasonableness) review within administrative and common law. For a recent assessment of this division, see: J. N. E. Varuhas, 'Against Unification' in H. Wilberg and M. Elliott, *The Scope and Intensity of Substantive Review* (Oxford: Hart Publishing, 2015) (Cf. *Pham* v. *Secretary of State for the Home Department* [2015] UKSC 19; [2015] 1 W.L.R. 1591).

[45] T. Hickman, *Public Law After the Human Rights Act* (Oxford: Hart Publishing, 2010), p. 225.

[46] See e.g. *Dimes* v. *Grand Junction Canal Co Proprietors* (1852) 3 H.L.C. 759; *R.* v. *Bow Street Metropolitan Stipendiary Magistrate, ex parte Pinochet Ugarte (No.2)* [2000] 1 A.C. 199.

[47] See e.g. *Cooper* v. *Wandsworth Board of Works* (1863) 14 C.B. (NS) 180; *Ridge* v. *Baldwin* [1964] A.C. 40.

had been frustrated by the decision.[48] Similarly, procedural defects in decision-making may also give rise to a challenge on the basis of a decision's illegality; taking decisions on the basis of irrelevant considerations[49] and the use of an allocated power for an improper purpose[50] both amount to essentially procedural grounds of illegality.

The common law jurisdiction of judicial review has therefore traditionally eschewed review of the substance, or merits, of executive or administrative decisions; judicial review permits intervention in defective public body decision-making. It does not permit the court to substitute its own decision for that which has been challenged. As Mead has argued, 'only if the challenge is based on irrationality has there been any level of substantive review'.[51] The law relating to judicial review of *administrative* action developed in this way in order to ensure that powers delegated by Parliament to officials were validly exercised in accordance with the terms of the statutory delegation.[52] The corollary of this *ultra vires* approach to review of administrative power is recognition of the necessary (and *intra vires*) policy autonomy of public bodies and elected officials. Judicial review in English law has therefore traditionally reflected a 'conception of limited judicial authority, recognising that in most cases a public authority may exercise a genuine choice between competing public policy objectives and contrasting methods of implementation'.[53]

10.3.2 Legislative and/or Constitutional Review

The principle of parliamentary sovereignty and Article 9 of the Bill of Rights 1688 provide the pillars on which the traditional non-justiciability of both legislative content and legislative process are based. Parliamentary sovereignty and the consequent (and concurrent) supremacy of primary legislation have served to focus judicial attempts to

[48] See e.g. *R.* v. *Liverpool Corporation, ex parte Liverpool Taxi Fleet Operators' Association* [1972] 2 Q.B. 299. It should be noted that the modern doctrine of legitimate expectations extends beyond the protection of purely procedural interests (see: F. Ahmed and A. Perry, 'The Coherence of the Doctrine of Legitimate Expectations' (2014) 73 C.L.J. 61).

[49] See e.g. *Roberts* v. *Hopwood* [1925] A.C. 578.

[50] See e.g. *Wheeler* v. *Leicester City Council* [1985] A.C. 1054.

[51] D. Mead, 'Outcomes Aren't All: Defending Process-Based Judicial Review of Public Authority Decisions under the Human Rights Act' [2012] P.L. 61, 63.

[52] For analysis, see: P. Craig, 'Competing Models of Judicial Review' [1999] P.L. 428.

[53] T.R.S. Allan, 'Human Rights and Judicial Review: A Critique of "Due Deference"' [2006] C.L.J. 671, 679.

interpret the law around the specific statutory language adopted: 'what the Queen in Parliament enacts *is* law'.[54] This constitutional presumption of statutory legality has conditioned (self-)perceptions of the judicial function, as well as the legitimate targets of judicial review.[55] As a result, in *British Railways Board* v. *Pickin*, having been asked to set aside a statutory provision on the basis that Parliament had been fraudulently misled into enacting it, the Appellate Committee of the House of Lords emphatically found that the court enjoyed no competence to examine the propriety of parliamentary procedure. Lord Morris of Borth-y-Gest said the following:

> It must surely be for Parliament to lay down the procedures which are to be followed before a Bill can become an Act. It must be for Parliament to decide whether its decreed procedures have in fact been followed. It must be for Parliament to lay down and to construe its Standing Orders and further to decide whether they have been obeyed: it must be for Parliament to decide whether in any particular case to dispense with ampleness with such orders. It must be for Parliament to decide whether it is satisfied that an Act should be passed in the form and with the wording set out in the Act. It must be for Parliament to decide what documentary material or testimony it requires and the extent to which Parliamentary privilege should attach. It would be impracticable and undesirable for the High Court of Justice to embark upon an inquiry concerning the effect or the effectiveness of the internal procedures in the High Court of Parliament or an inquiry whether in any particular case those procedures were effectively followed.[56]

The decision in *Pickin* drew on a series of established common law authorities, not least among which was *Edinburgh and Dalkeith Railway Co.* v. *Wauchope*. In that decision, Lord Campbell had made the following remarks:

> no court of justice can inquire into the mode in which [primary legislation] was introduced into Parliament, nor into what was done previous to its introduction, or what passed in Parliament during its progress in its various stages through both Houses.[57]

[54] V. Bogdanor, *Politics and the Constitution: Essays on British Government* (Aldershot: Dartmouth, 1996), p. 5 (emphasis added).

[55] For an overview, see: R. Masterman and J. E. K. Murkens, 'Skirting Supremacy and Subordination: The Constitutional Authority of the United Kingdom Supreme Court' [2013] P.L. 800.

[56] *British Railways Board* v. *Pickin* [1974] Q.C. 765, 790.

[57] *Edinburgh and Dalkeith Railway Co.* v. *Wauchope* (1842) VIII Clark and Finnelly 710, 725.

As a result, courts have treated parliamentary process as lying beyond the legitimate realms of judicial inquiry.

That judicial interpretation of statute is a process which is, in a sense, disassociated from the legislative procedures which saw the legislation enacted is confirmed by the Bill of Rights 1689, Article 9 of which provides that 'freedom of speech, and debates or proceedings in parliament, ought not to be impeached or questioned in any court or place out of Parliament'. Article 9 is, Kavanagh argues, commonly 'understood to preclude any judicial recourse to *Hansard* for the purposes of statutory interpretation'.[58] In other words, the evidence from which courts derive their understanding of statutory purpose is the output of legislative deliberations – the legislation itself – rather than from arguments advanced (or not advanced) during the course of the legislative process. The extent to which the courts have held themselves to respect the procedural and substantive legislative autonomy of Parliament can be seen in the relatively narrowly drawn circumstances under which it is regarded as being legitimate for courts to utilise *Hansard* as an aid to statutory construction. It is only since the seminal decision of the House of Lords in *Pepper* v. *Hart* in 1992 that judicial reference to parliamentary debates has been permitted, and even then, only in order to illuminate legislative intent in those circumstances where the apparent interpretation of the statute would lead to an ambiguity or absurdity.[59]

10.4 Process Review and the Influence of the Human Rights Act

That the HRA was not intended to vest disproportionate authority in the judges, to the detriment of the elected branches of government, is well-documented.[60] To the extent that it is a meaningful term of constitutional discourse, the HRA is a 'dialogic' instrument, which allocates responsibility for the realisation of the rights it protects across the branches of state. To this end, the processes of public body decision-making were almost certainly intended to be impacted upon by the enactment of the HRA.[61]

[58] A. Kavanagh, 'Proportionality and Parliamentary Debates: Exploring some Forbidden Territory' (2014) 34 O.J.L.S. 443, 453.

[59] *Pepper* v. *Hart* [1993] A.C. 593.

[60] See for instance I. Leigh and R. Masterman, *Making Rights Real: The Human Rights Act in its First Decade* (Oxford: Hart Publishing, 2008), chs. 1, 2 and 5.

[61] See generally P. Boateng and J. Straw, 'Bringing Rights Home: Labour's Plans to Incorporate the European Convention on Human Rights into UK Law' [1997] E.H.R.L.R. 71.

As Lord Irvine of Lairg QC, former Lord Chancellor and one of the architects of the Act, argued before the Joint Parliamentary Committee on Human Rights in 2001:

> a culture of respect for human rights is to create a society in which our public institutions are habitually, automatically responsive to human rights considerations in relation to every procedure they follow, in relation to every decision they take, in relation to every piece of legislation they sponsor.[62]

It was clear that the Labour government's intentions were that the HRA precipitate a step-change in governmental decision-making; as the Home Office Minister, Lord Williams, echoed in the House of Lords:

> Every public authority will know that its behaviour, its structure, its conclusions and its executive actions will be subject to this culture.[63]

Enforcement of the HRA therefore imposes upon public bodies (including courts, but excluding Parliament) a statutory obligation to act in compliance with the Convention rights.[64]

Though the Act excluded Parliament from its definition of public authorities to whom section 6 would apply,[65] it is clear that some modification of legislative process was envisaged. The Act requires that draft legislation be stated compatible with the Convention rights upon being debated in Parliament (although it makes provision for proposals which cannot be so endorsed to proceed).[66] The HRA has also seen the establishment of a Joint Parliamentary Committee on Human Rights[67] and, in the event of a judicial finding that primary legislation cannot be interpreted in a way which would achieve Convention-compliance,[68] more importantly provides that the locus of remedial action should be within a legislative process administered by the elected arms of government.[69] It is this characteristic of the HRA which emphasises the conceptual and practical distance between the compact between

[62] Joint Committee on Human Rights, Minutes of Evidence, 19 March 2001, 38 (Lord Irvine of Lairg, QC.).

[63] HL Debs, 3 November 1997, Vol. 582, Col. 1308.

[64] Section 6, HRA 1998.

[65] Section 6(3), HRA 1998.

[66] Section 19, HRA 1998.

[67] For a summary of the role and early work of the Joint Committee, see I. Leigh and R. Masterman, *Making Rights Real: The Human Rights Act in its First Decade* (Oxford: Hart Publishing, 2008), pp. 36–42.

[68] Section 3(1) HRA 1998.

[69] Sections 4 and 10, HRA 1998 (Section 4 provides for the courts to make a 'declaration of incompatibility' in the event that primary legislation cannot be interpreted compatibly with the Convention rights).

branches that it seeks to engineer and the judicio-centric precedents of many of its constitutional comparators.

Whilst the Act itself makes few prescriptions as to how public decision-makers are to go about the processes of achieving compliance with the protected rights, section 2(1) does impose a burden of process upon the courts who, in determining questions arising in connection with the Convention rights, must 'take into account' decisions of the ECtHR. The judicial approach resulting from this obligation initially saw domestic courts positioned as domestic proxies for the ECtHR, with the consequence that the substance of the emergent HRA jurisprudence very closely replicated its Strasbourg counterpart. The development of this so-called 'mirror principle'[70] fed criticisms of the HRA scheme which argued that the jurisprudence of the European Court was afforded too great an influence in the domestic sphere to the exclusion of distinctly domestic approaches to human rights adjudication.[71] Examination of the extent to which the European Court's use of methods of process review have been translated into domestic adjudication reveals an important disconnect between rights adjudication at the supranational and national judicial levels (as well as between pre- and post-HRA approaches to judicial review).

10.4.1 Away from Process-Based Review of Administrative Decisions?

Section 6 of the HRA renders it unlawful for public authorities or private bodies exercising public functions to 'act' in a way which is incompatible with the Convention rights.[72] The primary focus of section 6 is on the substance of a public body's decision:

> The first question that section 6 asks is result-orientated – were the claimant's Convention rights violated by the public authority? If the

[70] J. Lewis, 'The European Ceiling on Rights' [2007] P.L. 720. See also R. Masterman, 'Deconstructing the Mirror Principle' in R. Masterman and I. Leigh (eds), *The United Kingdom's Statutory Bill of Rights: Constitutional and Comparative Perspectives (183 Proceedings of the British Academy)* (Oxford: Oxford University Press, 2013).

[71] On which see: R. Masterman, *Supreme, Submissive or Symbiotic? United Kingdom Courts and the European Court of Human Rights* (London: Constitution Unit, 2015).

[72] Section 6(1) HRA provides: 'It is unlawful for a public authority to act in a way which is incompatible with a Convention right.'

> answer is affirmative the process by which the public authority came to violate his or her Convention rights is irrelevant.[73]

While it is certainly arguable that 'acts' of public authorities encompass the processes by which decisions were taken, adjudication under the HRA has seen a judicial reluctance to impose specific procedural requirements on public body decisions impacting on the Convention rights. The compliance with and/or proportionality of public body decisions with the Convention rights is a matter of an *ex post facto* assessment by the courts which is primarily directed towards the result or outcome of public body decision-making.

Two cases in particular have served to emphasise an approach to Convention-compliance which is primarily based on the outcomes of public body decision-making. The first of these decisions, *R. (SB)* v. *Governors of Denbigh High School*,[74] concerned a challenge made to the imposition of a School's uniform policy on the grounds that it prohibited the wearing of certain forms of religious dress and was therefore an infringement of the claimant's Article 9 rights.[75] The second, *Belfast City Council* v. *Miss Behavin' Ltd*,[76] concerned the denial by a local authority of a licence to use premises as a sex shop. In both decisions, the apex court found against a process of review which would have imposed overly onerous procedural obligations on the relevant public body.[77]

To contextualise this debate, the Court of Appeal in *Denbigh* – per Brooke LJ – would have seen the public body decision-maker respond to the following series of questions:

> (1) Has the claimant established that she has a relevant Convention right which qualifies for protection under article 9(1)? (2) Subject to any justification that is established under article 9(2), has that Convention right been violated? (3) Was the interference with her Convention right prescribed by law in the Convention sense of the expression? (4) Did the interference have a legitimate aim? (5) What are the considerations that need to be balanced against each other when determining whether the

[73] I. Leigh, 'Taking Rights Proportionately: Judicial Review, the Human Rights Act and Strasbourg' [2002] P.L. 265, 283.

[74] *R. (on the application of Begum)* v. *Governors of Denbigh High School* [2006] UKHL 15; [2007] 1 A.C. 100.

[75] Specifically, the policy did not permit female Muslim students to wear the *jilbab*, instead permitting them to wear the *shalwar kameez*.

[76] *Belfast City Council* v. *Miss Behavin' Ltd* [2007] UKHL 19; [2007] 1 W.L.R. 1420.

[77] A third case reiterated the findings in *Begum* and *Miss Behavin'*: *R. (on the application of Nasseri)* v. *Secretary of State for the Home Department* [2009] UKHL 23; [2010] 1 A.C. 1.

> interference was necessary in a democratic society for the purposes of achieving that aim? (6) Was the interference justified under article 9(2)?[78]

On appeal to the House of Lords, the Senior Law Lord, Lord Bingham, found that judicial enquiry should focus on 'the practical outcome, not the quality of the decision-making process that led to it'.[79] Echoing the approach to the interpretation of section 6(1) noted above, Lord Bingham found that '[t]he unlawfulness proscribed by s.6(1) is acting in a way which is incompatible with a Convention right, not relying on a defective process of reasoning'.[80] As the House of Lords subsequently confirmed in the decision in *Belfast City Council* v. *Miss Behavin' Ltd*, the central question for the courts must always be to adjudge whether the relevant decision infringed the applicant's Convention rights. Even in adjudication over those Convention rights with 'procedural content':

> the question is still whether there has been an actual violation of the applicant's Convention rights and not whether the decision-maker properly considered the question of whether his rights would be violated or not.[81]

The House of Lords advanced three primary reasons for the avoidance of requiring public bodies to adhere to specific structural requirements in the making of decisions which might impact on an individual's Convention rights. The first of these reasons might be labelled 'constitutional', the second 'practical' and the third 'institutional'.

First, the Law Lords noted that imposing a procedural burden on public authority decision-makers would be inconsistent with their understanding of the requirements of the Convention. The Convention rights require that the substance of the right (e.g. family life, freedom of religion) is guaranteed. When speaking to substantive rights, the Convention is not prescriptive about the process to be followed by the public authority; what is mandated is the protection of the right in substance. As explained by Lord Hoffmann in *Begum*:

[78] *R. (on the application of Begum)* v. *Governors of Denbigh High School* [2005] EWCA Civ 199; [2005] 1 W.L.R. 3372, at [75]. On which see: T. Poole, 'Of Headscarves and Heresies: The Denbigh High School Case and Public Authority Decision Making under the Human Rights Act' [2005] P.L. 685.

[79] *R. (on the application of Begum)* v. *Governors of Denbigh High School* [2006] UKHL 15; [2007] 1 A.C. 100, at [31].

[80] *R. (on the application of Begum)* v. *Governors of Denbigh High School* [2006] UKHL 15; [2007] 1 A.C. 100, at [29].

[81] *Belfast City Council* v. *Miss Behavin' Ltd* [2007] UKHL 19; [2007] 1 W.L.R. 1420, at [15].

> [A]rticle 9 is concerned with substance, not procedure. It confers no right to have a decision made in any particular way. What matters is the result: was the right to manifest a religious belief restricted in a way which is not justified under article 9(2)?[82]

The approach of the House of Lords on this point was informed by an approach to the interpretation of the HRA which viewed the purpose of the Act being to give better effect to rights (and remedies) which would otherwise only be available to claimants at Strasbourg.[83] The approach is neatly summarised by Lord Nicholls in the decision in *R.* v. *Secretary of State for Foreign and Commonwealth Affairs, ex parte Quark Fishing*:

> The [Human Rights] Act was intended to provide a domestic remedy where a remedy would have been available in Strasbourg. Conversely, the Act was not intended to provide a domestic remedy where a remedy would not have been available in Strasbourg.[84]

The House of Lords' decisions are therefore grounded in an approach to the interpretation of the HRA which sees domestic courts positioned as local proxies for the Strasbourg Court, their task being to 'assess how a claim by [an] appellant . . . would fare before the European Court of Human Rights'.[85] (Given the failure of the House of Lords to acknowledge the procedural turn of the Strasbourg Court, it should be noted that the apex court's approach extends to replicating the adjudicative outcome that could be expected at Strasbourg, rather than the adjudicative methodology of the European Court.)

Secondly, it would be impractical and/or inefficient to expect public authorities to engage in detailed, legalistic analysis measuring the requirements of the relevant Convention right against the measure under consideration.[86] Lord Hoffmann in *Miss Behavin'* argued that, as a result, the HRA could not impose such obligations on public bodies: '[a] construction of the 1998 Act which requires ordinary citizens in local government to produce such formulaic incantations would make it

82 *R. (on the application of Begum)* v. *Governors of Denbigh High School* [2006] UKHL 15; [2007] 1 A.C. 100, at [68].

83 Compare R. Masterman, 'Aspiration or Foundation? The Status of the Strasbourg Jurisprudence and the Convention Rights in Domestic Law' in H. Fenwick, G. Phillipson and R. Masterman (eds), *Judicial Reasoning after the Human Rights Act* (Cambridge: Cambridge University Press, 2007).

84 *R.* v. *Secretary of State for Foreign and Commonwealth Affairs, ex parte Quark Fishing* [2005] UKHL 57; [2006] 1 A.C. 529, at [34].

85 *R. (on the application of Al-Jedda)* v. *Secretary of State for Defence* [2007] UKHL 58; [2008] 1 A.C. 332, at [55].

86 *Belfast City Council* v. *Miss Behavin' Ltd* [2007] UKHL 19; [2007] 1 W.L.R. 1420, at [13].

ridiculous'.[87] The third ground for the avoidance of the process-focused approach acknowledges that public authorities will often not possess the competence or expertise to conduct a precise, legalistic proportionality analysis. As Lord Hoffmann put it in *Begum*, 'teachers and governors cannot be expected to make such decisions with textbooks on human rights law at their elbows'.[88]

As to the departure from the traditional process focused approach of judicial review, in *R. (on the application of Begum)* v. *Governors of Denbigh High School*, Lord Hoffmann made explicit the divergence between review on the basis of the Convention rights and the orthodox approach to judicial review:

> In domestic judicial review, the court is usually concerned with whether the decision-maker reached his decision in the right way rather than whether he got what the court might think to be the right answer. But Article 9 is concerned with substance, not procedure.[89]

As Lord Hoffmann continued, 'no display of human rights learning' by public bodies could render compatible a decision which, in the view of the court, violated the applicant's rights.[90] It was also clear from the speech of the Baroness Hale that HRA review should be regarded as being conceptually and procedurally distinct from judicial review as ordinarily conceived:

> The role of the court in human rights adjudication is quite different from the role of the court in ordinary judicial review of administrative action. In human rights adjudication, the court is concerned with whether the human rights of the claimant have in fact been infringed, not with whether the administrative decision-maker properly took them into account.[91]

It follows from this that, while the requirements of proportionality could prompt public authority decision-makers to analyse the potential impact of (less intrusive) alternatives to the proposed policy decision, this analysis need not impose an undue burden on public authorities and need not be explicitly Convention-based. While it may be open to public bodies to consider the potential impact of a particular policy or decision

[87] *Belfast City Council* v. *Miss Behavin' Ltd* [2007] UKHL 19; [2007] 1 W.L.R. 1420, at [13].

[88] *R. (on the application of Begum)* v. *Governors of Denbigh High School* [2006] UKHL 15; [2007] 1 A.C. 100, at [68]

[89] *R. (on the application of Begum)* v. *Governors of Denbigh High School* [2006] UKHL 15; [2007] 1 A.C. 100, at [68].

[90] *Belfast City Council* v. *Miss Behavin' Ltd* [2007] UKHL 19; [2007] 1 W.L.R. 1420, at [13].

[91] *Belfast City Council* v. *Miss Behavin' Ltd* [2007] UKHL 19; [2007] 1 W.L.R. 1420, at [31].

in substantive human rights terms, and while there may be good reasons for doing so, it is not a requirement of the decision-making process which will be imposed, or policed, by the court. Section 6(1) of the HRA does not therefore seem to require public bodies to engage with the substance of the Convention rights themselves during the decision-making process; it is the outcome of that process which the courts will assess for Convention compliance.

The appropriateness of this outcome-focused approach has, however, been widely contested. One view suggests that the potency of the HRA as a tool of rights protection can be evidenced in the ability of the courts to 'make authoritative determinations as to what the Convention rights require'.[92] Poole's criticisms of the process-focused approach of the Court of Appeal in *Begum* therefore accuse the court of making a 'fetish of procedure' and warn against the 'excessive judicialisation of the public sphere'.[93] By contrast, the apparent absurdity of the outcomes approach is effectively captured by Hickman:

> The effect of the House of Lords' judgments…is that even where a decision-maker decides a case by an irrational process of reasoning, or even without any consideration at all, it will be compatible with the Convention rights and it will be consistent with the decision-maker's responsibilities under the Human Rights Act, as long as the outcome is compatible with the Convention rights.[94]

Given that one of the stated objectives of the HRA was to fully integrate human rights considerations in the processes of public authority decision-making, this view categorises the outcomes approach as being based on 'judicial exclusivity'[95] and therefore unable to fully account for, or give credit to, public body decisions which consider human rights considerations, and an inadequate characterisation of the HRA's rather more 'diffuse' scheme.[96] As a result, Dickson has argued that the failure of the courts to encourage rights-respecting processes in public body decision-making 'strikes at the heart of the mission of the Human

[92] T. Poole, 'The Reformation of English Administrative Law' (2009) 68 C.L.J. 142, 160.

[93] T. Poole, 'Of Headscarves and Heresies: The Denbigh High School Case and Public Authority Decision Making under the Human Rights Act' [2005] P.L. 685, 691 and 694.

[94] T. Hickman, *Public Law after the Human Rights Act* (Oxford: Hart Publishing, 2010), p. 228. See also D. Mead, 'Outcomes Aren't All: Defending Process-Based Judicial Review of Public Authority Decisions under the Human Rights Act' [2012] P.L. 61, 81.

[95] D. Mead, 'Outcomes Aren't All: Defending Process-Based Judicial Review of Public Authority Decisions under the Human Rights Act' [2012] P.L. 61, 63.

[96] D. Mead, 'Outcomes Aren't All: Defending Process-Based Judicial Review of Public Authority Decisions under the Human Rights Act' [2012] P.L. 61, 63.

Rights Act, which is to inculcate an appreciation of human rights in all public authorities'.[97]

10.4.2 Towards Judicial Examination of Legislative Process?

The HRA was also intended to embed rights concerns into the pre-legislative and legislative processes of the United Kingdom Parliament.[98] Given that a stated aim of the HRA's authors was that the doctrine of parliamentary sovereignty remain undisturbed,[99] and the traditional reluctance of courts in the United Kingdom to explicitly engage with issues of legislative process, it might readily be assumed that questions relating to the Convention compatibility of primary legislation would also be primarily oriented towards an outcomes-focused assessment.

The increased willingness of courts to (prior to enactment of the HRA) utilise purposive methods of interpretation had already prompted a movement away from the highly positivist approaches that had dominated judicial reasoning during much of the twentieth century.[100] But the obligation imposed upon courts by section 3(1) of the HRA required further refinement of the judicial approach, with judges required to assess the compatibility of primary legislation with the requirements of the Convention rights. Inherent in this task, and assuming engagement and a *prima facie* interference with one of the protected rights, is the requirement that courts ask whether the extent of the interference is proportionate to the aim pursued by the legislation. It was clear from the outset that the approach of the courts to the application of section 3(1) was not to be so focused as to require only linguistic assessment of statutory purpose:

> In enacting section 3(1), it cannot have been the intention of Parliament to place those asserting their rights at the mercy of the linguistic choices of the individual who happened to draft the provision in question. What

[97] B. Dickson, *Human Rights and the United Kingdom Supreme Court* (Oxford: Oxford University press, 2013), p. 46. See: *Doherty* v. *Birmingham City Council* [2008] UKHL 57; [2009] 1 A.C. 367, at [109]: 'public authorities are bound to take account of human rights. . .this should be seen as a normal part of their function, not an exotic introduction.' For an early sketch of the effects of the HRA on the policy-making process, see: Department for Constitutional Affairs, *Review of the Implementation of the Human Rights Act* (2006), esp. pp.19–28.

[98] See Section 19, HRA 1998. [99] HC Debates, 16 February 1998, Vol.306, Col.772.

[100] See J. Steyn, 'Does Legal Formalism Hold Sway in England?' (1996) *Current Legal Problems* 43.

> matters is not so much the particular phraseology chosen by the draftsman as the substance of the measure which Parliament had enacted in those words.[101]

As the House of Lords noted in *Ghaidan* v. *Godin Mendoza*, the task of the court in applying section 3(1) is to 'concentrat[e] on matters of substance, rather than on matters of mere language'.[102] In the sphere of statutory interpretation, as with questions of public body decision-making, the courts have taken outcomes to be the focus of their enquiry into the Convention-compatibility of an Act. The point was reiterated in *R. (Williamson)* v. *Secretary of State for Education and Employment*; 'the proportionality of a statutory measure is to be judged objectively and not by the quality of reasons advanced in support of the measure in the course of parliamentary debate'.[103]

The European Court's reliance on process review has emphasised that the content of legislative deliberation can support a finding of proportionality. Direct and routine engagement with *Hansard* for the purpose of assessing the quality of legislative process is, however, impermissible. In the Court of Appeal's decision in *Wilson* v. *First County Trust*, the suggestion that the justificatory questions posed by proportionality analysis required a more interventionist approach was discernible:

> It is one thing to accept the need to defer to an opinion which can be seen to be the product of reasoned consideration based on policy; it is quite another thing to be required to accept, without question, an opinion for which no reason of policy is advanced.[104]

By analogy, the court appears to acknowledge the artificiality of a proportionality assessment which is premised on the orthodox approach to statutory interpretation by the courts, that is, a sovereignty-driven acceptance of the legality of the measure under which the assessment of arguments advanced, or not advanced, during legislative debates is non-justiciable.

In spite of this, indications that the courts indirectly acknowledge parliamentary deliberation of legislation affecting the Convention rights are not difficult to find, and it is relatively commonplace to see reference

[101] *Ghaidan* v. *Godin Mendoza* [2004] UKHL 30; [2004] 2 A.C. 557, at [123].
[102] *Ghaidan* v. *Godin Mendoza* [2004] UKHL 30; [2004] 2 A.C. 557, at [123].
[103] *R. (Williamson)* v. *Secretary of State for Education and Employment* [2005] UKHL 15; [2005] 2 A.C. 246, at [51].
[104] *Wilson* v. *First County Trust* [2002] Q.B. 74, at [33].

to the 'great weight'[105] which the courts acknowledge should attach to legislative decisions, and the presumption of parliamentary competence to determine how competing societal interests be balanced during the legislative process; 'line[s] must be drawn, and it is for Parliament to decide where'.[106] In those cases involving social and economic policy and the allocation of governmental resources, the highest courts have similarly indicated that 'the choices that are to be made can easily be seen as falling within the discretionary area of judgment best left to the *considered opinion* of the legislature'.[107]

Examining the extent to which the courts are engaging with the 'forbidden territory' of parliamentary process and debate, Kavanagh has asked whether such statements are 'rhetorical flourishes to emphasize the superior status of legislation' or whether 'they have a greater practical significance for judicial assessments about whether legislation complies with Convention rights'.[108] Kavanagh concludes that, in parallel with the flexible approach of the ECtHR, the Law Lords and Supreme Court have drawn both positive and negative inferences from the extent of parliamentary engagement with the implications for the protected Convention rights in the process of proportionality analysis. Some caution is needed here, however, as even though the Supreme Court has explicitly acknowledged that parliamentary process can affect the intensity of review,[109] the extent to which legislative process is susceptible to judicial examination is subject to ongoing limitations.

The leading case remains the House of Lords decision in *Wilson* v. *First County Trust*.[110] As Lord Nicholls outlined in that decision, in statutory review under the HRA, the court must ask 'whether the means employed by the statute to achieve the policy objective is appropriate and not disproportionate to its adverse effect'.[111] While, as a result, it may be necessary for a court to consider *Hansard* in order to be in a 'better position to understand the legislation', the House of Lords was careful to

[105] *R. (on the application of Animal Defenders International)* v. *Secretary of State for Culture, Media and Sport* [2008] UKHL 15; [2008] 1 A.C. 1312, at [33].

[106] *R. (on the application of Animal Defenders International)* v. *Secretary of State for Culture, Media and Sport* [2008] UKHL 15; [2008] 1 A.C. 1312, at [33].

[107] *Kay* v. *Lambeth LBC* [2006] UKHL 10; [2006] 2 A.C. 465, at [77] (emphasis added).

[108] A. Kavanagh, 'Proportionality and Parliamentary Debates: Exploring some Forbidden Territory' (2014) 34 O.J.L.S. 443, 445.

[109] *R. (on the application of SG and others)* v. *Secretary of State for Work and Pensions* [2015] UKSC 16; [2015] 1 W.L.R. 1449, at [92]-[96].

[110] *Wilson* v. *First County Trust (No.2)* [2003] UKHL 40; [2004] 1 A.C. 816.

[111] *Wilson* v. *First County Trust (No.2)* [2003] UKHL 40; [2004] 1 A.C. 816, at [62].

note the modesty of the change in approach the HRA would require. Lord Nicholls made the following observations:

> Beyond [the] use of *Hansard* as a source of background information, the content of parliamentary debates has *no direct relevance* to the issues the court is called upon to decide in compatibility cases and, hence, *these debates are not a proper matter for investigation or consideration by the courts.* In particular, it is a cardinal constitutional principle that the will of Parliament is expressed in the language used by it in its enactments. The proportionality of legislation is to be judged on that basis. The courts are to have due regard to the legislation as an expression of the will of Parliament. The proportionality of a statutory measure *is not to be judged by the quality of reasons advanced in support of it* in the course of parliamentary debate, or by the subjective state of mind of individual ministers or other members. . .*Lack of cogent justification in the course of parliamentary debate is not a matter which 'counts against' the legislation on issues of proportionality.* The court is called upon to evaluate the proportionality of the legislation, not the adequacy of the minister's exploration of the policy options or of his explanations to Parliament. The latter would contravene Article 9 of the Bill of Rights. The court would then be presuming to evaluate the sufficiency of the legislative process leading up to the enactment of the statute.[112]

While the court is ultimately concerned with the proportionality of the statutory measure under debate, the extent to which Parliament has or has not considered alternative and less intrusive measures would not appear to be a legitimate line of judicial inquiry. Whether a statute is considered to be Convention compliant is largely an objective judicial assessment which 'must be judged primarily by what the legislation provides'.[113] Judicial examination of legislative process within such a proportionality analysis is very much confined to a quantitative, rather than qualitative, assessment of parliamentary deliberations.

10.5 A Medial Approach?

In the context of HRA review of public authority decision-making, considerations regarding the process by which the public authority arrived at the decision are not, and should not be, dismissed as irrelevant. Considerations of substance and process are not mutually exclusive;[114]

[112] *Wilson* v. *First County Trust (No.2)* [2003] UKHL 40; [2004] 1 A.C. 816, at [67] (emphasis added).

[113] *Salvesen* v. *Riddell* [2013] UKSC 22, at [39].

[114] On which see: A. Kavanagh, 'Reasoning About Proportionality under the Human Rights Act 1998: Outcomes, Substance and Process' (2014) 130 L.Q.R. 235, 247–249.

the courts are grappling with the extent of the relevance and weight that ought to be attributed to process when deciding whether a measure or decision has unjustifiably interfered with a Convention right. Decision-making process will not impact upon a court's assessment of whether a Convention right is engaged, or whether there has been a *prima facie* interference with the right in question. Rather, as with questions relating to the extent to which the expertise or constitutional competence of the primary decision-maker should carry weight, considerations of process may factor in judicial analysis; a thorough, consultative process can positively influence the court's assessment of proportionality, while a procedurally deficient process can weigh against such a finding. In the sphere of public body decision-making at least, while a structured proportionality analysis will not be judicially required of primary decision-makers, evidence that a 'Convention-like' analysis had taken place might weigh in favour of the decision-maker in the court's assessment. As Lord Neuberger suggested in *Belfast City Council* v. *Miss Behavin' Ltd*:

> it seems to me . . . that where a council has properly considered the issue in relation to a particular application, the court is inherently less likely to conclude that the decision ultimately infringes the applicant's rights.[115]

On this reading, process, it would seem, is not entirely irrelevant to the court's assessment of proportionality. Developing Lord Neuberger's approach to the weighing of process considerations, Baroness Hale went some way towards outlining what 'proper' process might entail. The primary question for the court to resolve, Baroness Hale observed, was whether or not the claimant's Convention rights had been infringed.[116] The court's response to that question was not, however, to be completely disassociated from the decision-making process undertaken by the primary decision-maker:

> the court has to decide whether the authority has violated the Convention rights. In doing so, it is bound to acknowledge that the local authority is much better placed than the court to decide whether the right of sex shop owners to sell pornographic literature and images should be restricted – for the prevention of disorder or crime, for the protection of health or morals, or for the protection of the rights of others. But the views of the local authority are bound to carry less weight where the

115 *Belfast City Council* v. *Miss Behavin' Ltd* [2007] UKHL 19; [2007] 1 W.L.R. 1420, at [91]. See also at [37].

116 *Belfast City Council* v. *Miss Behavin' Ltd* [2007] UKHL 19; [2007] 1 W.L.R. 1420, at [31].

> local authority has made no attempt to address that question. Had the Belfast City Council expressly set itself the task of balancing the rights of individuals to sell and buy pornographic literature and images against the interests of the wider community, a court would find it hard to upset the balance which the local authority had struck. But where there is no indication that this has been done, the court has no alternative but to strike the balance for itself, giving due weight to the judgments made by those who are in much closer touch with the people and the places involved than the court could ever be.[117]

Both Neuberger and Hale point towards an approach which maintains the HRA's focus on substance, without fully jettisoning the established procedural concerns of domestic judicial review. Both also indicate that the integration of Convention rights reasoning into public authority decision-making can weigh affirmatively in favour of a finding of compatibility. Decisions taken in the aftermath of *Denbigh* and *Miss Behavin'* illustrate that a failure to consider the rights implications of a decision might also permit adverse inferences to be drawn from the failure of decision-making processes to engage with the Convention implications of a decision.[118] Given the apparent primacy of outcome-focused judicial analysis highlighted by the above discussion, it is important to note that the language of section 6 does not foreclose a broader interpretation which would view 'acts' of public bodies as including decisions taken and the broader processes through which those decisions were generated. As a result, the ability of courts to scrutinise administrative processes is not definitively precluded by the HRA itself, even though the primary

[117] *Belfast City Council* v. *Miss Behavin' Ltd* [2007] UKHL 19; [2007] 1 W.L.R. 1420, at [37]. While T.R.S. Allan challenges Lady Hale's suggestion that judicial review and HRA review are conceptually different, he shares her sensitivity to the contextual dynamics and differences between public body and judicial decision-making processes: 'The greater the dependence of legal analysis on a sensitive judgment of complex and contested matters of empirical fact, especially where competing imperatives of constitutional right and public interest are finely balanced, the closer the court's intervention must move to a species of procedural review. The court's role must be to examine the quality of the administrative process, in which the public authority will enjoy a limited power to make its own appraisal of all the relevant circumstances, subject to the normal demands of rationality or reasonableness. The court has the final say on the appropriate reconciliation of public and personal, or general and particular, interests; but the judicial process should not be the only means of preserving the requisite balance between citizen and state'. (T.R.S. Allan, *The Sovereignty of Law: Freedom, Constitution and Common Law* (Oxford: Oxford University Press, 2013), p. 264).

[118] See: *R. (on the application of Bashir)* v. *Independent Adjudicator* [2011] EWHC 1108 (Admin); [2011] H.R.L.R. 30; *London Borough of Hillingdon* v. *Neary* [2011] EWHC 1377 (COP); [2011] 4 All E.R. 584.

focus of the judicial enquiry has tended to be taken, on the basis of both section 6 and the perceived approach of the European Court, to be primarily directed towards decision-making outcomes.

By contrast with section 6, the target of section 3(1) HRA is, linguistically, rather more precise: 'primary . . . *legislation*'. In spite of this, the implementation of the HRA has also prompted a subtle revision of the orthodox understanding of the courts' approach to examination of legislative process. Courts will afford weight to the judgment of the legislature over the legislative resolution of 'controversial and complex questions of fact arising out of moral and social dilemmas'[119] on the basis of Parliament's expert judgment and capacity to accommodate diverse perspectives *and* have been prepared to draw inferences from the apparent depth and diligence of legislative scrutiny. But the extent of this change should not be overstated. The degree to which courts might, to use the wording of Article 9 of the Bill of Rights, 'question' the quality of the parliamentary process remains an area within which the courts are cautious. As much has been observed most recently in the UK Supreme Court's decision in *HS2* (albeit in the context a dispute concerned primarily with the influence of EU law):

> Scrutiny of the workings of Parliament and whether they satisfy externally imposed criteria clearly involves questioning and potentially impeaching (i.e. condemning) Parliament's internal proceedings.[120]

The abiding judicial view that an assessment of 'the quality of ministerial consideration of the policy options available in the context of the evolution of a particular legislative measure' would 'contravene article 9 of the Bill of Rights 1689'[121] makes detailed scrutiny of legislative process constitutionally impermissible.

Given this significant limitation on the use of parliamentary debates during the adjudicative process, it is unsurprising to find that 'British courts are much more content to elicit the legislative mischief or purpose from other "external aids" to construction', including Select Committee documents, White Papers, Law Commission reports and so on.[122] While

[119] *R. (on the application of Nicklinson)* v. *Ministry of Justice* [2014] UKSC 38 [2015] A.C. 657, at [232].

[120] *R. (on the application of HS2 Action Alliance Ltd)* v. *Secretary of State for Transport* [2014] UKSC 3; [2014] 1 W.L.R. 324, at [86].

[121] *International Transport Roth GmbH* [2002] EWCA Civ 158; [2003] Q.B. 728, at [114].

[122] A. Kavanagh, 'Proportionality and Parliamentary Debates: Exploring some Forbidden Territory' (2014) 34 O.J.L.S. 443, 455.

such sources may well illuminate a courts' assessment of legislative intent, the inability of courts to carefully examine the adequacy of the primary reasons advanced for legislative change ensures first that judicial focus remains on the outcome of parliamentary deliberations, the legislation itself, and second that attempts to 'give weight' to parliamentary consideration of competing interests will continue to be blighted by suggestions of institutional 'servility, or perhaps gracious concession'[123] to the superior constitutional position of Parliament. For so long as assessment of the adequacy of legislative process remains beyond the constitutional Rubicon, domestic courts will be ill-positioned to fully appraise the proportionality of a legislative measure; a court's assessment of the quality of the legislative process will necessarily remain impressionistic, rather than forensic. As such, the domestic proportionality exercise will continue to display the artificiality highlighted above, given its potential disconnection from the content of relevant parliamentary debates, and the informed judicial accordance of weight will be compromised through the inability of the court to fully examine the available evidence advanced (publicly) in support of a chosen legislative course. While courts are rightly concerned to avoid the subversion of the democratic process, it is also recognised that the extent to which a decision might be legitimately referred to as the 'the considered judgment of a democratic assembly will vary according to the subject matter and the circumstances'.[124] Judicial recourse to proxies for the quality of legislative consideration may be appropriate, but cannot always provide the justificatory evidence which would underpin effective proportionality analysis. It may be more obviously acceptable to, for instance, afford positive weight to a legislative decision taken following a manifesto commitment, consultation process and lengthy parliamentary process than it would be to afford weight to emergency legislation drafted and debated in the absence of broader deliberation. But to deny, in the latter circumstance, the courts the ability to evaluate what primary evidence in favour of the proposals may be gleaned from the parliamentary debates is to constitutionally impose an obstacle to informed proportionality analysis which denies the court the ability to fully assess whether the claimant's (or any other) interests have been considered in sufficient (or indeed any) depth. It might be suggested that a quantitative assessment of

[123] R. v. *British Broadcasting Corporation, ex parte ProLife Alliance* [2003] UKHL 23; [2004] 1 A.C. 185, at [75].

[124] *R. (Countryside Alliance)* v. *Attorney General* [2007] UKHL 52; [2008] A.C. 719, at [45].

legislative process might well be appropriate for a supervisory supranational court seeking to give effect to principles of subsidiarity. Whether it is appropriate for a domestic court to conduct a similar exercise and comprehensively examine the proportionality of a legislative measure is open to question.

10.6 The Interplay with Strasbourg: Subsidiarity, Complementarity or Confusion?

The above analysis suggests a lack of continuity between the approaches to review adopted at the Strasbourg and domestic levels, and as between the standards of and approaches to judicial review of administrative action at common law, and the legislative and public body judicial review sanctioned by the HRA. The procedural focus of judicial review at common law has not been fully replicated in the species of legislative or judicial review prompted by enactment of the HRA. Nor has the European Court's willingness to inform its proportionality analysis through examination of the adequacy of domestic decision-making processes been consistently acknowledged in HRA review. That domestic courts operate under the misapprehension that the European Court is largely unconcerned with matters of process speaks to both the lack of certainty as to circumstances in which process review is appropriate and provides evidence of a disconnect from the Strasbourg case law (contrary to common perceptions regarding the linkages between human rights laws at the domestic and supranational levels[125]) which might be seen to limit the potential of the HRA to instil a broad-based culture of rights.

Regardless of the administrative or legislative target of judicial review, a focus on outcomes, to the exclusion of process, 'flies in the face of collaborative – dialogic – approaches to resolving rights disputes'[126] and can increasingly be seen to be in tension with the reasoning processes of the European Court, and with broader attempts to fully integrate subsidiarity into the fabric of the Convention system.[127] The tendency

[125] For an overview, see: R. Masterman, *Supreme, Submissive or Symbiotic? United Kingdom Courts and the European Court of Human Rights* (London: Constitution Unit, 2015).

[126] D. Mead, 'Outcomes Aren't All: Defending Process-Based Judicial Review of Public Authority Decisions under the Human Rights Act' [2012] P.L. 61, 84.

[127] See the text of Article 1 of Protocol 15 to the ECHR: 'Affirming that the High Contracting Parties, in accordance with the principle of subsidiarity, have the primary responsibility to secure the rights and freedoms defined in the Convention and the Protocols thereto, and that in so doing, they enjoy a margin of appreciation, subject to the supervisory jurisdiction of the European Court of Human Rights established by this Convention.'

towards an outcomes-focused approach 'reinforces the idea of the HRA as a juricentric constitutional document'[128] at a time when the ECtHR is consciously seeking to demonstrate that respect for the considered decisions of national legislatures and governments is an embedded feature of its reasoning processes.[129] While the signs are emerging that a medial approach is emergent at the local level, it has yet to be fully and/or consistently realised. The judicial self-denying ordinance which appeared to oppose the accommodation of procedural concerns into proportionality analysis under section 6 HRA has shown itself to be more flexible than initially presumed. This is to be contrasted with the rather more immoveable constitutional obstacle which, in the context of statutory review, precludes full judicial engagement with the content of legislative process. In the light of these parallel developments, it should be recognised that the examination of administrative and legislative decision-making processes by the domestic judiciary can be facilitative of subsidiarity and can serve to support a finding by the Strasbourg Court that a potential infringement of the Convention rights falls within the discretionary area of judgment afforded to national authorities. For so long as domestic courts lack the willingness or competence to fully consider the adequacy of administrative or legislative decision-making processes in their assessments of proportionality, an opportunity to fully benefit from the Convention's new 'age of subsidiarity'[130] will remain tantalisingly out of reach.

128 D. Mead, 'Outcomes Aren't All: Defending Process-Based Judicial Review of Public Authority Decisions under the Human Rights Act' [2012] P.L. 61, 63.

129 See e.g. *National Union of Rail, Maritime and Transport Workers* v. *United Kingdom* (2015) 60 E.H.R.R. 10, at [99]; *SAS* v. *France* (2015) 60 E.H.R.R. 11, at [129].

130 Joint Committee on Human Rights, *Protocol 15 to the European Convention on Human Rights*, 2 December 2014, HL 71/HC 837, at [3.17].

INDEX

For EU product safety concerns, contact us at Calle de José Abascal, 56–1°, 28003 Madrid, Spain or eugpsr@cambridge.org.

www.ingramcontent.com/pod-product-compliance
Lightning Source LLC
LaVergne TN
LVHW011525200926
848484LV00001B/149
9781107183773